D1385123

CRUISING
RIGS
AND
RIGGING

CRUISING
RIGS
AND
RIGGING

Ross Norgrove

INTERNATIONAL MARINE PUBLISHING COMPANY
Camden, Maine

© 1982 by International Marine Publishing Company

Typeset by Journal Publications, Camden, Maine
Printed and bound by The Alpine Press, Stoughton, Massachusetts

Published by International Marine Publishing Company
21 Elm Street, Camden, Maine 04843
(207) 236-4342

Library of Congress Cataloging in Publication Data

Norgrove, Ross.
  Cruising rigs and rigging.

  Includes index.
  1. Masts and rigging. I Title.
VM531.N67 1982   623.8'82   81-82489
ISBN 0-87742-145-5

Contents

Preface

This book answers the questions of the person who is looking over the market for a cruising boat, but who isn't sure what rig to decide on. What rig will be best for me? Will I settle for nothing but a ketch, a sloop, a cutter, a yawl, a schooner . . .? Or perhaps one of the exotic rigs, with lateen or wrap-around sails? What should I do? What rig is the most suitable for my purpose? For my pocket?

It is easy to become confused, especially when attending a boat show where everything is glittering, and everything looks so efficient, so *safe*. It's hard to conceive that the gleaming sailing machine being drooled over by thousands might be blessed with a rig that would have you chewing your fingernails down to the first knuckle before you're a hundred miles clear of the land, or have a rig that, if only one small part carried away, might go over the side in the first real gale. Or, on a lesser note, might chafe the living daylights out of your sails. Or a rig that might be no good when running before the wind unless balanced by a spinnaker, or on the wind unless pandered to by constant changes of headsails as wind strength varies. Or need a permanent crew of four or more to handle . . . . On the other hand, the rig might be ideal for cruising. But how do you know? I mean *really* know?

A lot of sailboats are sold secondhand, and this can sometimes be a great advantage to a buyer. Such a vessel often comes equipped with cruising gear that was purchased as "extra" by someone who laid down money for a new boat. But how about the rig? Is it the right one to take cruising, year in and year out?

After scrambling through a boatyard behind a broker and finally arriving at a boat, either afloat or high and dry, how do you judge the suitability of her rig for *your* particular purpose? Or how do you decide what needs to be done to the rig to make it better, safer? Unless you *know* — or, at the very least, have some guidelines to follow — you could end up purchasing a vessel with a rig totally unsuited to your needs. The decision of whether the rig is safe, could be improved upon, or is just plain wrong for deep-water cruising — especially shorthanded cruising — should be made by someone who has an idea what he or she is looking for.

It is my hope that the information contained in the following pages, in "layman's" terms, will assist in the sometimes difficult task of assessing the suitability of a cruising rig for particular needs.

Acknowledgments

While working on the manuscript of this book, I found it helpful on occasion to check with various experienced yachtsmen, sailmakers, sparmakers, and riggers for sundry up-to-date information. I would like to sincerely thank the following (some of them friends and shipmates over the years) for the help they gave so unstintingly at such times: Ralph Naranjo, Max Carter, Dave Ferneding, Chris Bouzaid, Garry Hoyt, Lars Strom, Warwick Tompkins, Dean Taylor.

CRUISING
RIGS
AND
RIGGING

one

Different Rigs
Advantages and Disadvantages

It is a pleasure to see a cruising boat with an efficient, no-nonsense rig — a rig that, capable of using the wind effectively on every point of sailing, supplies the motive power to take the vessel competently to any port in the world.

Unhappily, not all rigs foisted upon cruising boats can claim this distinction. Some are good, some are barely adequate, some leave a lot to be desired. Upwind or downwind, some rigs are dependable and trouble-free. Some, most decidedly, are not.

Some cruising rigs are so unsuited to the hull in which they've been installed that they are a continual source of frustration to the owner at sea and an embarrassment when sailing in company with boats on a coast. Such a rig can be the reason why, once he's in the bay, the owner's conversation centers around a bigger auxiliary engine. Some way, somehow, he's just got to get his vessel moving faster through the water. And the only way to do it seems to be with a more powerful auxiliary.

Possibly, with an efficient rig, his ship might perform quite satisfactorily under sail.

In addition to cruising rigs that give a vessel an acceptable turn of speed under sail, and those that could be improved upon, are others that add little more than character. A brigantine rig planted in a 42-footer, for instance, can be a great talking point, and the little lady will probably cut a picturesque figure when anchored in a bay. But getting to windward — and let's not kid ourselves that when cruising we won't face a smart beat to windward now and again — might be as easy as climbing a wall with a pound of butter in each hand. If the ship were 80 feet or so longer, however, the rig might be a winner.

So rig is important. It is one thing to have a strong, seaworthy hull to go cruising in — and that is the first priority (see my earlier book *The Cruising Life*) — but it is quite another thing for the same hull to have a rig that suits. The standard to aim

1

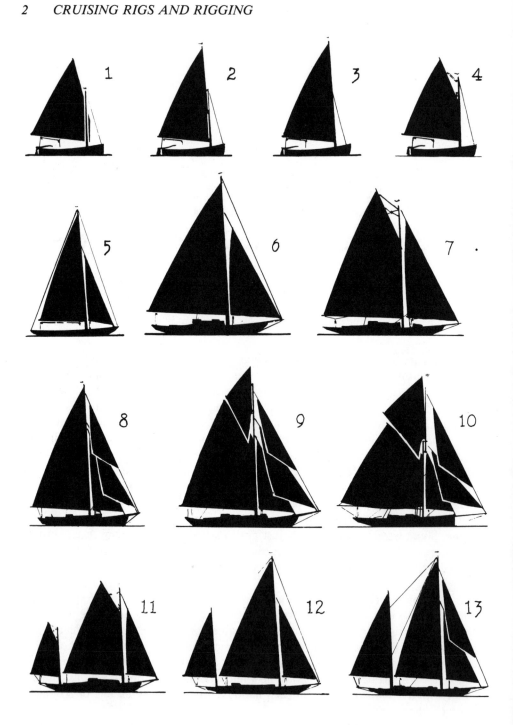

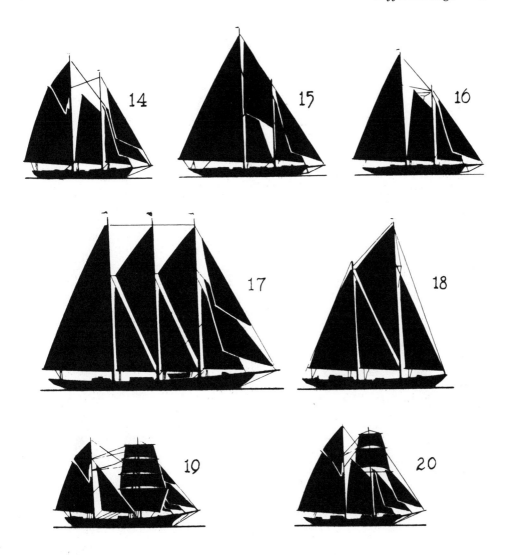

DIFFERENT TYPES OF RIGS. *(1) Standing lug rig. (2) Sliding gunter rig. (3) Jibheaded cat-boat. (4) Gaff-headed catboat. (5) Jibheaded knockabout with genoa (overlapping) jib. (6) Jibheaded sloop. (7) Gaff-headed sloop. (8) Jibheaded cutter. (9) Gaff-headed cutter with jackyard topsail. (10) English cutter with club topsail. (11) Gaff-headed yawl. (12) Jibheaded yawl. (13) Jibheaded ketch with jib topsail. (14) Gaff-headed schooner with working topsails on fore and main. (15) Staysail schooner with fisherman's staysail above main staysail. (16) Schooner with jibheaded mainsail, gaff-headed foresail, and Queen staysail. (17) Three-masted staysail schooner. (18) Staysail (wishbone) ketch. (19) Brigantine (formerly her-maphrodite brig). (20) Topsail schooner with upper and lower square topsails on foremast. (Drawings by W.H. de Fontaine. Reprinted courtesy Dorothy de Fontaine.)*

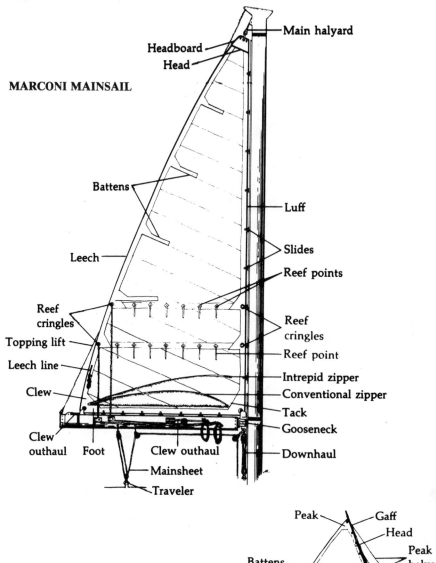

MARCONI MAINSAIL

Main halyard

Headboard

Head

Battens

Luff

Slides

Leech

Reef points

Reef cringles

Reef cringles

Topping lift

Reef point

Leech line

Intrepid zipper

Clew

Conventional zipper

Tack

Gooseneck

Clew outhaul

Foot

Clew outhaul

Downhaul

Mainsheet

Traveler

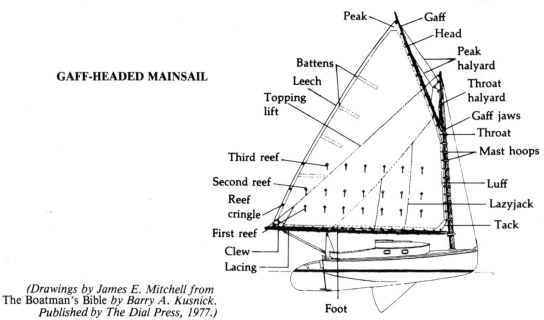

Peak

Gaff

Head

Peak halyard

Battens

Throat halyard

Leech

Gaff jaws

Topping lift

Throat

GAFF-HEADED MAINSAIL

Mast hoops

Third reef

Luff

Second reef

Lazyjack

Reef cringle

Tack

First reef

Clew

Lacing

(Drawings by James E. Mitchell from
The Boatman's Bible by Barry A. Kusnick.
Published by The Dial Press, 1977.)

Foot

for, especially when shorthanded cruising is contemplated, is a rig that extracts an acceptable performance from a cruising sailboat, a performance that doesn't necessitate a half-dozen hirsute characters bounding about the decks, constantly fiddling with sails and things.

When assessing the capability of a cruising boat's rig, a buyer should always assume that an engine is nonexistent, that he is going to have to rely solely on sails for motive power. That way he stands a good chance of ending up with an efficient sailing vessel. Then, if the auxiliary is a good one, he'll achieve the best on two counts.

The wise would-be owner will ponder all this before buying or building a dream-ship to cruise in or live aboard. It's a comfort to have a strong, efficient rig that you have confidence in, that requires little maintenance, that suits your vessel, and that can, with a minimum of fuss, take you and your cruising home under canvas wherever you choose to go.

There are many rigs, of course. From the earliest example, which was probably a man standing on a log, optimistically hoping the wind blowing against his body would enable him to "sail" short distances, rigs have come a long way. Some of the old ones, tried and true through the ages, have stood the test of time and are still able to give a good account of themselves. As I write this, I am 20 feet away from the water on Beef Island in the British Virgins, looking out at the Sir Francis Drake Channel. A mighty distracting spot! The *Antares,* a big gaff schooner carrying top-sails, has just put about with a thunder of canvas, 200 yards away. Perhaps I should take this as a hint and start with a discussion on gaff rig.

GAFF RIG

Gaff rig gets its name from the spar, known as a gaff, to which the head of a fore-and-aft sail is secured or, to be strictly nautical, "bent." The gaff, which is hauled aloft taking the sail with it, is held at the mast by jaws, a collar that encircles the mast, or a fitting on a strong track. Whatever type of attachment is used, it must allow the gaff to pivot or swing on a horizontal plane so that the sail may be presented at a correct angle to the wind; the fitting must also allow vertical adjustment of the angle between the spar and the mast. The peak halyard holds the gaff at this angle; the throat halyard is used to haul the inboard end of the gaff aloft. Gaff rig has been around for so long that an attempt to hark back to where and when it evolved would, at best, entail a generous quantity of guesswork. Suffice it to say there is still a lot to be said for the rig, for several reasons.

A mast in a gaff-rigged vessel is usually sturdier and shorter than its marconi-rigged counterpart. Except for backstays (and we'll come to these later), it's also easier to stay. The lower center of effort is touted as advantageous by gaff-rig adherents; it must also be said that a gaff mainsail gives excellent drive when running. A gaff main really catches the wind, and the feel of a vessel sailing downwind with a well-cut gaff mainsail is intensely satisfying. (Doesn't make you feel a bit guilty about not having a jib boomed out the other side.) A gaff sail may also be hoisted with the vessel sailing before the wind — a real advantage in some situations.

Although the rigging of a gaff mast is relatively simple as compared to a lofty

White Squall *and* White Squall II *meet in Suva, Fiji. After 29 years of cruising — great festivities.*

marconi spar, there are some disadvantages. High on the list comes chafe. Chafe can start with the lead of the throat and peak halyards, which must run free in the blocks and never bind — no matter how the gaff swings. When a gaff sail is set, the peak blocks on the mast and gaff must be such a distance from each other that the halyard is given a fair lead into and from each block. To a lesser extent, the same applies to the throat blocks. Adjustment of halyards means everything to the efficiency of this rig. A well-peaked gaff and a drum-tight luff are necessary for windward work. To "scandalize" a gaff mainsail and use only its lower half when coming to anchor, or to reduce sail temporarily in a squall, one eases the peak halyard, allowing the leech of the sail to collapse, thus reducing drive.

Sometimes the reason for chafe is not easy to find aboard a gaff-rigger. I remember a peak halyard that chafed in a ketch-rigged commercial sailing vessel in which I was crew in New Zealand. I was a young able seaman at the time and, along with the rest of the crew, I would spend all sorts of time aloft standing in the ratlines up near the gaff jaws, trying to locate the cause. The efficiency of that big mainsail meant everything to us. We carried 120 tons of cargo and our auxiliary engine was a mighty 66 horsepower (about 50 of them were dead). The ship's owners, however, secure in the knowledge that their vessel had motive power in her vitals, treated her like a fully powered motorship. No matter what the weather, we were expected to run to a timetable.

Finding where that peak halyard chafed nearly drove us around the bend. It was discovered eventually that when we were on the starboard tack, one of the masthead peak blocks didn't twist far enough when the heavy 40-foot gaff was pushed to port by the wind on our starboard side. The halyard chafed on the block cheek. We fixed it quickly enough by sending up a new block, shackling it onto a mast band and re-reeving (and end-for-ending) the peak halyard. I forget now who discovered the trouble, but I didn't.

There are other things besides chafe that have been detrimental to the popularity of gaff rig. It takes longer to set. There is the necessity to sway the gaff aloft and control it. In light airs, this last can be achieved with a topsail (see Chapter Eight) and/or with vangs, but a fair amount of work is involved. Furling, too, can be done shorthanded, but not as quickly as with a jibheaded sail. Gaff rig also means that a permanent backstay cannot be carried; running backstays often are necessary. But most important of all, the rig is not as close-winded as marconi; you just can't point as high.

This last fact may seem unimportant to some would-be members of the cruising fraternity, who have it all figured out that the way they'll cruise is with eased sheets — the hell with windward work. These are brave thoughts and we wish the person indulging in them all the luck in the world, because he's going to need it. Admittedly, we're not racing, so it's not necessary for our cruising vessel to point like a 12-meter would. When we put her about, her keel shape prevents her from spinning like a pinwheel. She'll never dislocate anybody's neck in stays, but even so, she *must* be able to go to windward under sail.

Sometimes, no matter how conscientiously we consult the wind charts and plan our cruise with respect to seasons and any other information we can conjure up, our expected fair wind comes from dead ahead. (The weather god forgot to read the wind chart.) Our cruiser, deeply laden with perhaps six months' supply of food aboard, is even less efficient to windward than she was before she had all this cargo to lump along. But she's still got to get there.

I remember one time in the Roaring Forties — an area where the "brave west winds" are supposed to reign unchallenged — beating tack for tack into a 25-knot easterly, day after day. I was in my 33-foot yawl, *White Squall,* and, for her type and size, she was a close-winded little vessel. I must have been starting to think wild thoughts; a few days ago I came across a daily navigational page in a musty, old, exercise book. It was the one I was using on the voyage and it projected me right back to that time.

Now, I'm not a great one for a log at sea. I reckon that when a boat is a man's home and he's going away for pleasure, he might as well slough off all he can that smacks of regimentation. Entering daily events in a log on a pleasure boat that's a home is a bit like a householder noting in a book every time he drives his car . . . .

Now and again, however, and usually under the stress of a powerful emotion, I would jot down a few remarks at the bottom of the navigational page.

The words at the bottom of this much-stained sheet tell anyone interested that " . . . on one tack we're headed for bloody China and on the other, the bloody South Pole . . . ." In a vessel that was a dog to windward, God knows what my comments would have been.

I've often wondered whether the low center of effort, which is sometimes eulogized when the gaff rig gang starts chewing the fat about this rig and that, is all it's cracked up to be. Again, I'm talking about windward ability. A vessel beating to windward in the open ocean *has* to carry sail high enough to catch the wind, especially when it's blowing. It seems she needs to carry more sail in these conditions than she would carry to go the same distance in sheltered waters. Going to windward in rough water may even be likened to a runner being faced with a number of hurdles as opposed to a piece of flat ground.

The larger the sea, the more one must crack on sail to get to windward. A too-low rig is at a distinct disadvantage here, for the vessel can lose quite a lot of drive in the troughs. In a sheltered sound, or within the confines of some island groups, you get every puff — you get all of it — but in the same breeze on the open ocean you can lose some in the troughs. The ship's motion can even shake some of the wind out of the sails. A stiff beat to windward at sea in a small gaff-rigged vessel, with her relatively short mast and low center of effort, can be mighty frustrating at times.

Along with most cruising yachtsmen, I favor the jibheaded or marconi rig, even though I've owned three gaff-rigged vessels and sailed in a number of others. In addition to its close-windedness and the ease with which a mainsail can be furled and set, the marconi rig has three additional features that clinch the matter for me. These are the single topping lift from the boom end to the masthead; the permanent backstay (you can't beat a permanent backstay to stiffen up a rig); and, finally, there's only one halyard to ease when reefing.

SLOOP RIG

The largest number of new boats seem to be marconi rigged and have one mast. Their use, in general, is confined to sailing in sheltered or semi-sheltered waters, with maybe some weekend or occasional overnight racing and perhaps a coastal cruise each year.

For this type of sailing, there is much to be said for a marconi-rigged sloop. Nearly all modern cruising sloops have a forestay going to a masthead fitting, and from the aft part of this fitting, a permanent backstay leading down to the stern. Such wasn't always the case. For many years, a sloop or cutter owner just wasn't with it unless his vessel was three-quarter or seven-eighths rigged, that is, unless his forestay led from the bow or bowsprit-end to a point approximately three-quarters or seven-eighths of the way up the mast. On the foreside of the mast at this point, jumper

Marconi sloop. Note anti-chafe patches each side of jib leech to prevent damage from spreader tips. (Ralph Naranjo photo)

struts braced stays leading from the masthead to the strut tips, to sometimes as far down as the spreaders. Their job was to stiffen the mast against the pull of the permanent backstay. Running backstays leading to the point where the forestay and jumpers were fitted were needed to take the pull of the jibstay.

All that paraphernalia is mostly in the past, and today the all-masthead rig has the limelight among cruising vessels. (I can hear the howls of Freedom 40 cat-ketch followers on the sideline, and I assure them we'll be coming to their vessels soon.) There are some fractional (usually three-quarter) rig buffs who don't use jumpers and who aren't happy unless their mast is bending like a banana. A discussion on such a mast and its suitability on the long-range cruising scene will be found in Chapter Two.

Setting only two sails — a mainsail and a jib — a sloop can be off and sailing in jig time. An owner can arrive at his boat fresh from the office or the factory, the sails

Sloop with a fractional rig, a luff spar, and a controlled mast bend. Note common shroud anchorage, single headstay, position aft of running backstays. (Courtesy Yachtspars)

are bent on in minutes, and the boat is underway. With a modern sloop, the only lines that need handling when tacking are jib sheets; the mainsheet is self-tending and any adjustment to the mainsheet traveler can be done at leisure; usually there are no running backstays. It's a simple, handy rig.

At the risk of being sniped at by various ketch, yawl, schooner, and possibly exotic rig enthusiasts, I'll repeat what I said in *The Cruising Life* and go on record as still being of the opinion that no vessel under 50 feet need have more than one mast, unless the mainsail is then going to be too large for one person to handle comfortably.

If you can, keep to one mast; your vessel will be faster, you won't have precious room on deck taken up by an extra mast and its attendant rigging, and you won't have the cost of it, either. My 33-foot cutter, *White Squall,* was a handy, capable little vessel when I launched her in 1948. Four years later I converted her to yawl rig and I always regretted it. For the life of me I can't remember why I did it; something I read impressed me, I suppose. Anyhow, I made a slower boat out of her, and that little mizzen was more nuisance than it was worth.

Advancing age and the lack of physical ability to handle sails of any size are often reasons for equipping a boat with two masts. I have often wondered if it wouldn't be better, when either building from scratch or redesigning a rig for cruising, to shorten an existing single-mast rig to the point where the vessel would be of the same speed as if she carried two masts.

A reason sometimes advanced for splitting up the rig on a small (under 50-foot) boat, so that two masts carry the sails instead of one, is that if the vessel loses a mast, she still has another that can be jury-rigged to sail her to safety. While this theory is interesting (and only practical if the two masts are not joined by a triatic or other kind of stay), I can't help but wonder: Do the owners intend to sail in the constant expectancy that one of their masts will go by the board? Isn't it better to settle for the simpler rig that is a little shorter, a little heavier, and a little better stayed? Especially if the single mast carries sails that move the boat as fast as if she had a split rig?

I consider that the size of sail that can be set, reefed, and furled by one (or at the most, two) increases with the displacement of the vessel. For example, a 280-square-foot mainsail on a 38-footer can be as hard to lower and furl as a sail twice that size on a larger, heavier-displacement boat. The reason is that the bigger boat is a steadier platform. My wife and I, when chartering or cruising our 70-foot, 60-ton schooner, *White Squall II,* never experienced difficulty either setting or furling the 900-square-foot mainsail. We had no fancy reefing gear, either. To reef, we would lower the main completely, tie in a reef, and hoist away again. The ship's 16-foot beam and hefty displacement helped make the job an easy one.

CUTTER RIG

A cutter rig is a good one for ocean cruising. With a true cutter rig, the mainmast is farther aft than in a sloop — sometimes even as far back as amidships. If the vessel has a bowsprit (and this can be quite short), the mast can be shorter and a greater amount of sail can be set than if the boat were rigged as an inboard sloop. Care must be taken here, however, that we don't end up with the center of effort too low — a fault sometimes found in small gaff-rigged vessels. Another point worthy of attention with a cutter is mainsail size. The neophyte cruising person on the lookout for a cutter must make sure the vessel eventually purchased does not carry too small a mainsail. If she does, constant headsail changes to keep her moving will plague the new skipper's life.

Great drive comes from the two headsails of a cutter with a well-balanced rig; a sudden, drastic reduction of sail area can come from dousing either the jib or the staysail. Some cutters will heave-to beautifully under staysail alone. That the mainmast is farther aft than in a sloop means that the mainsail, boat for boat, is smaller and consequently easier to handle. (As mentioned, however, it shouldn't be too small.) Something that completely sells me on cutter rig compared to sloop rig for cruising is the number of stays hanging from the mast. I received a concussion when beating up Auckland harbor in a small sloop when I was 16 years old, and I've been a "cutter man" ever since. The *Merlin* had one forestay leading from the masthead to the end of her bowsprit, and on this the jib was set. The bobstay carried away, the bowsprit and mast went by the board, and I was ducking my head fast, but not fast enough.

Ever since that day, the more stays hanging from a mast, the more it suits me. I would never have a cruising boat with only one stay forward of the mainmast. There are many sailboats relying on one stay to keep the mast from peeling back and clobbering the crew, and many owners who declare that one well-set-up piece of wire is all that's needed. Have at it, mate, and may you never get your mainmast down around your ears!

If you have a cutter with both a forestay leading to her masthead and a staysail stay (or inner forestay, as some prefer to call it) several feet below this and well back from the point where the forestay is secured below, you won't have all your eggs in one basket. In addition to having a permanent backstay, which is standard equipment aboard either a marconi sloop or a cutter, a cutter usually has running backstays coming from the same point on the mast to which the staysail stay is attached.

In some circles there is a hatred for running backstays, and an individual mentioning them is regarded as something of a pariah. Be that as it may, a running backstay is mighty handy and gives valuable support to a mast when it's blowing. It doesn't need to be used in light weather. In anything up to a moderate breeze, port and starboard backstays can be tied forward each side to an aft shroud. There is more than one vessel that would have been saved a dismasting if, in addition to her permanent backstay, she'd had a running backstay set up to windward. I remember when the schooner *Zambezi* was dismasted in the West Indies. She was running before a fresh breeze and a fitting on her bumpkin bobstay let go (exactly the opposite to what happened to us in the *Merlin*). The *Zambezi*'s bumpkin tore out and the mainmast went over the side, taking the foremast with it. One well-set-up running backstay would have saved the whole rig.

Not long after she lost her spars, the *Zambezi* nearly had another accident. It was in the worst weather I ever remember in the Virgin Islands. We had sailed across to St. Croix from Peter Island in the British Virgins in the *White Squall II,* and we had a charter party aboard. In increasing rain and wind, hour after hour ticked by, until we eventually hove-to under reefed mainsail and forestaysail. Visibility by then was only a few hundred yards.

I was contemplating the joys of a night at sea in a gale of wind with a full charter

Marconi cutter with double-spreader masthead rig. Forestay, inner forestay, running backstays, permanent backstay. Two shrouds each side locate beneath base of lower spreader. Intermediate shrouds take in the tips of the lower spreader and locate at the base of the upper spreader, which is also the junction for the inner forestay and running backstays. Cap shrouds take in the tips of both spreaders. It is doubtful whether the loss of any stay or shroud would cause this vessel to lose her mast. (Ralph Naranjo photo)

group aboard, when the murk lifted and I got a bearing on a radio mast ashore. So we proceeded in through Christiansted's reefy, dogleg entrance and anchored behind Protestant Cay, among what looked like half the vessels in creation. Around midnight it was blowing great guns and boats ahead of us were starting to drag, so I decided to move before something came down on us.

We fired up our Gardner diesel, hove in the anchor, and proceeded out. My intention was to steam to windward through the channel between the island and the town, and let go our big CQR over near the shipyard. It was a position more exposed to the wind but protected in great measure by the barrier reef; the holding was good and there were very few boats there (the dismasted *Zambezi* was one).

The wind and rain were trying to outdo each other as we passed slowly through the narrow channel between the island and the town, but the compass and echo sounder were both doing a good job, so "all parts were bearing an even strain."

The three couples in our charter party all owned boats on the Great Lakes and, thus far during the charter, had shown themselves competent hands. So, just before leaving the anchorage behind Protestant Cay, one of the men offered to station himself up in the bows and act as lookout. I told him to fire ahead, but to keep a sharp eye peeled for the *Zambezi*.

We were a few minutes clear of the island, we'd crossed the main ship channel, the echo sounder was showing the water starting to shallow, and I started to feel uneasy. I slowed down until the vessel was just stemming the elements, handed the wheel to my wife, and ran up the deck to the bows where my lookout, hand clapped above his eyes like Sinbad, was peering into the night. Dead ahead, about 50 feet, was the long, black, unlighted shape of the *Zambezi*. He was looking straight at it.

"Can't see anything yet!" Over his shoulder.

"There she is, right there!" I point.

"Where?" Staring right at it.

"Dead ahead — can't you see it?"

"No. My eyes aren't too good at night."

Which, I thought, as I made my way aft to the wheel in the rain and the howling wind, was one hell of a time to tell me. But I digress.

The fact that a cutter can be used as a sloop in light to moderate conditions is a great advantage. A quick-release lever on the staysail stay enables this stay to be taken back and secured to a shroud on whichever side of the ship is convenient. Some boats have a small, wooden cleat screwed to the forward side of the port and starboard spreaders, some two-thirds of the way outboard. The staysail stay is prevented from swinging and causing chafe by resting in a niche in this cleat.

In the days of commercial sail, cutters came in large sizes. I used to stand many times in San Francisco's Golden Gate Park and marvel at the size of the *Gjoa* in her berth on dry land. (She's since been moved to the Norsk Sjofartsmuseum in Oslo.) *Gjoa*, with famous Norwegian explorer Roald Amundsen and six of his countrymen aboard, navigated the Northwest Passage in the years between 1903 and 1906; they were icebound for three winters on the voyage. Tough, mighty tough men.

A true, workaday cutter of about 50 tons, *Gjoa*'s mainmast is well aft toward amidships. Her main boom is long and her gaff mainsail must have been a fair spread. In this day and age, such a vessel would probably have two masts and a

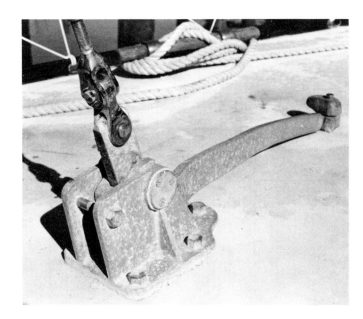

Quick-release deck fitting for staysail (inner forestay). (Courtesy Yachtspars)

powerful engine. It says a lot for the cutter rig that it was the one chosen for this heavy, rugged vessel as the most suitable for the sea conditions around Norway and in the Northwest Passage. *Gjoa,* though, had a large crew; no lack of Norwegian steam that trip.

KETCH RIG

Every rig has its followers, and from the number of ketches around, it would seem that this must be one of the good ones. A vessel is termed ketch-rigged when her mizzenmast is stepped forward of the rudderpost or the aft end of the waterline. If the vessel is over 50 feet long and will be cruising shorthanded, she is usually given another mast to split up the rig and so reduce the area of the mainsail to a size that can be handled conveniently. Ketch is the rig frequently chosen, and though the ship is a slower boat with two masts, the convenience of her individually smaller sails makes the choice an acceptable one to a lot of people.

We do, however, see ketches of a much smaller size than 50 feet. Some of them look pretty, too. My little *Kiwi,* an Offshore 31, was a sloop; I bareboat-chartered her in the Virgin Islands at the same time I ran the *White Squall II* as a term charter boat. I used to admire how the *Kiwi* got about her business and think how well she looked — until I saw an Offshore 31 with a ketch rig. There was no doubt about which was the prettier vessel: the ketch-rigged 31 had my *Kiwi* whacked to a frazzle. But it stopped right there. Under ketch rig, the hull was much slower, the mizzenmast was in the way in the cockpit, and its shrouds made for awkward walking on the side decks around the cockpit. It was very disappointing.

Maybe it was the comparison of those two differently rigged Offshore 31s that first gave me the notion that some people buy or build a ketch for no other reason

Marconi ketch. Visibility from the helm is restricted a bit by the low-cut foot of her overlapping jib (particularly when it is trimmed in flat), to say nothing of the obstacle to looking ahead presented by her high-wide-and-handsome doghouse. (Ralph Naranjo photo)

than that vessels carrying this rig often *look* good. Or that it *sounds* better, when describing your boat, to be able to say she's got two masts. Or maybe just to be able to say she's a *ketch*. You can't really knock this. We are, after all, in the game for pleasure, and if a guy has it figured that his ship is the best-looking craft ever to float down the channel, who is anyone else to say otherwise?

From a practical point of view, a ketch rig foisted upon the hull of a cruising boat — a boat that under cutter rig would have a mainsail of, say, not more than 450 square feet — will slow the boat considerably. The extra mast, with its boom, blocks, and standing and running rigging, can cost a fair piece of change, too.

Another thing. The mainmast of a ketch is positioned farther forward than that of either a cutter or a sloop, and the fact that this part of the vessel is (frequently) narrower makes the mast just that much harder to stay. Another strike against her is that the largest spar, in addition to being in a narrowing part of the ship, is also at a point where there is more motion than if she were a single-masted vessel. Setting and furling sail forward can be difficult; every foot farther aft usually increases the beam and lessens the motion. In order to enlarge her foretriangle and save her from being hardmouthed on the helm, a ketch is often given a bowsprit.

A large number of ketches have their cockpits amidships, which takes away the novelty when at the helm of trying to look forward with one eye each side of the mizzenmast — as is the case when the cockpit is aft. An amidships cockpit also saves the helmsman from beaning himself on the mizzen boom when he stands up.

I have only sailed in four pleasure boats that were ketches, and I found that hard on the wind the mainsail backwinded the mizzen to some extent, and off the wind the mizzen blanketed the main, so we hauled it down. On a broad reach, some ketches require a degree of helm compensation that makes them hard to hold as the wind tends to drive the stern to leeward; to drag the rudder at an angle through the water is detrimental to the vessel's speed. The whole idea of being able to drop a sail to shorten down is attractive, especially when advancing age influences the decision of whether it's time to split the sail area (no matter how small) by having two masts — or give the game away. For that reason alone, I suppose there will always be ketches.

YAWL RIG

Even though *White Squall* was a yawl for 10 out of the 14 years I owned her, and I always regretted the changeover from her cutter rig, if a person feels his small vessel *must* have two masts, no matter what, then yawl is to be preferred to ketch. There are a number of reasons: (1) The mainmast is farther aft, and this makes for easier staying. (2) The foretriangle can be larger, and a bowsprit can be shortened or dispensed with. (3) When running before the wind, with the mizzen lowered to keep it from blanketing the mainsail, the yawl doesn't suffer as drastic a speed reduction as a ketch — which has a larger mizzen than a yawl and a smaller mainsail. (4) When sailing on the wind in a hard breeze with the mizzen lowered and furled, a yawl's mizzenmast and rigging doesn't offer as much windage as would be the case if the vessel were a ketch.

This last is not a snide remark calculated to curdle the ire of any ketch-rig buff; it just happens to be a fact. Some of the ketches I see (and sometimes I see them every-day) hobbyhorsing to windward in a fresh breeze with the mizzen furled and dragging a tall mizzenmast with its attendant rigging upwind make me feel sorry for the boat. It just isn't fair to the vessel.

The small mizzen of a yawl can be backed this way or that to veer the stern when letting go a mooring and getting underway under sail; it depends on how many hands are aboard and how acrobatic you happen to be. It is not, however, a strong enough reason for me to put a mizzen in a boat.

Some ketch and yawl skippers sheet their mizzens hard amidships and leave them up at anchor, maintaining that this keeps a ship headed into the wind. Perhaps it does; but most well-designed vessels lie head-to-wind anyway, without any sail up. Unless, of course, a contrary current or tide rip is influencing the way the vessel lies. In such conditions, hoisting a sail (even a mizzen) can make the ship sail all over the place and, if you're sharing the anchorage with other boats, put an uneven strain on your popularity.

One fact touted by some mizzenmast enthusiasts as being an absolute clincher when discussing ketch versus yawl rig (and this includes me before I owned a mizzenmast) is the ability to carry a mizzen staysail. I seldom got mine to work; in fact, after the first few experiences, I gave it the title of "Providence" — because that's what I tempted whenever I used the thing.

We'd be bowling along with the wind aft of the beam and (with great excitement at first) I would bring the mizzen staysail on deck. Tacked up to windward, sheeted to the end of the mizzen boom, hoisted to the mizzen masthead, it would blanket the mainsail to a certain extent, but it would draw.

And then the wind would change, usually for the worse; it would come ahead. The most I ever got out of that sail at any one stretch was about 10 hours. Then a month or so would go by before, bending a crafty eye to windward, counting my beads and muttering, I'd give it another go. I wouldn't place the anticipated use of a mizzen staysail high on the list of reasons to foist a mizzenmast on any cruising boat.

Sloop and cutter owners can rig a "mizzen staysail" without going to the expense of another mast. A block with a halyard rove can be hung from about one-third of the way (or whatever height suits) up the permanent backstay. The sail is tacked and hoisted in the usual manner. Sheeting is more of a problem because there is no mizzen boom-end to take the sheet to, but the lead can be run to the extreme lee quarter of the vessel. The cruising man or woman doing this can then sample the special delights reserved for owners of mizzen staysails.

SCHOONER RIG

At one time I scorned schooner rig, but after having owned one for 15 years, I've changed my tune. Schooner rig suits larger vessels — say, 55 feet on up — very well. The big question becomes whether to settle for gaff rig on both masts, gaff on the fore and marconi on the main (a once-popular combination), or staysail schooner.

A gaff-rigged schooner, especially with topsails set, presents a magnificent sight — to me, the best sight of all. But while I may stand riveted at the picture she makes, I'm always conscious of a great feeling of relief. I'm glad she isn't mine.

Yawl with a tiny mizzen. Worth it . . .? (Ralph Naranjo photo)

Ah . . . mizzen staysails! (Ralph Naranjo photo)

There are two reasons for this. First and foremost is maintenance, which can be high. Second is the number of people it takes to set all those sails and pull all those pieces of string. I know Arthur Holgate sailed the 96-foot gaff-on-both-masts schooner *Antares* singlehanded from Capetown to the Virgin Islands without a winch aboard, but that was a one-shot deal — and there are not many around like Arthur. To the person who is all fired up to own a schooner with gaff sails on both masts, I say have at it and more power to you. Unless you're a cross between a circus strongman and an acrobat, however, you'll probably need a bigger crew than if the ship were rigged any other way — but under sail or at anchor, you'll cause a few sighs.

Staysail rig with a marconi mainsail seems about the simplest for schooners. When we first bought *White Squall II,* she was gaff-rigged on the foremast and marconi on the main. After the first year we sent the foresail ashore and converted to staysail rig. This moved the center of effort slightly farther aft, but it didn't make any difference to the helm. What it did mean, though, was that we always had to carry plenty of sail area in our headsails, for she was a heavy-displacement vessel. Without a generous amount of drive forward, she would have been slow on the wind. There was a small loss of sail area with staysail rig, but no noticeable difference in speed.

The bonuses we did enjoy with staysail rig were windward ability (she would point higher with the main staysail than with gaff foresail) and the ease of setting and furling. I would say we'd set the staysail in a tenth of the time it took to hoist and swig up the peak and throat halyards of the gaff foresail. We would furl it in about a quarter of the time.

The disadvantage with schooner rig seems to be the blanketing by the mainsail of the forward sails when running. It is possible to goosewing a foresail or main staysail by guying it out the opposite side to the main boom when running dead before it, but while this *sounds* good, it can be a different piece of cake when put into practice. If any sort of a sea is running, great care must be taken when steering a "wing-and-wing" schooner — otherwise one of the sails (usually the foresail) will be taken aback and a merry mix-up will ensue. Much beating of gums and gnashing of teeth.

When running dead before it on an ocean passage in *White Squall II,* we would haul the main staysail amidships to try to dampen down the roll; then we'd boom a large, roller-furling jib out forward on the opposite side to the mainsail. When running any distance in the tradewinds, we would lower the mainsail, leave the main staysail up and drawing, and boom a genoa out each side of the foremast. Then we'd set the big awning aft of the mainmast, and with "Iron Michael" (our Wood-Freeman autopilot) doing the steering, open a couple of cold ones. You won't break any records under this rig, but you'll have a lot of fun and all without the specter of chafe.

A schooner can set a fisherman staysail from her masthead, or even a larger — usually much larger — sail known as a gollywobbler. This sail, sometimes hoisted on a track on the foremast, has a second halyard to the main masthead and sheets to the end of the main boom. It can pull like a team of horses. With the mainsail and main staysail (or foresail) furled, a gollywobbler doing its stuff, and a boomed-out genoa or spinnaker forward, some schooners have made marvelous runs; it is a matter of the size of your vessel and the number of crew. Handling a large gollywobbler short-handed can call for some smart organization.

A schooner rig is generally magnificent with wind abeam or broad reaching. The position of the mainmast amidships, or just aft of this station, enables the mainsail to give good drive and, being in a wide, steady part of the ship, lend itself to easy setting and furling.

CAT KETCH

A rig that looks more like a schooner than a ketch, but that its designer describes as a cat ketch because the after mast is slightly shorter than the fore, is that of the Freedom line of cruising sailboats. When Garry Hoyt first brought out his Freedom

Gaff schooner carrying a fisherman's staysail. Note absence of backstays. (Ralph Naranjo photo)

40 a few years back, cruising buffs (including me) were curious, but not impressed. A boat thus rigged, with free-standing spars, would never be suitable for crossing oceans (we said). Since then, Freedoms of various sizes have crossed any ocean their owners desired. By romping home in first place in several Caribbean regattas, they've proved they can do it with speed, too.

We see many Freedoms here in the Virgin Islands, sailing along with other boats in the usual balmy weather. Once, though, from a perfect vantage point, I was able to get a bird's-eye view of how one of these cat ketches handled "a bit of a breeze." It was in July 1979, during tropical wave Claudette, and I was up on the southeast side of Little Mountain in the British Virgins. It was blowing 30 or 35 knots and gusting at 45 or more, and I could see about 50 boats sheltering behind islands and in various bays. There was only one boat out sailing, and it was handling the conditions with ease. The sailboat was a Freedom 33, and through binoculars I watched her beat up the Sir Francis Drake Channel under full sail. There was only one man aboard. I didn't know it at the time, but it was Garry Hoyt, out taking some of his own medicine.

An aft-cockpit Freedom 40. Note the wrap-around sails. The wishbone boom acts as a vang and also allows the curve of the sail to come right down to the foot. (Courtesy Freedom Yachts)

When it started to rain and blow pretty hard, still the cat ketch with the free-standing spars continued to slog into it without reducing sail. She beat the full length of the channel and then turned to run down around the islet of Marina Cay, through about 20 anchored boats, to finally pick up a mooring among a great cluster of boats sheltering from the blow at Trellis Bay on Beef Island. It was a performance that left me mightily impressed with the efficiency of the cat-ketch rig and the dependability of the free-standing spar. The fact that there was no jib to handle when the vessel came about — all that needed to be done was to put the helm down — was enough to give the most hard-nosed adherent of conventional rigs pause for thought.

WISHBONE KETCH

Each rig has its champions. One rig that has a small but devout following is the wishbone ketch. Popularized by the late Frits Fenger, it has the masts and rigging of a regular marconi ketch. The headsails and jibheaded mizzen are normal, as is the main boom. Instead of a marconi mainsail, a staysail is hoisted on a stay that runs from the mainmast gooseneck to the mizzen masthead. Its foot and sheeting are controlled by the "main" boom. (Aboard some wishbone ketches this sail is boomless.) A wishbone pivots about two-thirds of the way up the mainmast and is controlled by a sheet that runs through a block at the mizzen top and then to the deck. The wishbone sail, termed "main trysail," is hoisted on a mainmast track and fills the space from the mainmast gooseneck to the main top, to the wishbone end, and back down to the gooseneck. This sail stows in a bag at the bottom of the track.

It's possible to become completely sold on this rig, because each sail is small enough to be handled by one person — an attraction to those getting a little long in the tooth or such souls who just aren't as strong as they used to be. Harry and Oceana Scott cruised from Sydney, Australia, to various parts of the Pacific, including the United States West Coast, in their wishbone ketch, *New Silver Gull,* with Harry on the shady side of 70. A competent couple, they lived aboard and cruised for years and swore by their ship and her rig. So did Blue and Dot Bradfield, who sailed a large slice of the world in *D'Vara,* which, with her white masts, tan sails, and wishbone rig, was about as pretty a sight as a man could wish to see.

With the strain and sheeting of the main trysail taken from the wishbone end by the mizzen masthead, it is important that this be well stayed. It is not unusual for a wishbone ketch to be rigged with a bumpkin and for a permanent backstay to run from the mizzen top to the end of this. There is, of course, a bumpkin bobstay and, on most vessels carrying this rig, a triatic stay tying the mastheads together. The triatic stay, coming from the main masthead to opposite the point where the forestay is attached, gives continuity to the rig; it is not unusual for the backstaying of the whole setup to depend upon the wire from the mizzen top to the bumpkin end and the bobstay, with its attendant fittings.

Now, you can't beat optimism (a large chunk of it is important if various of our endeavors are to succeed), but this is carrying it a bit far. The number of terminal fittings, turnbuckles, toggles, shackles, plus the stay wire itself, give too many chances for something to be faulty — and cause the whole kit and caboodle to disappear over the side. And this can happen.

I have a friend (and no names, please) who left a month later than I did to sail up to Tahiti from Auckland, New Zealand, in 1953, in his wishbone ketch, which he'd built in his own backyard. When he and his three companions didn't show up, we thought they'd probably called at some other island. Six months went by before we met up in Suva, Fiji, and we found he'd been dismasted in the Southern Ocean. They'd headed down south to pick up a fair westerly wind and had been sailing along in fine style, when a bobstay fitting on the bumpkin let go and the whole rig went over the wall. They jury-rigged the ship, sailed more than a thousand miles to Tonga, and then another 500 miles through the reefy Lau Group to Suva — a pretty

The aluminum wishbone ketch on the left was custom built in Holland and single-handed around Cape Horn by 64-year-old Eilco Kasemier. Although choosing wishbone as the rig for his vessel, the lone sailor stated, after completing circumnavigation: "If I were 10 years younger, she would be a cutter!" The vessel on the right is a wishbone schooner, or, should we say, half-wishbone schooner, since her wishbone spar is one-sided. (Ralph Naranjo photo)

good act in itself. When I met my buddy in Fiji and asked him what happened, he said, "Well . . . er . . . you know, Rawss . . . er . . . I dunno!" (If you've read *The Cruising Life,* you can probably guess who he is.)

The moral of this story is: If you're bound and determined to own a wishbone ketch, make sure you have running backstays on your mainmast — and *use them!* The rig has a lot going for it; it can fill the whole area from bowsprit-end or stemhead to main top to mizzen top to bumpkin with sails of manageable size. I have often wondered why we don't see more wishbone ketches out on the cruising beat.

STANDING GAFF RIG

The standing gaff rig is seldom seen nowadays, but it is one that allows a large vessel with a loose-footed mainsail bent permanently to the mast and gaff to be handled by a small crew. One of the best-known world girdlers with this rig is the *Havfruen III*. I remember seeing her in New Zealand in the early 1950s and at various West Indian islands about 12 years later. Batchy and Anne Carr were still handling their hefty, 70-ton ketch with dispatch, furling the gaff topsail as they sailed into a bay and then brailing the big mainsail to the mast and standing gaff in a twinkling.

The brails on a standing gaff rig are secured to points on one side of the mast and gaff some four feet apart or less, depending on the size of the sail. A brail extends across the sail to the leech where it passes through a cringle and then back across to the other side of the sail to a sheave on the mast or gaff immediately opposite the point where its standing part is made fast. The brail then falls to the deck. Sometimes two or three brails are joined after passing through their individual sheaves so that the hauling comes on one or, at the most, two parts. Some small vessels with this rig have all brails spliced to a single common part, so that the whole sail can be brailed in by heaving on this.

When choosing a rig for a cruising boat, future owners should think long and carefully. If they are *really* going cruising, their craft first of all should be able to take the knocks. The rig the vessel carries should be strong and not too complicated.

Perhaps it's time now for a word of caution about exotic rigs, such as junk, dhow, pirogue . . . there are many. All too often we see rigs that impress us when cruising in outlying places, rigs that send local craft flying along and have us admiring their ability and lack of sophisticated, expensive fittings. Take my tip and take photos of them, even go for a sail in the boats if you will, but leave it right there.

Stick with the rig you've got, the one that's popular back home, the one that's proved it can beat into a bay or off a lee shore or sail around the world (uphill if necessary). Always try to improve your rig by all means, but don't go swapping it just because a different rig has been used for a few thousand years in the South China Sea, or on a Pacific islander's canoe.

There are lots of rigs that are the result of conditions existing off the coasts or around a group of islands where the craft evolved, conditions that are responsible for spawning a certain arrangement of spars and sails. These conditions might be particularly short, steep seas; constant wind abeam from off the land (a soldier's wind); a long run with wind abaft the beam, with a wait for a seasonal change such as a monsoon while cargo is loaded, and then a run home again. One of these rigs, taken away from the conditions responsible for its evolution, installed aboard a sailboat, and expected to perform conpetently alongside similar vessels with modern cutter or sloop rigs, can often result in an expensive disappointment; she might be a dog to windward.

In an attempt to hammer the point home, I might mention that it's possible that one day you may want to sell your dreamship, if only because something bigger or better has taken your eye. Provided, of course, that you can get a good price for your vessel, this new one would be the total end. If you've gone and planted a way-

Cutter with standing gaff and mainsail neatly brailed to mast. Note the way bobstay is slacked and pulled aside for anchoring, rode is hove forward clear of stem, jib club on pedestal, channels, and battened deck awning. (This is Claud Worth's old Tern IV.) *(Ralph Naranjo photo)*

There is often a great difference in the rigs of the vessels one sees along the cruising way. (Ralph Naranjo photo)

out rig in your present boat, you might have to almost give her away to get rid of her. All of which makes the chance of a quick sale for the purchase of a bigger, better craft — or anything else — a mighty slim one.

Another point I hope has been made in this chapter during the discussion of the advantages and disadvantages of various cruising rigs is the need for acceptable windward ability. These days, most cruising boats have auxiliary engines; some of these engines are dependable, some are not. It's not good enough to say, "Oh, when the wind comes ahead, we'll motorsail." If your engine quits and your vessel has a rig that won't drive her to windward, you're dead in the water. Even cruising motorsailers should be able to get to windward. To equip any vessel with a rig that will sail her only downwind is to get her into trouble faster.

two

Spars

A mast is not just any old pole to hang sails on. It is a spar that must be able to take high compression loads, while at the same time accepting such bending stresses as are imparted by the pull of sails from any direction and moments of inertia transmitted by the vessel's motion and the spar's own weight. In addition to fulfilling its prime function — that of supporting sails correctly — the mast of a *cruising sailboat* must be able to take all these strains year after year for 30 years or more. And if it won't, it's the wrong mast.

If a stay or shroud lets go aboard a cruiser, it's nice to know that the mast is rugged enough not to break, buckle, or go over the wall before you can do something about it. For cruising, the strength and absolute dependability of the mast must be beyond question. High ideals? Well, let's see what we have to do to get such a spar. Let's take a look at what we have to choose from.

SPAR CONSTRUCTION

It would be safe to say that nowadays most masts for either production-line or custom-built boats are aluminum alloy. In fact, it is a pretty safe bet that many present-day yachtsmen and women have never been shipmates with spars built of any material other than aluminum. Fair enough; there's a lot to be said for an alloy spar. The owner of an aluminum mast is not faced with the problems that go hand-in-glove with ownership of a wooden mast. The joys of scraping, sanding, and painting a wooden mast, and trying not to think about dry rot aloft, are not experienced by the bloke with an alloy spar. He or she still has things to contend with, however; it's not apples all the way. Alloy spars *can* bend, they *can* break, and unchecked electrolytic corrosion can make an aluminum mast look as if a hungry rat had been on the job.

Wooden Spars

The advent of really good alloy masts heralded a much-needed breakthrough in sparmaking. To appreciate just what this has meant, it is necessary to look back to the days of wooden spars, when, in an effort to cut down weight aloft, hollow wooden masts and booms were replacing solid spars. The specter always haunting the maker of hollow wooden spars has been dry rot; one reason for this was the quality of the glue used to hold a mast together. A glued seam would separate and fresh water would seep through into the mast — leaving the yachtsman sailing around with rot eating away at the spar above his unsuspecting head.

I had a friend, a professional boatbuilder, who glued up the hollow spars for his 44-foot schooner in the late 1940s. He drilled a little hole for a wooden plug just above the solid butt of each mast, and he was forever pulling out these plugs to see if any condensation had collected. I was aboard his boat one day when a little dribble of water ran out when he pulled the plug on his mainmast. It was the sort of thing that gives a man bad dreams and has him counting his beads twice over when he wakes up. This plug-and-water exhibition was the deciding factor in my whittling solid spars for my yawl — spars that are still going strong.

Even as better, stronger glues became available, some hollow wooden spars still contracted dry rot, and the reason, I suspect, could be found in the use of lumber that wasn't seasoned properly. If you build a hollow mast out of wood that the birds were whistling in a short time back, there's a good chance that its moisture content will encourage rot inside the spar. I've an idea that this is how the *Kiwi*'s mast got dry rot. From the outside, all the glued seams in the varnished spruce spar looked in top condition, but the mast crumbled when dry rot ate its way from the inside out before the spar was two years old.

A hollow wooden mast should be built from well-seasoned lumber. Masthead, heel, and the various points where spreaders, tangs, and gooseneck attach should be solid. These solid load blocks may be drilled or grooved vertically before the spar is glued up, so that internal wiring for navigational and other lights can pass up through the inside of the mast. The inlets and outlets of electric wiring are places where water conceivably can enter a hollow wooden spar; these places must be completely watertight under all conditions. The safest way to have one less thing to worry about is to put external electric wiring on a hollow wooden mast.

A solid length of fir or spruce is apparently hard to come by these days. However, a solid mast can be laminated together from selected pieces of fir or spruce, say, 2-inch-by-8-inch pieces, 12 or 15 feet long. Joints can be staggered and scarfed, and additional strength over a natural-grown spar can be achieved by laying up the lumber with the "run of the grain" going opposite ways. With some of the glues available today, such a spar can be enormously strong. I remember seeing a spar made in this manner in the 1950s; it had even been fiberglassed for good measure.

Aluminum Spars

As much as aluminum spars enjoy great popularity, it is not just a matter of blithely planting an alloy mast in a boat, and that's that. Types of aluminum spars, sizes, weights, section, moments of inertia — all these come into it (as does rigging, mentioned in Chapter One). Fractional rigs, which many yachtsmen thought had disappeared from the scene forever (except in class boats), have been receiving their share of acclaim for some time now. It's a well-deserved share, too. The small-sectioned, baldheaded top of a mast designed to carry a three-quarter rig can be very much lighter than if the spar were meant to carry a masthead rig. Mast-bend to a degree that would alarm an ocean-cruising buff is accepted cheerfully — even arranged. A light racing boat with a bendy, fractionally rigged spar can really get up and go.

Here we get right down to the meat of the thing — the security aspect. Safety tolerances in the rigs of racers or even weekend cruisers are not always acceptable to the yachtsman or woman equipping a vessel for long-range cruising. For greater peace of mind over the long haul, it is best to have a stable masthead rig that will at all times keep the spar as straight as possible. A cruising man desiring a dependable, trouble-free rig should investigate fully the types of spars available. There are certainly masts that fulfill this criterion.

The most cursory investigation reveals that all alloy masts are not the same; some masts, size for size, are thinner-walled than others. Some masts are tapered, some are not. How many boatowners know the wall thickness of their mast? How many suspect that it may be of minimum thickness for the job it's expected to do?

In this book we are dealing specifically with cruising rigs. While a weekend, race-around-the-buoys owner might understandably tear his hair and bite a chunk or two out of his lower lip if his mast goes over the side, this is seldom a catastrophe. Even if it makes him sulk or puts him in a blue funk, he'll be curled up ashore in a warm, dry bed that night. By midweek, it's a nasty memory of last weekend, and it's his insurance company's turn to worry.

If the ocean cruiser loses his mast way out at sea, it's a different piece of cake; there's seldom anyone to lean on or to tow him in. There won't be any steady bunk that night, either. (The roll of a sailboat with no mast will make a believer out of anyone.) And a few days later it'll still be very much a fact of the present — which is a whole lot different from a nasty memory of last weekend. Our ocean wanderer will be fussing around with a jury rig, fully occupied with trying to get himself to some place where he can start making repairs.

The big thing, of course, is to do your best to ensure that your mast stays up there, no matter what. While the standing rigging plays an all-important part in this (and we'll come to that in the next chapter), the logical first step is to ensure that the mast itself is independently strong.

This basic principle that the lighter and smaller-sectioned a mast is, the less windage and weight there will be aloft — and consequently, the better the boat can be expected to perform — means less to an ocean cruiser than to a racer. A cruiser can't afford to have a marginally safe rig. A cruising boat must have an efficient sailing rig, but an aluminum mast should be of large enough section, and heavy enough wall thickness, that if a stay or shroud does carry away, the mast will not bend and stay bent. I don't know how many kinked aluminum masts I've seen over the years, but it must be a couple of dozen. While hollow aluminum masts have a lot going for them, it's not too easy to effect a repair when you're miles from nowhere. Can you imagine a stay letting go and your mast halfway up, tilting 30 degrees, and *staying that way* the day before you arrive at Suvarov or Niue. I don't know what you'd do

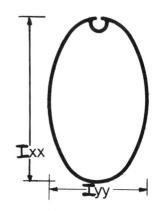

Above: *The top of a fractionally rigged tapered mast as compared with an untapered spar. (Courtesy Yachtspars)* **Right:** *Ixx is the mast's fore-and-aft dimension; Iyy is the athwartships dimension.*

in that case, other than your best — whatever that might be. Replacing the spar with a coconut tree isn't much of an alternative, but it's one you might find yourself considering. The best way around all this is to move heaven and earth first so that it doesn't happen.

To choose a mast for a *cruising boat,* consult every sparmaker's catalog you can get your hands on. The letters Ixx refer to fore-and-aft mast dimension, the letters Iyy refer to the athwartships dimension. If you have difficulty deciding on suitable dimensions for the mast(s) of your ship, write to a number of companies and stress the fact that your ship is going to be taken ocean cruising. Send a sail plan if you have one; always give waterline length, length of spar, beam of vessel, draft, ballast, and total displacement, and specify whether the mast is to be deck or keel stepped.

A plan of a vessel's hull shape is also handy for sparmakers to consult. In short, the more information supplied, the better a company can calculate suitable mast sections. The principal factors that govern the sections of an aluminum spar are:
   a) Displacement of vessel
   b) Ballast ratio
   c) Stiffness due to hull shape
   d) Height of foretriangle
   e) Angle of spread in shrouds
   f) Fore-and-aft staying
   g) Unsupported length of mast panel
   h) Manner of stepping
   i) Strength of material (see Table of Mechanical Properties on page 34) and distribution of same in the section

Some companies supply a recommended size (Ixx and Iyy) of spar for vessels of various lengths in their catalogs. Proctors of England supplies a handy, easy-to-consult graph in their catalog, and this gives the yachtsman a guide to the Ixx and Iyy dimensions suitable for the masts of his particular vessel. If the information you require is not in a catalog, write to the company; get as many particulars as you can from a number of companies.

Compare the recommendations; have a look at the comparable weights and thicknesses of the spars (see table). The racing man will be influenced greatly by the

(continued on page 36)

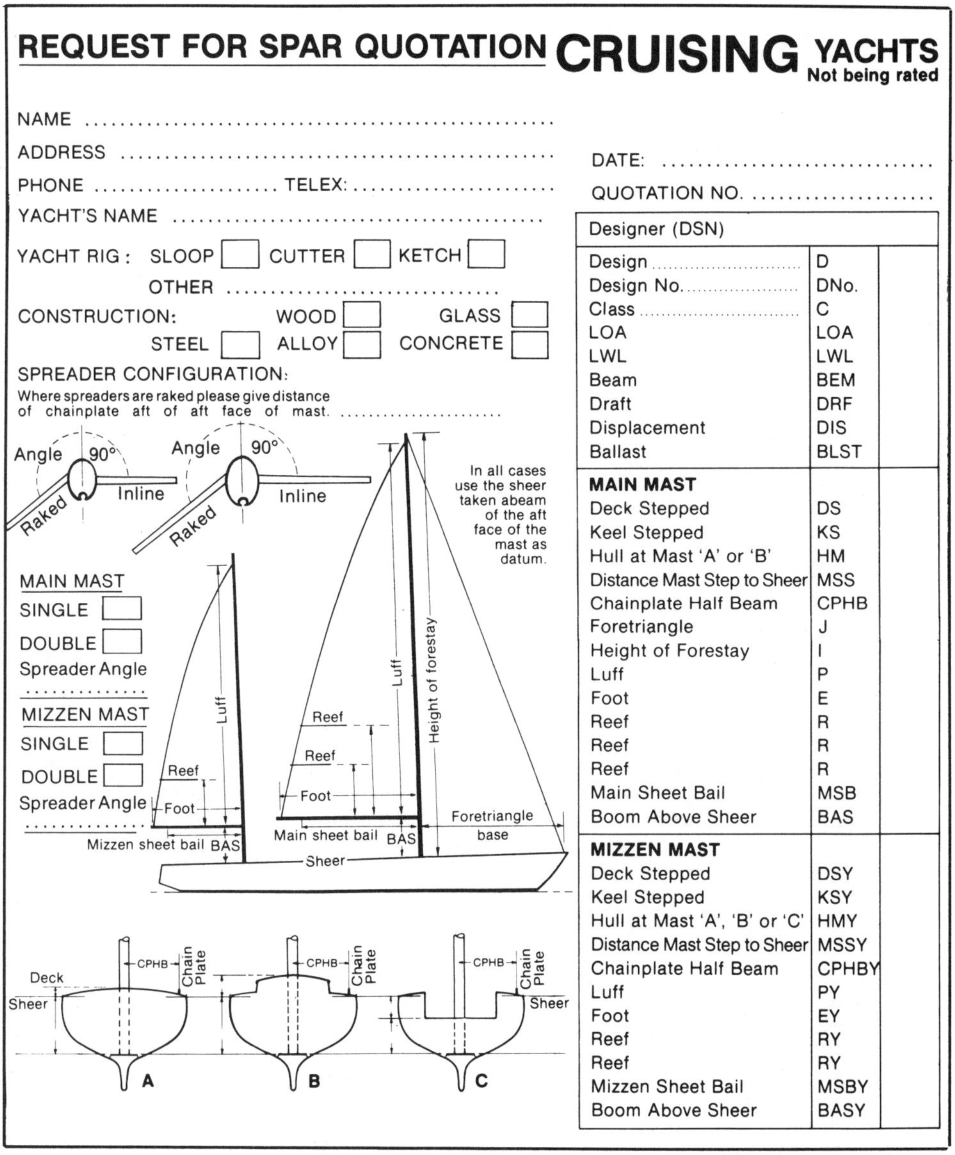

REQUEST FOR SPAR QUOTATION **CRUISING** YACHTS
Not being rated

NAME ....

ADDRESS ....

PHONE .... TELEX: ....

YACHT'S NAME ....

YACHT RIG :   SLOOP ☐   CUTTER ☐   KETCH ☐

OTHER ....

CONSTRUCTION: WOOD ☐   GLASS ☐

STEEL ☐   ALLOY ☐   CONCRETE ☐

SPREADER CONFIGURATION:

Where spreaders are raked please give distance of chainplate aft of aft face of mast. ....

DATE: ....

QUOTATION NO. ....

Designer (DSN)		
Design	D	
Design No..................	DNo.	
Class	C	
LOA	LOA	
LWL	LWL	
Beam	BEM	
Draft	DRF	
Displacement	DIS	
Ballast	BLST	
MAIN MAST		
Deck Stepped	DS	
Keel Stepped	KS	
Hull at Mast 'A' or 'B'	HM	
Distance Mast Step to Sheer	MSS	
Chainplate Half Beam	CPHB	
Foretriangle	J	
Height of Forestay	I	
Luff	P	
Foot	E	
Reef	R	
Reef	R	
Reef	R	
Main Sheet Bail	MSB	
Boom Above Sheer	BAS	
MIZZEN MAST		
Deck Stepped	DSY	
Keel Stepped	KSY	
Hull at Mast 'A', 'B' or 'C'	HMY	
Distance Mast Step to Sheer	MSSY	
Chainplate Half Beam	CPHBY	
Luff	PY	
Foot	EY	
Reef	RY	
Reef	RY	
Mizzen Sheet Bail	MSBY	
Boom Above Sheer	BASY	

MAIN MAST

SINGLE ☐

DOUBLE ☐
Spreader Angle ....

MIZZEN MAST

SINGLE ☐

DOUBLE ☐
Spreader Angle ....

When seeking a mast and rigging quotation for a cruising sailboat, supply as much information about your boat as is available. The more accurate the information you give, the more accurate the quote is likely to be. Above is a typical example of the information a company appreciates before working out spar sections and sizes of rigging. (Courtesy Yachtspars)

TYPICAL MECHANICAL PROPERTIES OF ALUMINUM
USED IN MAST FABRICATION

Alloy and Temper	Ultimate Tensile Strength	Yield Strength	Elongation %	Hardness (Brinell)	Shear	Modulus of Elasticity Mpa × 10³
A. 6061 T6	310	276	12	95	207	69
B. 6063 T5	193	145	12	60	117	69

Definition of Terms

Ultimate Tensile Strength is the maximum tensile stress that a material is capable of developing under a gradual and uniformly applied load.

Yield Strength is the stress at which a material exhibits a specified permanent set after being strained beyond the elastic limit.

Elongation is the increase in distance between two gauge marks that results from stressing the specimen in tension to fracture.

Hardness is a measure of resistance to indentation.

Shear is the maximum shearing stress that a material is capable of developing.

Modulus of Elasticity is the ratio of stress to corresponding strain throughout the range where they are proportional in an elastic material.

OPPOSITE PAGE: **Below left:** *Forward, starboard side of masthead. Suitable for cruiser/racer, or pure cruising boat with masthead rig, this four-sheave head with its twin spinnaker horns is welded to the top of a modestly tapered spar.* **Below right:** *Starboard side of masthead of an untapered spar for a cruiser or cruiser/racer. Note (from left) swage and toggle of permanent backstay; wire topping lift; rope-to-wire splice of main halyard just entering sheave; flag halyard and eye; angled stand on anemometer (top); jib halyards; 1/19 forestay, swage and toggle; and wire spinnaker halyard. Note also moused pin of shackle connecting spinnaker block to horn. Excellent practice! (Courtesy Yachtspars)*

THIS PAGE: **Below left:** *Port side of mizzen masthead for either ketch or yawl. Lug for a triatic stay on top if required. Note stainless steel guard around exit for internal staysail halyard and at the rear of the mast, the holes to take pins for a backstay, a mizzen topping lift, and the sheave for a mizzen halyard.* **Below right:** *Port side of masthead designed for mainmast of yawl or ketch or foremast of schooner with lug for triatic stay. Note strong, through-bolted shroud tang. (Courtesy Yachtspars)*

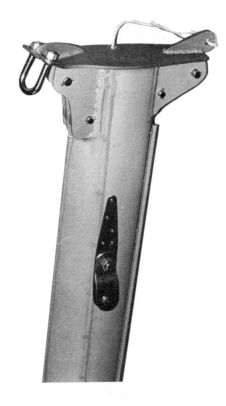

lightness of the wall of one company's spars as compared with that of another's. I advise the cruising man to take the opposite approach — and then go one size bigger if he feels inclined. Don't worry about the extra weight; your mast will still be one hell of a lot lighter than a solid wooden spar. (And vessels with wooden masts sailed around the world for centuries before the first aluminum job appeared.)

Sails and their various methods of hoisting, setting, reefing, and furling are discussed in future chapters; however, it is not too early to mention a system of sailhandling that has made life easier for a lot of cruising folk. This method is the Stoway. Manufactured by Hood Yacht Systems (P.O. Box 1049, Lime Street, Marblehead, Massachusetts 01945), the Stoway system enables a marconi sail to be set, reefed, or furled in almost as little time as it takes to think about it. The mast and sail are suitable for any rig that has marconi sails: sloop, cutter, ketch, yawl, schooner — straight sailboat, auxiliary, or motorsailer. A Stoway system used on a marconi sail makes sailhandling a joke.

The Stoway mast is an aluminum spar incorporating a partially enclosed section, inside of which a luff extrusion rotates to roll and stow the sail. All that's left outside is a tiny piece of clew (see photograph). The sail, which feeds in and out through a slot in the mast, can be raised or lowered in the usual manner if required. There are three options of sailhandling available: (1) A crank handle may be fitted in the for-

A Stoway mainsail being furled inside a mast by winding away at a crank handle on the forward side of the spar. Note weather cloths at each side of deckhouse and in lifelines aft of gate. (Courtesy Yachtspars)

ward side of the mast at gooseneck level to wind the sail in or out, and the clew outhaul line is led forward, so that this operation can be handled by one person; (2) Remote manual operation can be arranged by a control leading from either cockpit or doghouse to a mechanism within the mast that rotates the luff extrusion; (3) An electric drive unit (which has a manual back-up in case of power failure) will do all this at the touch of a button. (Wonder how many old shellbacks are turning in their graves?)

The aluminum extrusion method used by Hood for their Stoway rig makes a good, strong spar. The fact that the Stoway mast has an integral web running from top to bottom to confine the rolled sail contributes tremendously to its strength.

A lot of cruising sailors are do-it-yourselfers who like to work on the assembling of their own spars. A company catering to these preferences is the LeFIELL firm (LeFIELL Marine Products, 13700 Firestone Boulevard, Santa Fe Springs, California 90670). Spars are supplied either finished in every respect or in do-it-yourself kits. These kits, for many sizes of vessel, come with a complete set of step-by-step instructions that are easy to follow. The company suggests mast sizes and kits for various sizes and types of boat.

Steel Spars

Another type of hollow metal spar is the steel tube, and for the large, heavy-displacement cruising sailboat, it is well worth considering. Good, solid lugs can be welded to a steel mast for staying, and a welding rig can be carried aboard in case any additional stay or shroud anchorages are desired, or other fittings need to be installed. If you really want to be a sport, and you're not too worried about weight, pass a thinner tube up the inside of your mast and out one side at the top, and use this tube for your engine exhaust. One of the biggest favors you can do any engine is to give it a dry exhaust; this system saves the cruising sailor from wriggling a water-cooled exhaust around accommodations below — and saves one large hole in the hull of the ship.

My suggestion of a steel mast with exhaust might not add to my following among the "keep-down-the-weight-aloft-at-all-costs" gang, but it does work. With such an exhaust rig, you can whisper your way in and out of anchorages, and you never get a single whiff of exhaust smoke on deck. The cost of a steel-pipe mast is usually a whole lot less than an alloy job. For those whose boat is hefty enough to lump around a hollow-steel mast — and who are also keen to take this route — I say, fire ahead. A rigging failure is far less likely to leave you with a broken or buckled mast than with any other type of spar. A steel mast is cheaper; you can, if you so desire, lead your exhaust up inside; you can have lugs or anything else welded on in almost any port. It's a mighty convenient, tough piece of equipment.

Carbon Fiber Spars

Then there is the hollow, carbon fiber spar. Used as free-standing masts in the Freedom cat ketches, these spars appear wonderfully suited for this application. According to the designer of the craft, they have proved their superiority over

A 100-foot staysail schooner that sets a squaresail and raffee on her foremast. Note the reinforcing strip on the mainsail in way of the topping lift. Her masts are steel. The mainmast contains exhaust lines for main and auxiliary engines and the vent for a sanitary tank; the foremast has the flue for the galley range. This is the Westward, *designed by Eldredge-McInnis and now owned and operated by the Sea Education Association. (National Fisherman)*

aluminum. Garry Hoyt has told me he doesn't want a totally stiff spar. "Where the masthead of an unstayed aluminum mast would bend three feet from the perpendicular in a hard squall," he says, "the top of a carbon fiber spar bends only 18 inches under equivalent conditions — and this is ideal." He goes on to say: "It is perhaps not generally appreciated by most people how effectively a free-standing spar depowers when it bends backwards and off to leeward at the top. What happens is that the whole top of the sail goes completely flat."

A swiveling masthead fitting enables the sail to twist off in line with the wind. He continues: "This leaves only the bottom half of the sail driving — and yet the top half is completely stiff without the slapping that is often associated with twist. Thus, the free-standing spar is able to carry full sail much longer than the conventional masthead rig which has no way to allow the leech to relieve or the sail to flatten."

Carbon fiber, which is actually superheated rayon drawn into filaments as fine as human hair, is set in epoxy resin. The three important factors present in the manufacture of carbon fiber spars are heat, pressure, and tension. The spars are formed around a stainless steel mandrel, which is driven out after the epoxy resin is set. A most important part of the procedure is the tension applied to the longitudinal fibers while the epoxy is "taking." Used in a variety of applications, such as automobile drive shafts and tennis rackets, carbon fiber is touted to be " . . . as strong as steel and lighter than aluminum." If so, will hollow carbon fiber spars compete with aluminum for stayed masts? Will carbon fiber be able to take the enormous compression loads imparted by the small cap-shroud angles of some modern rigs? Or will these spars prove suitable only for special applications — such as ideal masts for a free-standing rig? Time will tell.

DECK-STEPPED VS. KEEL-STEPPED MASTS

Decide early on whether your mast is to be keel- or deck-stepped. A deck-stepped mast is often of heavier section than a spar supported at deck or cabintop level and stepped on the keel. Proponents of deck-stepped masts advance a number of reasons in defense of their cause. At the top of their list is its ability to keep below-decks accommodations clear, rather than having a mast appear in the middle of the saloon table or just where the head door opens.

Aboard a small weekend cruiser, where as much room as possible is needed for bunks and a place to cook and eat, space is at a premium. A designer or builder able to produce an uncluttered living area can be the one most likely to sell his product. The compression imposed by a deck-stepped mast is taken by a bulkhead, an I-beam running athwartships immediately below the point where the mast steps on deck, or sometimes by a pipe that doesn't offer as much physical size as the butt-end of a mast. Another "advantage" presented by the deck-stepped mast enthusiast is that if a vital stay or shroud carries away, the spar goes over the side all in one piece without bending or breaking. All he has to do is get it back aboard again — ho, ho! A deck-stepped mast is also shorter, and therefore cheaper.

Sometimes the reason for not continuing a mast through the deck and stepping it on the keel is that the vessel's cruising grounds include canals and bridges. The mast is going to have to be lowered to the deck at various times. This is the most valid ex-

Below: *The base of this deck-stepped mast incorporates a frame to which blocks may be snapped. Such a mast must be stayed very sturdily, for if any of the rigging wires or sundry fittings carried away, enormous strain would be imposed on the coach roof.* **Right:** *Hinge for base of deck-stepped mast on small cruiser. (Courtesy Yachtspars)*

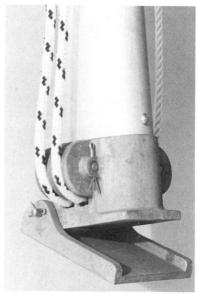

cuse of all for a deck-stepped mast. A housing on deck, inside which the butt of a mast pivots, allowing the spar to be laid fore-and-aft along the deck, is known as a tabernacle, and it is easy to arrange.

There are several manufacturers of aluminum spars (Proctors of England and Yachtspars of New Zealand are two) who will supply masts in tabernacles. The yachtsman who wishes to cruise in places where bridges or overhanging vegetation dictates that he lower his mast and proceed with it lashed on deck should, if he intends to use a tabernacle, choose this fitting with care. A tabernacle should be rugged beyond all question, and the whole installation should be arranged so that the crew of the vessel can lower and raise the mast without any outside help. This last is most important. There are limits on a vessel that has its mast hinged in a tabernacle but needs the services of a shoreside crane to lift the spar so the rigging can be set up. An important point to observe when the butt of a mast pivots in a tabernacle is that, when the spar is fully raised, the load is transferred to the deck. To achieve maximum stability at this point, slotted holes are sometimes utilized at each end of the pivot-pin; alternatively, wedges are sometimes driven between the mast heel and the base of the tabernacle frame.

A keel-stepped mast, firmly supported at deck or cabintop, gives a far greater safety margin than any spar stepped on deck. If a stay or shroud lets go, there is a good chance that such a mast will stay in the ship; with a deck-stepped mast, there is almost no chance. If you intend to do a lot of canal or under-bridge work, then so be it — a good tabernacle setup is probably the best. But if your venture through a series of canals or up a river is a one-shot deal — or something you only intend to do

A way of "jazzing up" a mast below decks. The odd elbow, knee, or head that contacts it in a seaway will think it's pretty good, too. (Courtesy Yachtspars)

every few years or so — install a keel-stepped mast in your ship and have a crane lift it in and out at the beginning and end of each trip. As mentioned, this limits where you can go, as the availability of the services of a crane at each end of the cruise is the deciding factor, but at least when the mast is stepped and rigged, it is part of the ship. There is no way a deck-stepped mast or a mast carried in a tabernacle can qualify as such.

An objection sometimes heard regarding a keel-stepped mast is the possibility that water will leak below through the hole where the mast passes through the deck or cabintop. There is no more need for this joint to leak than any other on the ship, whether the mast be constructed of aluminum, wood, or any other material. A completely watertight mast boot for a wooden spar can be made from a piece of cheap canvas, fiberglass cloth, burlap, or anything with a stretchy weave. The material is wrapped around the mast a few inches above deck level and glued to both mast and deck with Arabol. (Arabol is a white, rubbery mixture used in ships' engine rooms for sticking asbestos lagging to steam and exhaust pipes; it can be purchased from any supplier of asbestos lagging.)

Some makers of aluminum spars recommend that their keel-stepped masts be held firmly at deck or cabintop by hard rubber or wooden wedges, and that a watertight seal be achieved by a piece of inner tube clamped to both the mast and an upstanding

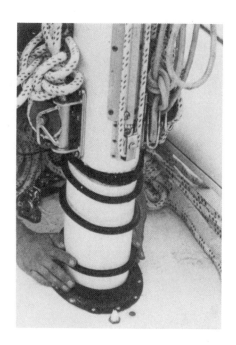

The rubber compression O-rings in this illustration should be placed on the mast a minimum of three inches apart. The rings should be so arranged that the bottom one enters the collar when the mast is nine inches off the step and the last one enters the collar when the mast is 1½ inches off the step. On no account should water or any other lubricant be used on the rings; they should be inserted dry. When the mast is stepped and the rigging set up, the space between the top ring and the deck collar can be filled with flexible seam compound. (Courtesy Yachtspars)

deck collar by hose clips. To protect the rubber from the sun's rays, and for cosmetic purposes, a fabric cover is sometimes installed over the rubber boot. The best deck-mast seal I've ever been shipmates with is the one used on both of the *Rigadoon*'s aluminum masts. Three large rubber O-rings (see photograph) are a tight fit inside the company-supplied through-deck fitting. Deck seam compound is used to fill the space around the mast (about one-half inch wide by one inch deep) from the top O-ring to the brim of the deck fitting.

Deck Collars and Mast Heels

If the mast is aluminum, the collar and mast heel should be of the same material. Otherwise there is every chance of massive corrosion. Salt air is enough to get electrolytic corrosion going at great guns between an alloy spar and a stainless step. (I have a friend who was recently faced with a great and expensive amount of surgery on the heel of his mizzenmast for just this reason.)

The yachtsman putting an aluminum mast in his boat should realize that water gets inside these spars. This especially applies to those with internal halyards. Internal halyards that are wet by rain and spray and are then hauled over sheaves, on down the inside of a mast, and out to a winch, can take a lot of water in with them. The more openings a spar has, the more water is going to get inside. The cruising yachtsman, concerned with the longevity of his rig, should make certain that any moisture can drain out as quickly as possible.

Some aluminum masts have a drain hole above the heel plug to enable any water that has accumulated inside to drain out and into the bilge. The cruising sailor would

Top left: *Mast deck collar for a small (up to 32 feet) cruising boat. If the eyebolts as shown are used as anchorages for turning blocks, the deck should be strengthened with tie-rods between deck and keel.* **Top right:** *Rubber mast boot with deck collar.* **Above:** *Mast bases for deck-stepped spars. The top three bases are fixed and have boom-vang fittings. The three bases at bottom can be used with a deck-hinge tabernacle fitting. (Courtesy Yachtspars)*

do well to regard this with suspicion. First of all, allowing water to drain out of the mast in this manner ensures that the mast, heel, and step are frequently wet — sometimes for quite long periods, and always to their detriment. The drier you keep your mast heel and step, the less likelihood there is of corrosion. My other objection to a drain hole is that it's inviting water into your ship, which doesn't make sense.

The best tactic I've ever seen to ensure that water drains out of an aluminum mast above decks is the one involving a tight-fitting plug as installed by Yachtspars of New Zealand. This waterstop is constructed of "memory-retentive" plastic about two inches thick, and, after being cut slightly oversize, is pushed up inside the spar to the bottom of the lowest halyard exit before a cast aluminum heel is fitted. The plug is positioned exactly so that water running down the inside of the mast will drain out the lowest halyard exit. This plug is sealed in place by self-leveling Thiokol, and the procedure for using this rubbery material on the job is as follows. The mast, complete with its plastic waterstop, is installed in the boat, and the rigging is tensioned (see Chapter Three). The vessel is then heeled away from the lowest halyard exit, which is invariably at one side or the other of the mast. This list can be induced by a halyard made fast to a dock (this must be watched carefully if the area is tidal); a distribution of ballast; or, easiest of all, by putting a weight at the end of the boom and guying it square off. The Thiokol is poured in through the halyard exit until it is level with the bottom of the slot, and then it is allowed to set for a few hours. The finished job ensures that, when the vessel is upright, there is a slope or "fall" toward the halyard exit. Water trickling down inside the mast from any cause has no option but to run down the slope of the Thiokol, out through the halyard exit, and onto the deck.

All this means that there is every chance that the mast heel and step will remain dry — unless, of course, the vessel leaks enough for bilge water to reach the spar end or there are halyards exiting below decks. In any case, whether or not a plug is present in your mast, keep a weather eye cocked on the mast heel and step: don't let the bottom of your mast remain uninspected. The butt of a mast takes enormous strains, and the harder a vessel is sailed, the harder is this pressure. Dissimilar metals, damp wood touching the spar, intermittent or constant immersion in salt water, or a stray electric current can all start corrosion, and the sailor could find himself in dire straits.

Great care should be taken to ensure that the base of a mast fits absolutely perfectly on or in its heel plug. If the plug is an indifferent fit, and if, for instance, one side of the mast heel takes the full weight of the rig, this stress will be distributed unfairly along the length of the spar. In some cases, an ill-fitting heel plug and consequent unequal distribution of compression stress can cause great difficulty in the correct staying of the mast. If your mast insists on kinking one way — no matter how you adjust the rigging — run a check on the fit of the heel. Could be the mast is only bearing on one side.

Care must also be taken over the type of step the heel plug sits in. An aluminum mast sitting in a bronze mast step, for instance, is asking for trouble because of the

The corrosion at the heel of this mast occurred within a few months from sitting in a stainless steel step and getting wet. That wiring doesn't look too healthy either, does it? (Courtesy Yachtspars)

dissimilar metals. Stainless steel is bad, too. So is wood, if it's allowed to get damp. In all of these cases, the mast must be insulated from the step by Formica, PVC, or some similar inert material. A galvanized steel mast step shouldn't need insulation. If your vessel is aluminum — which means the step will be that material, also — you're probably in good shape. If there's a smidgen of doubt, however, insulate the heel plug from the step — and don't forget to inspect it regularly.

MAST TRACKS AND THEIR FITTINGS

Traditionally, gaff-rigged vessels have wooden masts, especially if sail hoops are used. Sail hoops mean chafe, and even though a cruising sailor may go all ancient and crafty by slathering linseed oil and tallow up and down his mast, there will still be chafe. Some gaff-rigged vessels with steel masts have a hefty steel track welded to the mast or fastened on with machine screws. This track is strong enough to take the gaff gooseneck and sail slides (see photograph). An aluminum gaff has a lot to recommend it, especially in light weather at sea when the vessel is rolling and sails are slatting. Under these conditions aluminum is much easier to control with topsail, vang, guy, or all three, than wood or steel. Its light weight is a bonus when hoisting and furling sail, too.

Gaff gooseneck and custom-built slide for track welded to a steel mast. Note eye on top of gaff for throat halyard, sheet for topsail clew, and custom sail slides. The track on this schooner sits on a hollow "square" tube, which is welded to both track and mast. Inside of tube takes electric wiring for mast lights. (Dave Ferneding photo)

Strong gooseneck fitting for wooden boom of gaff sail. Sail tack shackles to eye of fitting, which swivels on knuckle pin. Lugs that confine pin are welded to the steel mast. (Dave Ferneding photo)

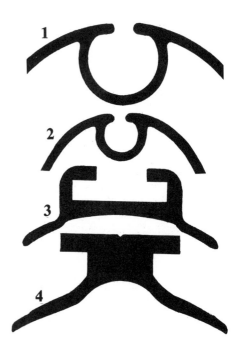

Mast tracks (actual size).
1. *Integral track cast into mast. A sail using this track must use slugs shackled or lashed to luff eyelets.*
2. *Integral track cast into mast. The wire luff of the sail may be fed directly into this track.*
3. *This flanged track may be fastened to any mast.*
4. *Spinnaker pole track. Suitable for fastening to any mast.*

Some manufacturers of aluminum spars supply their masts tapered toward the top. Others do so only by special order. It is kinder to a mainsail for the spar to be tapered where the sail is narrowest: a small-sectioned spar at this point reduces the area of turbulence and panders to airflow across the sail in a manner not possible for a large-sectioned spar. It also cuts down on weight and windage aloft. With a tapered mast, there is often chafe from external halyards, but for all that, I like to see a modest taper in the masts of a cruising boat.

Some aluminum masts are supplied with a sail track or slot already extruded in the spar for the bolt rope of a sail. There are several ways of viewing this. The first reaction of many cruising folk (including me) is that this is best of all: it saves installing a track and it is strong, mighty strong. The second, more cautious, note advanced by the doubters is that if, for any reason, an integral mast track is damaged, how do you repair it? It'd be a hell of a job. The third objection (and one that isn't too impressive) comes from people who feel they want to choose their own track and slides.

Personally, I like an integral track for its strength, although this wouldn't be the deciding factor in my choosing a spar. The ocean-cruising nut who buys a mast with a track for a bolt rope extruded in it would do well to discount feeding the luff of his sail into the opening, and instead purchase slides, known as slugs, to be shackled or seized to sail eyelets in the usual manner. An integral track is fine for the racing crowd, where there is always someone to feed the sail luff into the track as somebody else hoists away. Aboard a racer there are also many hands to prevent the rag from disappearing over the side and into the drink when it scoots out the bottom of the track as sail is lowered.

Aluminum mast section showing flanged female track pop-riveted to spar. (Courtesy Yachtspars)

Probably the best type of track to affix to an aluminum spar that has no integral groove is one with a full-length flange each side. The track itself takes slugs or regular flat, male slides, and the flange is fastened to the mast with stainless steel machine screws or stainless steel pop rivets. It is important with a track thus secured to double up on the track fastenings where the head sail slide comes in at each reefed position, as well as when fully hoisted. If the same track is used for the trysail, extra fastenings should also be used at the position that the head of this sail will occupy.

Always carry a pop-rivet gun and a supply of the identical rivets used to fasten any mast fitting. You never know — you just might want to put in a few more rivets here and there, or, now and again, replace some. A better, stronger (though more expensive) way of fastening track or anything else to a spar is with stainless steel or Monel roundhead machine screws. Again, the cruising boat should carry a supply of such fastenings, along with the correct sizes of drills and taps for the threads of the machine screws. When installing these fastenings in a mast with internal halyards, care should be taken that the fastenings do not project so far inside the mast that they chafe the halyards. Owing to the possibility of electrolytic corrosion, bronze or copper fastenings should never be used on an aluminum spar. If you have occasion to move a cleat or any other fitting, put plastic aluminum epoxy in the holes previously occupied by fastenings. This will keep water from entering these points and will aid corrosion prevention, too.

The yachtsman with an aluminum mast can be lulled into a sense of false security by the appearance of his spar between spreaders, or above and between places where gooseneck, winches, and other fittings are installed. The open stretches of mast usually look perfect. The true condition of the spar, however, depends on how well sealed from water and air *every* fitting is. An insulating and bedding agent such as polysulfide or zinc chromate paste should be used between an aluminum spar and *any fitting,* no matter what material the fitting is constructed from or what protective coating the mast and/or the fitting already has.

Even a cast aluminum pad should have an insulating compound between it and an

Steaming light fitting (visible arc 225 degrees). All lights and their mounts where they fasten to a spar must be sealed with compound and/or gaskets so that water cannot get at the wiring. (Courtesy Yachtspars)

aluminum mast; otherwise, salt water will find its way between pad and spar, and in time corrosion will get going. A satisfactory way to insulate shaped winch pads (of any material) from a mast is to cut a piece of thin neoprene or rubber, goop it up both sides with polysulfide, and install this between pad and mast. As the machine screws or bolts are tightened, the polysulfide will squeeze out, leaving a perfect seal. Best of all are winch bases welded to the spar.

It is possible for a cruising man or woman to install aluminum spars and enjoy the strength and dependability of these spars for many years. This will only happen, however, if they've chosen the correct-sized spars in the first place, if they've rigged them stoutly, and if they are corrosion-conscious. The reason I'm hammering away at this corrosion business is that the intended cruising person outfitting his or her boat for a life out there on the briny often equips it in a temperate climate, where there are local marinas full of boats whose aluminum spars give little if any trouble at all. It's when you leave these conditions and sail to the tropics (and most cruisers do) that corrosion troubles are most likely to start. It is usually impossible, once you get away cruising, to wash down your aluminum spars with fresh water — a treatment recommended in almost every aluminum sparmaker's catalog. The only rinsing that the spars of a cruising boat receive is from rainwater.

The captain of a long-range, aluminum-sparred cruising boat used extensively in the tropics is well advised to carry a spare section of mast (a minimum length of four feet) and a sleeve for joining sections (see illustration). If the mast heel needs renewing, or if a piece needs to be cut out of any other part of the mast and the spar rejoined, it's nice to know that the wherewithal is aboard to effect a strong repair.

The careful reader will probably note that while I have advocated the insulating of winch bases, spreader bases, and the like by the use of a compound between these fittings and an aluminum spar, I have mentioned that stainless steel rivets or machine screws are used to fasten tracks to the same spar. This is standard practice by many companies, and when questioned, one company executive informed me

Mast-lengthening-sleeving operation. Sleeve is placed inside both pieces of spar and is then welded to spar through the holes. Surface of spar has been disc-sanded around each drilled hole so that clean, untreated metal is exposed for the welding job. An example of finished welded holes can be seen in the center of the sleeve. (Courtesy Yachtspars)

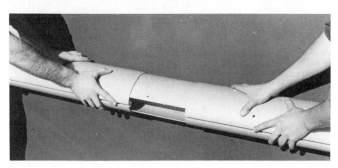

Another joining method. This sleeve is held in place by machine screws. (Courtesy Yachtspars)

that: "The head of a pop rivet is so small, and the position of the rivets such a distance apart, that even if one rivet *were* influenced by electrolysis, it could hardly spread to another." Be that as it may, I would strongly advocate that all spare pop rivets and machine screws carried aboard for the purpose of replacing fastenings in a spar, or adding extra fittings, be of Monel. This metal is excellent for its ability to do a strong job of holding a fitting, yet at the same time to be relatively unaffected by circumstances that lead to electrolysis.

BOOMS AND POLES

Hand in hand with aluminum masts go aluminum booms, and the same care applies regarding the insulation of fittings and mixing of dissimilar metals. Before choosing a boom, the cruising yachtsman should decide which system of reefing will be employed. Although reefing methods are discussed in Chapter Seven, the type of reefing used should be decided on early, as it will influence the choice of whether the boom is engineered for either roller reefing or slab reefing. If slab reefing is the chosen system, the spar manufacturer should be informed of the boom positions for the standing part and the sheave of each reef pendant. There will be other things, too. The position of bails is important. A cruising man might want a separate foreguy on each side of the boom (this usually depends on where the mainsheet is

Top: *Outhauling the foot of a mainsail. Note exterior cheek block, boom bail, mousing on topping lift shackle limiting movement of eye. (Courtesy Yachtspars)*
Center: *On this boom end, the outhaul is also used to put in a flattening reef. This illustration shows the wire of the outhaul emerging from the boom end, passing through the single block on the outhaul car, and so up to the reef cringle. This system enables the car to move at twice the speed of the flattening reef coming in, and thus automatically adjusts the tension between the two. There are not many cruising folk who bother with the niceties of a flattening reef, but for those who do, this isn't a bad rig. (Courtesy Yachtspars)*
Bottom: *These reef pendants pass through plastic grommets on their way into the boom. Note internal anchorage for mainsheet block. (Courtesy Yachtspars)*

secured). If he's going to utilize his boom as a derrick to lift a dinghy, auxiliary engine, or motorcycle aboard at times (see Chapter Eleven), he might want an extra lug on the boom end so that the topping lift can be doubled up.

Manufacturers of aluminum spars who cater to the sailor wanting roller reefing are not easy to find. Proctor (Proctor Masts, Duncan Road, Swanwick, Southampton, England) makes two sizes of through-mast roller-reefing gear for aluminum booms that are superb. This company also supplies slab-reefing booms with a track beneath the boom so that reef pendant positions can be changed quickly.

An aluminum boom is popular because of its minimum weight and for the reason that various lines, such as the outhaul tackle and reefing pendants, can be led along its inside. Line stoppers can be installed in the boom close to the gooseneck, and such gear is very handy. Another reason for the popularity of alloy booms is that they can be purchased "off the shelf."

There is nothing wrong with a wooden boom, though — especially if roller reefing is the system decided upon (see Chapter Seven).

In light weather, a little bit of weight at the bottom of a mainsail or mizzen — for those who are tardy about the use of a boom vang — can do some good. When the weather kicks up a bit, the extra weight of the wooden boom won't be noticed anyhow. Put it this way: If your vessel objects to the weight difference between an aluminum and a wooden boom, you've got the wrong ship to go cruising in, mate. You don't need to be a Grade-A wood butcher to whittle out a wooden boom; it's a job anyone can launch into after work.

Look through marine catalogs for boom-end fittings (gooseneck, outhaul, and track), boom bails (for guys, preventers, vangs, mainsheet), and track (for the foot of the sail). I like to see a boom-end fitting that slides over the end of the spar like a cup, and so protects the grain. A boom gooseneck fitting with a tongue each side should come at least a foot back along the boom and be riveted right through. When installing such a fitting, I prefer to shape the boom until the gooseneck is a snug fit; then, with a clear-cut bit in an electric drill, make a hole a little more than halfway through each side of the boom at the first hole in the fitting. With a hole right through the boom, a piece of copper rod is tapped on through until it is a good $\frac{1}{16}$ inch proud of the surface of the fitting. Then the rod is hacksawed off on its long side a similar distance from the surface of the metal, and the two ends are riveted over. When the first rivet is completed, the rest (three is a common number) can be installed. Always complete one rivet before drilling the next hole.

The rivet holes in the gooseneck fitting should be well countersunk to take the head of the rivet as it is peened over. The size of the copper rivets depends upon the dimensions of the boom; $\frac{3}{8}$- or $\frac{5}{16}$-inch-diameter rivets are suitable for a 4-by-4-inch boom. The fitting by which the gooseneck attaches to the mast or slider should enable the boom to swivel on its own axis, so that when sheets are eased, an unfair

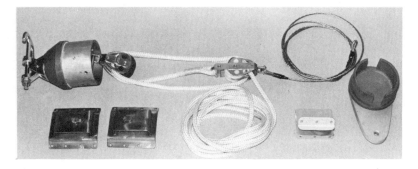

Boom gooseneck fitting, internal 5:1 outhaul tackle rove to advantage, boom-end fitting, sheave for outhaul wire, cheek blocks. (Courtesy Yachtspars)

Top left: *Gooseneck fitting on a slide that is positioned by downhaul. Note tack shackle, reefing hooks.* **Top right:** *"Cup" end and gooseneck fitting for wooden boom. Sail tack locates between flanges and is secured by pin (hanging from lanyard). Luff reef cringles lash to eyes formed by rod brazed to flanges and fitting.* **Above:** *Simple gooseneck fitting. Sail tack lashes to spindle, leaving reef hooks free. (Courtesy Yachtspars)*

twisting strain is not placed on the gooseneck. Another gooseneck fitting for wooden booms is in the shape of a cup. The boom is shaped to fit inside the cup and is held there by screws and/or rivets.

A gooseneck often locates in a fitting that slides on a heavy, cast piece of track, well secured by machine screws to mast bands, and to the mast itself with wood screws of a generous gauge. In order to avoid putting a line of screws in the masts of my yawl, I had mast bands cast out of aluminum bronze. Each band had a hefty lug cast in its aft side and these lugs were tapped with ¾-inch thread for the mainmast and ½-inch thread for the mizzen. Thus, the main boom gooseneck fitting could slide up or down a ¾-inch bronze rod between bands securely bolted around the mainmast. The vertical distance between the bands was one foot. The mizzen boom gooseneck was similarly treated; the distance between mast bands was nine inches, and the rod was ½-inch bronze.

A lot of fittings — especially on spars whittled out by do-it-yourselfers — are fabricated out of mild steel and galvanized. There's nothing wrong with this. Old Man Sea won't care if your boom and mast fittings are galvanized steel instead of stainless steel or bronze. As far as ability to take wear and tear is concerned, it's a fair bet those galvanized steel fittings will still be going strong when you've been given the deep six.

Outhaul tracks and boom bails should be riveted or bolted through the boom. Don't trust screws for any of these fittings; they take a mighty lot of weight at times. The U of an outhaul slider or gooseneck fitting designed to take clew and tack cringles should always be of a generous width between the jaws. The sizes of sail cringles vary often enough for this to be important. Another system, of course, is to forget all about outhauls and special gooseneck anchorages for sail cringles, and secure tack and clew with lashings.

Although a spinnaker pole is not carried as conscientiously aboard an ocean cruiser as on a racing boat, it is still a mighty handy spar to take along. My advice to any cruising man or woman is to carry a modest-length spinnaker pole — say, three-quarters of the base of your foretriangle. Its uses, as will be seen, are manifold.

A popular place to stow a spinnaker pole is along one side of the foredeck, and this is a position that exposes both pole and end fittings to every bit of mischief that salt water, salt air, and an accumulation of salt deposit can conjure up. I'm all for an aluminum spinnaker pole: it's light and it's strong, and, given a little care and attention, it will last for years. Every time there is fresh water to spare, the pole and

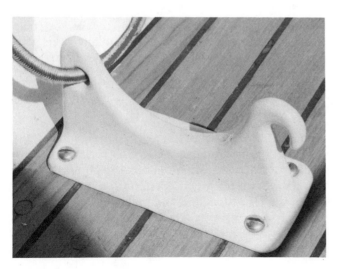

Deck cradle for spinnaker pole. (Courtesy Yachtspars)

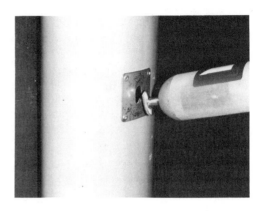

Slot on the mast to take the "T" fitting on the inboard end of this jockey pole is strengthened and protected by a stainless steel plate. (Courtesy Yachtspars)

end fittings should be given a thorough washing; when dry, any moving parts such as springs and plungers should be oiled.

Another spar worthy of mention — although its use aboard a cruising boat is limited — is the jockey pole or reaching strut. This is a short spar that, when needed, is attached to a mast and projects at right angles from the ship's centerline. Its purpose is to spread the angle between the spinnaker pole end and the after guy when the spinnaker pole is eased well forward toward the forestay. In addition to increasing this angle, the jockey pole keeps the guy away from the windward shrouds, and so helps prevent chafe. Most cruising yachtsmen won't give a jockey pole house room, even though a spinnaker might be set at times. If wind or course dictates that the pole be eased well forward, the cruising nut's more likely to have switched to a genoa jib — much less paraphernalia than a spinnaker and far easier to deal with shorthanded.

MAINTENANCE

Get in the habit of regularly inspecting your masts, booms, and attendant fittings. Buy or make a comfortable bosun's chair, and take an oil can aloft to lubricate any sheaves that may need it. Have a really good look at everything while you're up there. Is every pop rivet holding the mast track doing its job? Do any rivets need replacing? Are all halyard sheaves turning easily? How are the toggles, cotter pins, shackles (if any), and wire terminal fittings? Have all halyards got a fair lead? Nothing chafing? How about spreaders and spreader base fittings? Any signs of strain? No loose bolts or nuts? There's only one way to know all this, and that's to go up there — often.

While there are many variations in the design of bosun's chairs, there are basically two types. One type of chair is built of heavy, durable fabric. This chair has a fabric back, bottom, and sides, and often a front that clips or lashes across to keep a person in. Sometimes the seat is fabric-covered wood. Pockets for such things as wrenches, pliers, oil can, seizing wire, insulation tape, and sundry lashings are often sewn to the sides. One of these chairs is very handy when someone has to go aloft at sea; the "volunteer" who is swayed up a mast in such a chair has a pretty good chance of staying in it.

*As long as no one charges
by and sets up a roll,
it's often quite pleasant
working aloft. A lot of
work can be done from a
bosun's chair. Don't
forget to have a light line
falling from the chair to
the deck in case you forget
to take all the tools you
need and odd items have
to be sent up to you. Plus
a cold beer now and again!
(Ralph Naranjo photo)*

The other type of bosun's chair is simply a piece of board ¾ inch thick, nine inches wide, and 22 inches long. A hole is drilled near each of the four corners and a (typically) ½-inch line is led diagonally beneath the board from corner to corner and up through each hole to make a four-part bridle. The two ends of the line are finally spliced together beneath the chair. The four pieces of line are seized together at the top of the bridle to form an eye; this eye should be about two feet above the chair seat. The U of a strong shackle is held within this eye, and the pin fastens the chair to the terminal fitting of whatever halyard is used to swig the chair and the volunteer aloft.

I prefer this chair for use when at anchor because, if necessary, you can stand in it. It's almost impossible to inspect a masthead thoroughly — much less to work on the top of the mast — from a chair that holds you on all sides. It's difficult to climb up out of one of those fabric chairs. And the fact that the eye of the chair bridle comes two blocks at a masthead sheave often means that your eyes are below the top. Replacing the bulb in a masthead light, working on an anemometer, or anything else, can be a hell of a job, if not impossible. To stand in a chair at the masthead — and this can be done easily if the seat is a flat piece of wood — have yourself hove aloft until the seat is about three or four feet below the top. Bring one foot up to the *center* of the seat. Then, with a hand on a cap shroud each side, raise yourself into a standing position on one leg; adjust both feet carefully until your weight is distributed equally on the seat, and you're home free. If you have to work up there, pass a line around yourself and the mast, making a loop to lean back against. You can then work with both hands without hanging on. For those who desire a little bit of extra security, a safety harness can be worn, and this is attached to a separate halyard from that used to hoist the bosun's chair aloft. Slack, of course, must be taken up on the halyard leading to the harness as the wearer goes aloft in the chair. Once the chair is hoisted to the desired position, the "harness halyard" is belayed separately to the one used on the chair.

Makers of alloy spars are divided over which preparation (if any) should be used on the surface of aluminum spars. Some aluminum spars are anodized and the coating, which puts a thin, aluminum-oxide film on the surface of the spar, is often colored bronze or black. Anodized spars are sometimes left natural silver. It seems that anodizing, as long as the surface is not scratched or worn, is very good protection. (At the time of writing, the 53-foot *Zulu Warrior*'s bronze-colored anodized spars are still in excellent condition after 13 hard years of West Indies chartering.) If an anodized spar becomes scratched, and the sailor feels inclined to do something about it, the surface must be sanded down to bare metal, etch-primed, and painted.

Lacquer, polyurethane, and two-part epoxy paint are other coatings used by manufacturers on the surfaces of their aluminum spars. These coatings are easier to touch up than an anodized surface if the spar is scratched or fittings are moved. It's hard to avoid having a "touched-up" anodized surface look just that, so for aesthetic purposes, a regular, painted surface suits a lot of people.

As previously mentioned, the condition of the visible surface does not necessarily indicate the true health of an aluminum spar. It's what's going on under the fittings, at the mast heel, and *inside* the mast that counts. Inspection and concern over these places should take priority with a cruising yachtsman over touching up a few scratches. Don't worry too much if untreated parts of your aluminum mast are exposed to the salt air. Untreated aluminum forms a tough oxide film on its surface under these conditions; this film might look a little unsightly, but in fact, it is protecting the metal.

A solid wooden mast still has a place in the cruising game, maintenance notwithstanding. There are many solid wooden masts in cruising vessels; masts 30 years old and more that still carry the craft thousands of deep-sea miles. A moderate- or heavy-displacement cruising boat won't complain over the weight of a solid wood spar, believe me. I whittled out the solid fir masts, booms, and bowsprit for *White Squall* in 1948, and they're still going strong.

In an effort to prevent rot from attacking these spars, I cleaned out an old five-gallon drum and stirred together a mixture consisting of one part linseed oil to two parts kerosene. When the spars were all sanded and finished, I sloshed this mixture over them for weeks until the wood would soak up no more. The mainmast alone absorbed nearly three gallons. The spars were then given three coats of varnish and, of course, varnished every year thereafter. I had hoped the linseed and kerosene would be sealed in there, and I think that's what happened. I had steel caps made for the tops of each mast so that the end grain was always protected from fresh water. These caps, which were galvanized, had lugs for cap shrouds, forestay, permanent backstays, topping lift, and a half-inch clearance hole to take the bolt-axle for the Tufnol halyard sheave.

Masthead straps constructed of various metals — the most popular being silicon bronze — have been used by proponents of wooden spars for generations. Though straps do not offer the protection to end grain that one automatically gets with a cap, straps weigh less; to many yachtsmen, this is the deciding factor. A way of attaching tangs for standing rigging to a wooden spar is the pipe and through-bolt method. With this system, a pipe runs through the mast, and a bolt inside the pipe holds the tangs each side. The through-bolt must be a slide-fit inside the pipe; it should not be at all sloppy. Straps, which are part of the tang design, extend up the mast from the through-bolt for six inches or more (depending on the size of the spar). These straps are fastened to the mast with roundhead wood screws. Care must be taken, however, that the fastenings are staggered so that no two follow the same grain.

Another fastening method is simply to use a piece of thick-wall pipe as a bolt. The pipe is threaded at each end, and once the tangs are in place, nuts are run down the threads, securely tightened, and cotter-pinned. Both the threaded pipe and the pipe and through-bolt will do the job. The pipe, in either case, must be a tight fit in the hole running through the mast, for if fresh water can get between the outside of the pipe and the wood, it will create all sorts of mischief. Of the two methods, I prefer the pipe and through-bolt, for no other reason than that the idea of a pipe doing the work of a bolt doesn't sit well with me.

This fitting usually has to be custom-built, and the way I have done it (I was such a nut on these fittings that I even put one through the rudderhead of my yawl) was to have a ⁴¹⁄₆₄-inch hole machined lengthwise through a one-inch-diameter piece of bronze rod. The rod (now pipe) is a drive-fit through a one-inch (bare) hole in the spar and is cut off flush each side. A ⅝-inch-diameter bronze bolt is a neat fit through the pipe, and the tang fitting is bolted hard against the ends of the cut-off pipe. There is no through-compression on the spar with this setup, and the bolt can, at times, be removed for inspection.

In order to utilize the maximum shearing strength of a bolt, it is important that the tang fitting at either end be bearing on an unthreaded section of metal. A way of doing this, and of ensuring that a nut will seat against a tang before becoming "threadbound," is to cut two threads off the inside of the nut in a lathe. This allows the nut to travel a small distance past the end of the thread, and, if measurements have been taken carefully, tighten securely against the tang. All such nuts should be cotter-pinned.

BOWSPRITS

Despite the trend toward greater simplicity with the rigs of sailing vessels, the bowsprit is still with us, and it's not the fearsome appendage some would have us believe. A bowsprit enables such sailing vessels as ketches, schooners, and a great number of cutters to set a sensible amount of sail in their foretriangle: sail that gives the ship drive, brings the center of effort forward, and eases the helm. A short bowsprit with an integral pulpit can be very easy and safe to work on, too. Admittedly, such wasn't always the case. Muzzling the jib on the end of a 30-foot widow-maker sticking forward and skyward from the bows of some of the old-time commercial craft could make any sailor feel he was a long way from home. Especially at night in a breeze of wind.

I once sailed in a mullet boat with a jib that was set flying and that hauled out to the end of the bowsprit on a traveler. The bowsprit had a sheave at the tip, and the traveler was a galvanized steel ring that went around the bowsprit. The jib was attached to the traveler by a "ram's horn" — a curled finger of steel onto which the tack of the jib was coaxed. To set the sail, you hove the tack and traveler to the end of the bowsprit, belayed the line, and hauled mightily on the halyard. It was a rig that in no way endeared itself to me; battling that jib down at times took all hands and the cook.

Some of the old-time bowsprits on small craft sported a forestay on a traveler. The forestay was hove in to the stemhead, the jib hanked on, and the whole kit and caboodle sent out there again. The height of fashion at one time was to have a bowsprit offset to one side of the stemhead. This beauty was sent out by a tackle at its heel and retracted with another.

Thankfully, those days are in the past, and if we've got any sense at all, that's where we'll leave them. The best bowsprits these days are those constructed of pipe and welded to the bows of either steel or aluminum boats. An A-frame bowsprit (or

"Platform" bowsprit, stowage for two CQRs, sturdy pulpit, and roller luff spars for jib and staysail. (Ralph Naranjo photo)

bumpkin) attached in this manner is tremendously strong. Bowsprits for sailboats that are not built of metal generally are constructed of solid wood, and, while some cruising sailors prefer hardwood, I've never been able to get past Douglas fir for this job.

So it's a matter of personal preference. If you want to put a hardwood bowsprit on your vessel, then have at it; it'll probably do you proud. (It'd be a pretty dull world if we all agreed with each other, right?) Just make sure that whatever wood you choose for your bowsprit has a long, straight grain. This is another job for the do-it-yourselfer. (Bowsprit fittings and bobstays are discussed in the next chapter.) Make certain that the lumber of your choice is of large enough section, and that, when the spar is installed, it will be strong enough to take the knocks. Unless it leads a charmed life, or unless it never goes anywhere, a bowsprit really takes a beating.

If you are in doubt about what the Iyy and Ixx dimensions of your bowsprit should be, consult a naval architect. The factors used in deciding the size of bowsprit sections are: length of the sprit, displacement of your vessel, maximum amount of sail expected to be set off the end, and the material to be used in the construction of the spar. A good man should be able to tell you the suitable dimensions just by running an eye over your ship.

Aboard some wooden vessels with bowsprits, it is necessary to protect the end grain in the stemhead over which the bowsprit passes. This is a spot where fresh water can penetrate and start rot. If the deck (stemhead included) already has a waterproof covering such as fiberglass or canvas, then all is well. If, however, the end grain is exposed, it should be covered. Eighteen-gauge copper sheet, with a good compound such as polysulfide beneath, does an admirable job here.

While a bowsprit is a great help in distributing sail area over the length of a vessel, the sailor must make due allowance for it when maneuvering. He must never forget he's got that horn sticking out there. This may seem an unnecessary caution to some cruising sailors; *they'll* never forget, no sir! When maneuvering under sail or power, they'll remember the bowsprit and calculate things to a nicety! Maybe . . . but there have been some pretty capable seamen who have miscued.

Jibboom Jack, an old commercial skipper of my acquaintance, was one. Nobody earns a nickname like that unless he has done in a few bowsprits. Then there was old Bill, a fine master I sailed with as an A.B. On his first trip as skipper of the *Katie S,* a ketch-rigged cargo scow, Bill rounded up with a deckload of kauri logs aboard, stuck his bowsprit through a window of the company office, and knocked the manager off his stool.

Then there was the *Hero,* sailing down a river on her way to the New Zealand port of Wellington. The river, which ran through farming country, had many turns and twists. Situated fair on the tip of one of the bends was a farmer's corrugated-iron outhouse. As the *Hero,* with wind and current in her favor, swung around a turn in the river, her bowsprit speared the privy and whipped it away from its foundation. All efforts by the crew to free the outhouse from the end of the bowsprit failed, and she arrived in port with the privy impaled like a flounder on the end of her jibboom. There was a story going up and down the coast that the farmer was in the outhouse at the time it was snatched away, but I think that was only an attempt to make the tale a little more famous than it already was.

The sailors aboard a vessel equipped with a bowsprit are not the only ones who should treat it with respect. It works the other way around, too. Some years back the *Scot,* a small, ketch-rigged scow, sailed from the port of Auckland one black, wet, winter night. Gaff-rigged on both masts, 60 feet on deck, and with a modest 12-foot bowsprit, the *Scot* was on her way up the coast to pick up a cargo of lime. Her crew consisted of two men: Bert, the skipper, and a deckhand who went by the letters MBOSB (mate, bosun, ordinary seaman, and boy). It was a cold night with a fresh southwest wind sending the scow waddling along on a broad reach at a giddy six knots.

Bert was standing at the wheel peering from time to time into the oil-lit binnacle at the N-by-W compass course. Bert had a towel around his neck; the collar of his long oilskin was pulled up as far as it would come; his sou'wester hat was tied beneath his chin with a couple of lashings, which kept the side flaps over his ears. He was alone on deck and was as cold as a frog. Bert could hardly wait until he could put MBOSB (sound asleep in the cabin just forward of the binnacle) on a shake to stand a trick at "the bloody wheel."

A rainsquall came whistling across, heeling the *Scot,* sending sheets of water running down the old ship's sails and cold rivulets trickling down inside her captain's none-too-watertight oilskin. Bert hunched over the wheel and squinted into the binnacle at the compass course. Suddenly a fellow appeared from alongside the deckhouse and tapped him on the shoulder.

Bert always maintained, over the years, that anyone curious about the condition of his heart should have something like this happen to him. It would decide the issue right there and then. Bert vowed that his heart left his body, flapped around on deck for a while, and then leapt back into his chest again.

"Round 'er up! Round 'er up, for Chrissake!" said Bert's visitor.

"Wwwwhaffor?" asked Bert.

"You got me boat on the end of yer bloody bowsprit, that's whaffor!"

Apparently the bloke was beating home with a cargo of fish in his mullet boat, and he'd misjudged the closeness of the *Scot* as he tacked. Bert's bowsprit had skewered the mullety's mainsail dead center and he was dragging the vessel along sideways under the *Scot*'s bobstay and forefoot.

three

Standing Rigging

The standing rigging of a sailing vessel, made up of stationary shrouds and stays, keeps the mast straight and keeps it in the ship — in other words, keeps it standing. Shrouds hold a mast to port and starboard; stays hold a mast fore and aft. The standing rigging as a whole absorbs the strain imposed on the rig by the wind in the sails, by the windage of the mast itself, and by the motion of the vessel applied to the weight of the mast. A sensible arrangement of load points to which the rigging is attached around the deckline of the vessel (typically, chainplates, stemhead, and stern fittings) distributes strain.

During the course of an ocean voyage, the first 10 days or so can place as much strain and wear and tear on a vessel's rigging as is incurred in a year of sitting in a marina with only an occasional weekend sail. Loss or damage to her mast is a very serious occurrence to a cruising boat, and a lively awareness of this when planning or beefing up a rig before setting forth to sail can be worth it a hundred times over. For this reason, experienced cruising men and women often insist on a size bigger than the minimum for their rigging wire and attendant fittings.

When rigging a sailboat for cruising, it is wise to aim for the ultimate: that the mast or masts will continue to stand, no matter what. If this sounds like a lofty ideal or, at the other end of the scale, unnecessarily dramatic, I'll point out once again that when you embrace the cruising life, mate, you're more often than not all on your lonesome out there. It's the greatest game in the world, but if you intend to enjoy it to the full, do all you can, before you leave, to ensure that your stick or sticks will remain in your boat.

There are all too many people in cruising sailboats today who expect their whole rig to stay intact *all the time,* and if one part — any part — carries away, then over the side goes the pole. A few days before writing this, I spoke with the owner of a cruising boat at Trellis Bay in the British Virgin Islands. He gave me a great song and dance about his mainmast going by the board, and he left me with the impression that he felt he'd been shortchanged. But it was his own bloody fault. A turnbuckle had carried away — one turnbuckle. Apparently he was depending on every stay with all its connections — pins, toggles, shackles (if any), chainplates, tangs — to perform 100 percent every second of the day or night. And if any one fitting carried away, the whole lot could disappear over the side. The dependability of his entire rig was only as strong as its single weakest part — which isn't good enough.

When getting our cruising unit together, this vessel we are going to use as a home — a *safe* home to take us wherever in the world we choose to go — we endeavor to prepare her for whatever contingencies might arise by loading aboard all manner of stores and equipment. We have working sails for average weather, light extras such as genoas and spinnakers for use in light weather, storm sails for heavy weather. We carry several anchors aboard; we isolate the ship's water tanks from one another so that, if we lose the liquid out of one, there is another as a back-up, and we do the same with the fuel tanks. Fire extinguishers are studded around the boat in well-thought-out positions, so that in case of fire, one is always at hand. There's a spare compass, sextant, and so on. To go to sea without lavishing this same kind of attention on mast and rigging doesn't make sense.

Make every attempt to ensure that all parts of the boat's rigging are sound. Should any stay or shroud carry away, however, be sure, through prior planning, that the mast will stand until the faulty rigging is repaired. This means more stays up there than are generally accepted. It will probably mean a minimum of four chainplates each side instead of three, two stays forward instead of one, and running backstays as well as a permanent backstay.

All this is enough, possibly, to cause a really gung-ho racing man to throw up his arms in despair, but when your cruising boat is laid on her beam ends by a squall and you are umpteen miles from anywhere, you'll be happy about the security of that extra wire that is hanging up there. And if any shackle, toggle, terminal fitting, tang, or anything else carries away, you'll be ecstatic about the fact that a back-up stay prevented the rig from going over the side.

I know I was, one time when we were sailing from the island of Nuku Hiva in the Marquesas Islands to a neighboring island of Ua Pu in the *White Squall II.* We had a tradewind of about 20 knots aft of the beam, the day was bright and sparkling, and we sailed over the blue Pacific rollers with a feeling that we owned the whole world. We were about an hour out when we felt, more than heard, a sharp bang.

We almost twisted our heads off our shoulders examining the rigging. Nothing. Then Minine looked aft. "Look at the end of the bumpkin. It's lifting up and down every time we go over a swell." So I stuck my head over the stern and observed our chain bobstay trailing along behind us. It was hanging from the bumpkin-end. A ⅝-inch-diameter shackle only six months old that secured the bobstay to its chainplate had carried away. The A-frame bumpkin of four-inch-by-six-inch Douglas fir was pretty rugged. When I'd built it, I'd extended the legs nearly four feet inboard and bolted each leg down through two deckbeams with ⅝-inch-diameter stainless steel bolts. Without a bobstay, and in the breeze that was blowing, it was capable of holding the main masthead above the point on the mast where the running backstays attached — but just.

TYPICAL STAYING ARRANGEMENTS AND TERMINOLOGY

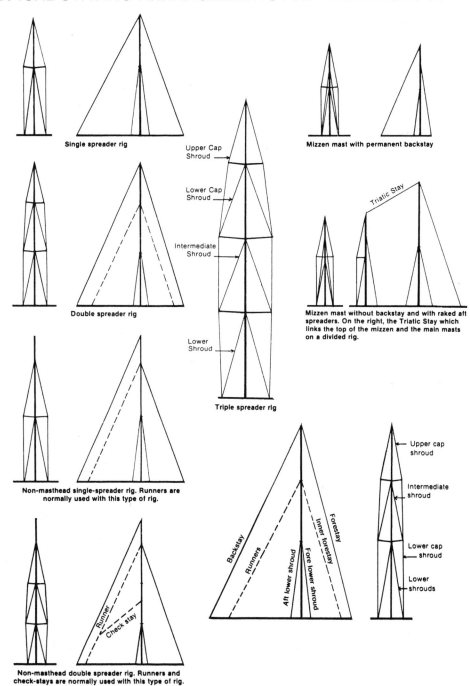

Single spreader rig

Mizzen mast with permanent backstay

Double spreader rig

Upper Cap Shroud

Lower Cap Shroud

Intermediate Shroud

Lower Shroud

Triple spreader rig

Triatic Stay

Mizzen mast without backstay and with raked aft spreaders. On the right, the Triatic Stay which links the top of the mizzen and the main masts on a divided rig.

Non-masthead single-spreader rig. Runners are normally used with this type of rig.

Non-masthead double spreader rig. Runners and check-stays are normally used with this type of rig.

Runner

Check stay

Backstay

Runners

Aft lower shroud

Inner forestay

Forestay

Fore lower shroud

Upper cap shroud

Intermediate shroud

Lower cap shroud

Lower shrouds

The port running backstay, set up to windward, saved the whole rig from going over the wall that day.

It is a wise precaution on the part of a cruising boat owner to satisfy himself that every stay or shroud on his vessel has a back-up. This doesn't mean that each length of rigging wire should have another piece running alongside it. This practice isn't necessarily the greatest anyhow. We often see sloops with twin headstays — two parallel stays with their turnbuckles secured to a common bow fitting and proceeding, a few inches apart, up to a masthead fitting.

If the bow fitting is rugged beyond any doubt and the load points are well separated, fine. But make sure that at the masthead, the stays are not secured to the one common tang, because no matter how wide or strong looking this tang is, if two stays are imposing their frequently uneven loads upon it, it will fatigue at a greater rate than if only one stay were using it. And when it lets go, one or two of the cockpit crowd could end up playing the harp. The lesson here is that every stay or shroud should go to an individual tang that, if it does carry away, won't start a chain of events (and these can happen mighty fast) causing the vessel to lose her mast.

The standard of rigging aboard a cruising sailboat, with most people, ultimately gets down to what they can afford. It's very easy to say that the cruising man or woman is well advised to fit out his or her vessel with larger-sized rigging than is usual. One size larger — say, ⅜-inch-diameter wire instead of ⁵⁄₁₆ inch — can, after all other parts have been beefed up proportionately, end up costing half again as much as the original size. I consider, however, that if your intention is to get out there and embrace the cruising life, then it's worthwhile skimping on furnishings and frills — such as an extra head, refrigeration (nice as it might be) — and instead pour the money into rigging. The standard of rigging of a boat that regularly goes off soundings should be secondary only to the seaworthiness of her hull. Load the other stuff aboard only if you can afford it.

The serious cruising man is sometimes influenced in his rigging selection by the rigging used aboard vessels belonging to various "one-trippers" he meets along the way. We're not knocking the one-tripper; more power to the guy who buys a boat, does a three-year trip around the world, and, at the end of it, squares his shoulders and looks around for other fields to conquer. That, in some measure, is what this human-life game is all about. But quite often, in addition to causing the dedicated cruising man to wonder why he's gone to all the trouble of a really strong rig when this other guy is getting away with murder, our one-trip man gets bitten to the bone by the cruising bug himself. He decides he's going to keep at it.

His rigging, designed for coastwise cruising with a bit of race-around-the-buoys-on-the-weekends thrown in, was new when he started three years ago, but it's had, say, 35,000 miles of wear. If the whole thing was minimal to start off with, it could be ready to quit.

Standing rigging, with its attendant fittings, should last a world-cruising boat a minimum of 10 years. For instance, the *White Squall II* was purchased from us in New Zealand and sailed back to the Virgin Islands to charter in the Caribbean once more. At the time of writing, the ½-inch-diameter galvanized rigging is 12 years old and still looks good. I don't know how many miles the rigging has taken the weight of the sails driving the 60-ton schooner, for I never bothered to count. But she's been to the other side of the world and back, crisscrossed up and down and back and forth among Pacific island groups, and now is doing the same thing again in the Caribbean. All this on the standing rigging we hung up there in St. Thomas a dozen years ago. Minimal rigging would never give this kind of service.

TYPES OF WIRE

There are three types of rigging wire used most often aboard cruising boats.

1. Wire made up of 19 single strands — a core of seven strands inside a covering of 12 strands — is called 1 by 19 wire, usually written 1/19. The core is laid in the direction opposing the outside wires. This 1/19 wire is very strong, has little stretch, and is available in both stainless and galvanized steel.

2. Standing rigging that has seven wires, each made up of seven strands, is called 7/7 wire. One of the wires is a core that has its strands twisted to oppose the other six laid around it. This 7/7 wire is also available in stainless and galvanized steel. While not as strong, size for size, as 1/19 wire, 7/7 is far more flexible.

3. A galvanized wire used for standing rigging some years ago, but which is seen very seldom nowadays, is 6/7. This wire had an oiled hemp core around which were laid six wires, each made up of seven strands. The hemp core, when squeezed by the wires under strain — as when the vessel was sailing — would cause that part of the strands lying against it to become coated with a light covering of oil, which helped prevent corrosion. If this rigging wire was treated regularly on the outside with a mixture of fish oil and paint, it would last 20 years or more. Its big disadvantages were that it wasn't as strong, size for size, as either 1/19 or 7/7, and that its stretch factor made it unsuitable for modern lofty rigs.

Rod rigging, the be-all-end-all for some of the racing buffs, is not often seen along the cruising way, even though some manufacturers claim that their rigging is as failure-proof as any wire. Maybe it is, and then again, maybe it isn't.

One day about 11 o'clock in the morning a few months back, at the Sheraton Marina in St. Thomas, various dockhoppers and members of the floating fraternity were startled by what sounded like a rifle shot up in the rigging of the 75-foot cutter *Southern Star.* Her sturdy-looking ⅞-inch-diameter stainless steel rod rigging cap shroud on the port side had parted some 30 feet above the deck while she was *at the dock!* I've never heard of any wire turning in a performance like that.

One dilemma that rod rigging presents for the serious cruiser is how to carry a spare length of rigging, say, twice the length of the longest stay aboard. Or even half this length. Some rod rigging can't be coiled in anything smaller than a six-foot-diameter circle. And even if a man is so happy with his rod rigging that he decides to keep it and do without a back-up, what does he do if it decides quite suddenly to let him down?

The most-available commodities at those paradise islands we cruise to are fish, yams, and coconuts — not rod rigging (or rigging of any other kind). Ordering and waiting for a new rod-rigging stay or shroud to arrive could take months, or could prove to be impossible. I think it's best for the cruising man to leave rod rigging to the all-out racing gang, who are not likely to be caught in a fix like this.

The wire standing rigging that most cruising boats use today is 1/19. Its size-for-

Stays on which sails are hoisted must take wear from sail hanks in addition to stress imposed by doing their part in keeping a mast standing. A strand carried away in this 1/19 stainless steel headstay while the jib was set. Skipper had to climb the wire and unhank the jib to get it down. Strong words etc. . . . . (Ralph Naranjo photo)

BREAKING STRENGTH WIRE

METRIC

| | 1 × 19 | 7 × 19 | | |
Diameter mm	Stainless kg	Stainless kg	Galv. kg	Wire Weights kg/m
3	952	862	816	.043
4	1497	1179	1134	.078
5	2132	1769	1723	.111
6	3719	2993	2948	.200
7	4671	3628	3583	.252
8	5669	4082	4399	.311
10	7982	5442	6485	.436
11	10612	7392	—	.593
12	13469	10340	—	.774
14	16780	12927	—	.981
16	20862	15875	—	—

IMPERIAL

| | 1 × 19 | 7 × 19 | | |
Diameter In.	Stainless lb	Stainless lb	Galv. lb	Wire Weights lb/ft
1/8"	2100	1900	1800	.034
5/32"	3300	2600	2500	.055
3/16"	4700	3900	3800	.077
1/4"	8200	6600	6500	.135
9/32"	10300	8000	7900	.170
5/16"	12500	9000	9700	.210
3/8"	17600	12000	14300	.294
7/16"	23400	16300	—	.400
1/2"	29700	22800	—	.522
9/16"	37000	28500	—	.661
5/8"	46000	35000	—	—

size strength comparison with 7/7 makes it a popular choice (see table). But 1/19 wire has two disadvantages. (1) If a strand fatigues and breaks, the wire has lost $\frac{1}{19}$ of its strength. (If a strand of 7/7 breaks for any reason, the wire has lost only $\frac{1}{49}$ of its strength.) Also, 1/19 wire cannot be spliced easily. It can, however, be used successfully with Nicopress or Talurit fittings (more on this later).

Although 7/7 wire is not as strong, size for size, as 1/19, and also has a greater stretch factor, it is a good wire, and it lends itself to more uses for the do-it-yourselfer than 1/19.

WIRE SIZE

Since the object is to keep the standing rigging hanging up there, no matter what, wire size is of prime importance. Speaking generally, the heftier the wire and the more there is of it, the longer it will last and the less chance there is of its breaking. We must arrive at a sensible compromise, however; otherwise we'll create so much windage and unnecessary weight aloft that we'll interfere seriously with the ship's sailing and seagoing abilities. It may be said that the heavier a vessel's displacement, the heavier her rigging should be — except for a qualification that applies to multihulls.

A stripped-out multihull can usually get by with light rigging, since every puff of wind is converted directly into the energy that scoots her over, not through, the water. A cruising multihull loaded down with equipment and stores, however, can become a very stiff vessel indeed; the higher her waterline rises, the more of an affinity she has with her heavier-displacement monohull cousin. She then tends to go through, not over, the water. The multihull that becomes such a "semidisplacement" vessel has her acceleration seriously affected; the sails, not able to convert the wind into energy as quickly as if the craft were flying light, place far more strain on the standing rigging. Also, a multihull, because of her beam, cannot take strain off her rigging by rolling with the punch in a sudden squall — as can a monohull. A seagoing multihull that is expected to carry her full quota of cruising gear should have rigging at least one size larger than if she were sailing stripped out. The same applies to her mast; it needs to be very strong.

I remember an occasion some 20 years ago when we hauled *White Squall* at Keehi Lagoon, Oahu, for a routine haircut and shave. We came off the ways early one afternoon and headed back to the Ala Wai harbor; a few hundred yards ahead of us was a big pink catamaran, her decks crawling with day-charterers. A rainsquall that came riffling across the water decided to liven up our day by putting us down to the rail. We nursed our little ship through by easing the helm and spilling wind from her sails, and when we came out of it, the big cat was still there — but her mast wasn't.

Maybe the weight of the crowd of passengers had converted the cat into a semidisplacement vessel and prevented her from utilizing the wind's full force to do one thing only — scoot ahead — thus easing strain on mast and rigging. Maybe the hollow wooden spar was just too light. The next day the waterfront scuttlebutt (usually mighty accurate) had it that the rigging had held. It had been the mast, set in the stiff, heavy vessel, that had been unable to take the compression forced on it by a bagful of wind and had given up the ghost. I can vouch for the fact that shortly after it happened, we sailed through a sea that seemed covered with splintered pieces of varnished wood.

There is a rough rule of thumb that has been around for many years that helps calculate wire size for the standing rigging of a cruising monohull. If you take the weight of the ballast keel of a moderate-displacement vessel and then double it, this figure may be used for calculating the ultimate tensile strength of cap shrouds for the craft. Thus, for a 35-foot ocean cruiser with a 6,000-pound ballast keel, cap shrouds of ⁵⁄₁₆-inch-diameter 1/19 stainless steel (12,500 pounds Ultimate Tensile Strength) would be suitable, though a size smaller would probably be considered adequate if she were sailing coastwise.

Lower shrouds, if there are two or more each side, may be of smaller-sized wire than the cap shrouds. Here, it depends on how gung-ho you happen to be. If you're a hotshot racing buff who has decided to have an offhand fling at the cruising life, you'll probably settle for lower shrouds of a smaller size. Any tiny bit of extra weight and windage in the spars and rigging does, of course, count against the performance of a boat, especially on the wind. But if you're like me, you'll standardize as much as you can by having all the standing rigging — as well as terminals, toggles, and turnbuckles — the same size. That way, one set of spares will do the whole job.

While light wire might make that tiny bit of difference to our speed and help us keep up among the front-runners in a race, it will fatigue and quit long before rigging of a heavier size. Ocean cruising with minimum rigging is like sailing on the edge of a knife blade: it's just plain unsafe. Quite apart from the safety factor, however, when we are paddling along all on our lonesome out there, is the fact that the average cruising boat is on a budget; we can't afford to be replacing gear forever. If you are a purist and cannot reconcile yourself to wire of a larger size (and more of it) than is the norm for a coastwise boat, and you suddenly find the mast down around your ears, you won't have to look farther than the nearest mirror to find someone to sheet the blame home to.

TERMINAL FITTINGS

Originally, the method by which wire rope was terminated in the rigging of sailing ships was to parcel and serve the wire, bend it around a deadeye (more recently, a thimble), and seize it to itself for a fathom or so up the shroud or stay with soft, galvanized wire. The seizings were about a foot apart. This type of terminal never gave trouble. I've seen shrouds terminated in this manner shuddering, slacking, and becoming bar-tight again during cargo loading and discharging operations, which put far more strain on the wire and its terminal than at any time we were underway. Although it would still work, this type of wire termination is rather ponderous. It's not quite "the thing" in this day and age; something a little more pleasing to the eye is required.

Swages

It seems that the perfect wire terminal fitting — the fitting we'd like to be as confident of as the wire itself — just doesn't exist. Swaged terminal fittings are the ones

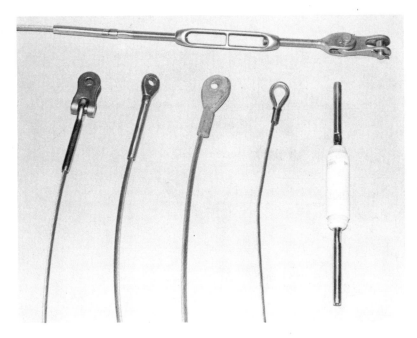

Top: *Open-barrel turnbuckle with fork-end and toggle one end, threaded stud and swage at the other.* **Bottom, left to right:** *Eye swage with toggle, eye swage terminal, Talurit sleeve holding wire around solid thimble, Nicopress sleeve holding wire around open thimble, "in-line" insulator. (Courtesy Yachtspars)*

we're most likely to see when inspecting the rigging of boats at a marina, boatyard, or boat show; either fork (jaw) or eye fittings are neat, handsome attachments. They are also probably the worst end fittings for any stay or shroud aboard a long-range cruising boat — especially a boat intended for tropic cruising.

Swaged terminal ends just don't last along the cruising beat. The top ends of standing rigging equipped with swaged fittings seem to stand up moderately well, but the bottom swages, the ones the salt water can really get at, often develop visible cracks. Some of the cracks even open up enough for the end of the swage to splay out in a bell shape. If you don't believe me, and you have a chance to inspect the rigging on cruising boats in some tropic port — a port such as St. Thomas, Papeete, Pago Pago, Suva, Vila — see how many of the vessels are using small hose clamps in an attempt to keep swages on some of the lower ends of their standing rigging from splitting further.

There is always the exception, of course, but we're not concerned with exceptions. When we focus upon standing rigging for a cruising boat, our undivided attention must be taken up not with how pretty it looks, but how dependable it's going to be *for years.* At least 10 years.

There is no doubt that a swage fitting looks the part: it's the neatest wire terminal to arrive on the scene, and it arrived nearly a half-century ago. The swage fitting used on sailboats is stainless steel; on standing rigging, the tube extends from an eye

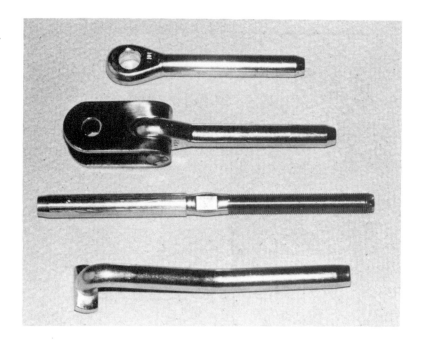

Above: *Swage terminals. From top: Swage with "eye" end; "eye" end swage with toggle; swage with threaded stud end, which screws into either closed- or open-barrel turnbuckle; "T"-end swage ("T" locates in mast slot at upper end of stay or shroud). (Courtesy Yachtspars)* **Right:** *Split swage terminal in lifeline. (Ralph Naranjo photo)*

or clevis and fits around the wire. This tube is then squeezed with great pressure, and if the operator knows his onions and his machine is hefty enough, the swage could last a long time. But if he has to run the swage through the machine a few times to achieve a satisfactory diameter, the fitting might quit years before the wire. Too many passes through the machine will fatigue the metal.

Cracks and misshapen swages can usually be traced directly to the machine used in the operation and to the skill of the operator. Swaging requires enormous pressure; the hollow shank of the terminal is squeezed until the metal of the fitting actually

"Squeezing in" a swage terminal. (Courtesy Yachtspars)

flows into the lay of the wire. Roll swaging, where the terminal is compressed between two grooved tools, needs a minimum of two passes between the wheels to achieve the correct finished diameter (the fitting is rotated 90 degrees between passes). If the pressure and the lead of the fitting are *exactly* equal on each pass, there is a chance that the residual strains in the metal of the terminal will be equal also. There's also a chance that they won't. If the terminal has been passed through several times — and this often happens — there's almost no chance.

Residual strain is always present in metal that is tightened, or forced (such as with a nut and bolt), to hold something in place. This strain is perfectly acceptable in correctly apportioned quantities. Four or more bolts (instead of one or two) holding each of an automobile's wheels in place is an example. Then there is the residual strain left within a swaged rigging fitting after it has been pressed to such an extent that some of the metal actually "flows" into the lay of the wire. It is possible for such pressure to alter the molecular structure of the metal. If the pressure is equal within the metal, the molecular alteration will be equal. If the pressure used on one part of the fitting differs from that used on another part, the molecular alteration will be unequal between the two, resulting in the possibility of one part of the fitting being loaded with more residual stress than another. In any case, there is an imbalance, which in some instances can cause cracks to appear in the fitting.

If either the terminal or the lead of the wire to the fitting isn't spot-on in the

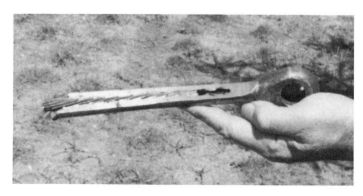

This swage was a shroud terminal fitting aboard the 85-foot trimaran Wanderlust. *When the swage started to split, the owner ground off the sides in an effort to preserve the length of the shroud so that a new terminal could be fitted. After he'd pulled the shroud approximately 1 inch out of the swage (as shown), he discovered that most of the 12 outside strands of the $\frac{9}{16}$-inch 1/19 wire had broken inside the swage. The only course he could follow then was to condemn every swage — an expensive business! This rigging was only four years old. (Minine Norgrove photo)*

machine, the finished job might assume a slight banana shape. (Ever see one of these?) Other factors contributing to this "banana-shape" are an oversize hole in the shank of the terminal and/or an undersize wire; as little as $\frac{1}{100}$ inch off the correct size will do it. Sometimes unevenness appears on the surface of the terminal along a line of unequal swaging. If the terminal is ever going to crack, there's a fair chance it'll be along one of these lines.

Rotary swaging is another method of squeezing a stainless steel terminal onto a wire end. With rotary swaging, a die subjected to controlled hammer blows (10,000 per minute) is rotated around the fitting. Then there is the machine activated by hydraulic pressure. In every case, there are enormous residual stresses in that innocent-looking terminal. Some rigging companies run a micrometer measurement on the terminal both before and after swaging. Another highly recommended practice is to buy wire and end fittings from the same company. Don't forget to specify *marine* terminals, *not aircraft* ones! Those skinny little aircraft swages have caused more than one sailboat to lose her rig.

Even when compressed onto standing rigging by a powerful hydraulic press capable of swaging in one operation — once in and once out — the bottom ends, which will receive much salt water over the years, should be regarded with mistrust. It is possible to keep up to date on the health of your swages by smearing Spotcheck on them, wiping it off, and examining them minutely with a magnifying glass. Spotcheck is used by engineers when examining spindles or crankshafts for flaws, and it'll tell if your swages are up to snuff. But what do you do if you arrive at the Cocos (Keeling) Islands, decide in a fit of enthusiasm to give your swages the Spot-

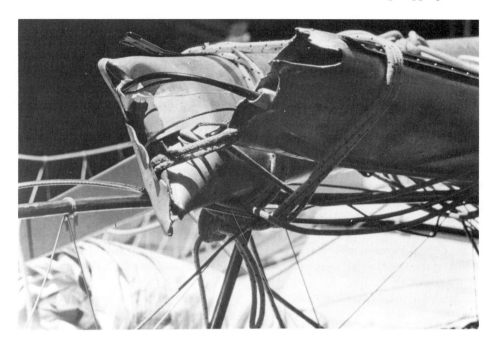

The Whim-Wham, *a Cal 39, lost her rig after an eye pulled out of a swage. (Ralph Naranjo photo)*

check treatment, and discover that a few of them are sick? It's like having appendicitis pains in the Gobi desert.

The owner of a cruising boat equipped with swaged terminal fittings is well advised to take each stay and shroud to the nearest rigging loft and have it tested at double its recommended safe working load before leaving on an extended cruise. Testing, it seems, is more advisable than X-raying. The *Whim-Wham,* a Cal 39, had had all her swages X-rayed at considerable expense before the 1976 Victoria (B.C.)-Maui race; and when the vessel was sailing back to Vancouver after the race, an eye pulled out of a swage and the rig went over the side (see photograph).

In addition to having her swaged rigging tested, the owner of a cruising boat can do himself a favor by stowing aboard a length of rigging wire equivalent to twice the length of the longest stay. Each end of this wire should have a terminal already fitted. These terminals can be Talurit, Norseman, Sta-Lok, Castlok, poured socket, swaged fitting, or a splice — whatever your favorite might be. The idea of carrying a wire twice as long as the longest piece of standing rigging is simply to have a spare on top of a spare. The reason for a fitting already installed at each end is that the wire can be cut to length and only one terminal need be installed at sea. This leaves a spare length of wire still longer than any piece of standing rigging. Regarding suitable terminals: Norseman and Sta-Lok are ideal for a job that has to be done underway. If the standing rigging is 7/7 and the operator is adept at splicing, then this can be done at sea, too. Talurit and Nicopress are as good as any, but if the wire exceeds ⅜ inch in diameter, this will call for a heftier machine than the average cruising vessel has room for. It would cost an arm and a leg, too. Bulldog clamps (discussed in detail later) are excellent for running repairs and have a place aboard every cruising boat.

Poured Sockets

A properly poured socket has several counts in its favor that are hard to pass up. A poured socket is something you can make yourself, which means you've got control over its quality. If, for any reason, you have to renew a length of rigging when you're away on a cruise, you don't have to content yourself with a temporary, lash-up affair. A permanent job can be done with a minimum of equipment, and you can use the same socket again and again.

The wire within the terminal itself is not held in any crushed or crimped manner, as is the case with a swage or compression-type fitting such as Norseman, Sta-Lok, or Electroline; the wire, its ends fishhooked back, is held within a zinc cone by a metallurgical bond, the same bond that makes the zinc part of the socket body.

Wharf cranes, their lifting wires terminated by poured sockets, lift cargo weighing tons and swing it over the heads of men on board ships. That used to mean something to me when I was one of those men: confidence. If you examine the termination of the wires in almost any elevator shaft, you'll see that the wires that haul elevators up and down are, in most cases, terminated by poured sockets. The Department of Buildings in New York City is responsible for inspecting all the elevators in Manhattan. According to this department, all wire-end fittings in the elevator business are poured sockets. Think about that the next time you board an elevator to be whisked up a dozen or so floors. Then give a little thought to the type of terminals that you'll use on the standing rigging of your cruising boat.

Poured sockets are available with both eye and fork ends. It is recommended that hot-dipped, galvanized sockets be used for galvanized wire, and bronze sockets for stainless steel wire. It may be necessary to hunt around a bit to procure bronze sockets, but they can be found. If enough yachtsmen start asking, perhaps companies such as Merriman-Holbrook, which once stocked an excellent range, will start handling them again.

The equipment needed to do a poured-socket job on standing rigging is as follows:

(a) Enough sockets for the ends of each stay or shroud. Whether the sockets are fork or eye is a matter of personal preference. I've used both.

(b) Metal for melting and pouring. In the United States I've used first-quality zinc; in New Zealand I've used capel metal, a zinc composition that seems to be sold specifically for this job. (The reason for the name may be that sockets are sometimes referred to as capels "down under.")

(c) Small ladle to hold the melted metal.

(d) Acetone or any other liquid that will cleanse the wire strands of grease, oil, or dirt and then evaporate without leaving a residue.

(e) Flux. For stainless steel wire and bronze sockets, phosphoric acid was once recommended to me by an ex-Royal Air Force wallah I knew, but while the job it did was 100 percent, I found it damnable stuff to use. Since then I've used any of the fluxes suitable for use with stainless steel and regular lead solder, and with wonderful results. For galvanized wire and galvanized sockets, I've used either spirits of salts or any other flux suitable for soldering galvanized iron.

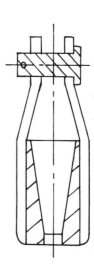

Drawing of poured socket with fork-end and clevis pin. Whole unit is prefabricated from mild steel and then galvanized. Sides of socket are flat bar stock welded to a piece of round bar hollowed in a lathe. (Barry Sexton)

(f) Asbestos string about ¼ inch thick, or asbestos clay.

(g) Torch. A blowtorch will do, as long as the flame does not leave a sooty deposit, for if any of this gets into the socket, it may prevent the zinc from adhering to the wire. A small propane torch is an ideal tool and far cleaner than a blowtorch. If a big rigging job is looming, such as a complete replacement of standing rigging, be a sport and buy yourself a plumber's torch, complete with a long, flexible hose and a fitting that will screw into a regular butane bottle. With a rig like that, you'll get all the heat in the world, and, provided your bottle is full, there'll be no likelihood of running out of gas partway through the job.

I always carried this kit aboard both *White Squall* and *White Squall II,* lending it out and using it several times myself while cruising in both vessels. A typical instance was an occasion in Papeete when we fitted a new wire topping lift and main halyard with poured sockets aboard *White Squall II.*

It's almost as easy to do 20 poured sockets as it is to do one; it's setting the job up that takes time. A nice, quiet anchorage helps, too; nobody in his right mind would tackle a poured-socket exercise in a roll or at sea. When Dave Ferneding and Minine and I replaced all the standing rigging on the *White Squall II* in St. Thomas, 12 years ago, we poked an oar through the center hole of a 1,000-foot drum of ½-inch-diameter 7/7 galvanized wire I had ordered from Miami. We slung it up under the main staysail boom so that the drum rotated on the oar. A 20-pound butane bottle on deck and the hose from a plumber's torch were connected to this. The torch and the rest of the kit were in the engine room.

When replacing a stay or shroud, we'd pull wire off the drum and then poke it down into the engine room via an open skylight. A seizing, a minimum of 1¼ inches in length, was then secured at a predetermined distance up from the end of the wire.

This distance is arrived at by measuring the hollow inside of the socket and adding ⅜ inch to it. The seizing of 1¼ inches in length (or not less than twice the diameter of the wire) ensures beyond all doubt that the wire, once pushed through the socket and unlaid, does not unlay further.

Although some riggers prefer to use wire for seizing, my favorite is flat, waxed Dacron. Whatever type of seizing is used must be small enough so that it won't be damaged when the wire is pushed through the hole at the small, tapered end of the socket. The seizing must be very tight and bound *against* the lay of the wire; the natural tendency of the wire to unlay causes the seizing to become even tighter. (The old shellbacks' jingle says, "Worm and parcel with the lay; turn and serve the other way.") If you see a poured fitting with the wires slightly unlaid after leaving the socket, most likely it will be because either this seizing (serving) wasn't long enough or it was put on with the lay — or both.

Once the seizing is on, push the wire through the hole in the tapered bottom of the socket, and out a foot or so from the large end. Grip the socket firmly in a vise. Unlay fully each strand of the wire and splay it out in the shape of an inverted cone to an included angle of 60 degrees. Now, with a pair of needle-nose pliers, take a little more than ⅜ inch of each wire and turn it back 180 degrees. (With 7/7 rigging, this means that you will turn back, or "fishhook," 49 wires.) You turn back slightly more than ⅜ inch because the wire "grows" in length when it is unlaid.

Thoroughly wash the splayed-out wire in acetone, or whatever cleansing fluid is being used, right down as far as the seizing. Shake the fluid off the wire, and when dry, dip the wire in the flux. Then pull the wire back through the socket until all the seizing is outside; that part of the seizing nearest the splayed-out wire should be flush with the tapered bottom of the socket. This wire, with every end fishhooked, should now be inside the hollow of the socket.

The system of pushing the wire through the socket, splaying the strands into a brush, fishhooking the ends, and then pulling the brush end back into the socket should only be done with the typical nongreasy stainless or galvanized wire rope used for rigging in sailboats. Wire rope that is the least bit greasy should not be pulled through the socket, because some of the grease inevitably would coat the inside of the fitting and prevent the zinc from adhering.

Installing a poured socket as a terminal on oily or greasy wire rope is a slightly different procedure. The socket is clamped in a vise and heated to dispel any residual moisture. The wire end is splayed out as far down as the seizing to an included angle of 60 degrees, and the resulting brush is cleaned in a solvent such as SC-5 methyl chloroform. (Be careful not to breathe in any of this stuff — or you'll think *you* are being operated on!) After the solvent has dried and the wire has been dipped in flux, the brush (which cannot be fishhooked) is seized tightly at its wide end and carefully pushed into the small end of the socket. The seizing holding the brush together is cut and the wire is distributed evenly around the inside of the socket. From this point on, the procedure is the same as for wire that has been fishhooked.

Bind asbestos string over the seizing and up a quarter of an inch or so onto the socket itself. This string protects the seizing from the flame of the torch, and also prevents the melted zinc from leaking out of the socket — so do a good, tight job here. You can use asbestos clay instead of string or, alternatively, a beer can previously threaded onto the wire through a hole in its bottom.

Filled with sand, the can is pushed up the wire until the socket bottom is sitting ¼ or ⅜ inch into the sand. I've used all three methods and this is as good as any. It also gives you a marvelous excuse to be drinking beer on the job.

To provide an extra bit of strength, a strand or two of asbestos string may be wound around the top of the socket so that the zinc can overfill the socket right to the top of this. With the stage now set, a chunk of zinc should be placed in the ladle and melted. The socket should then be heated carefully to remove any residual moisture. The zinc, which should be skimmed for dross, is ready to run when a small piece of paper touched onto its surface chars. While all this is going on, apply flux generously inside the socket with a small brush. Take care not to play the torch flame on the wire inside the socket, because it can be detrimental to the temper of the metal.

Many riggers caution against overheating the wire and annealing the socket to the point of weakening the metal. So don't get carried away with heating up the socket to the extent that this happens. Make sure the socket is no warmer than a temperature comfortable to hold, and you'll be doing exactly what I've done. And I've never had a failure with a poured socket as a terminal fitting for any type of wire.

When the socket is warmed and the zinc is hot enough, pour in the zinc all at once. It is important to tap the sides of the socket with a light hammer or spike so that any air bubbles can rise to the surface of the zinc before it sets. It is sometimes surprising to see the quantity of air that bubbles out of even a small socket. Failure to get all the air out can result in a void and consequently a faulty job.

And that's it. It may sound like a big deal, but once the gear is assembled to do the job, it can be done with dispatch. In the time it has taken me to write this, we could have done a dozen sockets. I have already stated that galvanized sockets should be used for galvanized wire and bronze sockets for stainless steel wire — but this is a case of "do as I say, not as I do." Dave and I hung all the new stays and shrouds on the mainmast of the *White Squall II* before we started on the foremast, and it was about this time that I stumbled upon an entrepreneur who wanted to unload a dozen or so ¾-inch bronze turnbuckles, each one incorporating a poured socket at its upper end. So we used these bronze jobs with the galvanized wire.

There doesn't appear to have been any trouble with electrolysis or any other type of corrosion, even after 12 years. This might be because immediately after we'd done the job, we blacked the rigging down with a mixture of one-third fish oil and two-thirds black anticorrosive paint (after initially washing the new galvanized wire and sockets with vinegar to provide a "tooth" so the mixture would hang on). Turnbuckles, shackles, sockets, mast bands, every metal fitting in sight — galvanized, bronze, stainless, you-name-it — got this treatment once a year.

Bronze and galvanized sockets are usually constructed of cast metal, and for this reason, they should be inspected annually for flaws. Spotcheck can be used for this, but the sockets must be shined and polished first. If a socket proves suspect, it should be replaced. The fact that the job can be done aboard ship, however, is a point in favor of poured sockets, in my opinion, for the same convenience just doesn't apply to swaged terminals.

Over the years I've seen plenty of swages with fearsome cracks in them, but never a poured socket like that, even though reports have trickled through from time to

Poured-socket rigging terminals and open-barrel turnbuckles. Little thread to spare on the center turnbuckle. Could that life ring be released and used in a hurry? (Ralph Naranjo photo)

time of sockets developing cracks. I suppose I've been shipmates with poured sockets for 25 full-time sailing years. All of these sockets I did in the manner described, sometimes with help but more often with no assistance, and never have any of these terminals given the slightest trouble.

A word of caution to anyone getting all fired up to do a poured-socket job is not out of place here. Wear shoes. When we did that re-rigging job on the *White Squall II,* Dave and I didn't own a pair of shoes between us. Our feet were as bare as mine are now, as I sit typing this with the Caribbean breaking on the coral 20 feet away.

My reason for recommending footwear is that once or twice in the schooner's engine room I got a bit heavy-handed when filling a socket, and it overflowed. I can still see that molten metal disappearing down between Dave's toes as he tapped the side of the socket with a marlinspike. Much leaping and bounding about, strong words, etc. Now and again I poured some between my own toes with an identical result. Minine, who'd like as not be holding the beer can of sand up under the socket, had some narrow squeaks, but she always escaped. (For continuing marital bliss, it is highly recommended that if you're going to pour molten zinc over anyone, pour it over yourself or your mate — never your wife.)

The reason that 7/7 wire was chosen for the job instead of 1/19 is that several of the shrouds and stays had to be spliced at their top ends to fit over a masthead, and while I'd spliced 7/7 perhaps a hundred times, I'd never had a go at 1/19. The old wire we were replacing was 6/7 galvanized and had had an innings of at least 25 years, so I figured that the new 7/7, stronger because of its wire core, was adequate.

Norseman and Sta-Lok

Stainless steel Norseman and Sta-Lok fittings have been given a good hand for many years now, and they've got a lot going for them. For a start, they are machined out of stainless bar stock, and so are very strong. Possibly their greatest virtue is that an entire rigging job may be accomplished quickly; the only tools necessary are a couple of wrenches, wire cutters, and pliers. Seizing twine, applied in the same manner as has been described for poured-socket preparation, is also necessary.

I first became acquainted with Norseman fittings 18 years ago when I sold my yawl in the West Indies. The new owner decided to re-rig the vessel, and he ordered the stainless steel wire and Norseman fittings from England. I think stainless steel rigging is a whole lot better today than it used to be; I always used stainless on my yawl, but extensive tropic sailing seemed to cause it to splinter, or "sprag." While my poured sockets and splices never gave me cause for concern, I had the minimum amount of confidence in the wire. It was a measure of doubt that more than once caused the hairs on the back of my neck to separate and stand at attention when a hard squall laid my ship down.

When Alan said he was going to replace the wire, I was all for it, even though he put my nose out of joint when he refused to re-use my precious poured sockets. We were tramping up and down the islands in the *White Squall II* with charter parties aboard at the time, and since Alan owned the resort on Marina Cay and used the smaller *White Squall* for day-chartering his guests, I had a fair chance to observe how the Norseman fittings were holding up.

From minimal enthusiasm, which included such comments as "His bloody mast'll go over the side — you wait and see!" I came around full circle to bragging about the rigging the yawl now sported. After a couple of years of this, Alan and Jean then sailed the vessel down through the Canal and across the Pacific to New Zealand, with the Norseman fittings still hanging on for dear life. We crossed tacks with the *White Squall* in later years at various Pacific anchorages, and the Norseman fittings, along with the 1/19 stainless steel wire Alan had used for standing rigging, were continuing to give good service.

A Norseman terminal fitting (see photograph, page 80) consists of a split cone that compresses and holds the wire inside a tapered body. This body, machined out of solid stainless stock, has flats at its wide end to facilitate holding the fitting with a wrench for assembling or disassembling. An eye, jaw (fork), or stud, complete with thin lock-nut, screws into the wide end of the fitting.

The initial drill when assembling Norseman terminals is identical to the preparation necessary for poured sockets. A thin, strong seizing is applied tightly to the wire at a predetermined distance back from its end. This distance varies with the size of

This Norseman terminal has seen a lot of service. Note classy clevis pin. (Dave Ferneding photo)

wire and fitting used, but it is indicated clearly in the instructions that accompany every Norseman. These instructions must be followed explicitly.

The wire is pushed through the hole at the tapered end of the body and carefully opened out as far as the seizing will allow. The cone is then slid down the center core of the wire. These cones vary, depending on what kind of rigging is being used, so it is important to specify exactly the type of wire when ordering terminals. The outside strands of wire fit around the cone and bend partway over its top. The cone and its wire are then carefully eased back into the body of the fitting, and the eye, fork, or stud end is screwed into the body. The tighter the cone and wire are forced into the tapered body by the end fitting, the better the wire is held.

There is, however, a fine line between sensibly tight and overly tight. If you happen to have the build of an Olympic weightlifter and you swing on a couple of oversize wrenches with might and main to tighten your Norseman fittings, you could place an unfair strain on the threads and the tapered body. Not long ago I heard that a member of the Seven Seas Cruising Association was talking of a stay letting go aboard his vessel when the tapered body of a Norseman terminal fitting exploded. The cause is unknown to me, but so much depends on the degree of strain applied when assembling these fittings that it is strange Norseman doesn't supply a torque chart for its various sizes of terminals. These fittings aren't cheap; a little bit of extra information as to the correct amount of torque to apply would remove any doubt when assembling them. Doubt is the last thing you need to have about any of your standing rigging.

Minine and I fitted new lifelines aboard the *White Squall II* in Bora Bora in the early 1970s, and for this job we used ¼-inch-diameter 7/19 stainless steel wire. The terminals we used were Norseman with a fork end. We slid the wire inside clear plastic hose to give the job a bit of style and to make the lifelines easier on the legs and arms of anyone falling against them. It was a simple exercise and the fittings were ideal for this purpose, but a few years later in the Fijis, when we were ready to renew the plastic hose (the tropic sun has a wonderful time with this stuff), it was a different piece of cake.

The pin in the Norseman fork screwed in with its head flush in a countersunk hole on one side of the jaw. To prevent its unscrewing, I'd walloped a centerpunch mark on the jaw at each end of the screwdriver slot to provide a burr to keep the pin from unscrewing. Getting that pin out after this treatment proved to be a terrible job. It was easy to disassemble the terminal, replace the plastic that had become opaque and hard, and assemble it again, but fiddling with those pins would have tested any man's blood pressure.

Norseman now uses a regular clevis pin in their fork-end terminal fittings, and this is a vast improvement over the slotted, threaded pin with the countersunk head. The clevis pin has a shoulder at one end and a hole for a cotter (split) pin at the other, and it is very easy to install or remove for examination. Also, the side of the fork that formerly was countersunk (and consequently weakened) is now just that much stronger.

Sta-Lok has always used a clevis pin in their fork-end terminals. Sta-Lok are compression stainless steel terminal fittings, machined from bar stock, as are Norseman. They are available with eye, fork, and stud ends and are designed specifically for the do-it-yourselfer using the same tools as are necessary for Norseman. When fitting Norseman or Sta-Lok terminals to standing rigging, the cruising yachtsman should, wherever possible, try to confine himself to eye fittings instead of fork ones. A fork fitting has a potential weakness at the base of each jaw, it has a hole in each jaw for the clevis pin, and finally there is the pin itself. All this seems a lot for a terminal that already has three component parts.

I remember when the 62-foot ketch *Mimosa* was sailing into St. Johns, Antigua, and a Norseman fork fitting broke at the side where the countersunk hole is drilled for the pin to screw in flush. More than 60 feet of 1/19 permanent backstay dropped from the masthead, and what was left of the fitting nearly made a believer out of a woman sitting on the coach roof when it parted her hair on its way to making a hole in the side deck. A thorough inspection of the rigging revealed that the side of another fork holding a port lower shroud to a mast tang was broken also, at each side of its countersunk eye, and was ready to let go. This rigging, fittings and all, was only two months old.

A terminal fitting with an eye that locates in the jaw of a toggle, a turnbuckle, or a double mast tang would seem a far better choice than a fork.

The sequence on the following two pages was taken during the re-rigging of the 42-foot cutter Coober Pedy *while at anchor at the Caribbean island of St. Martin. (Roz and Dave Ferneding photos)*

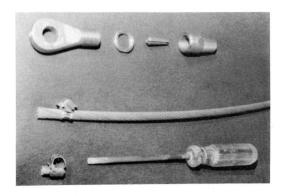

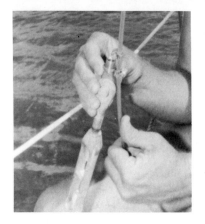

1. *Fittings used were Norseman eye terminals with 6 mm 1/19 stainless steel wire. Photo shows Norseman terminal components: eye, locknut, split cone, body. Small hose clips were used to keep the wire from unlaying.*

2. *A surefire way to get perfect measurement. A terminal fitting has been installed at the end of the wire, which has been taken aloft and secured in its tang. Norseman eye has been placed in turnbuckle, thus enabling the shroud to be measured accurately for length.*

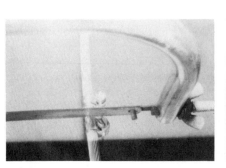

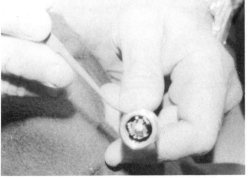

3. *Shroud is taken down and held securely in small vise, which is mounted on a piece of 2 by 6 fir. A hose clip is secured close to the one marking the correct length, and the wire is cut carefully with a hacksaw. Note several thicknesses of sailcloth protecting wire from jaws of vise.*

4. *After filing the severed wire-ends free of sharp edges, the hose clip is positioned a predetermined distance down the wire and tightened securely. Photo, looking into body of fitting, shows cone in position over center core and outside wires being spaced equally around outside of cone.*

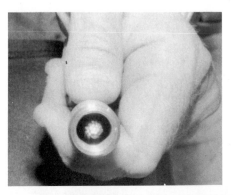

5. *Cone and wires after eye has been tightened securely and then unscrewed so that fit of wires and cone may be inspected.*

6. *Fitting being filled with epoxy glue. (Glue used was Resco, Miami Lakes, Florida 33014.)*

7. *Eye, with locknut in place, is screwed into body of terminal. Note hose clip at base of fitting preventing wire from unlaying.*

8. *Eye being tightened down securely onto the wire and cone.* **9.** *With locknut tightened and hose clip removed, mast end is secured in its tang, just-completed terminal fitted in jaws of turnbuckle, and shroud is set up. Excess epoxy that has squeezed out of base of fitting is being wiped away.*

10. *Spraying Soft Seal (C.R.C. Chemicals, C.J. Webb Inc., Dresher, Pennsylvania 19025) on terminal and wire. It is claimed that Soft Seal, which is a light amber transparent film 2 to 5 mils thick, is highly resistant to salt water and salt spray and will not craze or become brittle.*

Castlok

Castlok wire rope fittings differ from any other type of terminal in that the body is filled with an epoxy resin that forms a plug. The company's literature states: "The terminals use especially formulated resins of enormous compressive strength. To dispel a fallacy, the resin is not used as a glue. The wires are not held in the terminal by an adhesive mode. The function of the resin is to form a tapered plug to hold the wires in their natural unlaid helix. Since the terminal is completely sealed, it has unequaled resistance to saltwater corrosion."

In a pinch, a Castlok fitting may be applied to a wire end using only bare hands as tools, although a pair of needle-nose pliers makes the job easier on the fingers. The manufacturer's instructions, which include a thorough degreasing of the wire that the resin will flow around, must be followed explicitly. The splaying of the part of the wire that is to remain in the terminal into a "Coke-bottle" shape is one of the most necessary steps in the whole operation.

When the desired wire shape is formed (a diagram in the manufacturer's literature shows how to do this), the splayed end is pulled back into the body of the fitting in much the same manner as the fishhooked wire of a poured socket. The epoxy resin is poured in and agitated with a thin wire to remove any air and prevent a void. The body is allowed to stand for a full minute and then is topped off to the brim. The eye, stud, or fork end is then screwed firmly all the way in, hand tight. The fact that the body is fully topped up cancels out any chance that air will be introduced into the body chamber by this operation. Excess resin is squeezed out the bottom of the terminal, where it is wiped off, leaving a "fillet or drip-ledge at the juncture of cable and terminal."

It is recommended that the assembling and curing of Castlok terminals take place within a temperature range of 75 °F to 150 °F (24 °C to 66 °C). A full cure (the time it takes before a terminal can be put to work) varies from 24 hours at 75 °F (24 °C) to two hours at 150 °F (66 °C). The makers tell us that while curing, " . . . temperature may be maintained in the nominal range by a number of artificial means such as sunlight, a shrouded incandescent bulb or heat lamp, even body heat in an emergency."

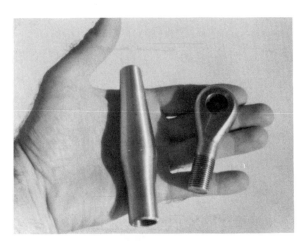

Components of Castlok fitting. (Jim Skoog photo)

Salt water, it would seem, has no more chance of getting into a well-assembled Castlok fitting than it has of getting into a poured socket; that fact alone makes this terminal worthy of consideration. I have not been shipmates with Castlok terminals for any great length of time. To go for an afternoon or for a few days' sail is not long enough to be able to give a positive report on any fittings: you need a minimum of five years of tropic cruising that includes occasions when it's blowing like stink and you're wondering how the hell your gear's managing to hang together.

There is another thing, too, for the do-it-yourselfer (and whether you are now or whether you're not, if you intend to stay out there cruising, you soon will be): The resin for any spare Castlok fittings you carry has an expiration date that, apparently, you must observe. So if you intend to use these fittings and take some spares along, keep an eye on the age of your resin.

Nicopress

The Nicopress fitting is a soft copper-alloy sleeve through which the two parts (the standing and the free) of a length of wire-rope rigging slide after passing around a thimble. The wires are pressed together securely below the apex (throat) of the eye as the Nicopress fitting is crimped between the jaws of a tool resembling a large bolt cutter (or, for large sizes of wire, in a hydraulic press). Usually two sleeves are applied to the wire, and the result is a rigging terminal that can hold like fury.

Nicopress fittings are popular for wire halyard terminals and to terminate standing rigging. They are suitable for small jobs, too. I used Nicopress for the staying of the mast on *White Squall II*'s nine-foot sailing dinghy and in the plywood sailing pram I built for my yawl. As terminals for ⅛-inch stainless steel 7/7 wire used for the rigging of both dinghies, the fittings were excellent.

The fact that the wire passes around a thimble before being crimped gives this fitting a head start on a terminal that merely accepts the wire and holds it as a straight pull. The Nicopress picks up a bit of buck-shee strength from the friction imposed on the wire as it passes around the eye. When using a Nicopress tool, make the first compression close to the throat of the thimble; rotate the tool 180 degrees for each successive compression. The number of compressions depends upon the size of the wire and the length of the sleeve. For a Nicopress fitting to achieve its full strength, the wire end should project one-half the diameter of the wire clear of the sleeve. Not only does this practice give the last "nip" in the sleeve more wire to grip, it keeps the buried ends of the strands from exerting a cutting effect against the standing lay, though unfortunately the projecting wire end will snag sheets, sails, fingers, and anything else that happens by.

The wire end can be taped, but it doesn't look the greatest, so in an attempt to kill two birds — the aesthetic and the practical — with the one shot, I worked Marinetex (a super-tough epoxy) down into the wire ends projecting from the Nicopress sleeves of the rigging on the *White Squall*'s sailing dinghy. It was a halfhearted effort, tackled from the point of view of having nothing to lose. The results astounded me. That rigging was used, abused, slacked off, tightened again, soaked, and dried in a tropic sun for four years until I sold the ship — and the wire ends were still smooth and sealed. I would definitely give this method a try on larger rigging.

A little tool can be purchased from the S & F Tool Company (P.O. Box 1546, Costa Mesa, California 92626) that enables the do-it-yourselfer to crimp his own Nicopress terminals aboard. The tool can be used on ⅛- through ¼-inch wire, although I have heard of a different tool used on 1/19, ⅜-inch rigging (No. 4 Swage-It, from the same company). Accompanying every tool are detailed and simple instructions, as well as micrometer readings so that a check can be run on the finished work. Universal Wire Products Inc. (Dept. UWS, 222 Universal Drive, North Haven, Connecticut 06473) also sells Nicopress tools. This company also sells cable cutters in three sizes: C-7 for up to ³⁄₁₆-inch wire, C-12 for up to ⅜-inch, and C-16 for up to ⅝-inch wire. In my opinion, suitable-sized cable cutters, Nicopress tools, and a selection of sleeves have a place aboard every long-range cruising boat.

A big attraction of Nicopress fittings is the price, which is a fraction of some of the expensive Norseman-type terminals, swages, or Castlok fittings. A criticism leveled at Nicopress when used with 1/19 wire is the need to bend the wire around a thimble. While the possibility does exist that the inside strands (those closest to the thimble) will crimp and that a stretch factor is present in the outside strands (outside as the wire passes around the crown of the thimble), these do not seem to affect good-quality wire.

Sleeve-type fittings, equally as good as Nicopress and with the advantage that they are also available for larger sizes of wire, are marketed under the British brand name of Talurit. They have the approval of the Board of Trade, too, which is not easy to come by. I've seen Talurits used as terminals on slings that lift cargo over the heads of men working on the decks and in the holds of ships. I've also seen them used as terminals on derrick guy wires and hold-down wires over deck cargoes of lumber, undergoing fearsome strains on merchant vessels, and have never known one to let go. And what more can be expected of any terminal? It would appear, however, that some types of sleeve fittings, when used on the lower ends of standing wire rigging that is constantly exposed to salt air and spray, just don't stand up (see photograph). The soft copper-alloy Nicopress sleeves, however, seem to be impervious to weather or corrosion.

Splices

I have never seen a wire splice pull and let go. But I've seen wire standing rigging break, leaving the eyesplices at each end of the wire intact and to all appearances as good as the day they were formed. Other people, however, tell of wire splices pulling out, and from time to time various writers cite the case of Sir Alec Rose's trouble with splices on his round-the-world voyage aboard *Lively Lady*. So it does happen, only proving once again that no method of wire termination is without its failures.

Wire rope, fitted snugly around a thimble and then spliced into its standing part, is one of the oldest methods of terminating a shroud or stay on sailing craft. It is also, in my opinion, still one of the best. As with other wire-rope terminals, though, the skill of the operator can make all the difference between a good splice that will hold and a bad one that will not. The type of splice matters, too; whether or not the termination is a lock splice makes a big difference in its dependability. So do the number of tucks taken.

Radar reflector installed at masthead of mizzen. Note rope-to-wire splice of halyard just passing over sheave at top of sail track. (Courtesy Yachtspars)

Whaling the daylights out of a splice with a hammer or mallet to make it look right can fatigue stainless steel wire and cause galvanized wire to lose some of its protective covering. Splicing stainless wire with a regular cold-drawn steel marlinspike is something else that can be detrimental to the job. Stainless steel wire is hard, and its strands can scrape infinitesimal pieces of steel from a regular spike. These, left buried within a splice, start rusting and cause oxidation to occur in the stainless wire surrounding them. Stainless steel wire should be spliced with a stainless spike.

There are many good types of splices, and every rigger has his favorite. Mine is the British Board of Trade (B.O.T.) lock splice, and it is the only one I've ever used on the rigging of sailing craft. I'm sure there are wire splices just as good — there may even be better ones — but this splice was approved many years ago as being suitable for use on wire that lifted cargo over men's heads as they were working, and that's good enough for me. I've never heard of a swage fitting rating this high.

The B.O.T. splice has a lock in its first tuck and is double-locked in its last two tucks; to the best of my knowledge and experience, the wire will break before this splice will pull. I used the B.O.T. splice on the 7/7 stainless steel $\frac{5}{16}$-inch standing rigging of *White Squall* when I launched her in 1948 (and on the galvanized rigging of two gaff-rigged vessels I had owned previously). I was aware at the time of other types of terminals that were pretty costly, but since I pushed my own splices in "for freebs" (and couldn't have afforded to pay for other terminals anyway), I carried on blissfully with the good old lock splice. Twenty years later, I was still using the same splice for various eyes in the rigging of *White Squall II*.

I've had trouble over the years with stainless steel standing rigging, wire suddenly sprouting a crop of splinters (the American term) or sprags (British), but the notion that a splice could pull just hadn't occurred until I started reading about it in books. These splinters or sprags appear as little broken ends of wire on the sides of shrouds or stays and are an indication that the wire is fatiguing, or "work-hardening." A tough, sharp, little end, sticking out perhaps a quarter of an inch to tear at sails and hands, is the result of the crystallizing and breaking of a wire strand.

A rule to determine whether a piece of splintered rigging should be replaced is: Multiply the circumference of the wire by eight to get a "test length" of the wire, and if in any such test length five percent of the strands are broken, the wire should be replaced. For example, if, in an eight-inch length of $\frac{5}{16}$-inch-diameter (near enough 1-inch circumference) 1/19 wire, one strand is broken, the wire should be condemned. In the same length of the same size 7/7 wire, it would take three strands broken before you'd have to chuck it. (This illustrates one advantage of 7/7 wire over 1/19.)

This is a mighty strict test on 1/19 wire, since it means that any time one strand lets go, you have to condemn the whole thing. If you don't want to be quite so strict, you can double your test length to 16 inches (for $\frac{5}{16}$-inch diameter), double your percentage to 10 percent, and thus go up to two broken strands in that length as the requirement for replacement.

The yachtsman or woman who wants to do his or her own wire splices is well advised to buy a book on the subject and practice at home. However, a few tips here are not out of place. Always work behind your marlinspike when splicing wire; don't go poking your eye out or sticking the spike into your hand. If the book tells you to push in three tucks and then taper off with the final two, give the splice another two full tucks for luck and then do your tapering. If a total of seven tucks gives you a splice an inch or so longer than you'd originally figured, don't worry about it.

If you want a wire terminal that won't give you grief, this is the way to get it. And as for looks, don't go biting your fingernails about that, either. If your splices aren't pretty, Old Man Ocean (the guy who counts) won't care; he treats us all the same, anyway.

A hollow marlinspike, a spike in the shape of a tapered tube, is popular in some circles because, when the spike is pushed between the wire lay of the standing part, a full strand may be pushed along in the hollow body of the spike and under the lay to complete that part of a tuck. It's all a matter of opinion, I suppose; I used a hollow spike on one splice years ago, and, though it was easy to use, never employed one again. I didn't like the way its two thin edges rasped under a strand as it forced it up out of the lay. I had the feeling that with some of the really hard-laid stainless steel wire, the strands could be damaged by the narrow sides of the hollow spike; with galvanized wire, some of that protective covering could be removed.

A regular, round marlinspike with a narrow, blunt chisel point seems a better bet to me. A round spike cannot under any circumstances leave a nick or score in the wire. You get a lot of mileage out of a good spike. I have a round marlinspike that a ship's engineer machined out of an old stainless steel pump shaft for me more than 30 years ago, and it's got a lot of work left in it yet. Again, though, it's all a matter of preference. A hollow spike, for the person who pushes in one or two (or fewer) splices a year, might well be his or her choice. For the amateur, it is certainly easier to use.

Solid thimbles cannot be pulled out of shape by the strain of a vessel sailing, and for that reason when some wire splicing is to be done, they are preferable to the open type of thimble (which is pressed from sheet stainless for stainless rigging or from steel, which is then galvanized, for galvanized rigging). A solid thimble is, however, a hard thing to come by, and it has been for years. I've used stainless steel "open eye" thimbles for both stainless and galvanized 7/7 rigging for many years, with never a failure or an incident of one pulled out of shape, so it would seem that these terminals are adequate.

A rigger's vise makes all the difference to a person putting in a wire splice. The wire, pressed firmly into the hollow of a thimble at the crown and at each side of the throat by the feet of a rigger's vise, is held very securely. A vise almost guarantees that the thimble will have a snug fit once the splice is completed and the vise is released. In the absence of such a tool, and if the thimble in use is large enough, three small Vise-Grips can be used in the same position as the feet of a rigger's vise and, if securely applied, will do a good job. On a thimble too small for the use of Vise-Grips — say, for ¼-inch wire — the wire is usually small and pliant enough to be held in the thimble with lashings at the crown and throat. The splice is then tucked in easily.

I've never owned a really good rigger's vise such as the Durkee, but a fellow charter skipper in St. Thomas had one of these monsters when we were chartering out of Charlotte Amalie, the port on that island. Along with various other charter skippers, I would borrow the Durkee from time to time. I was all fired up to put spliced eyes in the *White Squall II*'s rigging when the big re-rigging job was at hand, for the simple reason that the sockets I had ordered had gone adrift in Puerto Rico on their way to the Virgin Islands. So one day I headed brightly over to see Fergie, to put the bite on him for the use of his vise.

Unfortunately, he'd loaned it out a few days before to the Tahitian bosun of a big French schooner lying in the bay. This worthy then proceeded to have a spectacular tiff with his girlfriend ashore one night, and on his return to the ship, in a fit of pique, hurled all manner of stuff into the night, farther than the eye could see. Along with spikes, belaying pins, and other loose gear lying around on deck went the rigger's vise, to a watery grave.

A whole gang of us crawled around the bottom of the bay with scuba tanks on our backs for a couple of days. We found all sorts of things, but we didn't find the vise. Relations between the two local representatives of Tahiti and New Zealand (the bosun and me) were becoming a bit strained when Bob Smith, the dockmaster, appeared with an armful of sockets and some zinc. After that — except for the odd burn here and there — the rigging job was apples all the way.

Decisions

So — what is the best way of terminating wire rope? For a start, of course, it depends upon the wire. For reasons we've already covered, 1/19 wire doesn't readily lend itself to splicing. Because of the size of each individual strand, it is nowhere near as flexible as 7/7. It's not as easy to seat snugly in a thimble (there are the crimp and stretch factors already mentioned), and it's difficult to splice. However, nothing is impossible, and from time to time we do see 1/19 wire with spliced terminals, but such examples are few and far between. So the cruising man who wants spliced eyes had better content himself with 7/7 wire. If he does, and if his splices are tucked in well, he'll stand every chance that these terminals will last as long as the wire itself.

There are qualifications to this (as there are with most things, it seems). If the wire chosen is good-quality 7/7 stainless, the captain should be happy until the arrival of splinters on various stays or shrouds. A piece of rigging that cannot pass the five-percent test previously mentioned, or a test to twice its recommended safe working load in a rigging loft, should be replaced. (If the wire has been terminated with poured sockets, the fittings can probably be used again.) Good-quality stainless steel rigging should last, as I have said, for at least 10 years.

I don't consider that 7/7 galvanized steel wire of a diameter less than ⅜ inch should be selected as standing rigging for a cruising boat. The smaller the diameter of the wire rope, the smaller are the individual wires that make up the six strands in the lay and the center core. On smaller sizes of wire rope, the fine wires in the strands carry only a very thin skin of galvanizing, which just doesn't seem to last the distance on a cruising boat. In larger sizes of wire, however, from ⅜ inch on up, well-treated galvanized standing rigging will last a cruising vessel as long as, or longer than, any other. It should be remembered, when a decision is being made in choosing between galvanized and stainless, that galvanized wire will show its deteriorating condition with rust spots, while stainless steel will look great right up until the time it lets go.

Wonderful standing rigging, however, can be made with 1/19 stainless steel wire. If a good rigging job is done with properly poured sockets as terminal fittings, a boat will have standing rigging that is virtually maintenance-free and near perfect. Galvanized 1/19 wire is worth considering as standing rigging, too. The individual wires in 1/19 are of a diameter large enough to carry a generous skin of galvanizing, and if this standing rigging is treated once a year, it will go on and on.

By now it will be obvious that I am prejudiced in favor of splices or poured sockets, with Nicopress running a close third. I've been shipmates with splices all my life, in a wide variety of craft both commercial and pleasure, and have never had a splice let me down. The same for sockets.

But this, of course, is not enough reason to rubbish all other types of terminals. Norseman, for instance, has a good record. How do we know if misalignment of mast tangs wasn't responsible when the two-month-old backstay terminal on *Mimosa* let go off Antigua? Or if misalignment wasn't the reason for the cracked jaw in a lower shroud terminal? I have both the owner's and the skipper's report (they both agree) before me as I write this, and I remember when it happened. They are both mighty experienced seamen, but . . . you can never know. The most important thing to be learned from that incident, and from others like it, is that an eye terminal in a double mast tang is probably a better bet than a fork with its pin through a single tang.

A recent letter from Nautor of Finland, the Swan yacht builder, tells me of a rigging failure caused by a Norseman fitting aboard one of their boats. Lars Strom states, in part: "Upon examination, it was found that the outer strands had parted, while the inner ones, undamaged, had pulled out from the fitting. The reason was the Norseman cone design, which did not lock the inner strands effectively, letting the outer ones take all the load. A contributing factor was that Nautor uses metric wire, while Norseman is a British company and thus thinks in inches. The difference between 12-millimeter and ½-inch wire works out very unfavorably inside the cone."

Lars goes on to say that Norseman improved their cones after the accident, "making them less sensitive to variations in wire diameters." He concludes: "We feel that, properly assembled, Norseman terminals with the new cones give very reliable performance . . . . As you might know, swaged fittings are not without their problems either . . . ."

Terminals such as Norseman, Sta-Lok, and Electroline — and any others that hold a shroud or stay as a straight pull by its end clamped between a (usually) split plug and the body — would have an element of doubt taken from their performance if a torque factor for each size of fitting were supplied. When putting in a splice, the rigger can take another couple of tucks to really play it safe; with a poured socket, he can tie another strand or two of asbestos string around the top and overfill it with zinc. With Nicopress, he can use two or even three sleeves. But what does he do with a compression fitting? Tighten it a bit more? Ho-ho! What if he tightens it too much, to the point where after a year or so it decides that enough residual strain is enough — and it explodes?

Even the cheapest lawnmower engine has a torque chart supplied so that an engineer knows exactly how much to tighten head nuts, spark plugs, and brackets. Why don't expensive yacht fittings have such charts? If a lawnmower quits, you can walk back into the house congratulating yourself that you won't have to mow the lawn today. If a compression-type terminal explodes because it was tightened too much, or the wire slips out because it wasn't tightened enough, you won't be in the middle of the front lawn; more than likely, you'll be in the middle of the ocean in a gale of wind. And the only guy in line for congratulations is the one who made the fitting. He can thank his lucky stars that the sailor on the receiving end of the mishap can't get his hands on him.

UPKEEP

I have heard much discussion among cruising yachtsmen about keeping salt water out of a rig's terminal fittings; it is a point with which I concur wholeheartedly. The greatest number of swages that develop cracks, splays in the terminal where the wire enters the fitting, and rust marks (which sometimes creep up into the wire itself) are those on the bottom ends of standing rigging — the ones salt water can really get at. The terminals aloft are seldom affected as badly.

It might be worth a try to parcel the wire with friction tape (for six inches or so above each of the bottom swages and down an inch onto the body of the terminal) before serving tightly with marlin, and to treat this with a mixture of boiled linseed oil and varnish. There certainly wouldn't be much to lose. Although I don't know of anyone who has done this, if I were the owner of a newly purchased cruising boat saddled with swaged terminals, I would first of all have each shroud and stay tested at the nearest rigging loft; I'd then treat each bottom fitting in the manner just described. I would also remove all parceling and serving once a year and give the terminals the Spotcheck test. This rigmarole would take a day out of each year, but it just might prove to be a day well spent.

I have a friend who is the owner of a 48-foot steel cruising cutter that is now six years old. His 1/19 stainless steel standing rigging is terminated with Norseman

A little bit of tape here and there really helps in preventing chafe. (Ralph Naranjo photo)

fittings, which he assembled following their instructions. Before screwing the eye fitting of the terminal into the tapered body to finally tighten the wire and cone, he filled the body (which he'd warmed slightly) with melted beeswax. As the eye fitting was screwed in and bedded down, this wax squeezed out the tapered end. His object in saturating everything inside the terminals with beeswax was an attempt to nullify, as much as possible, any chance that the salt water would reach dissimilar or even the same metals within the fittings and cause corrosion or any other kind of mischief. This vessel has done a number of deep-water cruises and charters in the past six years, with no rigging problems. The 1/19 stainless steel standing rigging and the beeswax-filled Norseman fittings look as good as the day they first came aboard.

There is no way salt water can get into a properly poured socket. The metallurgical bond that forms between the wire and the socket, with the help of the zinc, establishes a solid body that is impenetrable. Castlok, if installed correctly, and assuming the resin keeps doing its job, also keeps itself dry very well. But what can you do about keeping water out of a splice?

With splices in stainless steel wire, you don't even try; at least I don't. I only serve the last couple of inches of a splice in stainless wire, to cover the tapered end where the cut-off strands are. For serving, I've used stainless steel seizing wire (when available) or marlin. The serving is only to protect sails, hands, or anything else from being snagged by the end of a strand. The idea behind minimal serving is that the splice is readily available for inspection.

With 7/7 galvanized steel rigging, I used stainless steel thimbles for more than 20

1. *Light stainless steel thimble.* **2.** *Heavy stainless steel thimble.* **3.** *Solid thimble for wire rope. (Courtesy Crosby-Laughlin)*

years. The wire would lie bare around the thimble, and the splice was served its entire length with marlin applied against the lay, over friction tape wrapped with the lay. Beneath the friction tape would be a generous smearing of red, butterlike Res-Q-Steel or anhydrous lanolin. Melted beeswax would probably be just as good. All this is to keep salt water away from any wires in the splice that may have had some of the galvanizing scraped off by the marlinspike during the splicing operation.

The fact that the galvanized wire lies bare around the stainless steel eye would seem, perhaps, to be an invitation to corrosion, but it has never happened. I attribute this to the treating of all standing rigging — eyes, thimbles, serving, wire, and so on — with a generous coat of one-third fish oil and two-thirds black anti-corrosive paint once a year. All nine splices and 31 poured sockets in the standing rigging of the *White Squall II* have had this treatment every year for the past 12 years, and three days before I wrote this, they still looked fine. And this is on a vessel in the tropics, out there earning her keep almost every day.

A dozen or more wire rope clips or U-clamps should be included among the bosun's stores of every long-range cruising boat. Known also as "bulldog grips" (depending on what part of the world you're in), they should be the correct size for the standing rigging of the vessel. A typical, good-quality clip is a piece of steel rod bent in a U and threaded at the ends of its arms. A drop-forged steel saddle slides onto the arms; its position is regulated by the nuts that thread on behind it (see photograph). The whole fitting should be hot-dipped galvanized steel.

A cruising man might go his whole life without needing a temporary rigging job, but if he suddenly has a rigging failure that calls for the use of wire rope clips, he's going to want them to be dependable. With this in mind, it is not a bad idea, when first bringing the clips aboard, to grease the threads and run the nuts down and back a few times. Place them in a plastic bag after this treatment and mark the contents on the masking tape you bind around the bag to close it. Then put the bag where you can reach it in a jiffy. If you do all this, there's a fair chance you'll never need them.

Properly applied wire rope clips will hold as well as almost any other type of terminal fitting. However, there is a right way and a wrong way to put them on. When

Hot-dipped galvanized wire rope U-bolt clip; Fist-Grip wire rope clip. (Courtesy Crosby-Laughlin)

using clips to hold rigging wire around a thimble, the U of the clip should be around the free (or short) part of the wire and the saddle should be tightened down onto the standing (or long) part. Always use two or even three clips about one saddle-length apart, and send the nuts securely home.

The Crosby-Laughlin Group (P.O. Box 3128, Tulsa, Oklahoma 74101) supplies a torque factor for each of their sizes of wire rope clips. It is recommended that the nuts of a clip be re-torqued for several days after installation to take up any slack occasioned by the wire settling in the clip. This company supplies distributors with forged steel, hot-dipped-galvanized, U-bolt clips for wire rope diameters from ⅛ inch through 3½ inches. Fist-Grip clips are available in galvanized steel for rope from ¼ inch through 1½ inches and in bronze from ¼ inch through ⅝ inch. This company also supplies solid thimbles for wire rope diameters ½ inch through 1⅜ inches, and heavy stainless steel wire rope thimbles suitable for wire diameters of ¼ inch through ¾ inch. These latter thimbles are ideal for use when splicing or using Nicopress fittings. Also available are galvanized forged steel and alloy cast steel sockets for wire sizes ¼ inch through 4 inches.

I have two friends who sailed their 53-foot schooner, *Whistler,* across the Pacific from California to New Zealand who will always place wire rope clips, plus a spare length of wire, high on their list of desirable bosun's stores. The *Whistler* is gaff-rigged on both masts, and when Pat and Polly were 600 miles out of Suva, their ship's port and starboard cap shrouds on the foremast started to strand. So they cut two three-foot lengths of wire from their spare piece of rigging and simply clamped one of these to each shroud with three wire rope clips above and below the weak part of the shroud. The U part of the clip was used on the new wire and the saddle was tightened firmly down onto the old shroud. Pat figured that the new wire should be able to stand any "nip" that might be imparted by the inside crown of the U better than the tired wire of the old shroud. This treatment was entirely successful and they completed the voyage with no further problem. They completely re-rigged the ship with ⁷⁄₁₆-inch galvanized wire and spliced eye terminals at Whangarei, New Zealand.

It was years ago, while reading an account of the tactics that old ships-of-the-line employed to train their guns at anchor, that I stumbled upon the way to black down my galvanized rigging without dropping a spot of paint on deck. I gave a brief account of the system in *The Charter Game,* but it's worth repeating here.

At anchor in a bay, a springline is led from well aft outside everything (lifelines, shrouds, etc.) and bent to the anchor cable or rode with a rolling hitch. With the springline fast aft, the anchor cable is slacked away until the ship is bridled off, side on to the wind. Then you go aloft in a bosun's chair and black down the lee rigging; any paint drops blow off into the sea to leeward. Repeat this procedure to do the rigging on the opposite side of the vessel.

A few tips. Minine would reeve a halyard through a snatch block and take it to a surging drum on our hydraulic windlass. Four turns around the drum (which would be revolving), and up aloft I'd go like a bag of fish. (Always be on the best of terms with your wife before you have a go at this; with little or no effort on her part, she could pull you right through the masthead sheave.) I would have a two-inch roller brush and a regular two-inch paintbrush, along with a half-gallon of my mixture of fish oil and black paint in a galvanized bucket, which would be hanging from the chair.

The regular brush was used to paint mast bands, sockets, and splices. The little roller was to do the wire shrouds and stays. I would also apply the mixture to the roller with the regular brush; it's practically impossible to distribute paint evenly onto a roller by dipping it in a can, and it's hardly feasible to take a tray aloft. It took one day a year to do all the rigging.

It must be pointed out that, while it's highly desirable not to drop any paint on your own vessel, it's nowhere near as important as making sure you don't spatter some other guy. Don't do all this with another vessel close enough downwind to cop a broadside of paint spots. Otherwise, your stratagem of bridling yourself off like a salty old man-o'-war may project you right back to those days: you might end up having to defend yourself.

TURNBUCKLES

The screw fittings used to apply tension to rigging are usually situated at the lower ends of shrouds and stays and are known variously as turnbuckles, rigging screws, or bottlescrews. Bottlescrews (also known as closed-barrel turnbuckles) have a closed barrel that has a righthand thread at one end and a lefthand thread at the other. This barrel accepts the threaded shank of a fork or eye, which, as the barrel is turned, slacks or tightens the wire. It is usual for closed-barrel turnbuckles (especially galvanized ones) to be filled with a heavy grease that squeezes out the two small holes in the barrel as it is tightened. (In days of yore, a mixture of white lead and tallow was used.)

When using closed-barrel turnbuckles, it is important to know the length of the screwed shanks; the shank disappears into the barrel, and the only way to check whether the full number of threads is being utilized is by measurement. I used galvanized closed-barrel turnbuckles aboard the *White Squall II* for 15 years and never had a failure. Also playing their part in the schooner's rigging without complaint for the past 12 years are those bronze, closed-barrel, ex-Navy jobs.

Most turnbuckles aboard sailboats are the open-barrel type; bronze, superston (an ultra-strong alloy), stainless steel, and drop-forged galvanized steel are all used in their construction. The advantage of open-barrel turnbuckles is that the amount of

Above: Any *turnbuckle can break — if it's put under enough strain, that is. (Courtesy Yachtspars)* **Right:** *The bow anchorage for these open-barrel turnbuckles incorporates a slot for temporarily securing the anchor cable. (Ralph Naranjo photo)*

thread being used is visible. Whenever a cruising man is buying turnbuckles, he should shop around to find what brand has the best record. "All stainless," for instance, *sounds* good, but turnbuckles machined from this metal are not always the best. Forged bronze turnbuckles have a good name, but every fitting that is used to tension your rigging, no matter what metal it is made of, should have a toggle that will allow movement of 90 degrees from the direction the bottom eye or fork is set after the screw is tightened. Otherwise there's a fair chance that it will fatigue and break.

Forestays that carry sails should have a toggle both top and bottom, since the distance a forestay moves (usually sideways) from its tensioned, pre-sailing position is often considerable. Sight up your forestay next time you're close-reaching in a breeze of wind and observe how far to leeward the stay is bellying from a straight line between the point where it's fast on your vessel and the place where it attaches to the mast. Allow for the fact that when on the other tack, it will sag the same distance the other way. Is an unfair strain being put on any fitting? If so, another toggle could be the answer.

Avoid using lock-nuts to prevent turnbuckles from slacking up. A lock-nut, tightened down onto a thread that is already doing a power of work, is not a fair go. Closed-barrel turnbuckles can be kept from unscrewing by a stiff, heavy wire or light metal rod passed through the holes in the center of the barrel. Open-barrel turnbuckles can be prevented from turning by cotter pins that slide through holes at the end of each threaded shank.

Spliced-eye shroud terminals and galvanized closed-barrel turnbuckles. (Ralph Naranjo photo)

While on the subject of the humble cotter pin, I might suggest that you carry aboard a good supply of the exact diameter(s) you need. Buy yourself a small, fine file. (I use the tiny files sold for cleaning the points of a magneto.) Take each cotter and file a nice round on the end of its longest leg; you'll find it a whole lot easier to use after this treatment. Your fingers will think it's great, too. Don't pry the pin apart and attempt to file its shorter leg; after it's installed in the shank of a turnbuckle, you can, if you want to be a sport, do a file job on it. It's not necessary to twist the legs of a cotter like a wishbone once it's in place. Spread the legs a quarter-inch apart and a cotter will stay put; this way it can easily be used again.

While I'm still up here on my soapbox for the cause of the cotter pin, I might add that it's not a bad idea to buy a small, good-quality engineer's drift for each size of cotter carried aboard. Driving a broken-off, frozen pin out with the right-sized drift is a piece of cake. Wondering how the devil you're going to do it in the absence of this cheap little tool is another story. Store the drift in the same place as your spare cotter pins.

Another type of turnbuckle worth more than a second glance is constructed in the following manner. Bronze half-barrels with fork ends (they're either forged or cast)

Well-designed turnbuckle fork-end and toggle. (Ralph Naranjo photo)

are tensioned by a rod that has a righthand thread for half its length and a lefthand thread the other half. The middle of this rod has a flat machined on each side so that it may be turned with a wrench. It would seem that this turnbuckle, especially if the rod is Monel, is as good as any.

In 1948, after I'd launched *White Squall,* I was in the process of whittling out the mainmast in my spare moments when the question of turnbuckles cropped up. I was a merchant seaman at the time, and on my next period ashore, I went to see a friend who was foreman of a machine shop attached to a foundry. He immediately started trying to talk me into the above-mentioned type of turnbuckle, or, to use his terminology, "rigging screw." He was also highly enthusiastic about using Monel for the threaded rod. I'd never heard of Monel, and my response was a skeptical one. In swift succession I'd been wrecked aboard a friend's boat in an ocean race, I'd been run ashore in a coaster when a man went to sleep at the wheel, and I'd had the *Merlin*'s mast try to drive me through the bottom of the ship after it walloped me on the head. A whole lot of things had gone wrong. Whatever I used aboard my boat had to be strong beyond all doubt.

Reg produced a length of half-inch Monel rod about a foot long, clamped one end of it securely in a vise, handed me a hacksaw, and told me to cut the rod halfway through. When this was done, he handed me a hammer and told me to hit the end of the rod to bend it down and open up the cut. That piece of Monel resisted every inch of the way. I pounded the end up and down, opening and closing the hacksaw cut half a dozen times. That rod didn't break. And that's how the *White Squall* came to have turnbuckles constructed of cast aluminum-bronze, fork-end half-barrels, with ⅜-inch threaded Monel rod in the center. They're still going strong, 33 years and umpteen-thousand miles later.

Riggers frequently experience difficulty in matching terminals, tangs, pins, toggles, turnbuckles, and shackles to each other. Some countries use the meter as a base for measurement, while others still calculate in inches and fractions. If the fittings come from different countries, it is not unusual for terminal eyes (especially swages) to be a bit smaller than the pins of toggles or turnbuckles. Drilling a terminal to enlarge the hole is not necessarily the answer, as this might weaken the fitting. When choosing the types of fittings to use when rigging his vessel, the cruising yachtsman is well advised to make certain that he won't experience trouble with incompatible parts.

Spliced eyes, Nicopress, and the large loop eye of some poured sockets will fit most turnbuckles or toggles, although they might be a tight fit in a jaw. The eye and jaw of some compression fittings are sometimes very difficult to match with a turnbuckle or toggle. Whenever possible, try before you buy. One time in Papeete I didn't do this. I bought some French-made turnbuckles that I intended to use for straining-up the *White Squall II*'s lifelines, and I had a devil of a time fitting them to the English Norseman terminals I was using on the wire. Take my tip and have all your sizes figured out before starting even the simplest rigging job; it can save a lot of grief.

Another method of setting up rigging, seen nowadays only aboard character boats with gaff rig, is with deadeyes and lanyards. Traditionally, lanyards were of either European or Italian hemp; deadeyes were lignum vitae. A shroud would be either spliced around the upper deadeye, or, after being served with spun yarn, passed around the eye and then seized to its standing part by three or more soft-wire sheer lashings spaced about a foot apart. The bottom deadeye was usually strapped around its perimeter with steel, the two eyes of the strap sliding each side of a chainplate and held there by a through-bolt.

The lanyard was rove from inboard of the foremost hole of the upper deadeye to outboard of the lower deadeye to inboard of the upper deadeye, and so on, until it was passed through all three holes, top and bottom. The upper end of the lanyard was kept from pulling through the deadeye by a Matthew Walker knot; the lower or hauling end was secured back to its own part with a rack seizing and three separate sheer lashings of marlin termed "throat," "quarter," and "end." They were a pain in the neck to set up and, especially when new, required continual adjustment; handy billies, gun-tackles, tallow — all sorts of salty stuff was pressed into use.

I remember a picturesque gaff-rigged schooner arriving at Suva, Fiji, from the U.S. West Coast. She was resplendent with deadeyes and lanyards on all her shrouds, so I took a pass close by in our dinghy to get a good look at all this. Practically hidden from sight inside the lanyards at the bottom of each shroud, each putting tension on the rigging independently, was a closed-barrel turnbuckle. The top and bottom deadeyes were strapped with custom-built galvanized fittings. Each of these straps was in two pieces, the top held by a bolt that passed through a spliced eye in the shroud, and beneath the deadeye by a bolt that passed through the eye of a turnbuckle. The bottom deadeye was similarly strapped: one bolt passed through an eye at the other end of the turnbuckle, and the bottom bolt through the top of the chainplate. Very, very crafty — not only did she look the part, but the turnbuckles were backing up the lanyards, and vice versa. It made a lot of sense to me.

STAYS

In these days of masthead rigs and stiff metal spars with generous fore-and-aft sections, the need for running backstays to keep a mast straight is not as important as it used to be. Indeed, designers of "cruiser-racers" almost never show running backstays in the rigging plan of their latest creation. If runners are shown at all, they are used purely as back-up stays and only in bad weather.

All this is fair enough for the weekend sailor. The ocean-cruising nut, however, should have another stay set up abaft his mast in addition to the permanent backstay, at all times. It's OK to have all your eggs in one basket (such as one stay forward and one stay aft) if you're always sailing in semisheltered waters with other boats in sight, or within radio distance of an understanding Coast Guard who'll leap out and hold your hand if your nasty mast goes over the wall. When you've got nobody to lean on, though, when you're off soundings, you can holler all you like and nobody'll give a damn. In my book, mate, this means you must have a good stay set up aft of your mast in addition to the permanent backstay, whenever you're at sea.

Aboard gaff-rigged yachts, running backstays have usually been part of the scene. Gaff-riggers with topmasts often have two runners each side, one to the hounds of the mainmast and one to the top of the topmast. Jibing with such a rig can be a big operation, calling for some crafty handling of mainsheet and windward and leeward backstays. Instead of jibing (especially when shorthanded), some masters would put the ship about; they'd come up into the wind, hardening in all the while until close-hauled. Then they'd put the ship onto the other tack, keep the helm down, and slack away until she was running off again on the other jibe.

Commercial gaff-riggers and some pleasure boats often manage to do without running backstays by having a hefty shroud led well aft on each side. This approach works very well, especially if the mast is raked aft a little. Care must be taken, however, that this wire not be led so far aft that it ceases to do its share of work as a shroud, prevents the boom from being well eased, or causes an unfair amount of chafe to the lee side of the mainsail.

Every cargo-carrying commercial sailing vessel I worked in solved the problem of backstays by having masts of massive proportions. The *Alma*'s mainmast, for instance, was of solid Douglas fir nearly 18 inches thick. Such a mast, though, had other uses in addition to holding up a few sails; a 1½-inch wire topping lift, or "span," lifted a swinging derrick for loading and discharging cargo. I served in this

They're having fun — and that's what it's all about! In addition, this small cutter has two stays forward, running backstays as well as a permanent backstay, and four shrouds per side. Not too much chance that mast will go by the board. (Ralph Naranjo photo)

vessel as an A.B. and in later years as master, and I'd say that the mast and rigging had a tougher time with our cargo-working antics than they ever had with the sails.

Racing yachts with large crews and carrying huge areas of sail forward of the mast sometimes have two sets of running backstays each side in addition to a permanent backstay; this is good insurance. My reason for advocating the use of running backstays as well as a permanent backstay for the cruising man is simply to have a back-up; the runner set up to windward is there "just in case." If, with a double-headsail rig, the running backstay comes from the same point on the mast as the staysail stay, it does a fair bit of work, too. With a three-quarter or seven-eighths rig, running backstays leading to the same position on the mast as the forestay (and sometimes inner forestay as well) are a necessity.

When sailing in my yawl, I would usually slack the runners away and tie them to the shrouds in calm conditions and in sheltered waters; for ocean work, however, they were always rigged, no matter what the weather. Aboard the schooner, I always had a runner set up to windward, even in a calm. I just cannot subscribe to having a 71-foot mast rely for its support on only one wire — forward, aft, *or* sideways. If a running backstay proves its worth as a back-up on only one occasion, if it prevents a mast's disappearance over the side just once in all the years of its owner's cruising life — as it saved ours in the Marquesas — then, in my book, it has more than earned its keep. A mizzenmast — especially one of any size — can often benefit from running backstays, too, and this applies particularly if a large mizzen staysail is carried.

Running backstays were traditionally set up with a block and tackle (commonly four-fold). The lee runner would be slacked away and a lot of line rendered through blocks as the stay was taken forward and tied to an aft shroud. When the ship was put about, all this line would be overhauled again to set up what was to become the windward backstay. This sounds like a big deal, but it's really not that bad. We had this rig for years aboard the *White Squall II,* and we got used to it. I suppose it's because nothing ever seemed to happen in a hurry aboard that ship. She had a long keel, and while she always came about, it was possible to put a becket on a spoke of the wheel and wander around the deck hauling on this and letting go that while the old girl swung steadily around onto her new course.

When we first acquired her, the schooner had one of the worst backstay rigs I've ever encountered. She had no permanent backstay. For aft support, her mainmast relied upon a stay each side that led from the masthead to a single block about five feet above the port and starboard rails, and back aloft again to shackle to lugs in a mast band that also accommodated the aft intermediate shrouds. The double block of a backstay tackle shackled to this single block. This rig was no better than a single wire, so after a year of watching it with a sour and skeptical eye, I added a bumpkin to the ship, ran a permanent backstay from there to the masthead, and retained a single wire each side as running backstays from the intermediate mast band.

The running backstay wires were led through heavy-walled plastic hose to save chafe on the lee side of the mainsail, and this tactic seems to have paid off. As mentioned, we used the existing block and tackle for eight or nine years, until the installation of Highfield levers in 1970 (more on these later) before leaving the Virgin Islands to cruise and (we hoped) ply our trade in the South Pacific.

Now and again one sees double backstays individually set up and led down from separate points on the mast to a triangular metal plate on each side of the ship. This plate, known as a "monkey face," is often located some five to eight feet above the deck on either side, and it has a block and tackle shackled to its bottom eye to enable the backstays to be set up. Sometimes a single wire leads via a deck block from the plate to a Highfield lever. Dodge this rig, Mr. Cruising Man; it's a pain in the neck!

When the purchase is slacked away and both wires are carried forward to the lee shrouds, they have to be lashed separately, because the lower backstay has more slack than the upper. If an attempt is made to lash them both together, the lower backstay can sometimes work a bit of slack into itself and make a mission out of flogging away at sail stitching, spreaders, shrouds — anything it can reach. The monkey face can take a bite out of things, too. One stay (usually the upper) is a set length and the other is adjusted (either at the mast tang or monkey face with a turnbuckle) to tension the wires. If the adjustment is at the monkey face, the whole business makes quite a package to carry forward on the lee side, especially if a bit of a sea is running. A smack in the ear from that lot will make a believer out of a pagan!

White Squall started her life with a backstay rig, which was common enough at the time but is almost never seen today. She had two running backstays each side and no permanent backstay. It seems incredible now, but that's how it was. A cast bronze track about eight feet long was bolted securely to the deck each side, just inside the rail; a bronze traveling car to which both upper and lower backstays were individually shackled slid forward and backward along the track.

The aft 12 inches of each track were solid, and five ⅜-inch-diameter bronze bolts each side fastened through the two-inch deck to a backing plate below. A line, its standing part located at a pad eye in the deck at the aft end of the track, led through a sheave in the traveling car and was used to heave the car aft and so tighten the backstays. After I changed from cutter to yawl rig and two permanent backstays, I discarded the upper runners and kept the lowers, which ran from the same point on the mast occupied by the staysail or inner forestay. These running backstays were shackled at their bottom ends to their old position on the traveling car.

Another type of backstay traveler employs a wire instead of a track; backstays are attached to a slide that is pulled forward or aft along the wire, which has a terminal fitting each end fast to an eye in the deck. I sailed a few times aboard a 6-meter named *Altair,* which had this rig, and to me it seemed a pretty hairy way of trying to keep a mast in a boat.

The Highfield lever — or better yet, the improved lever designed just after World War II by Laurent Giles and Partners for John Illingworth's *Myth of Malham* — is far better than any track or wire strung along the deck. A lever gives a running backstay the same positive tension every time it is set up.

Both types of levers operate on the principle of a flanged base bolted firmly through the deck, and an arm (lever) hinged to the base with bolts, cotters, or rivets. The backstay leads through a sheave on deck — which must also be "part of the ship" — and its terminal locates in a hook, bolt, or fork attached to the lever.

Adjustment of backstay tension with the original Highfield lever was achieved by moving the bolt that positioned the terminal to another hole in the body of the lever, which meant that when set up, a backstay would often be either too tight or too slack. The *Myth* lever is superior to the Highfield in this respect, because the terminal locates on a large, threaded hook, which means that the same fine type of adjustment provided by a turnbuckle is available.

Another advantage of this lever is its slotted body, which allows the hook fitting to slide almost the length of the lever when the lever is thrown over and tension is released. With the original Highfield lever, the only slack achieved when tension was released was double the distance from the pivoting point (the fulcrum) to the terminal. And the more this distance was increased, the less was the mechanical advantage. With the *Myth* lever, the hook fitting to which the backstay terminal attaches slides up close to the point where the lever is hinged to the base, and the improvement in mechanical advantage over the Highfield system is considerable. Also, the amount of slack when the lever is thrown is nearly double the length of the body.

Another company that manufactures an "improved" lever is Merriman-Holbrook. In this case, the backstay terminal locates in a fork whose body is threaded — providing the same fine adjustment as the *Myth* lever. When thrown, the fork fitting slides in grooves within the lever, providing approximately the same slack option as the *Myth* lever. The end of the Merriman lever "clicks" down into a spring-loaded catch (actually a hinged, inverted U with a rubber pad providing the spring), and this ensures that the lever will "stay put" when the backstay is set up.

The fact that a lever incorporates a sheave and the standing part of the flexible wire is located at the deck fitting means that when the lever is slacked, the backstay loosens up enough for it to be taken forward without being unhooked. This is highly desirable, especially aboard a shorthanded vessel. Unhooking a lee backstay and taking it forward to be secured to a shroud is all very well when there's a spare person available on deck. But when there's nobody on hand but Yours Truly, it often adds up to one more quite exacting job.

The lever method of setting up backstays that I used aboard the *White Squall II* — and that has been going strong now for more than 10 years — went like this: I hung a ½-inch 7/7 wire on the aft port and starboard lugs of the same mast band that the main-staysail stay was fast to; a poured socket terminal was installed at the bottom of each of these running backstays about four feet above the deck; shackled to each stay was a ½-inch-diameter 7/19 wire, which led down through a sheave in a deck fitting, along to a sheave in the lever, and back to the fitting; each deck fitting was held down by ½-inch-diameter silicon-bronze bolts.

An acceptable, and in some circles popular, way to tension a running backstay is to take it through a deck lead to a cockpit sheet winch. This method suits many boats, since there is often a windward sheet winch lying unused. A length of flexible (7/19) stainless steel wire rope with a rope-to-wire splice at its free end is shackled to the backstay a few feet above the deck. When the vessel is put onto a new tack or jibed, the rope tail leads the 7/19 wire through a sheave in a strong deck fitting to a winch that has been doing duty on the lee sheet; this winch's new job is to set up the running backstay.

A careful check is kept on tension by aligning a mark on the wire with a position on deck — stanchion, lead, filler cap — there is usually something. This system has a lot going for it, since it completely dispenses with such special equipment as levers, tackles, or hooks. It is especially attractive aboard a vessel where the setting up of running backstays only takes place in deteriorating weather.

Before leaving this discussion on backstays, we might as well draw attention to the triatic stay that connects the main and mizzen mastheads of so many ketches and yawls. The existence of this stay has been responsible, on occasion, for one mast following another over the side. Masts should, wherever possible, be stayed independently.

A perfectly tensioned rig in a cruising boat will keep the mast(s) straight on every point of sailing. With a modern, extruded aluminum spar, this is a whole lot easier than it used to be in the days when almost every mast was wood. Even though the light alloy mast is not prone to act like a piece of spaghetti — as its old-time counterpart would at times — in all fairness to the rig as a whole, we should do our best to ensure that each wire is taking its share of the weight.

Lengthy stays and shrouds, because of their stretch factor, should be tighter than shorter and lower wires. Set your rigging up at anchor or on a mooring by testing the tension on each wire with your fingertips. Cap shrouds should be tighter than intermediates, intermediates tighter than lower shrouds. A forestay should be tighter than a staysail stay (inner forestay). Permanent backstays should be tighter than running backstays when these are set up taut. Running backstays should be the same as a staysail stay (inner forestay). Forestay and permanent backstays should have similar tension.

Go for a sail and squint up the mast. Is it straight? Canted over at the top? Bowed in the middle? Feel the windward shrouds. Is the cap shroud earning its keep? Are the lowers? It is possible to adjust rigging tension while underway, but, although this is standard practice aboard racing boats (by cranking up or easing a hydraulic or other backstay tensioner), the cruising man is advised to proceed carefully and slowly here. It is a great temptation to put a vessel onto the other tack if a mast has a bit of a bow in it, and then fuss around with slack in the lee rigging. It can be done successfully, too, if great care is taken in the exercise and if turnbuckles are not tightened or slacked recklessly.

It is possible, however, to place enormous compression strains on a mast by over-tightening lee rigging while sailing. On an old wooden hull, you can start her leaking around the mast step as the spar tries to push its way down through the bottom of the ship. It takes a fine hand, and some people are far better than others at adjusting rigging while underway. I remember sailing back and forth in a Concordia yawl the day before the 1966 Bermuda Race, while a friend of the owner's tuned the rigging in this manner. He had the touch of Segovia; that pole was as straight as a die during the race, no matter what sails we hung on it. I couldn't have done anywhere near as well as he did, even on a bet.

The degree of acceptable tension in rigging depends upon a number of things. Is the mast stepped on deck? If so, the rigging must always be good and tight. There have been instances when deck-stepped masts have jumped out of the step at sea as the rigging slacked up, and if there's anything calculated to give a sailor bad dreams, it's an occurrence such as that. Generally speaking, the rigging on a mast that passes through a deck and locates in a mast step below can be set up less tight than if the spar is stepped on deck.

The age and construction of the boat come into it, too. The rigging on a mast set in a steel or aluminum hull can be much tighter than that of a planked wooden boat, especially if the wooden vessel is a bit long in the tooth. Fiberglass, ferrocement, and wooden vessels built on the molded, glued diagonal lath principle can usually have their rigging set up taut. Personal preference comes into it as well. I like to see a bit of give and take in rigging and have never been one for setting up mine like a guitar's E-string.

Before and during a session when you're engaged in setting up rigging, check the trim of your vessel. Make sure your boat isn't listing to one side or the other before getting involved in tensioning your shrouds carefully. A heel gauge — preferably one that was installed when the ship was under construction, and dead level — will tell you if she's straight up and down. It's also possible to sense it by standing aft with one foot on each side of the fore-and-aft line and facing forward. Row a couple of hundred feet forward of the ship in a dinghy and give her the benefit of a calculating eye; or, if she's in a marina berth, walk around to a dock on the other side of the boat harbor so you can see your vessel either bow on or stern on. If she has a list, you may have to move a few pigs of ballast, an an or — who knows what — from one side to the other to get her level. Once this is achieved, the setting up of rigging can proceed.

To check whether a mast is canted to one side or the other by wrongly adjusted shrouds, a plumb bob can be hung on a line made fast to the mast about six or eight feet above the gooseneck. The line should be tied carefully so that the plumb bob hangs from the exact center of the mast (usually the middle of the sail track). Immediately below this spot, the line should be pushed about an inch clear of the mast by any small object — the cork from last night's wine bottle will do fine — to ensure that the plumb bob hangs clear. While putting tension on the rigging, keep checking the point of the plumb bob in relation to the mast's centerline. Regarding mast rake: I have always aimed at a rake aft of one inch for every four feet of height, only for the reason that it looks right to me. If you decide on more rake, a plumb mast, or even a bit of a cant forward (and at one time with gaff rig this was *very* popular), then my advice is to go to it. After all, it's your boat!

Now and again we come across a yachtsman who either doesn't give a fig for all this or whose judgment is so tuned to the exigencies of the moment that he comes out on top anyway. In the early 1950s I was taking part in an Easter race across Auckland's Firth of Thames ("Frith" on the old charts). The distance is about 40 miles, and with some three miles to go to the finish, we were lying in fourth place. Along with every other boat, we were running dead before the wind with a spinnaker up and on the point of a jibe.

A slight variation in wind direction (it backed slightly to the west) caused the whole fleet to jibe — all except Bill (a great buddy), who was way out in front. Bill, whose spinnaker boom of 30 feet was a foot longer than his vessel, knew he would lose the first-to-finish prize money if he took time to go through the acrobatics necessary to jibe that pole.

So he slacked away his lee rigging and eased the sheet, allowing his main boom to swing way forward. He did, so help me. And roaring like a bull (nothing silent about our Bill), main boom kited at a prickly angle, no shrouds at all on his starboard side, he shot across the finish line to get the gun.

CHAINPLATES

The old adage that a chain is only as strong as its weakest link may sound a bit corny these days, but corny or not, it can be applied across the board to a sailing vessel's standing rigging. The final points to which rigging fastens must be beyond reproach. The chainplates to which shrouds and (usually) backstays attach, the stemhead fitting, the gammon and/or cranse iron that take the headstays — all these must be "part of the ship."

Chainplates in a wooden vessel should be carried well down either inside or outside the hull, and through-bolted. It is acceptable practice for these bolts to pass through a wooden filler that runs the full length of the chainplate inside the ship and butts up hard under the clamp. Wooden clipper ships carried their chainplates far enough down outside their hulls for the bottom bolt(s) to pick up a fore-and-aft stringer, an excellent practice.

A way to install chainplates securely in a fiberglass boat is to have pieces of metal welded at right angles across the part of the plate inside the hull. The welded-on pieces should be about six inches long and the same width and thickness as the chainplate; they should also be of the same metal. A chainplate with, say, 18 inches of its length inside the ship would typically have a piece of metal welded across the

CHAINPLATE SIZES METRIC					CHAINPLATE SIZES IMPERIAL				
Wire Dia.	A Pin Dia.	B Radius	C Offset	D* Maximum Thickness	Wire Dia.	A Pin Dia.	B Radius	C Offset	D* Maximum Thickness
3mm	6.4mm	9.57mm	1.6mm	6.3mm	1/8"	1/4"	3/8"	1/16"	1/4"
4mm	7.9mm	11.1mm	1.6mm	7.9mm	5/32"	5/16"	7/17"	1/16"	5/16"
5mm	9.5mm	12.7mm	3.2mm	9.5mm	3/16"	3/8"	1/2"	1/8"	3/8"
6mm	12.7mm	17.4mm	3.2mm	12.7mm	1/4"	1/2"	11/16"	1/8"	1/2"
7mm	12.7mm	17.4mm	3.2mm	12.7mm	9/32"	1/2"	11/16"	1/8"	1/2"
8mm	15.8mm	20.6mm	4.8mm	15.8mm	5/16"	5/8"	13/16"	3/16"	5/8"
10mm	18.8mm	22.2mm	4.8mm	15.8mm	3/8"	5/8"	7/8"	3/16"	5/8"
11mm	19.0mm	25.4mm	4.8mm	19.0mm	7/16"	3/4"	1"	3/16"	3/4"
12mm	22.2mm	30.1mm	6.3mm	22.2mm	1/2"	7/8"	1-3/16"	1/4"	7/8"
14mm	22.2mm	31.7mm	6.3mm	22.2mm	9/16"	7/8"	1-1/4"	1/4"	7/8"
16mm	25.4mm	34.9mm	6.3mm	25.4mm	5/8"	1"	1-3/8"	1/4"	1"

*NOTE: For Stainless Steel or Monel Thickness maybe reduced by 25%.   *NOTE: For Stainless Steel or Monel thickness maybe reduced by 25%

Bronze chainplate sizes. The chainplate sizes given exceed the breaking strain of the wire. (Courtesy Yachtspars)

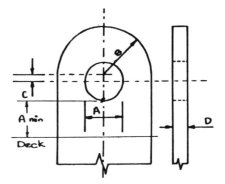

tip and so appear as an inverted T. Two similar pieces, spaced approximately six inches apart, would be welded to the plate above this in the same manner. The whole fitting is solidly bolted through the hull and then glassed in.

A steel vessel can have short, heavy pieces of Monel welded some eight inches down inside the hull plating and projecting far enough above the deck to form chainplates. The reason for Monel here, as opposed to the type of metal in the vessel's plating (typically mild steel or Corten), is to prevent rust where a shackle or toggle pin bears inside the eye of the chainplate. Also, since Monel is relatively inert, there is little chance of electrolytic action.

To cater to the sheeting angle of headsails, the shrouds — sometimes en masse, sometimes only the lowers — are often brought inboard of the rail on beamy vessels. The sheeting angle of a headsail, especially a genoa or genoa staysail, can be greatly enhanced by this treatment. Once again, it's all a matter of personal preference — and what you can afford. The price you put on ultra-efficiency is important, too, because there's no doubt that if the correct sheeting angle is attained, with the rigging arranged to pander specifically to this, you'll usually have a faster boat on the wind.

Pandering not at all to looks or possible drag, these well-fastened chainplates appear mighty strong. Now, if they were all the length of that long one . . . . (Ralph Naranjo photo)

A formula for calculating the minimum spread of a sailboat's shrouds each side of a mast's centerline at deck level is: "25 percent of J (base of foretriangle) plus three inches." A boat with a J measurement of 16 feet would thus have a minimum shroud distance of four feet three inches between the rail and the mast's centerline. On most vessels this would put the chainplates well inside the rail and enable a deck-hugging genoa to be carried.

I'm one of the ones, however, who refuses to move shrouds inboard on an ocean-cruising sailboat. To help ensure that your mast will keep right on standing up there, mate, I say cash in on every inch of beam you've got for the spread of your shrouds. Old-time sailing vessels even had sponson-like appendages known as channels built outboard on their hulls to increase their beam where the shrouds attached. A man would often stand there "in the chains," swinging the sounding lead as the ship sailed along a coast into what, perhaps, could be shallow water. A bit different from sitting in a comfortable cockpit, looking at an echo-sounder . . . .

A high degree of skillful engineering is needed if chainplates are to be brought in-board. It's not just a matter of a few eyebolts in the deck and — hey, presto — we'll make our shrouds fast to them. You need well-engineered brackets fitted inside the ship from the point where the chainplate passes up through the deck. Such a bracket extends beneath the deck from this spot, across to the hull, and is bolted to the ship's side as it proceeds down the distance of a normal chainplate. The longest side of what now becomes an obtuse triangle is bridged by a flat bar or rod from the spot

Above: *Plenty of shrouds, but those chainplates are on the short side. Well-proportioned open-barrel turnbuckles, toggles, and pins. Is there unfair strain on the toggle of the second-from-left turnbuckle?*
Left: *These shrouds are anchored to a common chainplate brought well inboard to cater to sheeting angle of headsail(s). Such an arrangement requires much strengthening below decks. (Ralph Naranjo photos)*

where the chainplate passes up through the deck to six inches or so above the bottom point it reaches inside the hull. An expensive deal, if done properly. Worth it? Some say yes, a thousand times. Others say you're out of your bloody mind.

STEMHEAD FITTINGS

Stemhead fittings, which take the strain of forestays and their sails, must be strong beyond all doubt. The load imposed by a large genoa, for instance, is considerable; a stemhead fitting accepting this strain should be well secured by bolts through the stem and each side of the bow. Permanent backstays are usually secured to chainplates.

Vessels with bowsprits generally have a metal fitting at the stem through which the bowsprit slides. This is known as a gammon iron –– even though, most likely, it's constructed of stainless steel, bronze, or Monel. My gammon iron on the yawl was bronze, and on the schooner, it was galvanized mild steel. I regalvanized the schooner's iron on one occasion in Panama (hell of a job getting it off), but the one on the yawl has never been disturbed. The legs of both these fittings go about 15 inches down each side of the stem and are through-bolted. The top of a gammon iron, above the bowsprit, is a common place for the staysail stay (inner forestay) to be attached. There is usually an eye here for the staysail tack, too.

A cranse iron ("crance" in some circles) is the fitting on the end of the bowsprit that the forestay, jib tack, bowsprit shrouds (if any), and bobstay attach to. This fit-

The bowsprit cranse or "crance" fitting gets it from all directions. (Ralph Naranjo photo)

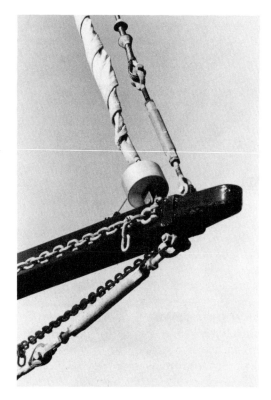

ting gets it from all directions, so it must be mighty strong. The best type of cranse iron is the one that slides over the end of the bowsprit in the form of a cap; there is no way it can be pulled aft by the strains of forestay and bobstay. It should be removed every few years and the end of the bowsprit inspected for rot. Saturate the wood with copper naphthanate (or its equivalent), smear some of your favorite bedding compound over it when dry, and slide the fitting back on again. If you have done a good job, the compound will squeeze out around the aft part of the fitting as forestay and bobstay are set up.

If the cranse iron is galvanized steel, it might need regalvanizing. This is a golden opportunity to build up with weld any wear in the eyes of lugs, and to take any stress out of the fitting by annealing. Have the fitting heated to 1200 °F. and allow it to cool gradually; then get it galvanized, and your cranse iron will be as good as new. This annealing business applies to any chain or fittings aboard that need regalvanizing. A mild steel fitting or chain can become work-hardened and brittle, as can stainless steel or any other metal. But all those strains disappear from mild steel once it is annealed. To regalvanize, without going through the heating and cooling process first, will only make the fitting look pretty. If it has reached the stage where it needs regalvanizing, it's probably pretty tired. Do yourself and it a favor by annealing first.

Bobstays, either bowsprit or bumpkin, must be able to take the knocks, because sometimes they really get them. I remember an occasion when, between charters in the *White Squall II,* we were lying on our mooring in St. Thomas. It started to blow up late in the day, and by midnight, the wind was playing a fine old tune in the rigging. I poked a bleary eye out a hatch about one in the morning and received a faceful of rain for my trouble; so I thought the hell with it, our mooring's a good one — we're OK. I turned in again. About an hour before dawn there was an almighty crash a few feet from where I was asleep in the forecabin.

I hopped up on deck to see what the latest crisis was, and fair across our bow, wedged in under the chain bobstay, was an old 54-foot two-master with a man and a girl aboard. I think their anchor cable must have carried away in a squall (we never did get to talk about the details of the situation), and they'd come down upon us at a great rate. Our chain bobstay was having a wonderful time sawing away at their port railcap and cabintop, but the main trouble was our cranse iron, which was wedged between their throat halyard (she was a gaff ketch) and their mainmast. The fellow managed to get his auxiliary going after a few threats and fiery oaths, but we couldn't get that damn cranse iron clear.

Our dinghy, its nose hard against his port bow and the 9½ h.p. Johnson earning its keep, managed to push his bow far enough upwind for our bowsprit to come clear. I kept giving her the gun on his bow just like my old tugboat days, and with his engine in gear ahead, he ended up managing a turn to starboard. The last I saw of them, they were being swallowed up downwind by the mother and father of the earlier rainsquall. The purpose of this narrative (I think) is to hammer home the fact that a bobstay must be able to take this sort of medicine without being damaged. On this particular occasion, the only proof that ours had been in a fight was the little bits of wood from the other guy's railcap, wedged here and there between its links.

It is worth discussing the different types of materials used for bobstays. Stainless steel and bronze rod are both popular and, it would seem, give good service. The ⅜-inch Tobin bronze bobstays I installed on both the bowsprit and bumpkin of my yawl, long ago, seem to have been able to take the knocks without complaint, and who can ask for more? Both ends of the bowsprit bobstay were screwed into cast bronze fork fittings similar in design to a half-barrel turnbuckle. The bumpkin stay had the same type of fitting on its bottom end; its top, or outboard end, after passing up through the bumpkin, was threaded to take a bronze eye fitting for the mizzen sheet.

Because of its strength and low stretch factor, 1/19 stainless steel wire is popular bobstay material with some yachtsmen. I tried it for the *White Squall II*'s A-frame bumpkin bobstay after I had finished building and installing this appendage. The bobstay wire was ½-inch diameter, and I used a bronze poured socket at each end. The outer wires started to strand in less than three years, so I replaced the bobstay with ⅜-inch chain (after melting the sockets off the wire and stowing them back on the ship). The bumpkin bobstay on the schooner used to get pretty tough use — especially when we were chartering. A cluster of dinghies under the stern, banging away at the bobstay, was a familiar occurrence; a couple of hundred such occasions finally caused the 1/19 wire to throw up its arms and quit.

A bowsprit bobstay can have a tough life, too, especially if an all-chain anchor rode is used. When a squall causes an anchored vessel to yaw, and the chain rasps and twangs away at the bobstay as the ship surges sideways, the strands (if the stay is wire) can really be damaged. A wire bobstay can, of course, live inside a piece of PVC pipe. The pipe takes the chafe whether the anchor rode is chain or rope. Two bobstays can be used to advantage, especially when a roller-furling jib is installed inside the forestay. The inner bobstay, immediately below the point where the drum

Rod bobstay with welded fork-end, through-pin, and cotter. One way of doing it. (Ralph Naranjo photo)

A chain bobstay is no friend to a rope anchor rode. Note traditional catheads and fisherman anchor "catted" on starboard bow. Rigging of this old-timer is festooned with baggywrinkle. (Ralph Naranjo photo)

fitting of the roller jib attaches to the bowsprit, can be 1/19 wire. The outer bobstay, there to take the knocks, can be chain.

Sometimes a forestay is taken to a sheave in the bowsprit just aft of the cranse iron and on down to a turnbuckle secured to an eye in the stem. The bobstay is outboard of the wire and affords it protection. The idea behind this scheme is to enable the jib to be lowered all the way down to the cranse iron. The trouble with this system, as I see it, is having the turnbuckle almost at the waterline. As soon as the vessel gets underway, this turnbuckle would be partially or totally immersed, and keeping it freed-up enough for adjustment could mean that its inspection would have to be a very regular affair.

A more sympathetic treatment of this turnbuckle is to arrange for the forestay to terminate six inches or so after passing through the sheave. The turnbuckle is secured to the forestay terminal by shackle or toggle, and a length of chain, rod, or wire connects the bottom of the turnbuckle with a regular bobstay eye in the stem of the ship.

When I first bought the *White Squall II,* her forestay passed around a sheave in the cranse iron, back along the bowsprit, and was tightened by a turnbuckle shackled to the gammon iron. (All this was done so the jib could be lowered right down and furled along the bowsprit.) When we renewed the rigging, we ran the forestay to a turnbuckle secured to the cranse iron, since I didn't like the sharp nip in the wire as it passed around the sheave. In any case, by then we had a roller-furling jib, and it was seldom that a sail was hanked to the forestay.

Sometimes, adjustment of both forestay and bobstay is achieved by having a bowsprit that can be moved inboard or outboard. The butt of such a bowsprit locates between two posts on deck and is moved by the adjustment of bolts that pass fore-and-aft through the posts and through the plate that the heel of the bowsprit rests against. Just as long as both bobstay and forestay each need exactly the same amount of tensioning, this system works. I prefer to see the heel of a bowsprit butted firmly into a samson post, and both bobstay and forestay tightened by separate turnbuckles.

A dolphin striker — which is simply a strut that does the same job for a bobstay that spreaders do for shrouds on a mast — is sometimes used between bobstay and bow. A dolphin striker is used to increase the downward angle where the bobstay secures to the cranse iron; its installation is usually necessary only if the ship has a long bowsprit. A dolphin striker must be able to pivot sideways where its fitting is attached to the hull, and so obviate the possibility that unfair strain will be applied to the fitting if the bobstay is pushed out of line by the anchor cable or anything else.

The fore-and-aft angles where the striker locates on the bobstay should be equal. The end of a dolphin striker, designed for use on a wire or rod bobstay, can have a piece of half-tube at least four inches long welded at right angles across its tip and bent to the angle that the stay will assume when it rests in the groove. The end of a striker for a chain bobstay commonly has a fork that slides each side of a link. Similar fittings to dolphin strikers, known as "cat's whiskers," are sometimes used to increase the spread of bowsprit shrouds.

The hull fitting or plate that a bowsprit or bumpkin bobstay attaches to must be very strong. A steel or aluminum vessel simply has a hefty lug welded to her hull at these points, and a fiberglass or ferrocement ship sometimes has the plate molded in as an integral part of her hull, in much the same manner as a chainplate. Wooden vessels should, whenever possible, have these fittings securely bolted through stem and apron forward and horn timber or transom (if it's up to it) aft.

I decided against bolting the bumpkin stay of the *White Squall II* because: (a) I had to do the job in the water; (b) the two-inch planking was hardwood and hard to drill by hand; (c) the horn timber was ironwood (as hard as a boulder) and tougher yet; and (d) the horn timber was more than a foot thick. I made up a Monel chainplate and drilled three ½-inch clearance holes in it to take the fastenings, and another hole to take the pin of the bobstay's ⅝-inch shackle. I hung a ⅝-inch Dacron line under the counter on a dead-calm day and sat in the bight of it, half in and half out of the water, with a brace and a few bits in my hand. The wood shavings came out clean and dry, and nobody hurtled by in a "fizzboat" to create a wash to wet the holes, which were only a few inches above water. So the plate ended up nicely bedded against the hull in Caulktex, held there by three ½-inch-diameter silicon-bronze coach screws, each seven inches long. The only strain on these fastenings would be from shear, so their use for this job was acceptable. For a straight pull, which is usually the case with a forward bobstay fitting, coach screws are unsuitable.

SPREADERS

The angle at which shrouds and stays lead from a mast determines the strain put on the spar itself, the hull of the ship, and the fittings. The smaller the angle, the greater the strain on the gear. Narrow spreaders, often installed to cater specifically to the sheeting angle of headsails, can reduce the angle of cap shrouds, with the result of enormous strain on load points and compression strain on the mast(s).

A sensible compromise must be reached for the ocean cruiser. A shroud angle of 10 degrees or less (acceptable aboard some all-out racers) should not, I feel, be considered for a cruising boat. An angle of 12 degrees is far more realistic but not always easy to achieve. If you have a narrow hull, the only way to increase your shroud angle will be either to shorten your mast or to increase the length of your spreaders. The first might be unacceptable (if sail area is too drastically reduced); increasing the length of your spreaders may be a more attractive prospect.

It is not unusual to see a set of spreaders as wide as or wider than the beam of the boat. If you have to fit extremely wide spreaders to achieve a good shroud angle, then do so by all means. If you can possibly avoid it, however, don't take your

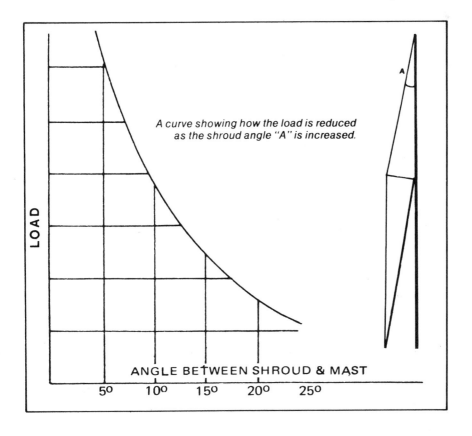

A curve showing how the load is reduced as the shroud angle "A" is increased.

ANGLE BETWEEN SHROUD & MAST

5° 10° 15° 20° 25°

LOAD

Fractionally rigged mast showing bald top and spreaders raked to increase fore-and-aft stiffness. (Courtesy Yachtspars)

spreaders out as far as the rail on a cruising boat. In some ports, a cruiser is ordered alongside a commercial dock for customs or immigration purposes; in other places you might have to raft up or lie alongside to take on water and fuel. Too-long spreaders can give you a lot of grief on these occasions, obstructing something or getting themselves tangled with somebody else's rigging. If only once in the course of a world voyage, one of your cap shrouds twangs away at a fender piling, or anything else — that's once too often.

Narrow spreaders certainly give a genoa jib a better chance of being flattened, and if the shrouds are moved inboard, they enable a deck-sweeping genoa to be sheeted inside the rail. But again we come to the expensive process of moving the chainplates inboard, and the lessening of the all-important shroud angle (with its resultant increasing strains).

An overlapping genoa, sheeted inside the rail, will tow a vessel up to windward like anything, and, since the foot of the sail is inside the rail, it won't scoop up the lee bow wave. But let's not kid ourselves; there's still a chance that the top of a sea might land in the sail from windward and do it in. It has happened to me, as will be

Not much chance of those headsails scooping up water. Note sturdy double-spreader masthead rig on mainmast, beam of vessel wide enough aft to dispense with spreaders on mizzen, mizzen's permanent backstay. (Courtesy Yachtspars)

discussed in Chapter Eight. And this was a genoa jib with the clew cut higher than the lifeline. A far better arrangement on an ocean cruiser, it seems, would be a high-cut Yankee jib, which can't be damaged by a sea, and inboard of this, a genoa staysail.

A single-spreader rig enables a larger genoa staysail to be carried than if the mast were equipped with two sets of spreaders (since the bottom spreader is lower in this case, it interferes with the staysail leech). A well-set-up double-spreader rig is hard to beat. Four shrouds (two each side) go from chainplates to (usually) tangs beneath the lower spreader base. Another shroud each side runs from its chainplate, up to and over the lower spreader tip, and locates under the upper spreader base. The cap shrouds take in the tips of both spreaders. With this system, should any shroud or spreader fail, there's still a good chance that the mast will stay in the ship because of the number of well-separated support points where shrouds fasten to the spar.

The double-spreader rig is sometimes seen in cruising vessels under 40 feet, but the rig is more popular in longer vessels with taller masts. A short mast, of course, can

Above: *Link plates. A single, fixed-length shroud goes from chainplate turnbuckle to spreader tip each side. Cap shrouds from spreader link plate fittings are also fixed length. Turnbuckles at the spreader tips adjust each intermediate shroud. The single shroud each side from chainplate to spreader tip does the whole job of supporting the mast from the lower spreader on up when the vessel is heeled. This shroud is much heavier than others, but there is no backup if a fitting carries away, so this rig shouldn't be particularly attractive to the cruising man. And there are the problems that fixed-length shrouds can't be adjusted to change the tension put on the mast and that turnbuckles aloft are hard to reach. Another strike against this rig is the chance that an eased mainsail or a close-hauled genoa will chafe against the link plate and its fittings.* **Right:** *Closeup of link-plate assembly. (Courtesy Yachtspars)*

be equipped with a double-spreader rig. If, for instance, a genoa staysail is not carried, the only real argument against the lower spreader is the extra windage it causes. A rig that has little influence on spreader height is the split-headsail arrangement with a staysail on a boom. (We'll have a "hate session" on this in Chapter Six.)

A system of staying a double-spreader rig that gets a big hand in the racing fleet is the one entailing the use of link plates (see photographs) at the lower spreader tips. Known as "panel rigging," this system has three chainplates on each side (some all-out fractional rigs have only two). In any case, the lower shrouds locate at the base of the lower spreaders, and a single shroud runs from a chainplate each side to the bottom of a link plate at each lower spreader tip. A cap shroud and an intermediate shroud (which goes up to an anchorage beneath the upper spreader base) secure to the top of the link plate. I advise the cruising man to avoid this rig like he'd avoid a port with cholera. All the eggs are in one basket — namely, the single shroud that runs to the link plate each side. If any fitting associated with this shroud carries away — any pin, toggle, terminal, turnbuckle, or the wire itself — the mast immediately loses its support from the base of the lower spreader on up.

I had a single-spreader rig in my yawl because of the relatively short mast length of 46 feet and because I wanted to carry a good-sized staysail — which the lower spreader of a double rig would have interfered with. I installed four bronze chainplates in the hull on each side to take the shrouds. Two shrouds each side led from the forward and aft chainplates to beneath the spreaders. An intermediate shroud went up over the spreader tips each side to the point where the staysail stay and running backstays were located (about six feet below the masthead). The cap shrouds lay against these wires in the spreader tips on their way to the masthead.

I'm sure we could have lost any shroud and still had the mast standing; I had sailed the ship as a cutter the first year with the mast baldheaded from the intermediate shroud on up. Nowadays it sounds like terrible practice for an ocean cruiser, and I can't say I was delirious with joy about the setup at the time, even though I was faithfully following the designed rigging plan. If I'd lost that intermediate shroud, I'd have been talking about my mast in the past tense. The fourth chainplate, which I'd installed each side "just in case," was utilized, and cap shrouds, along with foretopmast stay and two permanent backstays, changed the whole picture. All this may sound like a lot of wire to hang on a relatively short mast, but it did wonders for my peace of mind when I was miles from nowhere and a run of bad weather kept testing my gear.

The fact that the *White Squall II* carried only one set of spreaders on her 70-foot mainmast made me a bit uneasy at first, but she'd had the rig for 25 years before I assumed ownership — and that, I felt, meant something. Also, being a schooner with a gaff foresail meant that all that big mainmast had to do was carry the ship's mainsail — much different from the mast of a cutter, ketch, or yawl, whose mainmast is also expected to take the weight of a variety of headsails. When we changed to staysail rig, the mainmast was called upon to take whatever strain this sail imposed, but since the staysail stay was located at the point on the mast already supported by running backstays and intermediate shrouds, I felt the extra load would not be too much for these wires to accept. The foremast was sturdy enough and the beam of the vessel wide enough for this mast to stand without spreaders yet still have an acceptably large angle between the cap shroud and the mast.

The schooner's intermediate mainmast shrouds led from chainplates situated far enough aft on each side of the vessel to do a certain amount of work as backstays as well. That the mainmast was in the widest part of the ship meant that these shrouds were some eight feet from the centerline, proceeding up from this point to a solid mast band about eight feet below the masthead. Had we lost a cap shroud, an intermediate shroud probably would have taken over the job without a huff or a puff.

That's the whole thing right there aboard a cruising boat, as I see it — the ability of one piece of wire to do the job of another in a pinch, and so prevent the vessel from losing her mast.

Most spreaders have fixed bases, which are screwed, bolted, welded, or even pop-riveted (Glory be!) to the mast. Some aluminum sparmakers design the spreader base so that the struts are immovable. Others manufacture their equipment so that there is a small amount of flexibility where the spreader locates in the socket. Then there is the swinging spreader mounted on a vertical pin so it can pivot fore and aft.

All three can be seen out on the cruising beat, and all three work. Compression strain between a shroud and the mast is not the only weight a spreader (especially one with a fixed base) is called upon to take. When a mainsail is well eased, a lot of pressure can be exerted on a spreader as the sail is forced against it, particularly the

Swinging spreaders. (Courtesy Yachtspars)

upper strut of a double-spreader rig. This strain is transferred, in the form of leverage, to the spreader base. The longer the spreader and the more rigidly it sits in its base, the more sideways strain that fitting must accept. The base of a rigid spreader must be very strong indeed, and great care must be taken that these spreaders are never strained from their shrouds becoming snagged in any obstruction alongside a dock or in another vessel's rigging.

The swinging spreader does not, in general, enjoy great popularity; why this is so, I'll never know. When a mainsail is eased against the lee rigging, a swinging spreader will move forward as the belly of the sail presses against it. This takes strain away from the base fitting and chafe away from the sail, which, any way you look at it, is killing two undesirable birds with one stone. I had swinging spreaders aboard both my yawl and my schooner and they gave me no trouble. The tip would move about six inches forward when the sail was pushed against it; the spreader was prevented from swinging farther both by the lee shrouds taking up the slack and by the design of the base plate. This fitting was in the shape of a socket with two lugs that a pin passed through from top to bottom. This pin, on which the spreader pivoted, went through the strut about 1½ inches from its base; the sides of the socket limited its travel.

Spreader tips should be lifted slightly above the athwartships horizontal plane so that the top and bottom angles formed when they meet the shroud are equal. In the case of a double-spreader rig, where the lower spreader tips accept two wires each side, it is usual for these tips to be cocked up somewhat less than the angle formed by bisecting the intermediate shroud. The upper spreaders bisect the angle where they meet the cap shroud. Some spar companies arbitrarily cock their spreaders six degrees above the horizontal.

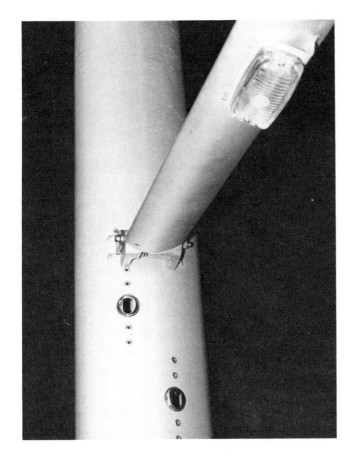

Spreader light and shroud anchorages for swaged "T" terminals. (Courtesy Yachtspars)

With the greater percentage of masts built of aluminum nowadays, it follows that spreaders, too, are commonly constructed of this material. This is good, as long as the spreader wall thickness is sufficient and the base and tip fittings are rugged enough. Wooden spreaders can give good service, but their nemesis, dry rot, is something a metal strut doesn't have to contend with.

In the search for lightness, a lot of wooden spreaders were commonly constructed of spruce, which just loves a drop of dry rot. The top of a wooden spreader — the part you can't see — gets good and wet in a shower of rain, or even a heavy dew. The sun faithfully dries this fresh water (sometimes several times a day in a showery tropical region), and continues to blaze down on the spreader top to eliminate its cover of paint or varnish. This allows fresh water to penetrate the wood, which the good old sun dries and heats up again, all ready for more fresh water. The dry rot spoor, ecstatic about all these preparations, enters the scene and eats down into the spreader from the top. This can happen in a few months, and all the while the spreader can look as good as new when viewed from below.

I constructed the spreaders for my yawl from jarra, an Australian hardwood — never mind the weight aloft. But as tough and rot-free as this wood is, every few months I'd be up there in a chair, inspecting suspiciously the upper varnished surfaces along with every other mast fitting. I never did get dry rot in the yawl's

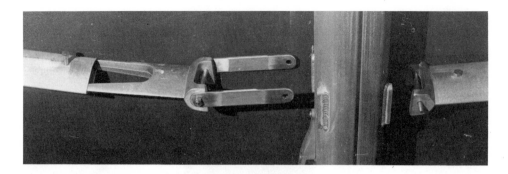

spreaders, but the schooner's hardwood spreaders, which always looked as solid and as tough as a rock, showed a case of rot on the port side after I'd owned her for nine years. I replaced that spreader with one I built from a piece of 2 x 4 teak. I suppose I really couldn't complain (even though I did moan and grizzle about it); the spreader I replaced was 33 years old at the time.

Some aluminum spreaders are beautifully shaped aerofoil section and others are merely pieces of aluminum tube. Base and tip fittings are usually stainless steel, although sometimes the plug used to solidify the hollow end is aluminum. Every spreader fitting, especially the base attachments that hold a spreader rigid, should be inspected thoroughly several times a year. Take nothing for granted here. Go up in a comfortable chair and take your big navigator's magnifying glass. If you see a crack in a fitting, you're going to have to do something about replacing or rebuilding it — and pretty soon.

Shrouds must be held securely in the spreader tips. I cut a ½-inch slot about 1¼ inches long in two short pieces of brass pipe to use in the tips of my yawl's spreaders. I squeezed the pipe in a vise to elongate its section; it was a drive fit over the spreader tip. I then carefully cut and rasped a ⅜-inch groove in the wood so there would be no chance that a shroud would bear against the sides or the end of the slot in the brass ferrule. To ensure that the wood would never have an excuse to spread, no matter what, I drilled a hole through each spreader from forward to aft immediately inboard of the ferrule and hammered home a solid copper rivet. Aboard the schooner, a bolt near each spreader tip, with its head well countersunk to prevent chafe, did the same job.

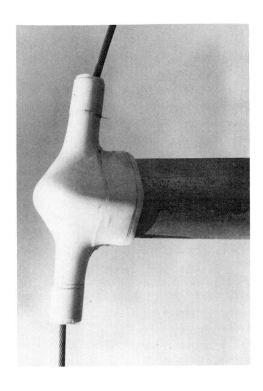

Taped-together spreader end fitting. Not too much chance of chafe here. (Courtesy Yachtspars)

I always serve shrouds where they locate in the tips of spreaders. Maybe you don't need to, but it's something I've always done. With galvanized wire, I would smear some anhydrous lanolin or Res-Q-Steel around a six-inch length of shroud, parcel it with friction tape, and serve it with marlin. The middle of this served piece would rest in the slot in the spreader tip. With a stainless steel shroud, I'd parcel and serve right onto the bare wire.

It's possible that some experienced yachtsmen will consider these tactics unnecessary, but when I was either cruising or chartering, I needed that mast to remain standing up there all year every year (and for plenty of them). The notion of a bare wire lying in a spreader tip just didn't appeal; the idea of one wire lying bare on top of another in a spreader tip was even less appealing. The stainless steel shrouds aboard the yawl were held in the spreader tips by a strong Monel wire seizing over the served marlin; with the schooner's galvanized rigging, soft-iron galvanized wire did this job.

Strips of sheepskin about two inches wide make good chafing gear for spreader tips. I've used them for the ends of ratlines, too. Any time I sailed down to New Zealand, I'd grab myself a sheepskin. They're easy to get "down under"; there are only three million people in my tribe (New Zealanders), but there happen to be 60 million sheep eating their heads off around the hills. A sheepskin here and there is never missed. You don't have to rush to a high-priced store, either; a sheepskin can usually be purchased for a song from any of the big slaughterhouses. Cut a strip off the skin as you need it, wind it like a bandage around each spreader tip, and sew it to itself with waxed thread. As an alternative, soft felt or even rubber may be used. Several layers of chamois leather would work well too.

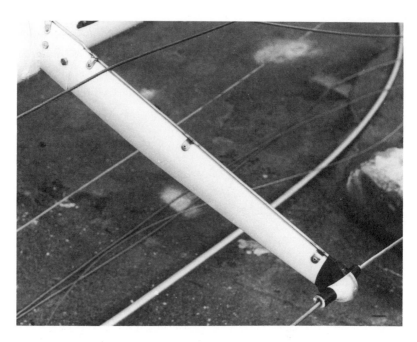

The cap shroud at the end of this spreader passes through a taped-in-position plastic tube. Note stainless steel anti-chafe bar fitted to prevent external wire halyards from sawing into the spreader. (Courtesy Yachtspars)

I like to see cap shrouds (or the intermediate shrouds of a double-spreader rig that pass over spreader tips) leading from chainplates positioned directly athwartships from the mast. Lower shrouds lead from chainplates installed forward and aft of these. The forward shroud each side, if its distance toward the bow is sufficient, can assist the headstays in supporting the mast, just as the after shrouds can help backstays. Don't go overboard on this, however. It is generally considered that the distance that either of these shrouds can be moved forward or aft, and still be expected to do its job in giving the mast lateral support, is one inch for every foot of height. Thus a shroud originating beneath the base of a spreader 20 feet above the deck can have a "spread" of 20 inches forward or aft of the position athwart the mast.

The forestaying of a mizzenmast on a yawl or ketch is sometimes assisted by a triatic wire from the ship's main masthead. It is a great temptation to run this stay across, but then, if something drastic happens to the mainmast, causing it to go by the board, it will usually drag the mizzen over with it. To dodge this unpleasant event and to make each spar independent, a mizzen can have intermediate shrouds running from chainplates that allow for one inch of forward "drift" for every foot of height.

Care must be taken here that these shrouds aren't led so far forward that they interfere with the main boom when it is eased. Assuming the mizzenmast has three chainplates per side, and that the spar itself is not lofty, the other two shrouds can be situated aft of the mast — again allowing no more than one inch of drift for every foot of height. If the vessel's lack of beam aft makes it necessary for the mizzen to carry spreaders to achieve an acceptable shroud angle, then these will have to be backswept to enable the cap shrouds to pass over their tips.

I can hear someone asking: "But won't these spreader tips chafe the daylights out of the mizzen when it is eased?" To which there seems only one reply: "Sure they will, mate, they'll chafe it to kingdom come — unless, of course, you haul it down!" Another alternative is to position the spreaders amidships and use running backstays to support the mizzenmast from aft. It's also possible to fit jumper struts and wires to a mizzenmast to keep the head from being pulled aft when the mizzen sheet is hove in, hard on the wind. Ah . . . mizzens!

The distance a permanent backstay should clear a boom end is critical. For a boom to clear a backstay by a few inches during a controlled jibe might mean that when (or if) the boom kites in a flying jibe, it will hang up on the stay. This can place a sudden unfair strain on chainplate, stay, terminal fittings, masthead — all sorts of things, including the skipper's heart. To check on this, slack away your mainsheet and heave-ho on your topping lift until the boom reaches a height that puts it perpendicular to the backstay. If your boom clears the permanent backstays at this height, you will be OK. If it doesn't, you're going to have to move the stays, shorten the boom, or sail very, very carefully.

ROLLERS, RATLINES, RADIO ANTENNAS, AND LIGHTNING RODS

Headsail sheets that pass around shrouds on their way aft to a winch or to a pair of powerful hands are prone to chafe on toggles, turnbuckles, cotter pins, terminal fittings, and wire. Also liable to chafe are the clews of overlapping jibs. It is possible to purchase split wooden rollers in some marine stores, and these, when installed on an offending shroud, rotate with the pressure of sheet or sail and greatly assist in reducing chafe.

Just as good as wooden rollers, which can put a hole in a poor yachtsman's pocket, are pieces of PVC pipe. With wooden end fittings to position them, these can be slid up the wire above the terminal and be held by split-round pieces of wood, which are either seized or glued together. The bottom piece of wood uses the terminal end, just where the wire enters the fitting, to spin on.

Shroud rollers vary in length with the size of the boat and the height of the sheet or sail-clew above the deck. Rollers between five and eight feet are typical. I've seen pieces of PVC pipe fitted on shrouds in such a manner as to serve merely as chafing pieces, not rollers, and I can't help but feel that there's a lot to be said for this. The "non-roller" has a similar wooden fitting at its top, and this is pushed an inch or so down inside the pipe to prevent its plastic end from chafing the strands of the shroud. The pipe's bottom end slides down over the terminal fitting, is held there by its jam-fit over the terminal, and is further prevented from slipping down by the length of toggle or turnbuckle pin it rests against. This chafing tube requires a bit more fiddling to position satisfactorily than does a roller, but at least there's nothing spinning or exerting a lateral pressure on the shroud wire where it enters its bottom terminal.

Open-barrel turnbuckles, whose screwed shanks are held from turning by cotter

Taped-together shroud rollers. Cotters are taped in terminal pins, toggles, and turnbuckles to lessen possibility of chafing head-sail sheets — or anything else. (Ralph Naranjo photo)

pins, can have a couple of turns of friction tape around the barrel at the position of the cotters if there appears to be a tendency for these to chafe jib sheets or anything else. If cotter pins of correct length have been chosen, however, this shouldn't be necessary.

Angled metal steps (see photograph), which are screwed or even pop-riveted onto masts, are popular with a lot of yachtsmen. The only experience I've had with them is as an onlooker, on a day Minine and I left our schooner in the bay and went for a jaunt aboard a 30-foot cutter in Fiji's Mamanutha Group. The ladies were after shells for their precious collections, so the day was dedicated to diving, and with engine ticking over, we threaded our way among a maze of coral reefs from one likely looking area to the next. One of the cutter's owners was a young, athletic doctor who scampered up and down the steps, which were screwed to the vessel's mast, as easily as if they were a flight of stairs.

I was mighty impressed by all of this — and by the thought of the bird's-eye view that Terry must have enjoyed as he conned the boat from aloft. The day was dead calm and conditions perfect for an act such as this. I couldn't help but wonder at the time, however, what it would be like to clamber up those steps in a breeze of wind

*Mast steps.
(Ralph Naran-
jo photo)*

when the vessel was heeling and a bit of a sea was running, as is sometimes the case when approaching a pass into a lagoon. I think a lot of people would be unable to use mast steps under those conditions. Other bogeys are the possible chafe of halyards and/or sails, and the chance that a halyard might become hooked in the steps. Windage is another consideration.

It is nice, of course, to be way up aloft when conning a ship by eye through a pass or an area studded with coral heads. For more than a few of the cruising gang, however, advancing age makes the masthead increasingly inaccessible; but they still want to sail into these tricky places. The question is just how high you have to be to conn a vessel safely.

Aboard my yawl, the lower shrouds were equipped with wooden ratlines to within a couple of feet of the spreaders, and at the slightest excuse, I would run up there looking for rocks, land, or anything else that might be waiting just over the horizon. By the time I'd moved aboard the schooner (some 14 years later), I'd settled for a few rungs up the main rigging, whose lowers were rattled down on both sides. After we replaced this rigging (nine years later), I decided to eliminate the ratlines. To achieve what was to us a satisfactory height of eye for eyeball navigation, one of us would walk along the deck, step onto a deckbox, up onto the upturned bottom of Minine's sailing dinghy, and then onto the main-staysail-boom gooseneck. This gave me a height of eye of about 17 feet and my mate exactly one foot less.

Traditionally, tarred hemp was utilized for ratlines aboard commercial sailing vessels, and these ladders in the shrouds were a lot harder to climb than the pieces of wood used nowadays. The old-time hemp ratline had an eyesplice at each end, made fast to a forward and an aft shroud with a cross seizing. The ratline was clove-hitched around shrouds between forward and aft, the hitches on the outside. The man putting on ratlines always had a stick (15 inches was a popular length) to standardize the distance between ratlines. Ratlines were usually installed parallel to the sheer pole, which is the first fore-and-aft wooden step in the rigging in line with the sheer of the vessel. The sheer pole commonly housed a number of belaying pins.

I put ratlines in the fore rigging of my yawl while tied stern-to at Papeete's waterfront in 1953. (We thought the place was crowded because two other cruising boats, *Moonraker* from England and *Novia* from California, were there. Over the next 25 years of visiting the port, I marveled at my naivete.) These ratlines, of some obscure Tahitian hardwood that was as red as fire, had their ends grooved so they could slide up between the shrouds. Once positioned, each end rested on a marlin serving two inches long.

A hole was drilled 1¼ inches in from the ends of each ratline, and many turns of marlin lashed it to a shroud. Lee Gregg of the *Novia* acquainted me with this procedure. The beauty of the system is that the ends are flush with the fore and aft side of each shroud; there is nothing projecting for the mainsail (or mizzen, if that's where the ratlines are) to chafe against. Despite that, I still covered the ends with small pieces of sheepskin. Ratlines on the lower shrouds of *White Squall II*'s mainmast were pieces of hardwood that were held in position by sheer-lashings of marlin. They projected about an inch forward and aft of the shrouds and caused me continual problems with chafe — another reason I wasn't sorry to see them go.

For those who are all fired up to rattle down their lower shrouds, the following advice might be useful. Carefully calculate the height of your lower ratline *on one side.* Don't worry about its being parallel to the sheerline of your ship; install it level, using whatever system you prefer to hold the ends in place. (Some people favor little stainless steel U-bolts in lieu of marlin.) Then stand off abeam in a dinghy or on a dock and see how it looks. If you're satisfied, put on the rest of the ratlines that side, using a stick of predetermined length to keep the separations constant between the ratlines as you work your way aloft. This is far easier than fiddling around with a rule or tape.

After you've done one side, fit your bottom ratline in the opposite shrouds; then stand off and see if it's exactly parallel to its counterpart across the ship. If it's not spot-on, and you continue to rattle down that side, measuring from the one you've just installed, the whole job will stick out like a sore thumb. If every ratline is parallel across the ship, however, you'll hardly notice they're up there.

Brails, inhauls, outhauls, vangs, guys, mast hoops — and the same ratlines as Columbus had. (Ralph Naranjo photo)

Some people take seriously the correct installation of ratlines. Along with a bunch of other seamen, I was marvelously entertained on the Auckland waterfront one day by an argument between two riggers who had just finished rattling down the fore shrouds of a large commercial sailing scow. They'd done a side each, and it was plain that the ratlines weren't parallel across the big old ketch when they finished. One rigger had started off measuring his side from the sheer pole, and the other guy probably eyeballed a level wharf stringer to set up his side. I thought at the time that they'd probably let fly at each other with a few terse words and leave it right there, but such wasn't the case. The argument became loud, highly personal, and studded with extravagant unprintable phrases. Then they ran out of words. Just as their audience (each individual highly appreciative) had concluded that that was that, the riggers decided to enter wholeheartedly into the spirit of the thing by shaping up and having it out man to man, right there on the dock. First class entertainment!

A useful function of a mizzenmast (some claim *the* most useful) is to carry a whip antenna for a transmitter. Aboard a ketch or yawl, the antenna can sit right up there at the mizzen masthead, clear of shrouds, stays, halyards, sails, and, if the mast is

In-line insulator. (Ralph Naranjo photo)

independently stayed, still be available for use if the main spar meets with an accident. A single-masted vessel can have a radio antenna installed well aft, just inboard of the transom, although this position makes it vulnerable to bodies falling against it at times.

The antenna can be installed, of course, at the masthead of a cutter or a sloop, but this position doesn't enjoy popularity, because: (a) it can seriously obstruct the visibility of any navigation light installed at the masthead; (b) a lot of skippers are unable to accept its weight and windage; and (c) some cruising folk use their radio so rarely that they can't stand the idea (or the sight of) the thing whipping around up there.

There are a number of "in-line insulators" on the market that can be installed in the rigging to convert a permanent backstay into an efficient radio antenna. I consider, however, that a vessel with one permanent backstay should not have the wire interfered with in any way, such as breaking it to fit radio insulators. One terminal at the top and bottom of a stay or shroud is enough, without adding the other four that the fitting of insulators demands. If you're all gung-ho to use a permanent backstay as a radio antenna, hang another stay up there especially for that purpose; this way, your rig will benefit from the support provided by an additional wire. If, for any reason, your antenna stay carries away, the permanent backstay will keep on supporting the mast.

I put a whip antenna on the foremasthead of the *White Squall II* for our VHF radio and found it quite adequate. The antenna for our regular transmitting set was simply a wire broken by two insulators that ran from the mainmast's starboard spreader to an insulated deck fitting and to the radio. Aboard the yawl, it never occurred to me to have a radio (I couldn't have afforded one, anyway), so the problem of a suitable antenna never arose.

A ship with a metal hull is far less likely to be damaged by lightning than a vessel constructed of any other material. Even so, all standing rigging, metal masts, and sail tracks of wooden masts must be well bonded to the hull. Lightning takes the most direct course to ground, and, unless it is led by the shortest distance possible to a ground plate no less than one foot square, it can cause serious damage aboard a vessel built of any material other than metal.

The bonding of all hull fittings isn't necessarily the answer either. It would seem, in fact, that in some instances bonding does more harm than good. I know of a case where a fiberglass sloop with a metal mast was struck by lightning when anchored among the San Blas Islands. The lightning melted several stainless steel fittings at the masthead, shot from one bonded fitting to another around the vessel, loosened up a through-hull fitting in the head, and blew the sink discharge clear out of the boat. The owner, who'd been standing in a hatchway, vows he was touching nothing, but even so, the tip of one forefinger split open and blood squirted over the nice teak grating on his cockpit floor. (Makes you want to reach for your beads and promise that from now on you're *really* going to be good.)

Anyway, he hopped over the side with a deck cushion, which was immediately sucked against the hull by water pouring into the ship through the hole left by the sink discharge. This completely stopped the leak, so he clambered back aboard, wrapped up his finger, and proceeded to get out his kit of tools, bolts, plywood, and bedding compound to make some temporary repairs.

I like the way Ralph Naranjo arranged the lightning ground aboard his 41-foot cutter *Wind Shadow*. Ralph took a heavy copper wire from the heel of his metal mast and soldered this to a bronze coach screw driven solidly into his encapsulated ballast. He ran a one-foot-by-eight-foot piece of copper sheathing fore and aft beneath his keel, drilled a ½-inch-diameter hole through copper, fiberglass, and ballast, and clear out the other side. A securely tightened silicon-bronze bolt, its head soldered to the sheathing, its nut head countersunk and glassed over, completed the bond to ground. In a sailboat where the ballast keel is bolted to the ship, the lightning conductor can run from the metal mast heel, or the metal track (if the mast is wood), to a keelbolt.

In Chapter Two we mentioned that some metal masts should be insulated from their mast steps with great care to prevent corrosion through electrolysis. When a copper ground strap is attached to a metal mast, the possibility of electrolysis must be kept strongly in mind. A successful method of bonding a copper strap to an aluminum mast can be achieved relatively easily. The copper strap is separated from the mast by a piece of PVC sheet, ⅛ inch thick. Stainless steel roundhead machine screws (a half-dozen will do), with stainless "star" washers between the head of each fastening and the copper strap, pass through clearance holes in the strap and the PVC into the aluminum mast. The threads of the machine screws may be smeared with silicone paste both to prevent the fastenings from binding in the tapped holes and to assist the bond. It is recommended that this mast-to-strap connection take place far enough above the mast heel (a foot or two) so that there is little possibility of its getting damp. The connection should be kept clean and dry and be inspected regularly.

It is almost always possible to beef up the standing rigging of a new or secondhand boat to give her a sturdy, well-stayed mast, so that if a wire or fitting does carry away, it will be an inconvenience, not a calamity. The big thing to remember is that nothing lasts forever. Stainless steel rigging and associated fittings look good and should give faithful service for years; for longevity, however, they can't compare with your wife's set of stainless pots she received as a wedding present 10 years ago. Those pots will probably go on another 10 years after that rigging needs replacing. Realize that a cruising boat's rigging is being tested constantly. Some of the nooks, corners, and roadsteads we hang on in when cruising fall far short of being tranquil, unruffled havens. While affording much-needed shelter, such an anchorage might contain a surge that keeps a vessel rolling day and night. Each roll places stress and strain on the standing rigging.

Tangs, terminal fittings, wire, toggles, turnbuckles — no matter what they're made of, keep a running survey going on them all. Don't forget your bobstay if you have one. Any fitting that's half in and half out of the water at times has a tough row to hoe. And try to fix things as they happen. It's difficult to do a lasting repair on a piece of standing rigging that gives trouble at sea, but, once you are in the bay, make it your first job — and make it a permanent one.

four

Running Rigging

Running rigging is the cordage and wire used aboard a sailing vessel to haul sails up, down, in, out, and any other direction that suits. Although most running rigging in sailboats is rope, it is seldom referred to as such. Even in accounts of the days of commercial sail, with their proliferation of "sticks and string," we find only a few "ropes." There were foot ropes hung along yards for seamen to stand on while bending, loosing, furling, or "passing a gasket." There were mast ropes for sending topmasts and topgallant masts up or down; a heel rope was rove through a block on the end of a bowsprit for heaving out a jibboom; a bull rope was set up to control a swinging derrick; a man rope was rove through gangway stanchions or hung alongside a pilot's or Jacob's ladder to assist a climber; there was always, nicely macramed, a bell-rope. This last is probably the only rope to be found aboard an American cruising sailboat these days, although the British still use the word more liberally.

Rope is purchased either in odd lengths or by the coil, which, if tradition is still exerting its influence, would be 120 fathoms. As soon as you start cutting off the lengths, however, they will have different names — such as halyards, which haul sails up and (if everything is going according to plan) lets them back down again; if you're wise, you'll have downhauls when cruising. Sheets heave sails in or let them out. Outhauls haul them out. There are pendants for reefing, lifts for supporting booms, guys for positioning booms, braces for yards, gantlines for temporary use in hauling someone or something aloft. Snubbers, stoppers, falls, dinghy painters — they all come from the one coil of rope (which, incidentally, is referred to as "line" as soon as it is lifted aboard).

Standing rigging is any fixed line or wire whose sole job is to support a spar permanently. Everything else is known as running rigging.

TYPES OF LINE

Running rigging (especially sheets, halyards, and downhauls aboard gaff-rigged vessels) traditionally was hemp, and some of it was pretty bad. Synthetic lines have done away with the headaches attached to much of the cordage available only 25 years ago; those problems just don't apply to the present-day sailor. To pander, however, to any shellback squirming jealously in his grave at the thought of how his modern counterpart has it so good, we'll touch briefly on what he had to put up with.

Most halyards, falls, and sheets were three-strand Manila, which was made from leafstalks of the Musaceae (*Musa textilis*) plant grown in the Philippines. This plant lent itself to the manufacture of "right-laid" rope; the fibers were twisted to the right and fell naturally into strands, which were also rolled to the right and laid tightly one against the other to make a rope. The correct way to coil this rope was to the right, or clockwise; it objected strongly to being coiled to the left.

Right-laid Manila *always* kinked or snarled, especially when wet; the day it stopped kinking and became pleasant to handle was the day it quit. Left-laid Manila was much more expensive and was beautiful to handle, and it didn't kink or snarl in the blocks. For this reason, left-laid (usually four-strand) Manila line saw great service as lifeboat falls in the merchant marine.

Manila halyards were notorious for shrinking when wet. More than one owner, after belaying his Manila halyards snugly, has found his pin rail pulled out of the deck or a gooseneck yanked up a mast because the hemp shrank after a shower of rain. Sisal, made from the Amaryllidaceae plant, was worse; flax was worse yet. Italian hemp and European hemp ("Europe") were good; both were stronger and harder and had far less stretch than Manila. "Europe" was generally used for lanyards when setting up shrouds with deadeyes; when tarred, it would last for years. Compared with Manila, it was expensive and so saw little use for sheets or halyards. However, an old skipper I shipped away with in my early years told me that the running rigging aboard the square-rigger *Herzogin-Cecilie,* in which he'd sailed as an able seaman, was all European hemp.

Cotton lines saw limited use aboard yachts, because, although cotton was easy on the hands, it rotted. Coir (a derivation of *kayar,* the Malayan word meaning "cord") was a brown, prickly line made from the fiber of coconut husks. Coir had marvelous stretching capabilities. Because of this, it saw great service as anchor rodes for small craft and even as springlines (they had wire tails) for large ships. I've seen eight-inch-diameter coir on the docks of some exposed, "surgy" ports, but it had a limited life. Nylon has replaced coir completely.

The synthetic lines available today have made a world of difference to the life of a sailing man. Quite apart from the no-rot and no-shrinking-when-wet factors is the strength of the present-day synthetic cordage. The cruising man these days knows that with reasonable care, his lines will last for years. Chafe, not rot, is the main enemy of modern lines. While there was always a good chance that hemp lines that were stowed away wet would rot, present-day cordage laps up this treatment.

There is a widespread belief that sunlight harms the fibers of synthetic rope, and, while this is true of polypropylene, it cannot be applied across the board. At the time of writing, the *White Squall II*'s ⅜-inch-Dacron mainsheet and main staysail sheet

	3-STRAND ROPE												BRAIDED ROPE					
	NYLON		SPUN NYLON		DACRON		SPUN DACRON		MULTI-LINE		POLY-PROPYLENE		DACRON		SPUN DACRON		NYLON	
	Wt.	Load	Wt.	Load	Wt.	Load	Wt.	Load	Wt.	Load	Wt.	Load	Wt.	Load	Wt.	Load	Wt.	Load
3/16"	1.0	135	—	—	1.2	155	1.0	120	—	—	0.70	120	1.0	180	1.0	180	0.90	135
1/4"	1.5	225	1.5	160	2.0	250	1.7	190	1.9	190	1.2	190	2.0	370	1.5	285	1.7	306
5/16"	2.5	345	2.3	245	3.1	390	2.7	295	2.6	295	1.8	290	3.0	560	2.3	435	2.6	459
3/8"	3.5	500	3.1	330	4.5	565	3.6	430	3.6	425	2.8	415	4.3	800	3.8	720	3.8	665
7/16"	5.0	675	4.5	480	6.2	765	4.8	565	5.0	575	3.8	535	6.0	1100	5.0	950	5.1	875
1/2"	6.5	865	5.7	610	8.0	980	6.4	655	6.5	735	4.7	645	7.9	1400	6.5	1230	6.4	1085
9/16"	8.3	1080	7.5	755	—	—	—	—	—	—	—	—	10.0	1820	8.4	1590	8.0	1345
5/8"	10.5	1404	9.0	960	13.0	1530	10.3	965	9.3	1070	7.5	950	13.0	2170	10.3	1950	10.0	1630
3/4"	14.5	1920	12.2	1295	17.5	1915	14.3	1315	13.0	1375	10.7	1300	17.0	3150	15.0	2840	16.3	2640
7/8"	20.0	2700	16.2	1730	—	—	—	—	17.5	1835	—	—	23.0	4130	—	—	19.5	3170
1"	26.0	3375	20.0	2135	—	—	—	—	22.5	2295	—	—	30.0	5370	—	—	25.5	4145
Elong.	17%		17%		8%		11%		9%		9%		2½%		3½%		12%	

Wt. = *Weight of rope in pounds per 100-foot length*   Load = *Recommended working load in pounds*   Elong. = *Elongation at recommended working loads*

LIMITATIONS: ☐ Specifications apply to new or unused rope of standard construction, manufactured and tested under Cordage Institute procedures.
☐ Weights are subject to ±5% variation.
☐ Recommended working loads are quoted as a percentage of tensile strength: nylon and spun nylon at 15% of tensile strength, all other ropes at 17%.
☐ Quoted working loads cover usage where there are no unusual shock or sustained loadings, severe abrasion conditions, chemical action or undue risk of personnel or property.

(Courtesy New England Ropes)

have been exposed to the elements constantly for 18 years, 16 spent chartering and cruising in the tropics. It seems that *good* synthetic line has an indefinite life; its only other enemy aboard ship, in addition to chafe, is the damage that results when the line rests on something rusty, such as a shackle in a rope locker or lazarette. If there's any one thing that synthetic fiber doesn't like, it's rust.

As can be seen from the chart of synthetic cordage shown here, three-strand nylon has an elongation factor of 17 percent at the recommended working load; at the other end of the scale is braided Dacron with a stretch factor of 2½ percent. This is with a working load of 865 pounds for ½-inch, three-strand nylon, and 1,400 pounds for braided Dacron of the same diameter. (Working loads, which are calculated as a percentage of a line's tensile strength, are 15 percent for nylon and 17 percent for other synthetic ropes.) It follows, therefore, that the particular duties a rope is expected to perform should be assessed carefully prior to its selection.

The strongest synthetic line is constructed from continuous filament: each filament is unbroken from one end of the line to the other. Of slightly less strength is spun synthetic line, which is constructed of pieces of fiber cut approximately six inches long and twisted in much the same manner as that used for making rope from natural materials. The difference between continuous filament and spun fiber can be noticed in the smooth, shiny finish of the former, compared with the relatively dull, linenlike appearance of the latter. I've used both, and I prefer continuous-filament line for everything except dinghy painters. The last statement, I must admit, is more the result of hardheaded prejudice than gentle reasoning.

In the early 1960s, before a charter, I spliced a new continuous-filament nylon painter onto the towing eye of the 12-foot-6-inch fiberglass dinghy we used as a tender for the *White Squall II*. The new painter was shiny and slippery — so slippery, in fact, that one night when at anchor at Norman Island in the British Virgins, the mysterious knot tied aboard the schooner by a crew member was tugged free by the dinghy.

The little boat then floated merrily on its uninsured way to Puerto Rico. I know this for a fact, because by the sheerest accident I discovered it there nearly two years later. It was lying on the beach below the Conquistador Hotel at Fajardo, on a day when another charter skipper and I headed in there from our vessels to quench a raging thirst. And the manager gave it back to me. Incredible. Not only that. When, a few hours later, we came to square up our bar bill, we found he'd paid it. A prince!

Most synthetic line is available in three-strand and braided construction; some of it can even be found with plaited strands. There is a lot to be said for braided line. Size for size, it is stronger than three-strand rope, it has less stretch, and, being torque-free, it can't get in a back-turn, or "hockle." On the debit side, it is harder to splice than three-strand rope.

Nylon rope has more than twice the strength of Manila. It has the greatest stretch factor of any synthetic line and is the strongest rope made. Its elasticity makes it ideal for anchor rodes, docklines, mooring pendants, and towing lines. While on the subject of this powerful cordage, let me encourage you to take great care when belaying, slacking, or letting go any line. A finger caught by a line and pulled into a cleat, such as when slacking a spring as a vessel comes alongside, will never be the same again. Be mighty careful rendering nylon under strain; it's wonderful stuff, but with a 17 percent stretch factor, nylon has all the properties of a rubber band. To flick the turns nonchalantly off a cleat where nylon is belayed under strain can cause it to go with a rush. Your favorite pinky, along with several of its mates, might get nipped off.

Dacron is DuPont's trade name for the polyester fiber used in the construction of this rope. The English equivalent of Dacron is Terylene. Either one is available to the yachtsman in both continuous-filament and spun-fiber construction; the line has much less stretch than nylon, and a slightly lower tensile strength. Dacron is available in three-strand, braided, and often plaited construction. It is wonderful rope for halyards, sheets, downhauls, tackle falls (as for vangs), reefing pendants, guys, and any job where minimal stretch is desired.

Color-coded braided Dacron (red, blue, or green flecks in the line) is popular with yachtsmen for use where several sheets or halyards lead to one location, such as a

Simple, well-designed blocks.
(Courtesy Yachtspars)

cockpit. If a staysail sheet is green-flecked, there is less chance that a sailor — unless he's color-blind — will confuse it with the jib-topsail sheet, color-coded red or blue. It is even possible to cater to the color-blind sailor with the line available today. A sheet or halyard can be either three-strand, braided, or plaited. Some yachtsmen, who like to be able to identify which line is which at night by feel alone, use all three types of rope aboard their boats. If the mizzen sheet is plaited, there is no way, even on the blackest of nights, that it can be confused with the feel of, say, a three-strand mainsheet.

Braided Dacron is getting a big hand for halyards and sheets, and deservedly so. In addition to having very little stretch, it is very "passive" when hove in: it lies flat, doesn't seem to get into a tangle all by itself, and is ever ready to be slacked off a winch drum or cleat without the chance of a kink or snarl. And, of course, it can't get into a backward hockle — as can three-strand line. I cannot help but wonder about its suitability for docklines on a cruising vessel, however. Once again, it's our old enemy, chafe.

I suppose that if a vessel ties up only in sheltered marinas, where the tidal range is taken care of by floating docks, and if chafe-guards are positioned carefully over each line at every chock and lead, then braided nylon is perfect. Along the cruising beat, though, these facilities are often hard to find. The cruising boat, alongside for customs inspection, water, or fuel, can find she's tied to something that's going to chafe the daylights out of her lines.

Even with my aversion for docks and anything smacking of floating suburbia, and being an old woman about the lead of my gear, I've had docklines chafed so badly I've had to cut out a piece and short-splice them together again. Easy enough with three-strand line. Braided line can be cut and joined, too, but it's a bigger deal. A cut splice, or a carrick bend with the tails spliced into the standing part, are two methods, but whereas the short splice in a three-strand line will render easily around winch, post, or bitts, the same cannot be said for braided line joined in the above manner.

Polypropylene line is the lightest of all synthetic lines. It has a low stretch factor and will float in either fresh or salt water. Polypropylene line is available in several colors, usually in three-strand or plaited construction. It is, however, susceptible to damage from sunlight, which greatly impairs its strength. Because of its buoyancy, it enjoys limited popularity for use as dinghy painters. (The boatman can't back down and wind a floating painter around his propeller.) I just plain don't like the stuff. Three-strand polypropylene is often hard and slippery, and the plaited line doesn't inspire confidence — not in me, anyway.

If you're worried about picking up your dinghy painter in the wheel as you go astern, thread a few little plastic floats along it, spacing them about three feet apart. That will keep it afloat, and you'll never know the sinking feeling that comes with looking aft as you back down and observe how the stern of your dinghy kicks in the air, its bow pulled under as the painter is wound around the ship's propeller. (Almost sounds as though it's happened to me, doesn't it?)

Make sure your dinghy painter is a good, strong nylon one that won't break, no matter what. And while I think of it, splice a generous-sized eye in the free end, so that the most unnautical crewmember can secure the painter simply by dropping the loop over a cleat or bitts aboard your vessel. Otherwise the dinghy might float to Puerto Rico . . . .

Another synthetic rope, Multiline, is worth mentioning. Multiline — and here I quote directly from information supplied me by New England Ropes — is "A combination rope. Each strand of Multiline has a polypropylene core with polyester yarn outside surface. It is lighter in weight than Dacron but offers the same general characteristics. Extensively used in the industrial and commercial fishing trades where low stretch and good rendering capability over winches is essential. Typical uses include tackle-ropes, bull-ropes, handlines, stringing lines and truck ropes."

Now, I've never been shipmates with Multiline, but it sounds pretty good, and well worthy of consideration by the cruising yachtsman. Multiline is used by commercial fishermen, and these guys give their gear merciless treatment at times. For such items as engines, generators, pumps, radios, automatic pilots — you name it — I've always had a good look at what the commercial fisherman uses year in and year out. When you sail off into the cruising life, you're putting your ship to work; you're expecting her to take you safely from country to country. In other words, you've given her a job. A bit of workboat equipment such as Multiline won't be found aboard a 12-meter, but as sea-anchor warp, gantlines, and spare running gear aboard an ocean cruiser, it could be right at home.

After selecting a suitable line for running rigging, attend to the lead of the gear. Chafe must be kept to an absolute minimum. The strongest line in the world can have its life halved, its fibers irreparably damaged, if it is led improperly to or from a sheave. A line aboard a cruising boat must never be allowed to rub day after day against another rope or piece of equipment.

HALYARDS

Yachtsmen are divided strongly on the use of wire and Dacron or Terylene for halyards. Talk rope halyards to a racing man, and there's a fair chance he'll look at you as if you've just crawled out from beneath a log. And well he might. The average racing buff, cranking away at his hydraulic backstay adjuster to rake the mast and get his forestay just a little better than drum-tight when hard on the wind, is able to see little humor in a rope halyard that stretches even the tiniest bit. The windage of rope as compared with wire comes into it, too. But champions of wire halyards are not necessarily confined to the racing gang. For many years, a large section of the cruising crowd have been vociferous (me loudest of all until recently) in their support of wire and only wire for every halyard except, perhaps, a spinnaker.

The flexible, 7/19 stainless steel wire rope can give good service, especially if it passes over a large, well-designed sheave. Some sheaves are aluminum with a bronze bearing, some are all bronze. Personal preference, combined with what's available, plays a big part here. I like Tufnol sheaves for wire rope. The sheave should have a deep groove for the wire to seat in, and be no less than 24 times the wire's diameter. The smaller the sheave's diameter, the quicker the small, individual wires will crystallize and break. The lead to and from a wire halyard sheave must be perfect, with the sheave or sheaves at the masthead separated one from the other and enclosed, so that under no conditions can a wire jump out of its groove.

This last is sometimes easier said than done. After 12 years of cruising in the *White Squall,* I figured I had a stranglehold on the wire halyard situation, simply because I'd had no trouble. However, one memorable day off Diamond Head, Oahu, at the start of a trip to the mainland, my turn came. We suffered a knockdown that morning from a puff that came out of nowhere, and we only managed to claw the mainsail down about two feet before the wire jumped the sheave and jammed solidly between the Tufnol and the copper-sided masthead slot. We managed to turn, and ran the length of the Molokai Channel with the main still stuck up there. Eventually we rounded up and anchored in Pokai Bay on the south side of the island.

Here, a "volunteer" went up in a chair on the genoa halyard to sort out the mess and unshackle the head of the mainsail. The wire halyard was carefully pried out and a copper U was fashioned from a piece of metal we had aboard. This was placed over the halyard on the forward side of the mast a few inches below the sheave, and fastened in place by a couple of bronze, roundhead wood screws. It did the trick. (Nothing's impossible, but we'd have had a merry time doing all this at sea.) I was only too well aware at the time that had the lead been there all along, the mishap never would have occurred. It was this experience that made me believe in halyard leads; I've had them all over the place in the form of bull's-eyes on spreaders and masts ever since.

The halyards of a marconi-rigged vessel are seldom damaged by chafe. If close attention has been paid to their installation, if the sheaves are a correct size and every lead is fair, chafe is hardly a consideration. The same cannot be said, however, for the halyards of a gaff-rigged vessel, on which the halyards move with the gaff. As this spar swings from one side to the other, the peak halyards go with it. Even the throat halyard just above the gaff jaws is influenced by the movement. Great care must be exercised, therefore, over the lead of both throat and peak halyards from the extent of one jibe to the other, to make sure nothing chafes.

A strong reason for all this concern is that aboard a gaff-rigged ship, we're usually talking about a lot of line. And line, any way you look at it, is money. While the main halyard of a marconi-rigged vessel leads up to the masthead and down, giving two parts, the peak halyard of a gaff-rigger, with a standing part at the masthead and two single blocks on the gaff, takes five parts — a length equal to five times up and down the mast when the gaff is lowered. The throat halyard may only go about two-thirds of the way to the masthead, but its three- or four-part tackle, when added to the peak halyard, makes for a lot of line.

It is possible to hoist a gaff sail on all wire, as my old friend Jim Squire did for years aboard his steel charter schooner, *Te Hongi,* in the Caribbean. Jim's vessel sported a huge, fearsome-looking winch bristling with cogs, dogs, and pawls, bolted to the deck at the base of both fore and main masts. These winches, built in Holland by De Vries Lentsch, were about 30 inches high; one person, by winding away and engaging this pawl and that dog with great expertise, could hoist or lower both throat and peak together.

There are three ways a sail can be hoisted on a wire halyard: (1) an all-wire winch; (2) a rope tail, connected eye-to-eye to the wire with a shackle or two eyesplices (the thimble of one eye inside the other); or (3) a rope tail connected to the wire with a rope-to-wire splice.

An all-wire halyard wound onto a winch located on the mast is a good arrangement, and once the sail is hoisted, a crewman doesn't have a length of line to coil and stow. Such a setup can, however, be tough on the wire. While the sail is being hove up, there is little weight on the wire as it winds layer upon layer on the drum. The last couple of feet — especially if the sail is starting to draw — often takes quite a bit of sweating up. The strain of winding down a final inch or two sometimes buries the halyard amid the part already wound onto the drum, which kills small, individual wires. Another strike against the all-wire halyard winch for a lot of yachtsmen is its slow speed. It cannot compete with heaving a sail up hand over hand.

After hauling away on halyards for a score of sailing years, I decided to install two wire-reel winches — one for the mainsail and the other for jib or genoa — on the mainmast of my yawl. Quite frankly, I liked them. They were slower, certainly, but then again, I was cruising, and the odd half-minute extra time it took to hoist a sail was of no consequence. Another thing in their favor, I found, was that I could hang on with one hand and hoist with the other. Heaving away hand-over-hand on a halyard aboard that little vessel in a seaway made a man wish he were Tarzan. The final clincher, as has been mentioned, is that once the sail was up, there was no length of halyard to coil down.

It must be said that all-wire winches should be used and treated with respect. The winches I installed aboard my yawl were standard Merrimans with no ratchet and a brake that was either on or off — but they needed constant maintenance to ensure that the brakes always held. While I personally had little trouble, the same did not apply to other yachtsmen I talked with. Tales of brakes suddenly letting go and handles having to be left in the winch and lashed to the mast to hold up a sail — which meant a very careful application of unwinding to get it down again — did crop up from time to time. In any case, as will be seen, my own approach to sail hoisting underwent a radical change in later years.

I hoisted every sail aboard the *White Squall II* with a rope tail, connected eye-to-eye with splices or a shackle to a 7/19 stainless steel wire halyard. Her hefty displacement and consequent slower motion made it a breeze to coil down the long Dacron halyard tails. Once coiled, the standing part of the halyard from the belaying pin would be passed through the coil and then half-hitched back over the pin.

It is a temptation with a long length of line to make it up in a big coil. Unfortunately, big coils don't like running free when you are lowering away; they're likely to pick up a couple of loops of their own part, just when you're in a hurry to get that sail down. Before you know it, there's a knot half the size of your girlfriend (and nowhere near as attractive) dangling partway up the mast. The smaller and tighter a line is coiled, the more chance there is of its running free.

One of the main bugbears in shackling or splicing a rope tail eye-to-eye with a wire halyard is that the travel of the wire when the sail is lowered is limited when the eye or shackle comes up hard against a mast lead or sheave. If, after you've hove away on the tail, the wire is long enough for a few turns to be taken around a winch on the mast, then this, of course, does not apply. In this case, you'll probably have all the wire you need to lower the sail. If the wire halyard is on a block and tackle with the hauling part led to a mast winch (as discussed in the next chapter), its length is severely limited.

A rope tail connected to the wire with a rope-to-wire splice looks very yachty, very "pukka." If it's well done, it's strong, too — as strong, some claim, as the rope. The big thing, as I see it, is that this type of join makes it possible for the rope tail to follow the wire over a sheave or around a winch. I can't help but question whether this type of wire-to-rope connection is one for the long-range cruising boat. We're not talking here of a boat going off on a six months' or one year's cruise — we're talking about a vessel out there on the cruising beat and staying out there — where marinas and rigging and sail lofts are far apart. A rope-to-wire splice might last for years, but if it suddenly goes on the sick list, how many yachtsmen can do this splice?

For anyone interested in splicing 7/19 wire to braided Dacron line, the following method shown me by my old friend Warwick Tompkins of San Francisco may be of interest. As "Commodore" says it: "The end of the wire is simply tapered by cutting each of the six strands progressively farther back along the wire, then wrapping the lot tightly and smoothly with a good brand of elastic, plastic friction tape (3M is best) to achieve a longish taper free of sharp bends. A couple of layers is best. A small splicing fid helps to insert the tapered wire into the core of the braid until the tape is completely hidden, at which point the core is separated into three or six strands and tucked with the lay, into either three or six strands of wire. Three strands is fine for the core tucking. The core tucks should be tapered for the best job, the cut made clean and close with a knife (not a hot knife).

"The sleeve of the braid may then be milked down over all, and its fibers made into six strands and tucked accordingly, also with the lay. The core may be tucked as often as you wish — four or five tucks are more than enough — but the sleeve ought not to be tucked more than four times. The strands of the sleeve should then be hot-knifed off, helping to prevent pulling out. This finish also aids the taper. Obviously, the lengths of core and sleeve need to be adjusted appropriately. A trick to preserve the pattern of the braid is to tape around the core and sleeve before separating into strands and tucking."

He goes on: "One further word about the braid splice: If one wished the wire to be covered, as for a wire genoa sheet or an after guy, the sleeve may be milked for any distance down the wire. The braided sleeve will constrict and cling close to the wire, acting like Chinese handcuffs to increase the strength (through friction) of the splice. If this is done, beware of too many tucks to secure the sleeve, as they will cause imbalance in the loading between the outer six strands of wire and the core. This, in extreme cases, can reduce the ultimate strength of the unit by about 12 percent."

A test for the confidence a cruising sailor places in his rope-to-wire splice comes when he is reefed. The splice, typically a few feet clear of the winch, must take the full weight of the sail and boom — and probably a hat-full of wind besides. It is possible to install a wire pendant of predetermined length between the head of the

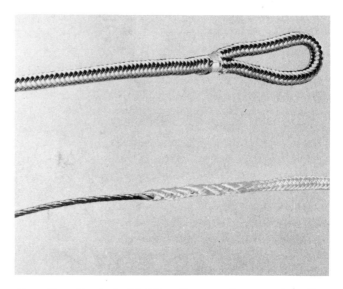

Top: *Eyesplice in braided line.* **Bottom:** *Rope-to-wire splice.*
(Courtesy Yachtspars)

sail and the halyard and so keep the wire on the drum, but this adds up to one more thing to do at a time when a man has enough on his plate as it is. To some, devout in their belief that the rope-to-wire splice will never let go, it may be perfectly acceptable that this connection take the full weight of sail, wind, and boom. Maybe I'm being an overly cautious nut when I say I won't buy it. (I can hear the reader exclaiming, "Here's a guy who's just spent all this time describing a good splice, and now he tells us he hasn't got the nerve to use it himself!")

You're right, mate! Tompkins' method is a good one, but no rope-to-wire splice is as good as an eye spliced to an eye because even though an eye-to-eye connection won't render through a sheave or block, it's right out there in plain sight. It might not look as pretty, but it inspires confidence — in nervous souls like me, at any rate.

The type of terminal fitting installed on the end of a wire halyard should be as rugged as that of a standing stay or shroud. A wire halyard terminal takes a beating. It must be able to stand a certain amount of lateral as well as direct pull, such as when hove close up to a masthead sheave; it must be able to take any amount of vibration, as when a sail is luffing, and be ready to come back for more. As with standing rigging, the type of terminal used is largely a matter of personal preference. I've always used my old favorites — splices, Nicopress, or poured sockets — and have never had a moment's trouble with any of these.

Until recently, all the cruising I've done has been in vessels equipped with external halyards. Apart from those early years in gaff-riggers, every halyard except the spinnaker hoist has been wire. I never thought I'd haul my flag down in the wire-versus-rope halyard controversy, but lately I've not only pulled down my wire flag, I've given it away!

During a recent Virgin Islands cruise with Carl and Jeanne Moesly in their 50-foot ketch *Rigadoon,* I came around full circle on the rope halyard issue. From regarding

Dacron halyards with a skeptical look and a curl of the lip, I became so enthusiastic about them that you'd think it was my idea all along. Carl and Jeanne had left Miami on their second circumnavigation in the 38-foot ketch *Rigadoon,* which they then sold in Auckland, New Zealand. There they had their new cruising boat built, the second *Rigadoon.* After 2½ years and 23,000 miles, they arrived in the Virgin Islands via the Cape of Good Hope, just as I was getting into this rigging book — which seemed as good a time as any to down tools and see how their dreamship was working out.

The *Rigadoon*'s 430-square-foot mainsail has a ½-inch Dacron halyard of regular three-strand construction; both this and the mizzen halyard are internal. A self-tailing winch, installed on the mast, handles the main halyard; it is thus possible to hoist away hand-over-hand to get the main as high as one feels inclined, and then crank away on the winch to set it up taut. After about 15 or 20 minutes of sailing, the halyard stretches a trifle, allowing a little slack to come into the luff. One crank on the winch handle, which has been left in, stiffens the luff again.

There are those who will observe wisely that a sliding gooseneck and a downhaul is the more correct apparatus for achieving this result. This may be so, but compared to the *Rigadoon*'s arrangement, it seems like additional paraphernalia and expense. For those who say that retightening a luff by cranking on a halyard is tough on this piece of equipment, it must be pointed out that the line in question has done a lot of work and come a long way, without showing any appreciable wear, and has not yet been end-for-ended. Any fuzziness on the halyard appears to have been caused by the grip of the self-tailer.

Self-tailing winch used for all-rope main halyard. When this picture was taken, this 3-strand spun Dacron halyard had seen 23,000 miles of use. (Carl Moesly photo)

Another advantage of all-rope halyards, especially with aluminum spars, is that being of a larger diameter than wire, they are far less likely to jump a sheave. And they are noiseless: there is none of this slatting or tinging business. External halyards should always be tied off to the shrouds so that they don't chafe against mast, spreaders — even each other — when a vessel is anchored. A combination of a slack wire halyard and an aluminum mast is a first-class arrangement for keeping ourselves and all hands aboard every other boat in the bay awake. All that's needed with internal halyards when the ship is at anchor is that they be set up taut. Half the halyard is inside the mast. No flapping, no windage, no noise.

The beauty of an all-rope halyard leading to a self-tailing winch is that it completely does away with the necessity of a rope-to-wire splice (along with its measure of doubt) or an eye-to-eye join (and the limit it imposes on the wire's travel). When hoisting a sail with an all-rope halyard, it is possible in the final stages to wind away on a self-tailing winch using one hand for the ship and the other for yourself. There is still a halyard end to coil and stow, however, which is something that's not necessary with an all-wire halyard winch.

An external mainsail halyard frequently will chafe the foreside of a tapered mast. An untapered mast, with a sensible projection of halyard sheaves fore and aft, will give halyards a clear fall, and, as a result, be far less prone to chafe. Not so with a tapered mast. It is seldom that a masthead sheave projects far enough forward to prevent an external halyard from wearing away the protective coating (varnish or paint if the mast is wood; paint or anodizing if metal) from the surface of the spar at the point the mast starts to taper. To avoid this circumstance, some spar companies install their masthead sheaves at an angle. A typical arrangement is a sheave box containing four sheaves (two forward and two aft with a fore-and-aft separation). This box locates in a slot so angled that the aft "port" sheave is positioned exactly over the mainsail track and the forward "starboard" sheave is directly under the jibstay. Thus the hauling part of the main halyard is led down the forward port side of the mast and is clear of chafing the spar where the taper starts. The hauling part of the jib or genoa halyard is led down the starboard aft side of the mast.

Various types and sizes of sheave boxes for use with internal halyards. (Courtesy Yachtspars)

An external wire halyard can sometimes cause real trouble when it is combined with a bendy, fractionally rigged mast. I know of an instance (and it might be best if I kept the ship's name under wraps) when the working of the vessel's backswept spar caused one of the fixed spreaders of the single-spreader rig to chafe against the mainsail's wire halyard. The wire cut through the aluminum spreader — and over the side went the pole. A strong reason this, for a bendy, fractionally rigged mast to have internal halyards.

Even vessels with masthead rigs are not immune from trouble if their halyards are external and the spars are tapered. When the Whitbread Round-the-World Race fleet reached Auckland in 1977, 11 of the boats had to have their masts lifted out for repairs, and a common reason was the chafing and sawing of wire halyards into spreaders.

It is touted in some circles as being a good thing for light messengers to be rove in the place of halyards that get little use. The idea is to save windage. When the halyard is needed, its end is married to the messenger, hauled up through the block and back down on deck. This is a great scheme aboard a cruising vessel where an extended stay in port (such as owners striking a blow ashore to build up the kitty) is anticipated. It would save the halyards from unnecessary weathering, and possibly from dirt.

As soon as the vessel puts to sea, however, it's a good idea for every halyard to be up there. Sometimes, no matter how we try to arrange it otherwise, there's a lot of work to do at sea. If any piece of equipment breaks, binds, or acts up, it'll be after you've left the bay, not before. In my book, the practice of leaving halyards or anything else to be rove at sea is unacceptable — unless of course a large crew is on

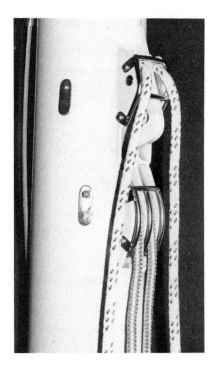

Fractional-rig hounds fitting for rope halyards. Note stainless steel anti-chafe guards. (Courtesy Yachtspars)

tap. That, as long as they're not seasick (a strong, well-rigged ship will stand more than her crew), changes the whole picture.

Whether a mast is equipped with external or internal halyards, there should still be a way of reeving an emergency hoist if needed. There can be many reasons for an extra line aloft. A halyard, chafed from being led wrongly to or from a sheave, might have carried away or suddenly expired of old age. A crewmember might have had an end whisked out of his hand on deck and, before his enthralled gaze, taken to the masthead.

There are many cruising boats with a "just-in-case" halyard rove permanently, and a down-to-earth skipper who cares not a whit for windage or the comments of those who might pass by. Then there's the guy who has his flag halyard rove through a healthy-sized block at the masthead. If the need arises to run up a gantline, he makes the flag halyard fast with a sheet bend to a small eye spliced in the rat-tailed end of, say, a half-inch line, and heaves it up through the block. If he's a seaman who likes to prepare for every conceivable contingency, he does this before leaving port.

Although I'm now an arm-waving rope-halyard advocate, I feel there is one circumstance that calls for all wire, and good wire at that. This is in the halyard of a roller-furling jib where the jib is hoisted independent of the stay. When this system of sailhandling appeared many years ago, it was known as the "Wykeham-Martin furling gear" and featured a light, twisted chain in the jib luff. This was advantageously replaced by 1/19 wire, which happily dealt with both the tension involved in setting up the rig and the torque generated by the furling of the sail.

The halyard of a roller-furling jib must be as strong as the luff wire of the sail. The luff wire, if installed independently, should be as strong as the forestay. In setting up the wire halyard of the roller-furling jib aboard *White Squall II,* I shackled the standing part of a 7/19 stainless steel wire to the foremasthead, a few inches below the forestay. The 7/19 wire was rove through a block shackled to the swivel at the jibhead, back through a block just below the standing part, and down to a well-greased, open-barrel turnbuckle at the foot of the mast. The bottom eye of the halyard was held by a pelican hook located between the jaws of the turnbuckle. The cotter pins holding the top and bottom shank of the turnbuckle in position were finger-tight.

This proved to be a good rig. The turnbuckle — about one-tenth the cost of a winch — was very accurate in adjusting tension. The idea of the pelican hook, the Dacron halyard, and the finger-tight cotters was to enable the turnbuckle to be slacked quickly in an emergency. The hook could then be tripped and the sail lowered. Although we had the sail on and off many times at leisure, there was only one occasion in our 14 years of constant chartering and cruising when it was necessary to get the jib down without delay, and that time the rig worked faultlessly. The swivel at the head of the sail was held about four inches away from the forestay by two hooked fingers of ¼-inch stainless steel rod, which curled, one from each side, over the stay. These fingers slid up and down the stay with the swivel whenever the furled sail was raised or lowered.

Above: *Halyard bitter end fast to mast anchorage with snapshackle and swivel. Note fitted mast boot, downhaul for spinnaker pole fitting, quick-release cam cleat on lower block of boom vang.* **Left:** *Every internal rope halyard should have a figure-eight knot at its bitter end. (Courtesy Yachtspars)*

The securing of halyard ends to pad eyes on the mast or on deck is sometimes given little attention aboard a cruising boat. It's a mighty frustrating feeling to be standing on deck and gazing at the end of a halyard that's floating in the air 20 feet to leeward. I'm one of the ones who knows exactly what it's like. About the only way to retrieve it is to alter course so that the wind will blow it back aboard. And if you're running before the wind, all vanged or guyed out, reaching out with a boathook to try to grab the halyard can be a dangerous business.

The bitter end of a halyard can be made fast by a shackle and swivel to an eyebolt on deck or a pad eye on the mast. Don't forget the swivel. It allows twists in the halyard to be removed easily. An internal halyard should have a figure-eight knot tied in its bitter end so there's no chance of its disappearing into the mast. There should also be locations for the hoisting ends of halyards not in use to snap or shackle onto. I have always seized 1½-inch-diameter rings, of bronze or stainless steel, to turnbuckles, terminal fittings, pulpits, or the like, for the hoisting ends of halyards that were temporarily out of work. If the yachtsman gets into the habit of using the same ring for the same halyard, he'll find it's a great advantage on a dark night.

If an internal halyard is lost inside a mast, it's a little more trouble to replace it than to replace an exterior halyard. Mast rake plays an important part in reeving the new halyard, since the spar must be as plumb as possible. A favorite way of doing this is to effect a transfer of weight from aft to forward to put the ship down by the head. Once this is accomplished, all remaining halyards are tightened, and a "volunteer" goes aloft in a chair to pass a thin weight fast to the end of a light line over the sheave of whatever halyard is being replaced. The weight is lowered down inside the mast to the exit box (which may have to be removed prior to the operation) and the messenger and weight hooked out. The halyard is then married to the messenger. (An easy way to do this is to stitch it end-to-end with sail twine.) The messenger, when overhauled, takes the halyard into the mast, up and over its sheave, and out into the light of day again. It is sometimes also necessary to go through this rigmarole to replace a halyard that was twisted around another one inside a mast.

It is all very easy to tell you to transfer some weight forward and put her down by the head. Such a project, if it entails carrying pigs of ballast, can add up to a lot of toil. Now, I've never had to plumb a mast so that an internal halyard could be rove, but if I were confronted with the job, I'd throw a cocktail party on the foredeck . . . .

DOWNHAULS

A downhaul, a line that goes up with a sail hoisted on a stay or track and can be used to haul the same sail down again when the halyard is released, can be very handy aboard a cruising boat. The extra windage of a downhaul prohibits its use when racing (the system of hoisting headsails in a grooved extrusion makes it impractical in any case). For the cruiser — the fellow who hanks his jib onto a forestay and, when the wind pipes up, scampers back out there to pull it down — a downhaul is worth the tiny amount of extra windage involved.

Aboard my yawl, I had downhauls on both jib and staysail. Lowering away was just a matter of letting go the halyard at the mainmast, and, without moving, heaving away on the downhaul, which was led through a block at the tack of the sail to where I was standing. With the sail down and the downhaul belayed, it was just a matter of passing a few sail ties (or gaskets, if one prefers that terminology) around the sail. In the schooner, the jib was roller-furling, but since both fore and main staysails were hanked onto stays, these sails were equipped with downhauls. This vessel is 70 feet long, with a 60-ton displacement, and she only had one winch (centrally located for the lee jib sheet) until just before we sold her a couple of years back. She was easy enough to singlehand, however, and one reason for this was the downhauls.

I always made a downhaul fast with a small bowline around the first jib hank down from the head of the sail. If the head is hanked to the stay, the downhaul can, of course, be fast to this point. It's all a matter of personal preference, just as long as the downhaul isn't tied to the head of the sail or halyard above the top hank. Otherwise, when the halyard is slacked, the downhaul will pull the head down past the first jib hank, which is likely to twist and jam.

All this hoisting and downhauling can, of course, be done without leaving the cockpit. It matters not whether halyards are internal or external; well-designed turning blocks that fit between flanges located on the mast at deck level are optional equipment with a number of spar companies. The halyards lead through these blocks and along the deck to a winch. Regular blocks, snapped or shackled to eyebolts in the deck, achieve the same result.

The weight-aloft-conscious racing man no longer studs his mast with winches. A halyard frequently leads through a turning block and then passes between the cams of a line stopper on its way to a winch that is bolted to the deck. A sail is hoisted, the lever of a stopper pushed down so that its cam may firmly grip the line, and the winch is free to be used for some other job. The once-clear deck of a racing boat is now a no-man's-land of winches, line stoppers, guides, cam cleats, and tracks.

Everything is a compromise, it seems, especially aboard a cruising boat. While the

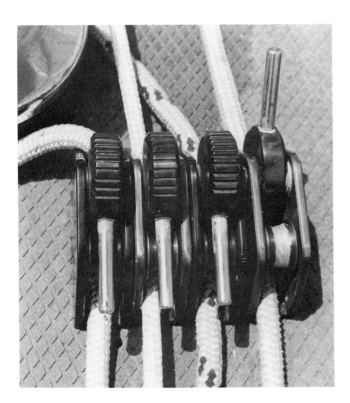

Line stoppers. The three lefthand stoppers are disengaged and allow the lines to run free. The righthand stopper is "taking the weight." (Courtesy Yachtspars)

A toe-catcher if ever there was one! (Courtesy Yachtspars)

rabid racing buff might go into transports of joy over the distribution of all this stuff about his decks, it can extract quite the opposite response from his cruising counterpart. The cruising man wonders where to carry his dinghy and spare gear, both of which contribute to the problem of handling sails from the cockpit.

Well-designed chocks to accommodate a dinghy can allow halyards to run unhampered beneath it from turning blocks at the mast to cockpit winches. The lead of such lines must be arranged carefully to avoid the gear stowed topside on an ocean-cruising boat. A look around any port where cruising boats gather will show vessels with anything from motorcycles to sailboards lashed down on deck. (Aboard my yawl, I carried a 175 cc B.S.A. motorbike on the port side deck, an 8-foot-6-inch dinghy on the cabintop abaft the mainmast, and a few jerry jugs of water on the starboard side — enough to cause a racing man to throw his arms in the air and pour himself another drink.)

Be that as it may, that's the way it is aboard a lot of long-range cruising boats. We are forever bringing gear aboard to make our cruising life more enjoyable, and some of this stuff just has to be stowed on deck, because there's no room for it below. The neophyte cruiser might spare a thought for all this before going overboard on running halyards and downhauls to and from his cockpit.

If the halyards and downhauls of jib, staysail, and mainsail are handled from the cockpit, you have six lines to coil and stow. Having jib and staysail sheets each side, plus the mainsheet, adds another five lines. But again, everything's possible. If you're confident that on the darkest, lumpiest night, you can unerringly do the right thing with the right halyard, sheet, or downhaul without a foul-up, then fire ahead

— you're an exceptional bloke. One little mistake with these lines, though, and your cockpit could look like a pot of spaghetti with someone (you) living in the middle of it.

There are several things that make a man wonder if all this "handle-everything-from-the-cockpit stuff is really worth the candle. Take, for example, a 40-foot cutter. If her cockpit is aft, the distance between its forward end and the mast will seldom be more than 15 feet; if the cockpit is amidships, the mast will be that much closer. Is it worth cluttering up valuable cockpit space with all those lines just to avoid stepping out on deck and traveling those few feet? Of course, getting out of the cockpit, especially in bad weather, means you have to climb into a safety harness, but if you're wearing it and are clipped onto something rugged, you're safe.

On the other hand, one benefit of handling everything from the cockpit is that you shouldn't have to worry about a harness. But if, on a night that's fit for neither man nor beast, you do get a foul-up on deck, you could be in trouble. You'll probably find yourself up there without a harness, sorting out the mess in extreme conditions — just the type of circumstance you've been trying to avoid. Not much chance of that? Not a good enough reason to forgo leading all halyards and downhauls to the cockpit? Maybe not, but having all the halyards at the mast and having to go there to hoist and lower sails is not really a big deal. And it does mean that you are seeing your gear at relatively close range. You'll be on hand to notice any unfair strain on the staysail sheet, hooked around a stanchion top. Or a jib sheet chafing under a sail hank, or caught under a windlass drum, or afoul of the spare anchor in its chocks on deck. All these things have happened to me, and if I dug deep enough, I'd discover a few more.

If, on the other hand, a physical handicap keeps you in the cockpit, that's a horse of a different color. By all means lead your halyards and downhauls to the cockpit, but do it wisely. Ask a good naval architect to tackle your special problem. And when you're finally out there, plan ahead; don't be too proud to shorten down while it's still daylight, so that in the event of a weather change during the night, you won't be in trouble.

TOPPING LIFTS

Every boom of a seagoing vessel should have a strong, adjustable topping lift. A gaff-rigged sail should have a topping lift each side of its boom so that when underway, the windward lift can be set up and the lee one slacked. (More of this later.) Some marconi-rigged stock boats are supplied with a short length of wire crimped to the permanent backstay with a compression fitting. It's there in lieu of a topping lift; the wire, which is of predetermined length, has a snapshackle at its free end, which is clipped to a fitting at the boom end to keep the spar from dropping and braining someone in the cockpit. This incredibly inefficient setup is surely one of the few Rube Goldberg ideas to have been commercialized, and Rube, wherever he is, must be getting a great kick out of it.

Beware of this rig! It may be OK for the weekend sailor, but it's not for the likes of you or me. With the boom end held captive within the limited swing of a short piece of wire, the vessel must be headed directly into the wind whenever sail is hoisted. And furthermore, as soon as the sail is up, the now quivering (possibly threshing) boom end must be unclipped. If, during a sail-hoisting exercise, the vessel falls off and the sail starts to draw, it could be impossible to let go the snapshackle, and an awful job getting the sail down so that the whole business can be started all over again. Dropping sail with this setup can make a believer out of a man, too. If someone isn't stationed aft ready to grab the boom end and snap on the wire, the boom, dropping unchecked, could drive the helmsman into the deck like a tack.

In my book, there are two acceptable ways an adjustable topping lift can be installed aboard a marconi-rigged boat. A wire — I have always used 7/19 stainless steel — is shackled to the masthead and led through a cheek block at the boom end. A terminal fitting is installed on the wire after it is passed about three feet through the cheek block. A handy-billy tackle is located on the boom with its traveling block shackled to the terminal fitting and its hauling part taken to the mast (a small sheet winch instead of a tackle is even better). Some yachtsmen end the wire lift a few feet above the boom end and set their tackle up with a standing part at the boom end, up through a single block on the lift (or a double block on large vessels), down through a cheek block on the boom and so along to the mast. I've always avoided this arrangement because of possible chafe of the blocks to the leech of the sail. There is no question that this method works just as well as having the tackle installed on the boom, however. Of course, it's a matter of personal preference.

The other method of rigging an adjustable topping lift, and about the only one that can be used with a roller-reefing boom, is to shackle a line to the boom end, take it to the masthead, and down to a tackle or winch. Great care must be taken, however, with the lead into the masthead block. The swing from dead before the wind one side to the same angle on the other can give the boom on some vessels a workable arc of about 160 degrees. It depends on how far aft the shrouds are from the mast. A masthead block or sheave that does not give a topping lift a fair lead from one extreme to the other of this arc will chafe the lift.

An all-external lift leading through a swivel block at the masthead can usually take care of this variation. A topping lift with an internal fall must lead into a masthead sheave that is very craftily positioned to avoid chafe from one jibe to the other. That this can be done successfully is evidenced by the $\frac{7}{16}$-inch Dacron internally led topping lift aboard the *Rigadoon,* which still looks good after 23,000 sailing miles.

A topping lift, whether it is taken from the masthead or the boom end, can chafe the leech of the sail. The amount of possible chafe depends in great measure upon the amount of roach in the sail. If your sail has a large roach that sticks out aft of the topping lift, you're going to have to get the sail re-cut to avoid chafe before you go cruising, or rig something to hold the lift clear.

One method of doing the latter is to seize a bull's-eye to the permanent backstay, opposite the point where the roach is closest to the stay when sail is hoisted. The lift is led through a smooth, stainless steel thimble, around which the end of a length of shock cord is seized. This thimble is then slid up the topper to the height of the bull's-eye, where a generous length is rove through the eye and down the permanent backstay. From here on, the positioning and seizing of the shock cord to the backstay is a matter of trial and error, as the length of cord needed varies from boat to boat. The whole idea is for the thimble to be under a small (but sufficient) amount of strain from the shock cord when the sail is hoisted, so that the lift is held clear of the roach. The cord must be taken down the backstay far enough (possibly 12 or 15 feet) so that enough stretch is available for it to render through the bull's-eye when the sail is eased.

Another system of keeping tension on a topping lift, and one that is suitable when a large roach is no consideration, is to seize one end of a three- or four-foot length of shock cord to the lift a few feet up from the boom end. The topping lift is slacked away a couple of feet (again, this differs from boat to boat) and the other end of the shock cord is seized on. Thus, whenever the topping lift is set up, this piece of shock cord is under tension. When sail is hoisted or eased and weight comes off the lift, the cord takes up the slack and the topper cannot chafe the sail. This method will work with a wire lift, too, if the wire is 7/19. A boom that continues a foot or more beyond the sail clew, combined with a masthead crane that has a generous aft projection, means that a topping lift, if led to or from both boom end and crane, is just that less likely to chafe the sail. Every little bit helps.

Gaff-rigged vessels have their own special problems with chafe, and if a lot of forethought is not devoted to this, the cruising yachtsman can find himself replacing equipment long before he'd originally planned. Topping lifts and lazyjacks are the perennial chafers of gaff sails. It is usual for the boom of a gaff sail to be rigged with two topping lifts, one on each side; when the vessel is underway, the windward lift takes the weight while the leeward one is eased. When tackling the job of rigging topping lifts for a gaff sail, care should be taken in choosing the points on both boom and mast where the lifts are secured and led. If the topping lifts are led to a band or tangs on the mast too high above the point where the gaff jaws rest when the sail is fully hoisted, an unfair amount of chafe can occur as the gaff presses against the lift when the sail is eased, even though the lift is slacked. A point immediately above the gaff jaws is a good choice for a strong mast band equipped with lugs from which topping lift blocks may be hung.

The lifts can be shackled to the same point on the boom where the mainsheet is fast. A band, with a bail for sheet blocks and a lug each side for port and starboard topping lifts, can be bolted around the boom two or three feet from the end. (This distance varies with the length of the boom.) The lifts can be 7/19 wire, leading through blocks on the mast above the gaff jaws and shackled to a line (or rope-to-wire splice) that leads down the line of either port or starboard shrouds to a winch. Alternatively, the wire can carry on down until a few feet above the deck, out near the rail, where it hitches onto a luff tackle (see Chapter Five). On smaller vessels (35 to 40 feet), a good, ½-inch Dacron line with neither tackle nor winch will probably be sufficient for each topping lift. It all depends upon the weight of the boom.

The system I've usually been shipmates with involves a single block, shackled to the top of each wire lift some three feet from the mast band. The mast band has a double block each side. A tackle is rove by passing a line up from forward through the outboard sheave of the double block, down through the sheave in the single block, up through the inboard double-block sheave, and securing it to the tail of the single block. The topping lift is set up or slacked by hauling or easing the line falling down the line of the shrouds, from the outboard sheave of the double block. It is belayed on a pin in the sheer pole.

When securing the topping lifts to the boom, be sure that when the sail is furled, the gaff lies along the boom with its peak projecting a foot or so between and past the lifts. This way, the gaff is always controllable; when either setting or dropping sail, it is confined within the lifts. If the gaff is very short, making sail and trying to coax that gaff up between the lifts — especially in a seaway at night — can improve the language of a saint.

A time-honored (and easy) way to furl a gaff-rigged sail is with the use of lazy-jacks, which are light lines hung from each topping lift and attached at specific points along the boom. Correctly rigged lazyjacks should be of such a length that when the lifts are set up, the jacks are taut. When a lift is slacked — such as on the lee side of a gaff sail when a vessel is underway — the lazyjacks on that side automatically slack, too. When the sail is lowered, it falls into the lee jacks, and this can be a great assistance in controlling and furling the sail, especially when short-handed.

A way to rig lazyjacks is to carve two pear shapes out of a couple of pieces of hardwood that are 1½ inches thick, two inches wide, and six inches long. Rasp out a groove about ⅛ inch deep and the same width around each of the two-inch ends. Drill three equidistant half-inch holes through each block from one 1½-inch side to the other, at right angles to the groove. A wire or rope (this must be of the same

Commercial all-sail oyster dredger with lazyjacks on jib and mainsail. Jib lazyjacks are rove through a "spectacle" iron (out of the picture, aloft) that rides on the outer headstay and has its own halyard. Main lazyjacks are four-legged. Note double bobstays, mast hoops, pole mast, block-and-tackle halyard. (Ralph Naranjo photo)

material as the topping lift) is laid in the groove and spliced tightly around each of these "camels," leaving a tail about a foot long. This tail is spliced into the lift about halfway up.

After all this you have two lifts with these pieces of wood (you can jazz them up with sandpaper and varnish) hanging from them. The lazyjacks are rove by passing a piece of ⁵⁄₁₆-inch line, or whichever size is decided upon, through each of the holes in the camels. From a point on the boom a couple of feet forward of where the lifts are secured, lead a piece of line up through the top half-inch hole in the camel and down to the same side of the boom just aft of the gooseneck. The distance remaining between these points on the boom (and this, of course, differs from boat to boat) is then apportioned so that the next lazyjack, which is led through the middle hole, and the last jack, which occupies the bottom hole, are an equal distance from each other.

When the lines are rove through both camels and cut to length, this gives six lazyjacks a side. When the topping lifts are set up, each lazyjack should be drum taut. Smaller camels with fewer holes than those described can be used; it depends upon your sail area. Three-hole camels giving six lazyjacks each side are adequate for a 1,500-square-foot sail. Lazyjacks for smaller gaff sails are sometimes spliced independently into Dacron topping lifts or hung off from the lifts by small loops of line that do the same work as camels.

The points where lazyjacks secure to the boom can be eyebolts, tangs, or holes in a long batten screwed to the top of the boom. If the latter method is used, a port lazyjack, for example, would be led through a hole in the batten from the port to the starboard of the boom and be held by a wall-and-crown knot; a Matthew Walker or a figure-eight can be used on the starboard side. The same, in turn, applies to the rest of the jacks.

The whole idea of having the batten screwed along the top of the boom, rather than the bottom or the sides, is so that if a sail is caught by the lazyjacks when lowered, it will be rolled right up *on top* of the boom when the lifts are set up. If, for instance, the lazyjacks are fast to points beneath the boom, the sail can be jammed against the sides of the boom when the lifts take the weight. If this happens, the sail can be difficult to furl. A track to take slides along the foot of the sail can, of course, be installed on top of the batten. In this case, the batten should be well glued to the boom and through-bolted at various points. Every commercial gaff-rigger I sailed in or commanded had foot stops (a separate length of line at each foot eyelet), which were tied in a reef (square) knot below the boom. The ends of each foot stop were always stitched back to their own part for the sake of neatness and the stops were tied at such a length that when the sail was hoisted, the bolt rope along the foot was just clear of the batten to which the lazyjacks were fastened.

In some circles it is popular to festoon the topping lifts and after shrouds of gaff-riggers with baggywrinkle or sheepskin chafing gear. Sometimes a marconi-rigged cruising boat, run by a skipper with an ocean-cruising gleam in his eye, will have clumps of this stuff all over his rigging. While sheepskin is far better for yacht chafing gear than baggywrinkle (which can wear the sail incredibly), any of these clumps of anti-chafe equipment catch all manner of dirt and dust, and when wet, they can really mark up sails. But dirt is better than holes. It must be said, however, that twin lazyjacks on a gaff-rigger equipped with sheepskin chafing gear will not make holes.

While still on the subject of chafe, we might as well talk about gaff jaws. Nothing, but nothing, can chomp into a mast quite like the jaws and butt of a gaff. In days of yore, consistent and liberal applications of tallow kept gaff chafe at an acceptable level, but for all that, it was still a major problem. Since those days, the tallow treatment has waned in popularity, there being a scarcity of yachtsmen who take the heating of a pail of tallow on the galley stove and the scampering aloft to slosh it over a chafed mast as the perfect way to start a day. Quite apart from the mess it makes, have you ever smelled this stuff? I remember a trip when we were sort of jury-rigged for food, and I was so hungry I could have chewed a clump of baggy-wrinkle, and the cook of the day served up eggs *fried* in tallow. . . . No, tallow is out; there is no place for tallow aboard a modern cruising boat.

Nor is there a place for the nice, traditionally curved gaff jaws, parrel balls, and pivoting butt-piece. If you have a wooden mast aboard your gaff-rigger and you don't want your dreams disturbed as pieces of wood are chewed out of the spar, think about sending the gaff aloft cn a length of stainless steel tube. The tube, a

This gaff has a leathered saddle and parrel balls. Luff of sail is seized to hoops. Note strong-looking fife rail, ratlines flush with fore and aft sides of shrouds, sheerpoles, and belaying pins. (Ralph Naranjo photo)

loose fit around the mast, should be slightly bell-shaped at top and bottom and be at least one-and-a-half mast-diameters in length. A regular gooseneck fitting on the gaff locates between two strong lugs welded to the outside of the tube, halfway along its length. The throat halyard shackles to another lug welded to the aft, top of the tube (above where the gaff gooseneck locates). This tube — call it a saddle, a traveler, a throat-pipe, any name you like — does not need to be leathered. As long as the inside of the tube is smooth and the ends are belled, that is sufficient.

If you're cranky (like me) about your gear, you'll still use something to prevent chafe on the mast where the tube lies when sail is fully hoisted. I prefer vertically placed ironwood strips. (Their distance apart varies with the mast's diameter.) These strips should be tapered top and bottom for appearance, and also to enable the tube to slide up without catching; they should also be well bedded to the mast with a compound such as polysulfide. Don't ever tack sheet metal around the mast where the gaff jaws rest; it invites rot. A steel mast is excellent for gaff rig, since a strong track to take a gaff gooseneck and sail slides may be welded to the spar. There's just no chafe at all with this setup.

When hoisting a gaff sail, send the throat and peak up horizontally. If only one person is hoisting, which means hoisting a little on one halyard and then a little on the other, always keep the throat a bit higher than the peak. Always set up the throat first (if you set up the peak first, you'll never get the throat tight). When lowering a gaff sail, ease the throat first and keep the throat below the peak as sail comes down. If the peak is eased before the throat, or the peak gets below the throat, the gaff butt or saddle can be jammed against the mast and you'll probably have to end up hoisting away on the peak before the throat will come down.

Lazyjacks are a great help in furling a gaff sail. For a "sea-furl," float the throat a foot or so above the gooseneck and the peak about three feet above the boom. Pull the leech into the belly of the sail and swing on the leeward (eased) topping lift. This will tighten the leeward jacks, which will roll the sail up onto the boom and against the windward jacks. Lower the gaff on top of the sail. For a "harbor-stow," float the throat and peak as previously mentioned, pull the leech into the belly of the sail, and, from either windward or leeward, pull the foot of the sail out at right angles to the boom and up over the folds of cloth. If someone else can set up the leeward topping lift at this stage, the lazyjacks will take over the job of holding the rolled sail. The gaff can then be lowered to hold all in place, and she'll have a skin on her like a sausage.

VANGS AND GUYS

There is hardly a sailboat launched today that doesn't have provision for a vang (American), or kicking-strap (British), to be rigged from the base of her mainmast up to her boom at an angle. This blanket statement refers to both stock boats and custom-built sailing machines. It doesn't apply to the Freedom boats with their wishbone booms, because with the wishbone, which splits the angle at the clew with a downward thrust, the sail is automatically vanged no matter how the sheet is trimmed. Someone not usually influenced by the boom-vang trend is the do-it-yourselfer — the guy knocking a boat together in his backyard. Chances are that this

Vang effect of a Freedom's wishbone booms is seen easily in this picture. (Ralph Naranjo photo)

bloke's got it all figured to carry his dinghy on deck just aft of the mast (the best position), which pretty well cancels out rigging a vang in that location.

Vangs appeared in sailing dinghies and small open classes before World War II. (I remember, as a boy, seeing one on an Australian 18-footer and being greatly intrigued by it.) The idea of setting up a tackle from a point along the boom to the foot of the mast is to keep the boom end down and so keep the mainsail from twisting as the sail is eased. Block-and-tackle vangs as well as the powerful, easily adjustable hydraulic vangs have now been popular in larger vessels for years. When rigging a vang, it is an advantage for the boom to be short, and high above the deck; the recommended angle of 45 degrees between the foot of the mast and the boom-vang location puts this point well along the boom. The smaller, more oblique the angle between boom fitting and vang, the more strain there is on the vang location at the foot of the mast and the gooseneck.

If, when a boom is eased, the sail begins to flog (and this happens), enormous jerking strains are transmitted via the vang to the mast and rigging, so there must be provision for immediate release of the vang. A short boom can usually handle this (even if the mast objects), but the leverage of a long boom on the vang's location point can, in some cases, break the boom. Some vangs can be released from the cockpit by flicking the hauling part of a block-and-tackle vang out of cam cleats or lifting the cam of a line stopper. With hydraulic vangs, a release of pressure will do the trick.

There is no doubt that a craftily tensioned vang makes a sail set better; in some instances, to race without a vang, to sail without being able to tension it for prevailing

Left: *Welded-on vang fitting on keel-stepped mast. Note eye for boom downhaul on strengthening web between vang-plate and mast, pop-riveted flanged trysail track, sheave for internal halyard to lead up to a winch.* **Right:** *Vang fitting at base of deck-stepped mast. (Courtesy Yachtspars)*

Block-and-tackle boom vang. (Courtesy Yachtspars)

conditions, is to lose the race. The present-day vang setup means that you don't have to be adjusting things continually. The boom can be eased or brought in and the vang will do its job faithfully all the while, and as long as the sail is not allowed to flog as mentioned above, the vang will make all the difference to the ship's performance without placing an unfair strain on mast and rigging. Weekend yachtsmen have every reason for being vang-conscious: even when "cruiser racing" home from a yacht club picnic on Sunday, having a vang (and knowing how to use it) can make a difference to their showing alongside other boats. For ocean cruising, though, it couldn't matter less; I say, leave vangs for the racing boys. Once an ocean cruiser's mainsail is up and drawing, and the boom, foreguy, and topping lift are set, the rig might not be touched for 24 hours or a week — or more. It's just not necessary to have the same, ever-available vang setup as that sported by the weekend racer or "cruiser-racer."

If you want to rig your boat safely and sensibly, and take her cruising for years, and you feel you must have a boom vang set up in what has become the approved manner as described above, then more power to you; have at it, mate. You'd better be pretty light on your feet in a wind change, though; an untended vang holding down a flogging sail can sometimes, in a very short period of time, cause real damage.

I've never had room for a vang, even if I had wanted one. The cabintop of my yawl was specifically designed so that an 8-foot-6-inch dinghy would fit snugly between the mainmast and the doghouse, so there was no way a vang could be installed. I would, instead, rig a boom guy to do the work of a vang.

A guy — preventer is another name for it — is a line or wire led forward or aft from a boom or pole end to assist in positioning the spar. A boom or spinnaker pole guyed fore and aft and held by its topping lift will, if thus rigged, usually behave itself. Our boom guy on the *White Squall* was a length of ¼-inch, stainless steel 7/19 wire, shackled to a lug on the boom end fitting a few inches forward of the double-sheave mainsheet block, which hung from a bail on the end of the boom. The wire was 12 feet long; the boom, 14 feet. The free end of the wire was shackled to a rope tail of ⅝-inch Dacron. When not in use, the guy was led along under the boom and turned up on a pin at the gooseneck.

At sea we used it all the time, even when close-hauled. My mate, Doug Duane (a tailor of stainless steel), made up a couple of mighty stainless cleats, which bolted through the side decks near the after shrouds, close to the rail. Backing blocks below decks distributed the load. Originally, these cleats were for springlines, but they proved ideal for our boom-guy-vang setup. Our system was to get the vessel on course and ease the mainsail a little more than necessary. The rope tail of the boom guy was then belayed around the cleat on the lee side. As the mainsheet was hove in, the weight would come on the wire guy and the boom end would walk on down, tightening the leech and taking the twist out of the sail. After we'd set up the topping lift, that boom would be on its best behavior; it was going no place. And it's nice to have a boom set up rigidly; if the mainsheet, foreguy, and topping lift all come from the boom end, it's easy on the spar. There is no point along the boom — a third or midway from the mast — taking any unfair strain. You've got to have a strong gooseneck with this rig, but the gooseneck on a cruising boat should be strong anyway.

Close-hauled or reaching, this system worked well. When running, the foreguy was led outside everything, up forward to a block on the gammon iron, and then back to the samson post where it was made fast. We used to debate the idea of leaving the wire guy on the big cleat so as to still keep the boom end down, and rigging another guy to lead forward, but we were all talk and never got around to it. We just didn't like the idea of vanging the beautifully varnished, 4½-inch, solid fir boom down to the cleat from a point, say, one-third or halfway along the spar.

We used the same setup on the schooner's main boom and were very happy with it. We couldn't have fitted a regular vang anyway; a big skylight was in the way. In any case, I did consider that the *White Squall II*'s main boom of 28 feet was too long for such shenanigans. Instead of making fast to a cleat just inside the rail, we would lead the vang-guy to a pin rail in the bulwarks that was "part of the ship." It needed to be, too; there was a mighty lot of weight on it at times.

I used to dodge any suggestions of vanging down from a point along the schooner's main boom in much the same manner as with the yawl (at such times you become very busy pouring drinks, or you become deaf). These tactics were highly successful until the time my wife shot me down with a present she brought back to the Virgin Islands after a trip to New York. The present was a rubber snubber of a size I'd never before seen, and she produced it from her bag with the air of a conjurer as soon as she got back aboard. She handed it to me and the conversation went something like this.

"Hmm . . . is it for me or the ship?"

"Both of you; I think of the two of you together."

"Oh . . . that's nice."

"Do you like it?"

"Yeah, oh yeah, it's great."

"You don't *look* as if you like it."

"Oh, but I do. It's just that our main boom is a pretty big one." (And, I'm thinking, mighty hard to replace.) I would have given an arm and a leg right then for a talk with the guy who sold the thing to her.

Minine didn't get a chance to see her famous vang in action for a week or so, until we were broad-reaching down the northern side of Tortola from Gorda Sound in the British Virgins. It was a "brochure day," and we were sliding along at eight or nine knots. We had a charter party aboard, too, and they watched me setting up the great, black piece of rubber with intense interest. I slid it between the foot of the mainsail and the boom about a third of the way along the spar, and from the two eyes of the snubber, took several turns of half-inch nylon down at an angle to the pin rail, just like they do in the magazines.

It was shortly after this that we saw the sharks — the biggest sharks we'd ever seen. They first became visible ahead and a little to windward as two large black fins cutting back and forth through the water. I thought at first from the size of the fins that we'd stumbled upon a couple of killer whales, but they proved to be sharks, all right, huge sharks, and they were feeding. Our party, cameras at the ready, gathered along the starboard side as we altered course a trifle to windward so as to pass close by.

The two huge fish were tearing at a great ball of minnows, which had huddled together in their thousands under the mistaken impression that this tactic was the safe one. We passed right over the top of one shark and had a good close-up view of all this, and as the ball of tiny fish was on our starboard side, Minine, at the wheel, gave the helm a touch in that direction to round the ship up a little and give all aboard a prolonged view of what was going on.

The mainsail luffed with a thunderous shake, followed by a brraannggg . . . a sound never before heard aboard the good ship *White Squall II*. The rubber boom vang was no more. My heart, which was branggging away all on its own, settled down as soon as I'd sighted along my precious Sitka spruce boom and run my hand lovingly where the vang had been. All was well. Now, I'm not known for my ability to say or do the right thing at the right time. Others can, but not me. This time, though, for the first time ever, I didn't flub a line. With one hand on the boom and the other clutching half of the rubber boom vang, I went on the air.

"Our beautiful present . . .," spoken to the boat along with much sorrowful head-shaking.

My bride, wide-eyed at the wheel and back on course once more, couldn't get over the terrible thing she'd done. (I mean, it's one thing to give a guy a present; it's quite another to go and break it.)

"The salesman must've sold you a faulty snubber, Cookie."

"That's right! He'll never see me in his store again!"

The next half hour or so was spent very satisfyingly by all hands (the charter party applying themselves wholeheartedly to the task) on a hate session directed at men in marine stores who sell faulty rubber snubbers to the wives of sailors: they should be ashamed of themselves, the whole lot of them!

The foreguy or vang on the boom of a gaff sail can be rigged in the same manner as its marconi counterpart; the gaff, however, demands its own specialized treatment. No matter how a gaff sail is trimmed, the gaff will sag farther to leeward than the boom. By overtrimming, the area of sail from immediately below the gaff jaws and extending across the sail to the leech and thence to the peak can be made to draw, but this puts the main boom farther inboard than is desirable and often causes weather helm.

The trick, then, is to be able to control the gaff on a vertical plane and keep it parallel to the boom. This is another thing that's easier said than done. On a single-masted vessel — a gaff-rigged cutter or sloop — a line is secured each side at the peak of the gaff. These lines change names with the tack or jibe of the vessel. The line to windward becomes a vang and the one on the lee side of the sail sometimes sees use as a foreguy. To take the twist out of a sail, to bring that gaff back above the boom, it is necessary to lead the vang to the windward quarter. Here it can be secured to the hook of a double block with a blackwall hitch (or better yet, a double blackwall). This four-part tackle is set up with a bit of huffing and puffing, or, to make hard work easy, is led to a winch.

Aboard some vessels, the vang is a wire with a terminal fitting or spliced eye in the free end, and the tackle is shackled or snapped onto this. The lee wire, when used as a foreguy, has a rope tail secured to its end in the same manner as on a boom vang. A lot of weight comes on a vang led from the peak of a gaff, so make sure all your gear aloft is in first-rate condition before electing to control your sail in this manner. Again, it's a matter of leverage; the wider the stern of your ship, the farther up to windward the tackle can be taken and the angle between peak and vang increased. The farther a sail is eased, the greater this angle becomes and the less difficult the gaff is to control. Aboard a narrow-sterned vessel, it can be impossible to vang the gaff over when close-hauled, because the angle between gaff and vang becomes almost nonexistent.

These wires or lines led to the peak of a gaff really come into their own in light weather. The thrashing around of a gaff in an ocean swell, when there's not enough wind to keep the spar quiet, can be felt throughout the whole ship. A big, light gaff topsail (see Chapter Eight) can work wonders in taming a gaff under these conditions, but so can a vang and foreguy. The vang is set up from its usual position on the windward quarter and the foreguy (which, when not in use, is belayed at the gooseneck) is led outside the lee rigging to the eyes of the ship.

Aboard a schooner, ketch, or yawl, a vang from the peak of the forward gaff sail (foresail on a schooner, mainsail on a ketch or yawl) can be led to a block on the after mast, as near as possible to the height of the peak. The fall of this vang is usually led to a pin in the gooseneck or fife rail below this block. This is an easier way of taking twist out of a gaff sail than setting up a vang to windward, and there is nowhere near as much strain on the gear — especially on the peak halyard.

With this arrangement, it is not a bad idea to still have another line each side made fast at the peak. This may sound like a lot of string, but if a foreguy is to be set up in light airs, there is no option but to have these lines. A vang from the peak of a gaff to an after mast, plus a foreguy set up like a banjo string, can save the gear from chafe occasioned by the gaff's thrashing around when there's not much wind. It can also prevent what wind there is from being shaken out of the sail and make life aboard just that much more peaceful.

SHEETS

The number of parts (total of the pieces of line running block to block) to a mainsheet depends upon several factors: the size of the mainsail, the length of the boom, the position of the sheet blocks on the boom, and the size of the winch (if any) that's used to handle the sheet. This last, of course, has a direct bearing on the mechanical advantage of a mainsheet. (Mechanical advantage in this case depends upon the amount of power needed to be applied to the hauling part to achieve a given result.) If the vessel doesn't sport a mainsheet winch and has a 900-square-foot mainsail (as we had aboard the *White Squall II*), she'd better have at least a 7-to-1 purchase. On the other hand, if your cruising boat has a high-aspect-ratio rig with, say, a 350-square-foot main and your sheet is on a bail at the end of your boom (which will be short), you're home free with a 3-to-1 purchase if you've got a good-sized winch. If there's no winch and good old Norwegian steam heaves the sail in, you'll probably be happier with a mainsheet of four or even five parts.

If the mainsheet does not come from the boom end — and many don't these days — a four- or five-part tackle plus winch almost certainly will be necessary. Some cruising boats, with the end of a boom positioned directly over the center of the cockpit (where a sheet would be in the way), have their mainsheet taken from a

Fixed mainsheet boom anchorage. Good-looking, large-sheave blocks. (Courtesy Yachtspars)

block that is snapped or shackled to a bail on the spar as much as a quarter or a third of the way along toward the mast. In many cases, the sheet is led to a block secured to a sliding car that is located on an athwartships track on the deck or cabintop just forward of the main hatch. The hauling part of the sheet leads to a winch. Such a mainsheet can interfere with the rigging of a boom guy. For instance, if a guy is to be rigged from the boom end forward when the sail is eased, this guy must be dipped around aft of the mainsheet after a jibe, or, alternatively, there must be two guys leading from the boom end, one along each side of the mainsheet.

Adjustable mainsheet boom anchorage. (Courtesy Yachtspars)

Mainsheet on traveling car. Purchase 4-to-1. Note unfair strain being imposed on coach-roof fitting by single block. Should this fitting be repositioned with its clevis pin 90 degrees to the direction it occupies in the picture — and a twisted shackle used to line up the block? What would you do? (Courtesy Yachtspars)

The farther toward the mast a mainsheet is attached, the more power it takes to get the sail in; it's a simple matter of leverage. Double-ended mainsheets are popular in some circles; I had one on my yawl more than 30 years ago and was quite happy with it. This sheet is commonly rigged by hanging a double block from the boom and installing a single block to a traveler on the cabintop or deck beneath. There is also a single block each side, usually well outboard. The tackle is rove by passing the mainsheet through one outboard block, up over a sheave in the double block, down through the single block on the traveler, up to the double block again, and finally down and through the other outboard block. The sail is trimmed or eased by heaving or slacking the sheet leading from either of the outboard blocks. This rig is popular because a mainsheet end is available on either side of the cockpit and because you don't always put wear and tear on the same part of the sheet when close-hauled.

The best mainsheet rig I've ever seen for deep-sea work, and one that completely does away with a traveler, while at the same time does the work of a boom vang on anything up to a close reach, is the one sported by the *Rigadoon*. As can be seen from the photograph, there are actually two separate mainsheets coming from the same bail at the boom end; the purchase of each is 5-to-1. In the picture, the leeward mainsheet is doing the work of a vang, while the windward sheet positions the boom.

This means that the cruising sailor doesn't take up precious dinghy stowage space by rigging a vang to the foot of his mast, and he doesn't have a traveler with its sliding car and positioning tackles cluttering up his deck or cockpit. This rig is really appreciated when jibing in a breeze of wind. To jibe, the lee sheet is steadily overhauled until it's hove down short — in much the same position as shown in the photo. The windward (soon to be leeward) sheet is brought in until the stern passes through the wind, at which point the lee (soon to be windward) sheet is eased and the sail jibes. This sheet continues to be slacked away as the now-leeward mainsheet is brought in until, once the boom passes over its deck block, it takes over the job of easing the boom out. It's a very smooth operation.

This rig isn't for the racing man or even the weekend sailor; even while tacking, there's a bit of fiddling around with each mainsheet, but after having spent a few days and nights sailing with this gear, I came away sold. For ocean cruising, it's way ahead of anything I ever used.

Rigadoon*'s mainsheet makes jibing a joke. (Carl Moesly photo)*

Above left: *Strong, fixed sheet lead installed on angled block. (Ralph Naranjo photo)* **Above right:** *Sheet lead on sliding car. (Ralph Naranjo photo)* **Left:* *"Bonnet" lead for headsail sheets. (Courtesy Yachtspars)*

Pay close attention to the lead of the sheets from your various headsails. Does the Yankee sheet chafe under the main boom when both are eased? If so, you might need to take a short length of line and tie a bowline around the sheet at that point. This line, after being rove through a pad eye on deck, can be used to pull the sheet a few inches below the boom. The lead of jib sheets between lifelines is equally important. If a genoa sheet bears against the middle wire of a lifeline on a Sunday afternoon sail, it's hardly worthy of consideration; keep going on that leg for five or six days, and the resulting chafe could be disastrous.

Because of the differing heights of headsail clews, it is almost impossible on a cruising boat to arrange jib-sheet leads so that the line itself is always clear of obstructions. Turnbuckles, stanchions, lifelines, deckboxes, cruising gear (such as jerry cans of water) stowed topside, or the particular type of deckhouse construction on a vessel — these are all potential line-chafers. I've always carried several pieces of ⅜-inch line, ranging in length from one to two fathoms, for use in temporarily pulling a sheet away from an obstruction that might damage it. A handy, mobile piece of equipment is a snatch block with a strong rope tail. The block is placed over a sheet chafing, say, under a boom; the rope tail is led to a cleat, pin rail, pad eye, or winch, and the sheet is pulled clear. This is the best chafe-killer of all.

Braided, prestretched Dacron (or Terylene) is wonderful line for jib sheets. This rope has minimal stretch, and the yachtsman using it knows, after setting up his sheet, that he'll lose very little power through fluctuations in wind strength. With elasticity as low as 2½ percent, nearly all the force of any wind increase will be transmitted to his ship as drive.

Apart from doing everything possible to ensure that no line chafes on anything, the biggest favor a sailor can do his running rigging is to lead it over sheaves of a generous size. While a lot of blocks available today are strong and well designed, quite often the sheaves are of a very small diameter. All this doesn't matter too much where the line is taken to a winch: a powerful winch couldn't care less what the line is led around, a fact I've long suspected of being an influence on the tiny sheaves sometimes touted as suitable for even large-diameter lines.

While the filament (either continuous or spun) of a synthetic line can take the sharp "nip" of a small sheave, it's a whole lot happier when it passes over a sheave of generous diameter. It will last longer, too — make no mistake about that! A big reason the *White Squall II*'s ⅝-inch Dacron mainsheet is still going strong after 18 years is that none of the sheaves that the line passes over is less than 4½ inches in diameter.

All this doesn't mean that the owner of a 35-foot cruising boat should rush out immediately and buy an armful of nine-inch blocks to stud around his ship (like I once did). Instead, he should carefully assess the amount of hauling he's going to have to do on various pieces of running rigging in the normal operation of his vessel. Some blocks he'll use often. *Those* are the blocks he should pay special attention to. The bigger the sheave diameter, the easier it's going to be to achieve something by heaving on a line. If he *really* wants to be a sport, he may want to find blocks a size bigger for all his lines.

All running rigging must be of a large enough diameter to handle easily. I consider that anything less than ½ inch for such lines is too small for an ocean cruiser. This observation will probably cause the owner of any 28-foot, light-displacement job

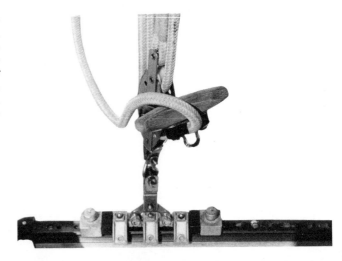

This lower mainsheet block has it own cleat and quick-release cams. Are the horns of the cleat long enough for this size line? Note use of twisted shackle between block and swivel on traveling car. (Courtesy Yachtspars)

currently cruising the world to regard me with a cynical look and a curl of the lip —
too bad. Even though ⅜-inch-diameter line or less may be strong enough, it's just
that much harder on the hands.

I know that when I was a commercial fisherman just after World War II, another
deckhand and I each used to hand-coil 10 miles of rope a day. We were Danish seine
fishing at the time, and the trawler carried a mile-and-a-quarter of ⅝-inch-diameter
seine rope on deck on either side of her wheelhouse. We did eight shots a day —
sometimes more — and at the end of each 12- or 15-hour period, after heaving the
line barehanded off a winch drum and coiling at quite a fair speed, we knew we'd
done a bit of work. Ever since then, I've been a fan of good-sized line. I don't think
our hands could have stood up to even ½-inch line.

When making a sheet fast to the clew of a headsail — be it jib, jib topsail, staysail,
genoa, drifter, or one of the ones with fancy names such as "gennaker" — use a
bowline. It's a great knot for this job. Don't go relying on any high-priced or
foolproof clips or snaps. They just might let you down when you need them most. I
remember a night when the *lashed-together* sister clips that secured the *White
Squall*'s sheets to the clew of the jib shook free in a wind change that put our mainsail in the water in the middle of the Tasman Sea. Our main hatch erupted bodies
that night as the crew fought their way up on deck (no sense going down with the
ship).

It was raining and blowing too hard to tell what was going on, but once we clawed
the mainsail off her and got her back on her feet, she turned willingly enough and
washed along before wind and sea. We were taking part in a race to Australia at the
time and wanted to lose as little ground as possible, but the flogging and flapping
that was going on up forward had to be attended to before we could even think
about reefing down and getting back on course.

We couldn't get the jib down, because after it shook itself free of the sister clips, it
wrapped itself around the outer forestay (a terrible rig, two forestays close together,
and one that shouldn't be foisted even upon a Philistine). And just to demonstrate
what they could *really* do under fire, several jib hanks had leaped across and clipped
themselves onto the outer forestay as well as their own piece of standing rigging. It
was sorted out in the end, with me standing on a "volunteer's" shoulders on the end
of the bowsprit, unwrapping and unclipping things. (It occurs to me now that Sid
must have gotten a trifle damp that night. With 380 pounds on the end of her
bowsprit, our little vessel was down by the head and plunging enough for salt water
to wash over *my* feet from time to time.) Ever since that night, I've been a confirmed
jib-sheet-bowline-tier.

Another thing. Make sure that all sheets aboard your cruising boat are handy to
the helmsman. I know that most long-range cruisers have self-steering these days,
and that being on watch means you'll probably be sitting in the hatchway while
behind you, the wind vane or the iron mike does all the work. So there may seem to
be some excuse for sheets led to a position unreachable from the wheel (oh, well,
we're never at the wheel anyway).

I say let's have all sheets handy to the helm for two reasons. First, if the self-
steering decides to quit, and standing a watch means you have to get out there and

steer the ship, it's nice to be able to play with the sails without leaving the helm or calling someone from below. For the singlehander, this is obviously a must. Second, even if the self-steering is fully operational, there might be cause to take the wheel or tiller to avoid an obstruction — a fish float, debris, another boat, a pod of whales, an island — so it's a big advantage to be able to slack away or harden in, all without leaving the helm.

A headsail sheet led to a track that has a sliding car with either blocks or fairleads for the line to lead through is excellent. The car can be positioned for whatever sail is being used. If the buying and installing of such equipment is financially over the horizon, as it was for me during the first 15 years or so of my cruising life, don't despair. Talk your sailmaker into coming aboard, and discuss, over a few cold ones, likely positions in the deck for installing a few bronze eyebolts. Shackle a block to each of these to lead a sheet through.

To keep a block from murdering the deck all around it in light airs or when a sail is flapping, lead a piece of shock cord from its tail to a lifeline, or use a wide spring of stainless wire from the eyebolt to the block to hold it upright. A method just as effective for taming a deck block is a short piece of rubber hose compressed end-on between the block and the deck. The hose must be cut very craftily to length and have a hole chopped in one side (a ⅜-inch wood chisel is an ideal tool for this job) so that the pin of a shackle can be inserted and screwed in. We used this system aboard my yawl and it never let us down.

Halyards of gaff-rigged vessels are usually rope, and aboard most pleasure or commercial craft, they always have been. In the days of commercial sail, the skipper and mates were as alert to the presence of chafe as a mother hen is to the safety of her chicks. As a matter of course, halyards and sheets were end-for-ended when a little wear showed. In some vessels with parsimonious masters, well-worn parts were sometimes cut out of halyards and another much-used piece of line was longspliced in. (If there's any practice that makes a poor sailor want to reach for his beads and say a few Hail Marys, it's that one.) Longsplices may look right and clever in a book, but aboard a vessel that's out there earning her keep, such a join in a line that's expected to take its fair share of weight is downright dangerous.

I was shipmates years ago with a skipper who, as a young man, shipped away in a five-masted schooner out of Newcastle, Australia, bound for Callao, Peru, with a cargo of coal. By the time they arrived at Callao (where the master of the vessel skipped off with the ship and their wages and left them on the beach), every throat and peak halyard had been end-for-ended *and* longspliced.

In the normal course of events, though, aboard well-run ships, chafe of halyards and other running gear was watched carefully, and lines were end-for-ended when necessary. Often this was done in some quiet little port for no other reason than to give the crew something to do. It was precisely this situation that existed one day aboard a husky ketch that made her way in the world by trading under sail between Australia and New Zealand. An old mentor of mine with the grand name of Francis B. McKenzie is the only performer I know in this scenario, and since Francis has been playing a harp on Fiddler's Green (or drinking up a storm in some other very warm place) for years now, we'll never know who the others were.

Anyway, the ship was tied alongside the wharf in a small port on the west coast of New Zealand's South Island, and Francis, along with the four other sailors in the crew, had been given the job of end-for-ending all throat and peak halyards and the main and mizzen sheets. They were to do this task without supervision, because the skipper and mate, who were brothers, had caught the early morning train to visit their old family farmhouse for the day.

Francis and his satellites were hard at work, and the job was forging ahead, when the pub, just across the railway tracks and the street, opened its doors at nine o'clock. This inspired one of the sailors to come up with the idea of hauling the ends of the lines over there to do the splicing with a fid in one hand and a schooner of beer in the other. Brilliant!

The only work involved in an end-for-ending job, apart from re-reeving, is splicing a new thimble in the bitter end, which, when this is done, becomes the standing part. A neat whipping, done with a palm and waxed thread, takes the place of the old spliced eye. So, pockets bulging with thimbles, sailmaker's palms, needles, thread, and beeswax, and wooden splicing fids stuck in their belts, our heroes traipsed over to the pub, dragging the ends of halyards and sheets with them. Everything went according to plan. The locals, greatly taken with this performance, pressed large tankards of beer upon Francis and his men. The sailors, not to be outdone, bought buckets of beer for the locals and regaled them with sea stories. The splicing and whipping was accomplished in short order. The halyards and sheets were so long that they snaked out the door of the pub, across the road, and over the railway tracks to the ship.

And so the day wore on. It was mid-afternoon when, scuppers under, and dragging the spliced halyard ends with them, the sailors headed for the door. The bartender announced a round of drinks on the house. Francis and the locals blew the froth aside to take a sample of this unexpected bonanza just as the train carrying the skipper and the mate came in and cut all the lines in two.

five

Handy Billies and Winches

A handy billy is a tackle (pronounced "taykel" in some circles) consisting of a double and a single block. Traditionally, the double block of a handy billy had a rope tail and the single block had a hook or shackle. This once-almost-indispensable piece of seafaring equipment now sees less use than in probably all the history of the sport. For those who feel they should have this small, mobile tackle in the bosun's locker "just in case," or for those among us who prefer to own a character boat with deadeyes and lanyards and who like to sweat up the shrouds as in days of yore, the following description of a handy billy might be of interest.

A handy billy is rove with the standing part fast (usually shackled) to the bottom, or "arse," of a single block. This line then leads over one sheave of the double block, back over the sheave of the single block, over the second sheave of the double block, and at this point becomes the hauling part. The tackle is used by hooking or shackling the single block to a fixed point, such as an eyebolt, pad eye, or strop, around a mast or samson post.

The rope tail of the double block is made fast with a stopper knot or rolling hitch to the point to be hauled — typically, halyard, backstay whip, jib sheet, or anchor rode. By heaving away on the hauling part, a mechanical advantage of 4-to-1 (less 10 percent for friction and the weight of block and line) is attained. This friction loss varies with sheave diameter and the condition of the bearings on the block pins; a tackle that can be heard squealing like a couple of alley cats is losing far more than 10 percent friction. Large-diameter line, bearing against the block cheeks, contributes to friction, too. Line used in a tackle should be of such a diameter that it has an unhampered passage through the swallow of a block and is a nice, easy fit in the sheaves.

It is important to understand that a tackle is "rove to advantage" (you're getting the most out of it) when the hauling part comes from the moving block. A tackle is

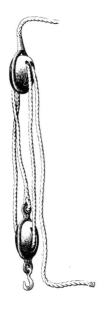

Handy billy (otherwise known as tail tackle or watch tackle). (From The Marlinspike Sailor *by Hervey Garrett Smith, © 1971. Published by John de Graff, Inc.)*

"rove to disadvantage" (you're getting the least efficient use out of it) when the hauling part comes from the fixed block. To calculate the mechanical advantage of any tackle, count the number of parts at the moving block, including the hauling part, and subtract 10 percent for friction and the weight of block and line. It would appear at face value that the more sheaves a block has, the more the mechanical advantage and the less force we have to put on the hauling part to achieve a given result. However, there is a point — especially aboard a cruising sailboat or in any situation where the pull on the hauling part is done by hand — when so much power is lost through friction that a constant adding of sheaves to the tackle is hardly worthwhile. An approximate connection between the weight to be hove in and the stress on the hauling part of a tackle can be found by the following formula:

Where:

S = stress on the hauling part,
P = theoretical power of the purchase,
W = weight being lifted, and
 n = number of sheaves in the purchase,

$\frac{nW}{10}$ = the allowance for frictional resistance.

The theoretical power or mechanical advantage of a purchase is equal to the total number of sheaves in the tackle when the hauling part comes from the standing block. It is increased to the total number of sheaves plus one when the hauling part comes from the moving block. Using the above equation, P = n if the tackle is rove to disadvantage, and P = n + 1 when rove to advantage.

The equation will show you, for example, that a pull of 100 pounds on the standing part of a four-part handy billy, rove to advantage, will produce a pull of about 308 pounds. Another way to say it is that the handy billy is 77 percent efficient, or will produce 77 percent of its theoretical mechanical advantage (given the 10 percent friction allowance per sheave).

With the number of sizes and types of winches available today, most of this block-and-tackle stuff can be left to history and to the few traditionalists who genuinely enjoy fussing around aboard their boats with such equipment. I say *most,* because not all tackles have disappeared from the sailing scene. Mainsheets, for instance, still use tackles, even though the hauling part may lead to a winch. We still have boom vangs and tackles that control the mainsheet traveler, heave down a staysail boom, haul out a sail, and so on.

Winches, though, are the workhorses of the sailing world. Not only do they haul sails up, down, in, out, and any other direction required of them, but winches do other jobs as well. While it was once standard practice aboard some vessels to drop an anchor and heave the stern lines banjo-taut to a quay with the use of a handy billy, the same boat will do the job now with deck or cockpit winches. Good, well-positioned winches are worth their weight in gold and make all the difference to the crew-drill of sailing any vessel.

But an aspiring cruising man shouldn't be coerced into thinking that unless the boat he has in his sights is "down by the head" with winches, she's no good. That's baloney. I sailed my yawl at least 12,000 deep-sea miles before Winch Number One went aboard. It took me years, in fact, to acknowledge that winches were worth more than a second glance. This milestone in my existence dates back to a time in the early 1950s when, during the course of an 8,000-mile Pacific trip, I prowled around the decks of Tom and Anne Worth's *Beyond* in the Fijis. Their 42-foot cutter was built of Birmabright, an aluminum alloy, and they had left England the year before to sail around the world with companions Pete and Jane Taylor.

Beyond didn't have many winches by today's standards; a couple of all-wire halyard winches (the first I'd seen) were on the mainmast, while two small bottom-action sheet winches and one tiny top-action sheet winch graced the cabintop aft of the center cockpit. That was it. Compared with my noble vessel, however, *Beyond* was studded with winches. On this particular occasion, Pete had disassembled one of the wire halyard winches, and I found myself mightily intrigued by its components.

"How often do you do this, Pete?"

"Too bloody often; this is the second time in nearly a year!"

"Hmm . . . and what about those other three, aft of the cockpit?"

"Haven't had to touch 'em yet, thank God!"

I left Pete at his routine maintenance job, feeling that if winches looked after themselves, they might be well worth installing at some future date aboard the good ship *White Squall,* but not winches that a man had to pull down twice a year. Our values change, however; while the average ocean-cruising yachtsman of those years might have been short on winches (most of us couldn't have afforded them, anyhow), it meant he didn't have the job of maintaining them, either. And the maintenance aspect of winch ownership, as will be seen later in this chapter, is something to consider.

So . . . how many winches should we have, what size do we need, and how do we go about choosing them? The number of winches a cruising boat should have depends, of course, on the size of her sail wardrobe. The winch inventory usually goes hand in hand with the depth of her owner's pocket. A cutter would typically carry three winches on her mast: one for the jib(s), one for the staysail, and one for

Winches can do more than one job. (Ralph Naranjo photo)

the mainsail. To the winch-conscious cruising man, this would be the minimum. If he's a sport and carries a spinnaker, he'll probably have a winch for its halyard and another for the pole. He might even have a winch for the main boom topping lift.

Add a mainsheet winch, in addition to four cockpit winches for headsail sheets, and the average cutter is well equipped. If the ship is a ketch or yawl, then a smaller winch for the mizzen sheet can be positioned at the aft end of the cockpit. A schooner can have her foresail or main staysail sheet leading to a winch near the one that handles the mainsheet. Depending on the amount of equipment on deck — and this, of course, varies from boat to boat — these last two sheets could possibly pass through line stoppers, which means that one winch would be doing two jobs.

This is an important point to keep in mind when installing winches: as much as is practical, use them for more than one job. A sheet winch, for example, can be pressed into all sorts of service. As mentioned in Chapter Four, a windward sheet winch can be used to tension a running backstay. Another job for a sheet winch is to set up the rode of a stern anchor to keep a cruising boat end-on to a swell so that she'll pitch instead of roll. With this type of use in mind (winches cost enough; get

This bottom-action winch has its own cleat. (Courtesy Yachtspars)

your money's worth out of them!), it is a good policy to place an eyebolt or pad eye here and there about the decks in strategic positions where a snatch block can be snapped on to give a fair lead to a winch.

I remember a time in the 1960s when in between chapters I was scarfing a piece in the stem of a buddy's boat at Hassel Island, St. Thomas (he'd come off second best in an argument with a coral head). I was diligently shaving away at this and that and hoping people would notice how clever I was, when news came to me that I'd just volunteered to give Don Street and Johnny Nissen a hand to lift the *Iolaire*'s rudder back up into its trunk. The yawl was hauled out on the same slipway, so it was only a few steps to where the big rudder was lying on the ground.

Don dropped a line down through the trunking and we made it fast to the rudderhead. After a great amount of huffing and puffing and calling upon our Maker to lend a hand, the stock was persuaded to enter the trunk. At this point there was a scuffle on deck, followed by a rapid clicking as Don took the line, via his mizzenmast and a snatch block, to a winch. The little red spots Johnny and I had had dancing before our eyes from the strain of holding the rudder disappeared like magic as the line took the weight. No two ways about it; a little effort with a winch by someone who knows what he's doing can make hard work easy.

When choosing winches, write to several winch companies, giving particulars of your vessel and the size of sails the equipment will be expected to handle. Ask their opinion on what size winches you should install aboard your ship. Don't forget to drive home the point that you have a *cruising* boat. A talk with a few knowledgeable salesmen can often help, but make sure the guys know their onions. I remember talking to a salesman at the Miami Boat Show a few years back. He was standing behind a counter displaying many sizes of a name-brand sheet winch. My mouth watering at the sight of all this stuff, I started asking him about construction, power ratios, types of materials used in bodies, pawls, springs, bearings. I also wanted to know about maintenance, lubrication, recommended spare parts for a cruising man to carry — and all he could do was hand me a few brochures. This isn't good enough. Choosing the right winch is serious business, and any person representing a company should *know* about them.

A talk with owners of vessels in your own size range can usually help in your decision. Once you've decided on the equipment you require, a few inquiries about secondhand winches in an area where racing boats live can sometimes bring results. Bigger or better winches, or winches with design innovations, can cause some racing boat owners to replace a winch here and there aboard their vessels. Sometimes a cruising man can stumble upon a bonanza.

However, while we're all in favor of picking up a perk here and there, and recognize that the secondhand winch market is sometimes responsible for landing a winch that a cruiser would otherwise be unable to afford, it must be pointed out that his acquisition might not be without its headaches.

SHEET WINCHES

Sheet winches, in my opinion, should be the first ones aboard. Sails are harder to sheet in than to hoist, so if money is a consideration when equipping your cruising boat with winches, start at the cockpit. A sail being hoisted is usually luffing, which greatly assists the job. A sail being brought in, however, quickly puts weight on the sheet, and the last couple of feet can prove impossible unless the line is taken to a winch or the ship is luffed, which is something we did for years, but it also takes way off the vessel. A tackle can be rigged, certainly — even a tackle on a tackle if the sail is large or there's a bag of wind. This last is gung-ho stuff, though, far better to read about than to do.

While it might be said that any winch is better than no winch at all, we can state in the same breath that the power ratio calculated as suitable for the winches of our particular vessel and our specific needs can really count, too. It is, for instance, far easier for a child or light person to crank in a sail with a winch of 50-to-1 ratio than 10-to-1 ratio. Drum diameter is a compromise. A small-diameter drum supplies more power than a fat drum, but less area on which a rope can grip. No matter how many turns are taken around a thin drum, it's still hard to tail off, especially if there's a lot of weight on the line leading to the winch.

When considering the type and power of sheet winches to install aboard a cruising boat, the strength of the weakest member of the crew should be used as a guide. A winch with a small ratio of, for instance, 10-to-1 may be all that is needed for the 200-pound skipper of a 40-foot cutter to sheet in any sail aboard his vessel, but such a ratio might not enable his 100-pound wife to get in an inch of line once the wind pipes up. Two good two-speed winches on either side of the cockpit make all the difference to the ease with which a vessel is handled and the speed with which headsails are sheeted home.

I remember over 20 years ago being shown the workings of a two-speed winch that Australian Dereck Bayliss was designing and building for the Barient (an acronym derived from the names of the ocean racers *Baruna* and *Orient*) Company of Sausalito, California. By that time I had a few (five) modest single-action winches on my yawl, and I used to preen myself about this from time to time. Until I gazed into the bowels of Dereck's winch, that is. Its insides looked like those of a Swiss watch when compared with the humble workings of the winches I owned. However, I consoled myself: classy and all as it may look, all it did was pull in a line. My winches could do that!

But after sailing on San Francisco Bay with that two-speed winch, I found I was kidding myself. How much easier it was than with the little single-action jobs I had! And when some real weight came on the sheet, all you had to do was start turning the handle the other way and the increase in ratio (the mechanical advantage) was such that the clew of a jib walked in, no matter how hard the wind was blowing.

The two-speed winch has now been around a long time, as have coffee grinders, pepper grinders, and the three-speed marvels. Racing and cruising sailors are well catered to. But aboard the average ocean-cruiser, typically operated by a man-and-woman team, you should not get too sophisticated in your choice of winches, because the more complex the equipment, the more specialized treatment it demands. You might load such a proliferation of gear aboard that most of your precious time is spent keeping it in running condition.

Two-speed winches will do everything needed aboard a cruising sailboat. The second (more powerful) gear must allow the weakest crew member to sheet home the largest sail unassisted. Some winches have a drastic increase in ratio between gears,

Self-tailing sheet winch. (Carl Moesly photo)

maybe 10-to-1 in "first," and, as soon as the handle is wound back the opposite way, 100-to-1 in "second." This means that a sail will come in quickly and easily in the first gear, and very slowly — but, because of the enormous mechanical advantage, very surely — in the second.

In the racing game, this is unacceptable to a lot of skippers, for the tiniest loss of time in any drill can send his chances of winning down the drain. For cruising, however, it doesn't matter at all. So what if it does take an extra 20 seconds to sheet home the genoa? What's the hurry, anyhow? One reason we've shaken free of the rat race and embraced the cruising life is to take things a bit easier. If you ever have to double up people on the crank handle of a winch to sheet a sail in, you've got the wrong winch.

Most winches today are top-action. The once-popular bottom-action winches seem to have fallen by the wayside and are seen less and less. They still have a place

Bottom-action winch on mast. Note angled installation of cleats, figure-eight knots in bitter ends of halyards, deck leads and bull's-eyes, powerful "Norwegian steam" mainsheet. (Courtesy Yachtspars)

aboard, however. I used a small bottom-action sheet winch for the *White Squall*'s mizzen halyard, and it was a great convenience to be able to leave the handle permanently in place. Another job a bottom-action winch is well suited for is heaving down the pendant when slab reefing (see Chapter Seven). The handle of such a winch, when installed on a boom, can be left in the base, to be ready for use. The handle can be prevented from hanging below the boom by a tight strop of shock cord around it and the boom.

WIRE HALYARD WINCHES

All-wire, or reel, halyard winches are worth considering. When deciding on the suitability of an all-wire halyard winch, imagine the worst possible conditions, such as a rainsquall at night and *you* having to use the winch for a quick reduction of sail. Picture the vessel almost on her beam ends and you and the winch on the lee side of the mast. If you think that the wire halyard winch you are looking at will perform faultlessly and safely under those conditions, then it's the winch for you. If you have any doubts, you had better keep looking.

It is important that a wire halyard winch have a good, positive brake, so there is no chance that the handle will fly around and injure someone. It must be possible to hoist a sail with the brake on. And if the person who is hoisting slips or wants a rest, the brake must automatically hold the winch. Beware of the type of winch requiring that a handle be inserted before freeing a pawl, then the brake engaged, and then the handle removed, before the brake can be slackened and sail lowered. This rigmarole is too dangerous.

Racing boats, their owners ever-conscious of the weight factor of equipment, are sometimes fitted with winches that have an aluminum body. Because of the combination of different metals used in their construction, these winches need to be washed inside and out with fresh water at regular intervals to prevent corrosion. This sort of attention is almost impossible aboard an ocean cruiser. Fresh water is at a premium on a small boat and is used only for drinking, cooking, and washing on some voyages, so such a winch may sometimes be sadly neglected.

In December 1979, an American vessel from California arrived in Durban, South Africa, on her way around the world. Aboard were a pair of three-speed winches with aluminum bodies; the working parts included bronze and stainless steel pawls and bearings. Both winches were frozen solid. The winches were manufactured by one of the best-known companies in the business, so the disillusioned skipper, after having an unholy time pulling the equipment to pieces and finding parts eaten away by corrosion, wrote to the firm, asking them what they intended to do about it. He received a reply from the company disclaiming any responsibility and stating that the winches were not designed to be on any vessel where there was the possibility of exposure to salt water and spray. Swallow that in one lump, if you can! What did they think he was going to sail on out there, anyhow? A servile ocean that wouldn't dream of wetting their precious winches?

A lot of old-time winches were sealed, and it was pretty difficult for salt water to get in and create mischief. Most of their present-day counterparts, however, while being many times more powerful, versatile, and pretty (and costly), freely admit "the playful vagrancy of every sportive wavetop." Water is encouraged to get in and get out. So, even though you're prepared to do your part with maintenance (and we'll come to that soon), be as certain as you can that all the metals in a winch that you beg, buy, borrow, or steal can get along well enough to keep from eating each other when the going gets wet.

Unless some exotic new material makes its mark before this book vies for a place on yachtsmen's shelves, this means bronze, chromed-bronze, stainless steel, or Tufnol. All-stainless (that is, stainless body, pawls, springs, gears, and bearings) is a wonderful ideal to aim for and usually gives less grief than bronze winches that have both bronze and stainless steel parts. But it depends on what the individual can spring for. If all-stainless isn't going to break the bank, then have at it, mate; you're in good shape. On the other hand, there is nothing wrong with bronze or chromed-bronze winches; they'll just need a little more attention.

INSTALLATION

The installation of mast winches is something that should be worked out very carefully. One important consideration is that the higher they are, the less weight a user is able to put on them. If a winch is so high that a person hoisting has to *pull down* on a winch handle to sweat up a halyard, the amount of working force is limited to the weight of the user — which is OK if you're a 250-pounder but not the greatest if you weigh in at 95, dripping wet. If a mast halyard winch can be mounted so that when hoisting, a user *pulls up* in the final stages, this is ideal; the average person can apply a whole lot more weight when lifting than when pulling down. The lower position will also gain its share of plaudits from the weight-aloft-conscious crowd.

The weight-aloft-conscious racing man no longer studs his mast with winches: he plants them around the deck and leads halyards and lifts to them via turning blocks and line stoppers. It is impossible to generalize that this predilection is being, or will be, followed by the cruising man. If a generality can be applied, it is that the cruiser seems more "efficiency conscious" nowadays. He expects more of his boat than just her ability to get out there and stay out there; he requires that the lady be able to give a fair-to-middling account of herself under sail, too. If he is following the keep-the-weight-low routine, he might want his halyard winches on deck, which is fine if it doesn't foul up his lounging, living, or stowing space — and if it keeps him happy. Most cruising boats, however, need deck space for dinghy and/or life-raft stowage, ventilators, and hatches — or perhaps their owners still carry halyard winches on the mast merely from habit.

Whenever possible, sheet winches should be mounted where the helmsman can reach them. If a sheet needs easing or cranking in a few inches, it's nice to be able to attend to this without leaving the wheel or calling someone up on deck. Aboard a large vessel with a large crew, this is not really a consideration; two people on watch at all times when underway means that an extra pair of hands is always available. Such is seldom the case with a small cruising boat, however; only one person at a time is on watch.

Most cruising sailboats have a system of self-steering, but even so, it should be assumed when positioning winches to handle sheets that there will be times when a person at the helm will need to trim sails. Even the blithe singlehander who sleeps his or her head off on an ocean passage can fall into a stint of hand-steering at times. In a busy shipping lane, when closing a coast, or when the possibility of a sudden course change is present, the term of a singlehander's wheel watch might be that of "go on and stop on." Having all the winches and sheets within reach at such a time can be very advantageous.

The admonition that all winches must be mounted securely applies especially to winches installed on decks, cabintops, and coamings. They must be part of the ship. Make sure that whatever location is chosen for a winch — be it deck, coaming, cabintop, strongback, or anywhere else — will not expose the structure to a force it may be unable to accept. Winches are built to take enormous strains; a two-speed winch with a 100-to-1 ratio in second gear will pull 4,500 pounds (5,000 pounds less 10 percent for friction) with a stress of only 50 pounds on the handle. Let's assume it's taken that much to get our genoa in, and with winch and jib sheet cheerfully taking the weight, the old girl pokes her nose into the sea and scoops a quarter of a ton

Sturdy, solid winch mount, quarter leads, and stern pulpit (pushpit). (Courtesy Yachtspars)

of water up into the sail. The mast, sail, sheet, and winch might not be wild with joy about this, but they should be able to take it. So should the fastenings holding the winch down, as well as the structure where it's mounted.

A winch mounted on deck should be held down by bolts that pass through a block bridging several beams below, so that the strain is well distributed. Whether the winch sits up on a pad depends on both the lead of the lines or sheets it will be called on to handle and the camber (if any) of the deck. Quite often, when camber is not a consideration, no pad will be needed, since the base below the drum of some modern winches is frequently at least two inches thick. When this figure is added to the inch or so of the bottom of the rope drum, the result is a drum situated high enough to handle lines (such as from turning blocks) at an acceptable angle. Where the deck has camber, it is necessary to have a shaped aligning pad to give the winch base a flat mounting surface.

While the bolts used to hold down a winch will vary in length from boat to boat, their diameter should be of the largest that the mounting holes in the winch base will allow. The bolts should also be compatible with the winch base: bronze if the base is bronze, stainless steel if the base is of that metal. Once the winch is bolted down solidly and bedding compound between winch, pad (where necessary), and deck has been squeezed until no more will emerge, the bolts should be locknutted.

Although bedding compound should never be omitted, no matter what surface the winch is bolted to, it must be emphasized that some cases warrant more attention than others. Water should never be allowed to lie between a metal or wooden deck and any object. A fiberglass deck can take a certain amount of abuse in this respect, but while the deck might not be damaged, water leaking down alongside bolts can play havoc with furnishings, electric wiring, clothes, books — many things. Water allowed to penetrate the foam sandwich or wooden core of some decks can have disastrous results: the core may be saturated slowly, with an unsuspecting owner none the wiser. I like to see a good synthetic rubber compound, such as Caulktex or 3M's 5200, used for bedding a winch to such a deck.

Cockpit sheet winches are commonly mounted on stands that fasten to both deck and coaming. Again, the principle of "stronger than strong" must apply. Wood can be used to fabricate a stand for a small winch, but for a winch of any size and power — which means most winches used today — a metal stand is preferable. A wooden stand takes a lot of (usually) expensive skill to build, is bulky, and is seldom as strong as its metal counterpart.

Small sheet winches are sometimes mounted on the outside of sturdy coamings, but this places great strain on the coamings and the winches can be hard to use. When a vessel is beating to windward, for instance, jib sheets leading to winches mounted on the outside of the lee coamings sometimes demand that the sail trimmer take up a stance with one foot in the cockpit and the other on the ship's rail. A large, powerful winch should never be installed in this manner. Not only is it tough on the coamings, it's also dangerous to use. A strong, cast-bronze or prefabricated stainless steel winch stand with its top bolted to the coaming and its bottom "legs" bolted through the deck to a solid backing plate, which spreads the load below, is the type of mounting a powerful sheet winch needs.

The method of mounting winches on masts or on booms (for slab reefing or

Left: *Drum-type winch bases on an aluminum mast. Note boom-vang fitting, trysail track led nearly to the deck, well-positioned cleats, gooseneck, and sail-slide entry. Also trysail slide entry.* **Below:** *Winch table welded to mast. Holes for winch base are drilled through the wall of the spar as well as the base. The holes in both winch base and spar are tapped to accept stainless steel machine screws. (Courtesy Yachtspars)*

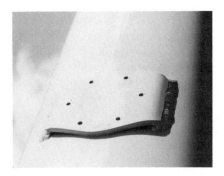

outhauls) depends upon the construction of the spar. The base of a halyard winch should be mounted on a table or pad that enables the winch to stand out far enough from the mast to prevent overriding turns. I like to see winch tables welded to a metal mast when the spar is built (as was mentioned in Chapter Two), but it's not always possible at that point to know the position of your future winches. Fitting a new winch on an existing mast is an exacting job. For a start, a winch should never be installed where the main boom will interfere with its use. If your wife has just given you and your boat a new halyard winch for Christmas, swing the main boom out square off one side and then the other and do some crafty thinking. Does the spot where you want to mount the winch allow it to be used no matter what the boom angle? How about the height and the leads of other winches? Or halyards?

Once the spot is selected, have at it. If the mast is aluminum, fasten the winch table to the mast with stainless steel machine screws. This table may be in the form of a cast pad of aluminum supplied by the manufacturers of the spar and shaped to fit the mast. It may be prefabricated out of aluminum or stainless steel sheet and supplied by the same source. On the other hand, you may have to have it custom-built from stainless steel or Monel (my favorite) sheet.

Tables for wire and rope halyard winches fastened to the wall of an aluminum mast with machine screws. Note nicely angled cleat below forward winch, gooseneck of worm-drive roller-reefing boom on slide with another worm-drive, which regulates height of boom, chain uphaul-downhaul on spinnaker-pole bell, shrouds well inboard to cater to headsail sheeting angle. (Courtesy Yachtspars)

Whatever material is used for the table, there should be a thin gasket of rubber, neoprene, strips of electrical insulating tape, or a compound like polysulfide between the pad and the mast itself. The purpose of a gasket is to discourage any corrosion that might occur between dissimilar metals, such as a stainless table and an aluminum mast. In cases where both table and mast are aluminum, a compound or gasket should still be used — even though both mast and table are anodized or painted. It will pay over the long haul to make every effort to keep salt water out. If the winch table is untreated aluminum, paint it or have it anodized before installing it on the mast, and don't forget the gasket.

Don't fuss around with countersunk machine screws when securing the winch table in its chosen location; use good roundhead stainless steel machine screws that have plenty of meat in the head. A powerful winch on a spar with a large dimension and corresponding thick wall may need six ⅜-inch-diameter stainless machine screws at each end of the table. A smaller winch on a smaller mast demands less.

There are several points worth considering before drilling and threading the holes:

1. Have any other holes been drilled in the mast close to the position you've chosen to mount your winch? Will the strength of the spar be impaired by the addition of the holes you intend to drill? A metal spar is very strong, but it can be

seriously weakened if a series of holes, especially on a horizontal plane, are drilled close together.

2. Where's the electric wiring? This is something the owner of every hollow mast should know. Electric wiring for navigation and other lights is often inside a pipe within an aluminum mast, which is a good arrangement. Make sure, however, that you're not in such an all-fired hurry to get your winch installed that you drill a hole through the wall of your mast and into the wiring. This is the sort of goof you'd have a tough job blaming on somebody else.

3. What length are your machine screws? If your mast has internal halyards, this is a very important question. Overlong fasteners sticking into the interior of a mast will chafe internal halyards. Machine screws need not project into the mast. You can cut a hand-hole in a mast and reach inside to put a nut on each machine screw (or bolt); while this method has been practiced, it makes me very uneasy. I know that a bolt is preferable to a machine screw, but machine screws are undeniably adequate, and nobody can tell me that a hand-hole doesn't weaken the spar. The hand-hole can have a cute little door with a gasket and screws around the edge to close it up, but in my book, that hole's still there and you're better off without it.

4. Are you going to put anything on the machine screws before driving them home? If you smear a little silicone on the threads, the fastenings won't bind, and if they ever need to be taken out, they'll unscrew without argument. The silicone will also provide insulation against corrosion between two dissimilar metals.

Mounting the winch base on the table only requires that short (usually), countersunk bolts or machine screws be used. Again, always use a gasket between the winch base and the table if they are of dissimilar metals; hard plastic, rubber, neoprene, and polysulfide are all acceptable here, as they were as a gasket between table and mast. About the only time a gasket isn't necessary is when a stainless steel winch base is being bolted to a stainless table.

A winch on a wooden mast is usually mounted on a wooden pad that has been shaped to the surface of the spar and glued into place. The fastening of the winch base through the pad and to the mast is achieved variously by long, heavy-gauge screws and/or bolts.

Now, while it's all right to talk about bolts, it must be remembered that a certain number of holes for the purpose of mounting winches or other fittings is permissible, but more than one wooden mast has gone by the board from a weakness induced by holes drilled at its base to install a cluster of winches. If bolting is considered, align the winch base so that two (of the common number of six) of the countersunk holes in the base plate are at the bottom of the mounting pad. The fastenings farthest from the point of strain are the ones that do the most work. Drill your holes through the mast so as to use bolts only in the two bottom holes. Use heavy-gauge wood screws in the other holes.

I have used only screws to mount rope winches on a wooden mast. The *White Squall II*'s solid Douglas fir mainmast is some 12 inches in diameter at its base, so when I installed a halyard winch about three feet above the deck, I first shaped a wooden block and glued it to the mast. The winch base was then secured to the block and mast by six seven-inch silicon-bronze wood screws of a mighty gauge. I did the same with a foremast winch. These fastenings have taken plenty of weight these last 10 years without complaint.

When ordering or building a hollow wooden spar, in addition to ensuring that solid wood is accessible for the installation of sheaves, spreaders, and tangs, you must make certain that the place where a winch will be mounted is even more solid. Always try to use bolts to fasten a winch to a wooden boom. If the fastenings holding a mast halyard winch let go, the winch will fly up the mast, which, startling and all as it may be, is seldom dangerous. But a winch pulling out of a boom and launching itself with tremendous force toward the cockpit can send some unlucky soul into orbit.

On the mainmast of my yawl I mounted three winches: two were the wire halyard winches previously mentioned, and they handled the mainsail and jibs. A single-action sheet winch was installed for the staysail halyard, which was Dacron. The wire halyard winches were mounted on the lower, heavy-bronze gooseneck bands with ⁵⁄₁₆-inch Monel machine screws (I'm a nut on Monel). No fastenings went into the six-by-seven-inch solid Douglas fir mast. The staysail winch was mounted on a bronze plate that was brazed to the upper gooseneck band on the starboard side. Again, no fastenings went into the mast. The mizzen was tiny enough to haul up with one hand behind your back, but after a few years I decided to spoil it with a little bottom-action sheet winch. This was secured to the mizzenmast gooseneck band with ¼-inch-diameter Monel machine screws.

A wire halyard winch should be mounted in the same manner as its rope counterpart, with a couple of additional qualifications relating to location and angle of the wire leading to the drum. A wire halyard winch and a rope winch don't have much in common. A single-speed rope winch has a ratchet incorporated in its design, so that even if a full 360-degree swing of the handle is not possible at all times (such as when mounted as a halyard winch and a boom or sail gets in the way), the sail can still be cranked up. The ratchet makes it possible for the handle to travel up and down through a free arc of 180 degrees or more, depending on the obstruction. Two-speed rope winches have no ratchet; when the handle rotation is reversed, another gear comes into play, and for this reason, they don't see much use as halyard winches. A two-speed winch installed on a mast should have a handle that incorporates a double-directional ratchet. No matter what rotation of the winch is used, a ratchet is thus available.

Wire halyard winches or their handles, however, often have no ratchet, so when mounting such a winch, a prime consideration is a full 360-degree swing for the handle at all times. If the wire halyard is external, the winch can be mounted on a table whose surface is parallel to the mast; the fall of the halyard, usually from the masthead, is given a fair lead with such an installation. When an internal wire halyard is used, the table must have an angle incorporated into its design such that the winch is canted to ensure a fair lead for the wire (see photograph). This is not as important with rope winches mounted on a mast; as previously discussed, it is desirable for a line to lead ''up'' to a drum, and an internal rope halyard leading from its sheave-box to a winch already does so at an acceptable angle.

In all the preceding recommendations on mounting winch tables on masts, I have specified stainless steel fastenings. Stainless steel is the metal most used by spar-makers to fasten tracks, tangs, and spreaders (and everything else) to aluminum

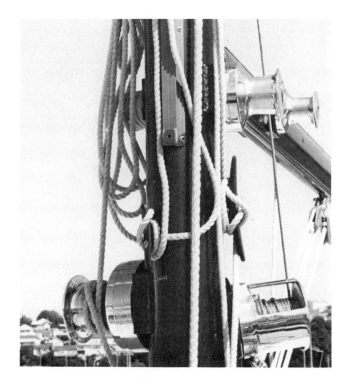

Wire halyard winch (lower right) installed on angled table. (Courtesy Yachtspars)

masts. Even though it is advisable to insulate stainless steel fittings of any size from aluminum spars, it is generally conceded that the small area presented by a stainless pop rivet or the thread of a machine screw is of small moment. My preference for Monel is something I'm stuck with; I just plain like the stuff. It's expensive and often hard to get, but in my book, for bolts, machine screws, wood screws, winch tables, chainplates, and propeller shafts, Monel has no equal.

If you decide to use stainless steel fastenings to mount winch tables on an aluminum mast, always make inquiries as to what series stainless you're buying. Stainless steel of the 300 series is the most popular for marine use. However, type 302/304 *is* magnetic. Type 316 is less magnetic and type 305 has a permeability low enough to qualify as nonmagnetic. The less magnetic the fastenings, the better. And don't forget to use a little goop on the threads so the machine screws can be removed easily.

POSITIONING CLEATS

With the advent of self-tailing winches, the faithful studding of cleats on deck is not the necessity it used to be. Carefully positioning a cleat so that a sheet or halyard can be belayed after leaving a drum is a dying art. Even when a winch is not a self-tailer, a line stopper and/or cam often takes the place of the traditional cleat. For the cruiser, though, the guy who prefers to make his sheet or halyard fast in what may soon be known as "the old-fashioned way," the correct way to position a cleat is worth mentioning.

Above: *A well-designed cleat. (Carl Moesly photo)* **Right:** *A strong, well-fastened cleat. (Courtesy Yachtspars)*

The axis of a cleat (see photograph) should be at such an angle to the line leading to it that when under strain, the line can in no way jam the turns on the cleat. Never point a cleat at a winch, think that'll do, and fire ahead to bolt it down. Chances are — unless the winch drum has a large diameter — that the line coming off the drum will not only get in the way when you're turning up on the cleat, it will make it difficult to get the turns off, too. Wherever possible, a cleat should be the type secured by four fasteners. On a wooden mast, four hefty bronze screws will usually do — bearing in mind the number of adjacent fastenings. A cleat on a wooden boom should be through-bolted. Install a cleat on an aluminum mast in the same manner as you would a winch table. A cleat should be bolted through a deck or coaming. Another thing: a cleat should, wherever possible, be installed on the opposite side of a winch to that which the rope under strain is leading. While the weight taken by the cleat is in no way comparable with that accepted by the winch, any attempt to take strain off the winch mounting bolts must be considered worthwhile.

MISCELLANEOUS CONSIDERATIONS

To guard against the possibility of an overriding turn, a line should lead up to a winch. That is, the line should lead up onto the drum from the base plate at a few degrees below perpendicular with the center shaft. Keep this in mind when installing either winches or deck leads, whether these leads come from sliding cars, snatch blocks, bonnets, bull's-eyes, or anything else. An overriding turn on a winch drum — and is there a seaman anywhere who hasn't experienced this? — can sometimes need quite a bit of clearing. If it happens when you're tacking (a favorite time), luffing may be necessary to gain enough slack to clear the foul. This could put the vessel in irons or even back on her original board, which — and you can almost bet on it — will be toward an obstruction, a shoal, or a lee shore.

When slacking a line around a winch drum, hold the free end of the line at an angle down toward the base. Again, you never allow any rope — and this especially applies to a rope under strain — to get even near perpendicular to the drum when slacking away. To allow the line being rendered up past the perpendicular is asking for trouble. There is always the possibility that the top turn of line will jump off and be followed quickly by another and another until the strain — which may be half a ton — is transmitted suddenly to the arms of the line-handler in one almighty jerk. Winches are wonderful pieces of equipment and make it possible for little people to do big things, but treat every one of them with respect.

The self-tailing winch has added another dimension to the cruising game. Where cranking and tailing in a weight of wind was once a two-person operation, a winch with a self-tailer makes this a thing of the past. It is no longer necessary to "put your mate on a shake" and get him (or her) growling and grizzling up on deck to tail off while you crank in a few inches on the jib sheet. If you've followed the dictum of calculating winch ratio according to the strength of the lightest crew member, sack time won't be interrupted to help featherweights, either. Self-tailing winches cost a bit extra, of course, but they've really made a big difference to the cruising life.

When installed on a mast to handle rope halyards, self-tailing winches are ideal. The fact that it is possible for one person to hoist a sail with ease, holding on with a free hand and cranking with the other, has converted this exercise into a picnic. The self-tailing attachment of one of these winches frequently "fuzzes up" the surface of the line, but this is no great consideration when compared with the convenience afforded.

Don't just throw your winch handles down or leave them "around somewhere" after using them. They are expensive pieces of equipment, and if you really need winches to handle your ship, you'll be dead without your handles, so look after them. If you can't spring for those classy soft-plastic holders for your winch handles, build a couple of plywood holders and fasten one to each side of the cockpit, a deckbox, or even the mast. Or you can make them out of pieces of PVC pipe.

More and more owners of sizable cruising vessels are putting electric winches aboard. There's no doubt that these pieces of machinery make life easier when it comes time to do some hauling, but there's also no doubt that electric winches are, by comparison with their manual counterparts, expensive and complicated to install and maintain. It's your choice, mate.

An element that enters into choosing a location for an electric winch to handle sheets and other lines is the room the motor takes below decks. This can be 12 or 15 inches, or more, depending on the size of the winch. Be extra careful where you mount one of these winches; an electric motor or anything else sticking a foot or so down into a cabin hasn't got a friend in the world. In a playful moment it might remove your hat or your toupee, or give you a scar you'll carry to the grave.

Don't be stingy about the size of wiring that's led to your electric winch, either. The biggest favor you can do for direct current is to give it a good-sized copper wire to travel along. Quite often, wiring sizes recommended by manufacturers are the minimum only. Try to go without your beer for a couple of days; spend the extra cash on heavier wiring — your batteries will love you for it. And make certain that after installation, there is no way the wiring or motor can get wet. Also, an electric winch should be mounted a minimum of six feet (preferably farther) from a magnetic compass. Failure to do this can result in drastic compass deviation on some headings, especially when the winch is in use.

WINCH MAINTENANCE

There is no piece of equipment with moving parts that is completely free of maintenance. Heavy advertising with a strong "maintenance-free" theme can influence people into thinking that all they have to do is walk aboard, use their boat, and never give a thought to most of the equipment. Then, when something freezes up or falls to bits through lack of grease or attention, they feel cheated.

If they're old hands, they have no excuse — it serves 'em bloody right. But if they are newcomers, who can blame them? Advertising, calculated more to sell a product than to present it honestly, can be responsible for a feeling of complacency on the part of the buyer: he has, after all, just bought something that's supposedly maintenance free.

I advise the cruising man or woman to regard *nothing* as being free of care and attention, especially equipment that is constantly exposed to salt air and that may, in addition, receive a dollop of salt water from time to time. Keep a running inspection going on all your gear and don't feel you're being shortchanged if you've got to turn to and do a bit of yackka (work) on the equipment now and again. The sailing game today is easier and safer than it's ever been, thanks to improvements in rig, rigging, and cordage — as long as we keep our eye on all of it. When you're on the receiving end of a knockdown, or suddenly find you have to beat your way off a lee shore in a breeze of wind, the fact that you know your rig is sound because you *regularly inspect every part of it* will do wonders for your peace of mind.

You can't beat knowing your boat and her equipment inside out. If your automobile breaks down, the fact that you know nothing about cars won't matter so much. You can get out and walk — you might mumble or complain — but there's a good chance that help is only a few minutes (or hours) away. If there's a breakdown of gear when off soundings, you are on your own, mate. So here we have two desirables, both of which should be attended to before sailing from home base: (1) make as certain as possible that the hull of the ship is a suitable design and strong enough to stand the rigors of cruising (see *The Cruising Life*); and (2) know every piece of equipment — masts, mast fittings, wire, terminals, turnbuckles, toggles, clevis pins, chainplates, tracks, eyebolts and pad eyes, winches (plus their components and fastenings) — from A to Z. And keep every moving part sensibly lubricated.

The winches available to the sailing man today are beautiful pieces of equipment. They are also expensive; a dozen winches of a hefty size can cost as much as a boat did a few years ago. So, quite apart from the practical aspect of usage while sailing, you need to protect what can amount to a considerable investment. Keep 'em turning, sport; they represent a lot of bread.

There are three kinds of maintenance. There's the preventive kind, which takes place at scheduled intervals. Preventive maintenance is largely responsible for the smooth running of a cruising vessel, with little or no excitement. Then there's the we'd-better-free-that-up kind, which occurs after a winch becomes hard to turn. The maintenance required in this situation is sometimes awkward, and if it has to take place at sea, it can sometimes result in smart chases after little ball bearings as they head for scuppers or cockpit drains. Then there's maintenance of the Rube

Goldberg kind, which takes place when an item of equipment has frozen or carried away. Temporary "maintenance" is effected with pieces of string and odd lengths of wire. This type of maintenance contributes more excitement to the sailing scene than the other two put together. For the bit of string holding the winch handle (which had been left in and tied because all the pawls were broken) suddenly to let go and give the skipper's girlfriend two black eyes as it wipes the binoculars away from her face and over the side enlivens what might have been a dull day. It all depends on how you want to live, of course, but in my book, preventive maintenance wins hands down over the other two.

Assuming that we're going to leave the excitement to the other guy and do our part in keeping the winches turning, we first of all read the book the manufacturer provides (or should provide) with his winches. "Thou shalt read the manual" is an important winch commandment. It's the twelfth commandment, in fact. ("Thou shalt not be found out" is the eleventh.) The manufacturer's literature will tell you the recommended disassembling procedures, as well as the proper lubrication and the intervals at which these should take place.

It is best to do the job in quiet surroundings with the ship as stable as she can be persuaded to be. Prepare the ground by plugging scuppers and cockpit drains to prevent the escape of anything that might be dropped. If you have a teak deck, froth up a bucket of salt water (or fresh, if you can spare it) with detergent and scrub the part of the deck chosen for the work area. Then spread an old piece of canvas or sailcloth over it. (When the job's finally done, slosh a bucket or two of water over the deck, and any stains will scrub away.) I have always cleaned engine or winch parts with a small, new paintbrush dipped in a half-gallon or so of diesel oil in a plastic bucket. If the manufacturer recommends something else, such as kerosene, fine — just as long as you don't use gasoline. Gasoline does a good job, but it is too dangerous to use it for such work on a boat.

Manufacturers' literature often advises you to "reassemble in the reverse manner," but when you've got bits strewn all over the place, these instructions don't help much. An unmechanical bloke can end up with a few pieces left over. It's not a bad idea for first-timers who aren't sure how they are going to get the thing together again to take a Polaroid photo of each stage of the procedure when pulling a winch down. After the first time, they'll probably be able to do it blindfolded, but if they keep the photos, there will never be the possibility of a mistake, no matter who does the job.

After being cleaned, the winch parts should be drained and dried on clean paper. The ideal stuff is absorbent white paper toweling on which every component is visible. If a winch has standardized roller bearings, then so much the better. It means that bearings of different sizes need not be carried as spares for each winch; one size will do. Properly lubricated bearings should last for years. However, if, after disassembling and cleaning, a bearing needs replacing, this task is simplified if the spare bearings for a particular winch are of one size only.

The worldwide availability of spare parts is something to consider when shopping for winches. A point to be realized here is that even though spares might be available in various countries along the way, it still pays to carry a sensible selection aboard. The farther from home base a part is purchased, the more expensive it is likely to be.

A winch manufacturer will recommend either in his literature or upon request just what spares a cruising boat should carry. Spare springs, in any case, come high on the list. Springs actuate pawls, and more than one sailor, fiddling around with his winch, has seen one of his springs take a flying leap over the side. If our mariner has a fistful of spares, he can treat this performance with a sneer. If it's his last spring, he could be dead in the water. Some winch manufacturers advertise their pawls as being heat-treated stainless steel and virtually indestructible. Even so, spares should be carried, and during a maintenance job the working pawls should be inspected thoroughly for cracks or flaws. If the winch pawls are bronze, this inspection is doubly important.

It is not generally advisable for the cruiser to use the same winch lubricant as that chosen by the racing man. In an effort to get as much free-wheeling speed as possible, the racer often uses a light oil (sometimes sewing machine oil) on every moving part. This practice demands that the winches be pulled down, cleaned, and re-oiled at short, regular intervals — something that's not always possible aboard a cruising boat. A cruiser should use a lubricant that will "hang on" on his winch bearings. The best kind is one that he knows will not be washed off, or, after a little use, disappear. A winch used with no lubricant in the bearings will suffer unnecessary wear; it might even freeze up.

I have always used marine Lubriplate A for winch bearings. In fact, I invariably carried a case of instant grease-gun refills of this lubricant aboard our schooner. After using the auxiliary engine, I would give a Zerk fitting in the engine room a few pumps, and this, via a thin copper pipe leading aft of the stuffing box, would put a thin skin of grease around the propeller shaft and prevent water that cooled the gland when underway from entering the boat. As soon as the engine was started and engaged in gear, this seal would be broken, and water would reach the gland within the stuffing box and proceed to cool both gland and shaft. The windlass bearings, via their Zerk fittings, existed on a diet of Lubriplate A, as did the bearings of the steering gear. The closed-barrel turnbuckles were also full of this lubricant.

My only reason for mentioning all this is to demonstrate that standardizing aboard a cruising boat can even extend to the type of lubricant used in the ship's winches. There are other excellent lubricants, of course, and it's possible for a winch manufacturer to be so sold on his own recommendations that he won't budge from the one he's touting in his literature. If so, OK; play along; if anyone should know what agrees with his product, it's the guy who built it. But the tropic sun can really heat up a winch drum, so a cruiser headed for warmer regions should consider this. A winch drum heated from any cause can be the reason why some lubricants melt out or break down.

After cleaning and drying the bearings, put them back on the winch spindle in the exact order in which they were taken off. Don't start in gaily slathering grease and oil over everything at this stage. Work grease into the bearings with clean fingers, making sure it penetrates between the rollers. In general, grease is used on the winch spindle, bearings, gear teeth, and ratchet teeth. Oil (I've always used 30-weight nondetergent oil) is used on the gear bearings, pawl axles, winch handle grip, and ratchet (if there is one) at the business end of the handle.

Allowing grease or oil to be smeared on a winch drum is no way to encourage the cooperation of a sheet or halyard led to it. Winch drums should be kept away from lubricants. So should the brakes and brake drums of wire halyard winches; these should be smooth, clean, and totally free of any slippery substance. Keep oil away from the parts that need grease, and vice versa. And try to clean up as you go.

Some people are better at this than others. My wife, for instance, can paint all day and get no spots on her face, her clothes, or the handle of the brush. After I've painted for an hour or so, I look as if I've dropped the brush in the paint and dove in to look for it. After a half-hour's work on the *White Squall II*'s engine, I looked as if I'd camped overnight in the sump. So, non-engineer cruisers, take heart. If, during the job of pulling a winch down and putting it together again, *I* can keep the greasy and oily parts nicely separated and the surrounding area spic-and-span, then so can you.

The above treatment applies in principle to all winches installed aboard cruising boats — or any other kind of boat, for that matter — and doesn't only concern manually operated equipment. More and more electric winches are earning a place for themselves in sailing craft, and along with their manual counterparts, they must be maintained. There should be a strict timetable for lavishing attention on an electric winch. The reason for this is that mechanically driven equipment seldom has a way of indicating to a user that its servicing schedule has been overlooked. A hand-cranked winch will tell a person bringing in a jib that it needs attention by becoming hard to use, and although maintenance should be arranged so that this doesn't happen, some sailors do wait for such a sign before getting out the tools. An electric winch with a powerful motor can do a lot of damage to dry bearings within a winch; spindle and gears can be worn unnecessarily, too. It can also be tough on the motor and increase the drain on the battery.

An electric winch aboard a long-range cruising boat calls for a selection of specific spares to be taken along. These may only be a set of brushes; in any case, the manufacturer will advise on this score.

An anchor windlass usually cops more salt water than any other winch aboard, and for this reason, it should be inspected frequently. If the windlass is a hand job, oil or grease every part that the maker recommends; wind the handle back and forth every which way and make sure the wildcat ("gipsy" in some parts of the world) runs free and doesn't drag. If the windlass has a sump (often referred to as an "oil bath"), keep it topped up. A windlass is often called upon to take enormous strains when cruising. Make sure it's well bolted through the deck to a backing plate that will distribute all this stress. Knock out a bolt every now and again and give it the eye; do this to the fastenings of every winch aboard. The same treatment should be applied to a windlass powered by mechanical linkage, hydraulic fluid, or electricity. Keep things free and keep them clean. Lash a cover down over your windlass at sea. It's practically impossible to keep water from swirling up under a cover when a vessel sticks her nose into a big one, but we can do our best. Any cover is better than no cover at all.

ALTERNATIVE ARRANGEMENTS

In many boating circles, it seems that winches for both halyards and sheets are regarded as indispensable. As was mentioned briefly earlier in this chapter, this need not be so. The availability of winches to assist in the handling of small sailing vessels is a fairly recent phenomenon. I'd never even *seen* a winch until I was in my late teens, and I'd had a good 10 years of coastwise sailing under my keel.

I had several years and many deep-sea miles in my yawl before the first winch came aboard. By no stretch of imagination could the schooner be regarded as over-winched, either. When I bought her, she was 26 years old, and the only winch she sported was her anchor windlass. So, I hear you cry, if a sailboat hasn't got winches, how do we get her sails up? And in?

Aboard my yawl, I hoisted mainsail, mizzen, and jib on 7/19 stainless steel halyards. A single block was shackled to each wire, and when a sail was lowered, this block would be at the masthead. A line, with a standing part fast at the gooseneck, led up the mast, through the single block, and down. This was the hauling part. The purchase with such a rig is 2-to-1, and although it took a bit of a huff and a puff and "bowsing" to get a luff tight at times, we managed. The staysail halyard was an all-rope gun tackle. A single block was shackled to a band immediately below the junction where the staysail stay secured to the mast. A standing part was shackled to the tail of this block, run down to a single block at the staysail head, up to the mast block, and down again to become the hauling part. This tackle, being rove to disadvantage, had a 2-to-1 purchase. (Always try to arrange that the block you are pulling on does the moving.)

The schooner had the same arrangement for her mainsail halyard. The only difference lay in the fact that soon after acquiring the ship, I installed a handy-billy tackle at what was formerly the standing end of the rope purchase to the wire halyard. The mainsail was shackled to the wire halyard and when sail was lowered, a single block at the other end of this wire was pulled to the masthead. To heave this block down again (and hoist the sail) was the job of the ⅝-inch Dacron rope purchase. That handy billy installed at the end of the standing part of the purchase made it easy to tighten the luff of the 900-square-foot mainsail.

Before hoisting, the handy billy would be slacked away until its moving block was about seven feet above the gooseneck. The ⅝-inch Dacron line that led from this block up to the single block at the end of the wire halyard and back down (to become the hauling part) was hove down until the sail was two or three feet from the masthead. This line, with its purchase of 2-to-1, was then belayed. The handy billy, giving a 4-to-1 mechanical advantage, plus the 2-to-1 advantage of the Dacron hauled through the single block — in other words, a tackle on a tackle — was brought into play to heave the sail up the remaining distance and tighten the luff. When, after about 10 years of this, I stumbled on a good buy and jazzed up our sail-hoisting arrangement with the addition of a winch, it made the exercise look a bit more sophisticated, but it didn't get the sail up any faster — or better.

Sheeting in the jib and staysail aboard the yawl (and the three gaff-riggers I owned before her) was accomplished by a couple of two-foot pendants, each with a single block at its end, shackled to the staysail clew. Two pendants were also secured to the jib clew — again, each pendant with a single block at its end — but these were longer. All these pendants were rope, and the length of the jib's pendants was determined by the distance from the clew (when this sail was sheeted hard in) back to the staysail or inner forestay, plus about a foot. The idea was that the single block at the end of a windward pendant should never reach the staysail stay, or be pulled around it. Sister clips, which look like two hooked fingers, were used to secure the pendants to the jib clew, the idea here being that these old-fashioned marvels would be less likely than a shackle to hang up on the staysail stay when tacking. However, after shaking free and giving us an occasion to remember that night in the Tasman, this arrangement was banished forever, and new, longer pendants were made fast to the clew with bowlines.

Each sheet led from a standing part, which was merely a wall-and-crown knot, hard up against a bronze eyebolt in the deck. From here, a staysail or jib sheet would lead forward to pass through a single block at the end of a pendant, back through a lignum-vitae bull's-eye bolted through the deck, and to a cockpit cleat. The purchase was only 2-to-1, which isn't much when bringing in a sail in a breeze, but again (possibly because we didn't know any better), we managed.

Something that helped was the size of the sheaves that the halyards and sheets passed over. During the year I was waiting for the lumber for my yawl to season (I'd had the kauri trees cut from the forest), I spent quite a bit of my spare time ashore, making blocks. Advice was scarce; the yachtsmen I knew used blocks I considered too small for my ocean cruiser, and the horny-handed shellbacks I was going to sea with disdained anything less than 12-inch blocks with nine-inch sheaves. My blocks ended up about the right size for a 100-tonner. They were internally strapped with galvanized steel; the cheeks, held at each of the four corners with a copper rivet, were 7½ inches long and four inches wide, and each sheave (they were all single blocks) was solid 4½-inch-diameter bronze.

Ridiculous? Right! But, boy-oh-boy, were they kind to a ½-inch line. The rope rendered so easily that on one occasion when I leaped forward to heave the staysail down, the monster of a block at its head came streaking toward the deck and landed on the top of my own mallet with a thud that furled me along with the sail. As the years passed and winches came aboard, I invested in smaller, more "yacht-like" blocks for my little 10-tonner. I kept the 7½-inch blocks with their 4½-inch sheaves, however, and when I acquired the *White Squall II,* I hung them about her 60-ton bulk and they proved none too big. Last time I saw her, she still had two of these blocks as part of her mainsheet tackle.

When I first walked aboard the schooner in 1962, she didn't have a sheet or halyard winch to her name, so after I'd allocated my blocks to this job and that, I installed a bottom-action, geared, Camper & Nicholson sheet winch (picked up at a St. Thomas locker sale) on a stand forward of the mainmast. The winch was centrally located and handled either port or starboard jib sheet. This lasted a half-dozen years until, by incredible luck, I acquired a Number 7 Merriman to take its place. The forestaysail didn't have sheets; it was on a boom, which I hated with a passion. Both fore and main staysails were hoisted by handy-billy purchases, and the jib, after a year of the same type of arrangement used for hoisting the mainsail, was converted to roller furling.

After a few more years I invested in a single block and winches for both staysails and replaced the block-and-tackle purchases on the running backstays with Highfield levers. I was never conscious, however, that these alterations made a big difference to the work of running the ship, and we chartered and cruised in the Caribbean and Pacific for many years. Just the two of us were aboard when sailing for fun, and only Minine and I handled the ship when catering to charter guests. And as far as ability is concerned, we're nothing special. I'm firmly convinced that in many cases a big vessel with a long keel and a hefty displacement is easier to run than some of the small ones on which a tiny variation in weather can call for sail changing and reefing. Maintenance on a large vessel, though, is another thing altogether; you can sometimes be running all day every day to keep up with it.

I might mention that when rigging various block-and-tackle purchases, it's handy to have a variety of shackles. Quite often, after a block is shackled to an eyebolt in the deck (such as for the lead of a mainsheet to a winch), the sheave might be at right angles to the lead required. Sometimes, alternative holes at right angles to each other at the head of the block will enable such a situation to be rectified by relocating a shackle pin. If this is not possible, and the use of a second shackle to turn the block 90 degrees brings the block to an unacceptable height from the deck, a twisted shackle (its pin is at a right angle to its crown) can often save the day. Shop around for a few of these and carry them in your bosun's stores.

A boat can be sailed perfectly well without winches, but it's sure nice to have them. As previously mentioned, it's nice to have a winch for each headsail sheet and a rope or wire halyard winch. With the cruising fraternity, it boils down in most cases to money. It's a great temptation to anyone writing a book such as this to recommend the studding and hanging of winches about the ship like so many bunches of grapes. Nothing could be more unfair to the neophyte cruiser. Don't be deterred by the fact that you can't afford winches to haul your sails up, and in. If your ship's not dripping with high-priced gear, it won't make one bit of difference to the distance you travel. It sure didn't make any difference to me. And if you need any further convincing, remember: Slocum didn't have winches . . . Dickens didn't have a typewriter . . . .

six

Sails

One thing a cruising boat's sails must be, above everything else, is durable. Cruising sails must be constructed from material that will stand up to the wear and tear of years of ocean sailing. They must be able to be furled or stowed away wet without losing their shape or becoming mildewed. These ideals, once considered a pipe dream, are now entirely possible. Such wasn't always the case; comparing the sailcloth of yesteryear with the synthetics available today is like comparing the old hemp lines of Manila, sisal, or flax with rope constructed from Dacron or nylon fiber.

MATERIALS

The good old days of duck canvas sails or sailcloth made from Egyptian cotton (which we used to consider the total end) have long disappeared — a fact for which even the most impious of us should let fly with a few Hail Marys now and again. That old sailcloth was a pain in the neck. Whenever a sail was lowered and furled or bagged wet, it was with the certain knowledge that the race was on — the object being to get the canvas hoisted and dried again before mildew set in. Sometimes this was a hard race for a cruiser to win. A few wet months in a humid climate — such as in some tropic zones — could take more strength from a suit of cotton sails through mildew than a year of hard sailing.

Mildew-proofing wasn't all it was cracked up to be, either. Tanning a yacht's sails, the same way fishermen's nets were treated, was moderately successful, but none of the do-it-yourself mildew-proofing seemed to work — *really* work. It didn't for me, anyhow. I remember a time, years ago, when I mildew-proofed a suit of new duck sails for my yawl before one of our trips to Tahiti. The experience left me with the impression that so far as the proofing gunk was concerned, a man couldn't trust the stuff. I was all fired up to do a good job, too. I mixed a big packet of mildew-proofing powder with 10 gallons of water, following the instructions to the letter. I did this in the bathtub at my parents' home, dunked the mainsail in the mixture for the prescribed length of time, dropped buckets of the white milky stuff through the house as I carried the sail out, and had an unholy time getting the thing dry. Even in our easygoing household, my shares were at rock bottom by the time the mizzen and headsails had had their dips.

Was it worth it? Not on your life! I couldn't spring for sail covers in those days, so after we reached Papeete and Quinn's Tahitian Hut, I left the main and the mizzen on their booms; they were, after all, mildew-proof! And while I was innocently enjoying myself in the manner of a young sailor in a port that was down by the head with girls and booze, the mildew-proofing (which had caused me to come within a hair of being banished from home and hearth) joined forces with the weather to *attack* my sails. A scurvy trick if ever there was one. I was constantly having to leave important unfinished business ashore to go back to my vessel and dry her sails. This couldn't happen today. Dacron, or Terylene, sails lap up this treatment of being left on spars to dry — giving the oceangoing sailor all the time in the world to "enjoy the sights" ashore.

Sunlight, not mildew, is the enemy of synthetic sails, so whenever possible, they should be covered, bagged, or stowed below. Even sunlight isn't as much of a bogey as mildew used to be, though. When I acquired the *White Squall II,* her 10-ounce Terylene mainsail was four years old. The sail had been built by Joe Pearce in Sydney, Australia, and had seen a fair amount of use, but this was nothing alongside the wear it received when we started chartering 30 weeks a year in the Caribbean.

I would protect the sail when furled by spreading the awning over it and clipping a "jacket" (which we had made on board) around the stacked part of the sail at the bottom of the mast track, and this worked to keep the sun's rays away from the material. There was nothing I could do about the exposure to sunshine when we were sailing, though. This sail lasted another six tough years before it gave up the ghost. None of the old cotton sailcloth could have come within a mile of a record like that.

Ironically, it wasn't until the end of the canvas-sail era, when synthetics were becoming the rage, that a truly mildew-proof canvas appeared and started to be used widely for awnings, sail covers, dodgers, and sails. This product was Vivatex, and I had a main staysail constructed of the material for the *White Squall II.* The Vivatex staysail didn't set as well as a Dacron or Terylene sail would have, but it required absolutely no care. It never had a sail cover and lasted for eight hard-working years before, in a capful of wind, it blew to pieces. Now, if only I'd had Vivatex canvas aboard my yawl in Papeete so long ago, instead of cotton duck and that do-it-yourself mildew treatment . . . .

The sailor these days needs to be a little more chafe-conscious with his synthetic sails than did his predecessor whose vessel sported a canvas wardrobe. The stitching of a Dacron sail — especially a stiffly resinated sail — sits proud of the surface, begging to be chafed. A soft Dacron sail has this trouble, too, although not quite to the same extent. The stitching of a canvas sail would pull in practically flush with the surface, which was a great advantage when a sail was eased and its lee side rested against the shrouds. The seam stitching was not nearly as likely to be chafed as is the stitching of a synthetic sail.

The lee topping lift of a gaff-rigged vessel can be tough on stitching standing proud of the surface, too. For this reason, soft chafing gear such as sheepskin should be used on the lifts of a gaff-rigger with synthetic sails. But don't make baggywrinkle out of hemp and hang it up there; this chafing gear can wear away stitching at a great rate.

CHOOSING YOUR SAILS

The sails for your world cruiser should definitely be of Dacron. The material should be as resin-free as your sailmaker can procure. My old friend Chris Bouzaid, twice the One-Ton world champion, and president of Hood Sailmakers, believes, "There is far less likelihood that a resin-free [pure] sailcloth will lose its shape, and although initially it is a little springier than the hard-resinated cloth, in the long run it is a much better investment."

There are three ways of cutting sails. The first is to run the panels from luff to leech in the usual manner. The second is the "up-and-down" cut, which has panels running from the foot, parallel to the leech. The third is "Scotch-cut." This cut has a miter, which runs typically from clew to luff, bisecting the angle at the clew. The sail panels below the miter run parallel to the foot; above the miter, the panels are parallel to the leech, as with the "up-and-down" cut.

The number of sails a cruising boat carries usually is based on three things: cost, number of crew to handle the sails, and stowage space.

The first priority — the sails an ocean cruiser *must* have — is a strong working suit. Storm sails come next, in my book. (None of us enjoys bad weather, but the possibility that we may get at least our share must be faced squarely.) A heavily constructed storm jib and a trysail that will hoist on its own mast track (and, in the event something goes wrong with the arrangement, separate parrel-ball "hoops" that go right around the mast at each luff eyelet) are well worthy of a place aboard. An extra jib, such as a Yankee, is a good investment. A working staysail that can be reefed should also be included automatically in a cruising boat's wardrobe. A genoa staysail can pull like a horse to windward and is a wonderful sail, but on a two-handed, ocean-cruising sailboat, it wouldn't see much use. (At least we didn't use ours much, despite all good intentions.)

While light sails and running sails are covered in detail in Chapters Eight and Nine, it is worth mentioning here the room necessary to stow these sails. I'm thinking about a little boat you intend to *live aboard*. Even if you could afford them, there just isn't room to stow unlimited bags of sails below decks after all the thousand-and-one other necessities (see *The Cruising Life*) are loaded into the ship. It's something in the nature of a vicious circle. A bloke who says, "The hell with this shorthanded stuff; I'm going to carry a crew and plenty of light sails so that I can always sail at top efficiency" can find he has no room to stow the bags of sails because the crew needs the space for living quarters. There's a big difference between cruising and racing. When cruising for months and sometimes years on end, people need their privacy; when racing, you can stack 'em in like cordwood.

Mainsails

The mainsail should be built of heavier cloth than the other working sails, for the reason that it's up there most of the time the vessel is sailing. An exception to this is a staysail with reef points that can be shortened down and still carried in a blow. Such a sail is commonly the same weight as the mainsail. The mizzen is likely to be dropped when the weather deteriorates; a headsail might also be furled. In light weather, the working headsails might be furled and a large, light jib brought into play. In each case, the mainsail is up there, doing its stuff, and the weight of its cloth depends largely on the weight of the boat it is expected to drive. Put a six-ounce mainsail on a 100-tonner and there's a good chance it'll be truly strained — or even disappear like a puff of smoke if it comes on to blow. Hoist a 14-ounce mainsail aboard an eight-tonner and you'll slow her down to a crawl.

A good sailmaker can advise on a suitable weight for a cruising boat's sails; however, a common rule of thumb is to go one weight heavier than would be usual if the same boat were engaged in occasional weekend sailing with, say, a three-week coastwise cruise once a year. This simply counteracts wear and tear over the long haul. Whatever weight is chosen, the mainsail should be reinforced well at head, tack, clew, and reef cringles. Make sure you insist on this; you'll bless those outsize strainer patches as the years go by. (I had eight-foot strainer patches sewn into the new mainsail for the *White Squall II.* One requirement was that the leech strainer

Mainsail well strengthened with strainer patches. Four rows of stitching in every seam. Note in-line batten above reef points, other battens at right angles to leech and in center of sail panels, running backstays as well as permanent backstay, main shrouds "rattled down" on both sides, roller-furling jib. (Ralph Naranjo photo)

went up past the first row of reef points, and I used to feel mighty smug about this whenever we pulled a reef down.)

The seams should be cut with a hot iron (which seals the edge) and triple-stitched. I insisted on four rows of stitching for each seam of the 12-ounce, 900-square-foot Dacron mainsail for our schooner. The seams of the yawl's 8-ounce, 260-square-foot Dacron mainsail were triple-stitched. Some yachtsmen and sailmakers consider that two rows of stitching to a seam is plenty, maintaining that any more than two rows doesn't leave enough cloth for the sail to be restitched without weakening the seam. I won't buy this. If the sailmaker doesn't stinge in his seam width, there should be plenty of meat left if restitching is necessary. As I see it, it's far better to triple-stitch initially, and then look after the sail, than to accept the fact that the sail is going to have to be resewn at some future date because it wasn't built strongly enough in the first place.

Another thing. Restitching a mainsail, especially a big, heavy one, just can't be done in some parts of the world. Rolling up the bunt of a heavy sail and passing this huge bundle under the arm of an average sail-stitching machine in a small loft can be a job for all hands and the cook. Sometimes, no matter how much help is available, it is impossible to reach the seams in the center of a big sail. When a sail is built, each panel is sewn on separately, so that all that passes under the arm of the machine is the width of one panel, often rolled to make the job easier. All the more reason for the sailor to insist on a minimum of three rows of stitching along every seam of his mainsail in the first place.

There is great controversy over the number of rows of reef points a sailboat should carry in her mainsail. The racer of today has a high-aspect-ratio mainsail of at least 3-to-1. (Aspect ratio is calculated by the number of times the foot of a mainsail can be divided into the hoist.) Her sail is like a bird's wing and commonly has three rows of reef points. The amount of sail left after the last reef is pulled down varies from boat to boat, but 50 percent or less is regarded as acceptable. Because of the number of crew carried aboard a racing boat, the acrobatics necessary during the tying in and shaking out of reefs is of little consequence; many hands make light work. That is the main consideration when calculating how many rows of reef points a cruising boat should have in her mainsail, and how much reduction in sail area each reef should account for.

I like to see two rows of reef points in a cruising boat's mainsail. The first reef should be a deep one, taking in 30 percent of the sail; the second reef should take in 20 percent. There are three reasons for this.

1. When it comes time to put in a reef aboard a cruiser, put in a deep one that takes in a generous amount of sail area; there's a chance it will be all you need. To take a hypothetical case, imagine that you and your wife (or husband) are sailing a 15-tonner and you've been standing watch for a few days and nights. If you pull down a reef that accounts for only a small reduction in sail area when the wind freshens, you'll feel like you're chewing a lemon if you have to climb out of the sack an hour or so later to put in another. You'll probably look as if you're chewing a lemon, too.

2. A cruising boat's well-reinforced mainsail should be capable of standing the strain of being reefed to 50 percent of its total area. This accounts for the second

reef taking in a further 20 percent of the sail. If a further reduction in sail area is necessary, it's time for a trysail.

3. If a cruising boat's mainsail has only one row of reef points, she'll have to carry a trysail with an area comparable to a double-reefed main. When it comes time for a second reef, she's got to lower and furl her mainsail to set a trysail. Quite a bit of sail drill to achieve only a double reef. With a reduction in wind strength, the trysail will have to be lowered and stowed (even if it's in a bag at the foot of the mast, still a job), and the mainsail has to be hoisted again. Aboard the usually shorthanded cruising boat, all reefing should be done on a mainsail that's capable of taking it (to 50 percent of its area) with the reefing equipment already rigged on the main boom. The storm trysail should be no more than 30 percent of the total mainsail area. It should be small enough and tough enough to do one job only — namely, to be used with confidence in gale conditions.

The strengthening patches in a mainsail, for both tack and leech cringles at the end of each row of reef points, should be more rugged than those at the foot of the sail, since these will be the load points in worsening conditions. A roll-reef — a line of eyelets or points running from the tack of a mainsail to a cringle a few feet up the leech — is sometimes used to cock the end of the boom up when running downwind in a big sea. I've never found myself wishing the mainsail was thus equipped in any vessel I've been aboard for an ocean cruise, but there's no doubt that in a boat with a long boom that's low to the water, such a reef would be a godsend. Seems to me, the higher the aspect ratio (and consequent shorter boom), the less the need for a roll-reef.

A cruising rig that is finding favor in some circles is a fractionally rigged spar with a reef in the mainsail. This is arranged so that the head of the mainsail (with one reef tied in) comes just below the point on the mast to which port and starboard running backstays are secured. The bottoms of these backstays are then moved aft so that the boom swings well inside them — doing the job, in this position, of twin permanent backstays. Proponents of this rig maintain that the big (unreefed) mainsail gives them drive in light weather without resorting to large headsails. An increase in wind sees a reef in the mainsail, which (A) obviates any necessity to change headsails, (B) has the desirable effect of moving the center of effort forward, thereby easing weight on the helm, and (C) results in a snug, well-stayed rig once the running backstays are taken aft.

Recently I was given a wonderful ear-bashing on the virtues of this rig by an old friend who is also an experienced hand; hence its mention in these pages. To him it is the total end. I can't help but wonder about the long boom that is sometimes used with the mainsail of a fractionally rigged vessel. Unless the boom is carried well above deck, it could, under some conditions, trail in the sea when eased. Perhaps a roll-reef would do a good job here.

The tabling, which protects and strengthens every edge of a sail, should be a long, sewn-together strip cut from the edge of the sail while it is being shaped. The strip should be folded over the edge of foot, luff, or leech, and then sewn to itself through the sail. On cheaper sails the edge is sometimes just turned over and sewn. This is not the best practice, because a seam still has continuity through the tabling. A far better system, after the tabling is cut, is to place it so that the joins come within a sail panel and the seam ends are covered with strong, unjoined cloth.

Dacron tape or rope strengthens the foot of a mainsail, the luff, and the leech (a sensible distance up past the top row of reef points, over the headboard, and a short distance down). Tape is strong, is a bit lighter and not as bulky as rope, and is popular for these reasons. I've used both and have been happy with both.

I like to see a jackline rove back and forth across the forward side of a mast through eyelets in a mainsail, from the top row of reef points down — or, instead of around the mast, back and forth between eyelets and slides. This jackline obviates the necessity of letting the mainsail slides run off the track (so that the tack cringle of a row of points can be hooked or lashed down) and then feeding them back on again when hoisting away. If you have a big crew falling all over themselves with eagerness to do all this, then forget about the jackline. If you're cruising shorthanded, a jackline is mighty handy. A jackline allows the easing of strain at the luff when a mainsail is lowered and furled, too.

I have always insisted on a leech line in a cruising sail, for it can be adjusted to prevent the leech from chattering, especially on the wind. The proportion of use a leech line receives depends in large measure on the amount of roach in the sail — and here we come to another area of controversy. Roach means battens. There ain't no way you're gonna have roach in your sail without battens!

The cruising fraternity is divided on the batten issue; many very experienced cruising folk wouldn't have a mainsail without battens. Others wouldn't let a batten aboard. Personally, I've swayed back and forth on the batten issue over the years —

Roach means battens. (Ralph Naranjo photo)

sometimes for, and, at other times, vehemently against (great strength of resolve). Lest the reader regard this with a curl of the lip and think, "Some guy to be writing a rigging book!" — let me present my reasons.

For a long time I was moderately happy but highly suspicious of battens in the mainsail of my yawl, until one dark night off Pukapuka in the Cook Islands, I was pounced on by a typical South Pacific rainsquall. I was lowering the mainsail in great haste when, halfway down and flogging like a whip, it managed to jam a batten between a cap shroud and the mast above the spreaders. I had to go up the ratlines in the lee rigging and onto the spreaders to free the batten before the sail would come down. I still remember tearing every batten out of the sail then and there, and with words to suit the occasion, hurling the lot over the side. There is nobody in this world or the next who could have discussed battens with me that night. I weakened as the years passed, though, and in the Caribbean's salubrious climate, I used battens again in the mainsail of my yawl and, later, in the schooner.

For the cruising man or woman who is all fired up to have battens in the leech of a mainsail, my opinion (for what it's worth) is that you should not hold out for too much roach; the bigger the "snapper-back" you insist on, the longer the battens will have to be. Settle for the minimum number of battens — certainly no more than four — and make sure every batten pocket is sewn to the middle of a sail panel at the leech — *not along or over a seam*. Otherwise, if the stitching of a sail seam needs resewing, the whole batten pocket must be "unpicked" from the sail, the repair on the panel effected, and the pocket sewn on again. A big, unnecessary deal.

Make sure that battens between rows of reef points are parallel to the points, and not at right angles to the leech. Otherwise, when a reef is pulled down and the batten gathered into the bunt, a strain could be placed on the top and bottom of the pocket as the batten is induced to lie flat. An alternative system is to have all batten pockets installed at right angles to the leech, and when reefing, to remove any batten that is in the way. The novelty of this last move will wear pretty thin after the first half-dozen reefs have been tucked in and the battens replaced before hoisting sail again. Far better to have the pockets built into the sail so that battens will lie flat along the boom when the sail is reefed.

Finally, for those of you who still intend to use battens in the mainsail of your cruiser, get out your palm, needle, and a length of waxed thread, and sew in each batten at the leech. Those cute pockets that have a V at the leech just can't keep a batten captive on a long trip. Batten pockets of this type are ideal for the weekender who bends on his sails Friday night and takes them off again Sunday. But they're not for the cruiser; someway, somehow, occasions arise when the battens pop out of their pockets. A favorite time is when hoisting sail again in a seaway after a bit of a blow: I've seen 'em going end-over-end downwind, time and again.

This section wouldn't be complete if I didn't point out that the cruiser who is content with a batten-free, hollow-cut leech will never have any of this strife. There is a lot to be said for a battenless mainsail. No matter how well batten pockets are built into a sail, those pieces of wood, plastic, reinforced nylon — or whatever the battens are made of — are still available to cause trouble. If, aboard any cruising boat, they go year after year without at some time causing their share of grief, then I'll volunteer to fly to the moon unassisted.

Battenless, partly reefed Stoway mainsail and partly reefed Seafurl jib. Note excess draft in luff of jib with sail partly rolled. (Courtesy Yachtspars)

I've always (often to my sorrow) been highly skeptical of push-button, patented, or newfangled innovations. (For instance, I had been deep-water sailing some 20 years before I allowed a roller-furling jib aboard. After I'd wound it in and out a few times, you'd think I invented the thing.) It's been the same with the Hood Stoway mainsail (see Chapter Two). This rig has been alive for years now — certainly long enough for the bugs to have been worked out of it. You wind a handle — or push a button! — and that sail sneaks out of sight into the mast, except for a tiny piece of clew. For the cruiser who is content with a battenless mainsail, this setup seems the ultimate.

There is, however (nothing is perfect), a little something we should mention about the Stoway mast. This has nothing to do with strength; the Stoway mast is plenty strong. It is, however, noisy. With the vessel lying head-to-wind, the mast is as quiet as any other. But with the ship in a marina, or anywhere where the wind can blow into the mast slot from a critical direction aft of the beam, the spar acts like the pipe of an organ and comes to life with a distinctive ululating cry. To throttle this down, you can use a contraption known as a "flute stopper," which is simply two long, sausagelike pieces (foam or rubber) about 1½ inches in diameter, which have been sewn around with material and joined together along one side by a piece of the same fabric. A halyard heaves the flute stopper aloft so that one sausage is inside the mast slot, the other outside, and everyone in the bay goes to sleep again.

Working Jibs

I like to see two sizes of working jibs in a cruising boat's wardrobe. The average boat, loaded down with her owner's belongings, plus all the gear and stores necessary for her own function as a long-range cruiser — a little workhorse — must always carry sufficient sail forward of the mast to give her drive. The heavier her displacement, the more she needs this. If such a vessel loses her jib, it'll make a dog out of her, especially on the wind. If there's any spare working sail a cruising boat should carry, it's a jib.

I carried two working jibs aboard my yawl for this reason. One jib was a high-clewed Yankee of 150 square feet, and the other, a smaller but similarly cut jib of 120 square feet. Both were originally eight-ounce Egyptian cotton, and in later years, six-ounce Terylene.

Aboard the schooner, we carried a 600-square-foot, six-ounce Dacron jib, and a Yankee jib of about half that area. The Yankee was eight-ounce Dacron. We would use the big jib when sailing a coast, or when among a sheltered island group; the Yankee was for an ocean passage, when we would use it in combination with a forestaysail.

The schooner's big jib was by no means a decksweeper; when sheeted hard in, it was still a good three feet above the rail. This didn't save it from Old Man Ocean, however, for one fine day between Tonga and the Fiji Islands, the top of a sea came curling over the windward bow and did it in. (Much beating of gums and complaints to the Almighty.) At the time I considered it most unfair, but the truth of the matter is that it served me bloody right. I should have swapped the big jib for the high-cut Yankee before leaving Vava'u.

A high-cut Yankee, with the clew eight or nine feet above the deck, is a wonderful jib for an ocean cruiser, but the lead of the sheet demands close attention. If the clew is so high that the sheet must be led well aft to give it a fair lead, this same sheet will chafe the underside of the main boom when the mainsail is eased. Also, when tacking, the flogging of that sheet around the cockpit area can give a man a smack in the ear that'll make his head ring for a week. Design your Yankee so that it leads to a point forward of the cockpit, and you'll win out on two counts.

The method by which a cruising boat's jib is hoisted, lowered, furled, or stowed is worth more than a moment's consideration. Roller-furling jibs are becoming more and more popular aboard cruisers each year. Both working jibs aboard our schooner were roller furling, and I never had cause to regret this. It's all a matter of preference, of course. Instead of roller furling, or the old piston hanks that clip a jib onto a headstay, there is the luff spar into which the leading edge of a headsail slides so beautifully. (It slides out and over the side beautifully, too, which is a serious

Roller-furled mainsail, jib, and staysail. Aboard this cutter, sail can be set, shortened, or furled in a jiffy. Note the stowed position of the twin running poles and the wide, flush deck. Hope the edge of that black mooring buoy isn't as hard and sharp as it looks! (Ralph Naranjo photo)

point for the cruising man to consider when choosing a system he can rely on aboard his boat.) A luff spar (see photographs) is a metal or plastic ''spar'' that revolves around a stay and that has one or more grooves to take the luff of a headsail.

You must be able to handle your sails in any conditions you're likely to encounter, with whatever crew you have aboard. If you figure you can manage to feed various sizes of jibs in and out of a regular luff spar at sea without any grief, then have at it. If you have any doubts, settle for piston hanks and downhauls like other sailors have done for years. A sail that is hanked to a stay is held captive whether it's up or down, so it's possible for a sailor to let go a halyard at the mainmast (or even the cockpit)

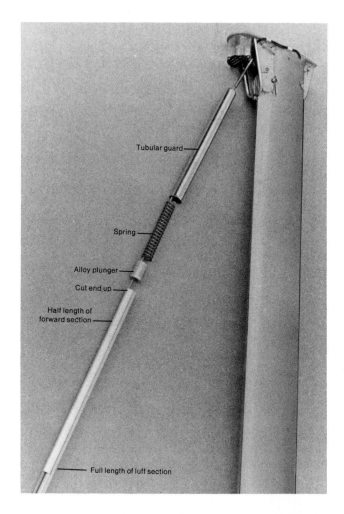

1. *An exploded view of the top assembly of the Gemini luff spar showing the tubular guard, the spring and alloy plunger, and the first lengths of aluminum extrusions. These extrusions are so placed in one full and one half length that joins will be staggered all the way down to the forestay. When assembling, the cut end of the short extrusion is placed uppermost. (Courtesy Yachtspars)*

Tubular guard

Spring

Alloy plunger

Cut end up

Half length of forward section

Full length of luff section

2. *Assembling interlocking pieces of extrusion for the luff spar around the forestay. (Courtesy Yachtspars)*

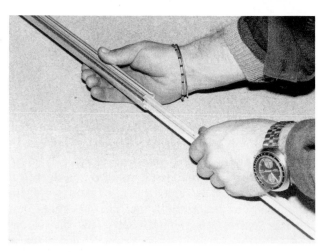

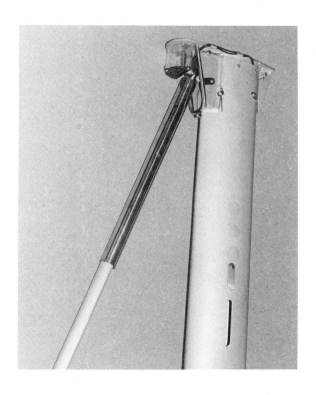

3. *Finished luff-spar
assembly with the tops of
both parts of the extrusion
inside the tubular guard
and the spring under com-
pression. The tubular
guard protects the spring
from the genoa and/or
spinnaker halyards and
protects the halyards from
chafe. (Courtesy
Yachtspars)*

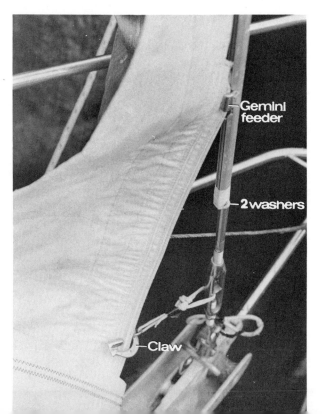

4. *Sail being fed
automatically into bottom
of a double-groove luff
spar. The sail must always
be hoisted through the
claw feeder, which lines it
up for the luff guide. The
lanyard should be fast at
least a foot above the stay
anchorage and be long
enough so the claw is never
closer than the same
distance from the luff
guide. (Courtesy
Yachtspars)*

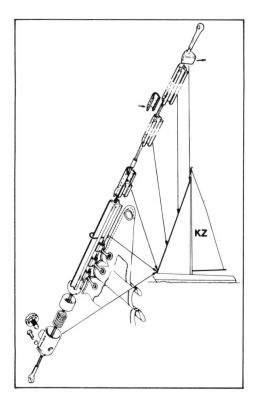

Drawing showing "Kayzee" removable cartridge at base of luff spar. (Courtesy Yachtspars)

and, without changing position, heave that sail down. And when it's down, it's still held to the stay by its hanks.

This could never be done with a headsail that feeds in and out of a groove in a luff spar. You've got to be right up there, bundling it into a bag or down a hatch as it slips out the bottom of the groove. and if a bight gets whisked over the side, you can hang on until your nose bleeds — and still be mighty lucky to get it back if you're out there alone. Picking up a jib that's gone over the side (and probably under the boat) is, at the very least, one hell of a job, and it's often tough on the sail, too. Anyone contemplating using a regular luff spar aboard a shorthanded cruising boat and indulging in a drop of singlehanded jib-changing at sea is well advised to secure netting between rail and lifeline from the shrouds forward to help confine the sail.

The same applies to a somewhat lesser extent aboard the vessel whose roller-furling jib is on a luff spar. Furling sail with this rig is so much easier than dealing with a hanked-on jib — or one that must be captured as its leading edge emerges from the bottom of the spar — that a comparison is ridiculous. However, if the intention is to change jibs at sea, the same care must be exercised as when taking a non-roller-furling headsail off its spar.

The Kayzee headfoil, with its removable magazines, seems to me to be an excellent way of controlling headsails on a luff spar during a setting or furling operation. The Kayzee is an aluminum extrusion that fits around the forestay in the usual manner. The foil has two continuous tracks; each track has a removable magazine at its lower end. A headsail, which has been fitted with Kayzee slides and loaded into its own magazine, is simply snapped into place at the bottom of the extrusion. The headsail hoists straight out of its magazine and, of course, lowers obediently into it. Both sail and magazine can be stowed below. With this system, there is just no chance that a headsail will slip out of its groove in a luff spar and over the side as it is being lowered. Kayzee foils, complete with magazines and slides, are distributed by Yachtspars (Auckland, New Zealand) and Alspar (Sydney, Australia).

The roller jib, which furls around its own luff wire, is different again. This is the system I've most often been shipmates with. We would usually hoist our roller-furling Yankee before an ocean passage, winding it in and out in the bay, making sure there were several turns of wire still on the drum when it was furled. Brimming with pride and confidence, away we'd go. Light weather during the voyage would often call for this jib to be furled — a 10-second job — and a lightweight genoa hanked to the forestay, which was 12 inches forward of the roller-furling jib at the tack and about six inches forward at the head.

The sheets of this non-luff-spar roller-furling jib have been coiled and hung at the tack of the sail to be out of the way during a stay in port. Note wire leading aft from open-type drum and generous distance between forestay and furled jib. (Courtesy Yachtspars)

Taking off this type of roller-furling jib at sea (something we seldom did) was not difficult; it was rolled up like a window blind and, all going well, would lower obediently to the deck. (In answer to the reader whose blood pressure shoots up on reading this, who is all ready to give me hell because he had a devil of a time with his gear last week, I'll temper that last observation by saying that *usually* this went like clockwork.) The only time we ever had any excitement getting the rolled jib lowered and out of the way was when the sail in use was the large (600-square-foot) jib, and the onset of a spot of really bad weather had made me feel guilty enough to take it down from where it should never have been in the first place.

The only times we used that large roller-furling jib on an ocean trip were when I cast an "experienced" eye at the weather before leaving and forecast an easy voyage — a practice that accounted for the complete demise of the jib on one passage. If it came on to blow at sea when the Yankee was in use, we'd roll it up and leave it where it was, even if we ended up hove-to under main staysail. The only time that weather influenced the lowering and stowing of the rolled-up Yankee was when we were huddled in some hole during the hurricane season and the barometer was telling us to get all sail below and stowed.

A roller-furling jib, which is rolled up by its own rotating luff wire, must be hoisted very tightly. The luff wire of such a jib should be strong enough to do the job of a forestay, since the only way the jib can be expected to set well on the wind is to have a drum-tight luff. As soon as the jib is full of wind, the forestay is apt to slack a little, placing the strain normally taken by the headstay onto the luff wire of the jib. The luff wire of this type of roller-furling jib should be 1/19 stainless steel wire rope, plastic covered or taped. (Don't encase the stainless in Dacron; they just don't get along.)

It is important on this type of roller jib that the terminal fitting at the head not be so buried and swathed in sailcloth and strengthening tape that the head of the sail becomes large in body. If the head of the jib is bulky, it can gather in the forestay when being furled and create something of a crisis. This can be avoided by having the throat of the luff terminal fitting just clear of the sail at the head. Attach strong Dacron lashings (or wire) from the throat of the terminal fitting to a well-reinforced cringle in the strainer patch at the head of the sail. The same type of fitting is also suitable at the tack. The insulated luff wire should be hand-stitched strongly to the luff inside the folded tabling.

Always buy a drum and swivels a size larger than are recommended for the sail area you intend to handle. Never purchase minimum-sized equipment for your cruising boat; for year-in, year-out performance, go at least one size heavier.

Some members of the cruising fraternity declare that the closed type of roller-furling drum is the way to go. I've only used the open type, and have found it easy enough to clear the occasional foul of overriding wire turns on the drum, which have been caused when strain is not kept on the wire as the jib unfurls. Seems to me that fiddling with a foul inside a closed drum would be an interesting experience.

Roller-furling luff spars have been with us for many years now. I saw one aboard a hefty 55-foot cutter in 1971 in Suva, Fiji. The vessel was on a delivery voyage from New Zealand to the Virgin Islands, and she had an aluminum luff spar that revolved around her forestay. I remember being interested, but not impressed, because of the

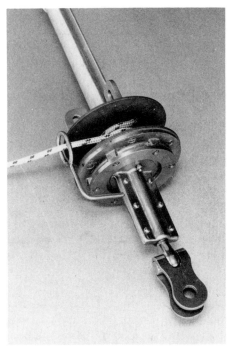

Left: *Partially enclosed drum using 7/19 wire at the base of a luff-spar roller-furling rig.* **Right:** *Open drum and rope guide at the base of a roller-furling luff spar. (Courtesy Yachtspars)*

diameter of the roll. The aluminum spar was of such a size that by the time the jib was totally wound around it, the spar was some six inches through at the thickest part, where the clew was rolled on.

It's a different ball game now. The luff spar extrusions being used these days can make even the most hard-nosed among us look twice. Since Phil Weld won the 1980 OSTAR in his trimaran *Moxie* with Hood's Sea Furl on both jib and staysail (he had a Stoway mainsail, too), the usefulness of luff spar furling cannot be denied.

There are considerable advantages to a roller-furling luff spar — just as long as its section is small enough not to add unrealistically to the diameter of the rolled sail. First, the extrusion fits over the headstay, which immediately takes away one of the biggest bogeys of a roller-furled headsail: winding the jib around the headstay when furling. Second, the luff spar minimizes headstay sag. Third, the strain on swivel bearings, which is always present when the luff wire of a roller-furling jib assumes the job of headstay, is considerably less. Normal halyard tension is all that is necessary.

This last, to me, is the greatest attraction of all. The weight that the swivel bearings have to take, on a roller-furling jib set flying, is extraordinary at times. Every few months would see me taking apart the drum and head swivels of our furling gear in the schooner's engine room, examining and cleaning the ball races, and regreasing them with Lubriplate A. Swivels with roller bearings are an improvement on the ball-bearing jobs, but even so, the strain on the fittings, the beefed-up luff wire, the two-part or sometimes three-part 7/19 wire purchase at the head of the sail — these are all part and parcel of a roller-furling jib whose luff wire acts as a headstay.

One of the greatest tests that can be given to any piece of seagoing equipment is to use it on a boat that works for her living. A lot of pleasure-boat equipment just can't take the exigencies of the commercial life. The type of luff spar furling used aboard *Moxie,* however, appears to be able to take anything thrown at it. For some time now, I've watched this type of furling aboard the bareboats belonging to two charter companies in the Virgin Islands; one outfit has its headquarters in the British Virgins and the other works out of St. Thomas. Charter groups, many of whom have never even seen the rig before, walk aboard and take these vessels cruising for a couple of weeks. And the bareboat charter companies are still sold on the rig.

There seems no doubt that this type of furling is efficient. The only reservations that I have about the suitability of luff spar furling for the headsails of the short-handed, long-range cruising boat (and that I feel bound to mention) are those outlined later in this chapter in the section on storm sails.

Forestaysails

Double-headsail-rigged cruising boats often use a boom, called a "club," on the foot of their forestaysail. I don't know whose bright idea it was to foist a club onto a staysail (and the crew of the vessel), because the bloke, whoever he was, has been out of circulation for some hundreds of years. (Just as well, because if some of us could get our hands on him . . . .) Staysail clubs think that ownership of the foredeck is their God-given right; they neither respect nor fear the crew of a sailboat. Woe betide the sailor who ventures onto the foredeck while that club is thrashing around. The clew of a staysail that has no spar can give a man a wallop he'll remember for a day or two, but the same treatment from a club end can make him think he's headed for the Promised Land.

The main idea of a club, of course, is to make the staysail self-tending. You can put the ship about and the club will swing faithfully to the other side. Here, held by its sheet, it will keep the staysail in its preset position on the new tack. On the face of it, this is fine and dandy, and it does work. As far as efficiency goes, though, it's another story. To get the best out of a staysail, the clew should come back aft of the mast and create a slot effect. If you want to do better yet, put the clew close to the deck and back as far as it can sensibly come (without letting the leech foul the lower spreader), and make a genoa staysail out of it. Being well inside the rail, the staysail can't scoop up water from the lee bow wave. Combine this with a high-clewed Yankee and you've got a mighty efficient double-headsail rig. The idea isn't new; John Illingworth, in his *Myth of Malham,* beat the tar out of the opposition in almost every British ocean race he entered in the late 1940s by exploiting this rig.

A staysail whose clew when sheeted home is aft of the mast cannot be on a club. The staysail sheet must be slacked away on one tack and hove in on the other in the same manner as a jib. This is the most efficient way of handling a staysail, but it entails more work for a shorthanded crew when tacking. It also means that another set of winches is called for — unless, of course, the staysail is small and single blocks on pendants are utilized to form a tackle, as described in Chapter Five.

This forestaysail has its very own lazyjacks, but the club rules the foredeck. Note the "stow" of the fisherman-type anchors. (Ralph Naranjo photo)

A working staysail (not a genoa staysail) is sometimes the same weight as the mainsail aboard a cruising boat; it is fitted with one, or even two rows of reef points. As the main is reefed, so is the staysail. A genoa staysail, which is usually doused and swapped for the working staysail when the wind freshens to above 20 knots, can be up to two weights lighter than the mainsail. A staysail is a real workhorse aboard a cruising boat. It should be very strong, with the same attention paid to strainer patches, cringles, stitching, tabling, and roping as to these parts on the mainsail. The alternatives for hoisting or setting a staysail are the same as for a jib.

This cutter uses a wishbone on her staysail instead of a club. Note dinghy stowage. (Ralph Naranjo photo)

If, despite all warnings, you are still determined to use a staysail club, make sure that the bottom block of the staysail sheet is on a traveler that crosses the full width of deck necessary to sheet the sail properly when hard on the wind. Otherwise great loss of efficiency will be felt when the end of the club lifts and slackens the leech. The sheet should be led forward along the underside of the boom to a block at the gooseneck of the club, and then aft to the cockpit (or whatever point is chosen to trim the staysail). This sheet, being rove to disadvantage, is sometimes hard to trim, especially on the wind in a breeze.

The owner of a club staysail also must contend with the necessity to slack the luff with a jackline, slack the clew, or install the gooseneck on a traveler or "horse" so that the club can be eased forward as the sail is lowered. Otherwise the staysail will not come down much farther than the point on the stay that forms a right angle with the club end. Probably the most common way to deal with this situation is to use a jackline as I did with the schooner's forestaysail (with which I had a running vendetta over the years).

A piece of Dacron line is spliced into an eyelet situated the sail's foot-length up the luff. It is possible to buy piston hanks that incorporate a large hole in the body to accommodate a jackline. With a piston hank clipped to the stay below the splice, the jackline is led through this hole. Seized at right angles to the bolt rope on the luff, at each eyelet toward the tack, are two brass cringles of a size to accept the jackline after leaving a hank. A piston hank is clipped to the stay between each pair of cringles — the jackline running from cringle to hank to cringle, and so on, until the tack is reached. Seizing the cringles at right angles to the luff gives the jackline a fair lead and prevents a twist in the staysail luff from the line passing through eyelets. Tension on the jackline is determined by hoisting the staysail and heaving the jackline taut before making it fast to the tack cringle.

In addition to limiting the size of a forestaysail, the staysail club — especially if the foot of the sail is fast to the boom along its length — interferes with the airfoil shape of the sail. The way to get a minimum measure of cooperation and efficiency out of a staysail is to hold the foot of the headsail to the club with a lashing, footstops, or a track, and then pivot the gooseneck on a fitting attached to the turnbuckle that holds the stay. That way, you'll not only muzzle the sail from drawing decently when eased, you'll also stand a good chance of damaging or breaking the turnbuckle as well. Incredibly, we do sometimes see this rig.

A way to give the foot of a club staysail an acceptable amount of flow, and at the same time salve one's conscience about having such a fiendish setup on the foredeck, is to pivot the club on a stand a foot or so aft of the tack and use the staysail loose-footed, with its clew the only part of the sail fast to the boom. This way, when the sail is eased, the foot will assume a shape more in keeping with the rest of the sail.

As long as there is plenty of wind, this arrangement is the one that sees the staysail boom at its best — out of the way and clear of the ship. The crew of the vessel, taking their courage in both hands and giving way to little cries of delight, can gingerly explore the foredeck now, if that is their wish. But they'd better be ready for instant flight. If the wind drops suddenly, or if, for any reason, the staysail becomes blanketed, the club that owns the area forward of the mast will swing violently inboard and dish out a helping of cuts and abrasions.

If the boat has a bowsprit, a foreguy can be rigged from the end of the club to a block shackled to the cranse iron; this is about the only way the staysail clew can be kept out there in a light breeze. The angle of the stay to the boom encourages the boom to assume an amidships position whenever possible. The crew of a vessel without a bowsprit, and consequently without a place to run a foreguy, are out of luck. The foredeck, for them, is taboo.

The end of the club should have a topping lift to keep the whole thing from dropping when the sail is lowered. I led the forestaysail lift aboard the *White Squall II*

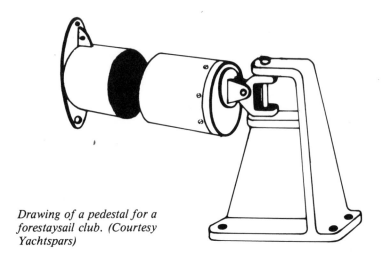

*Drawing of a pedestal for a
forestaysail club. (Courtesy
Yachtspars)*

from the boom end to a block below the staysail stay and down to a pin rail near the
port shrouds. Even when anchored in a bay, that boom was a menace. I installed a
snaphook on a two-foot pendant in both port and starboard shrouds to hold the
club when we were at anchor, and I would hook up whichever side was convenient.
The end of the club was just at eye level, and after I walked into it one night and it
trimmed my personal port lamp a rare shade of black with an artistic blue-orange
edge, I painted the end white. Another night, going forward in a crouch in a rainsquall to close the forward hatch, the block hanging from the end of the club slugged
me between *both* my lamps. After that, I hoisted the thing eight feet in the air
whenever we anchored. The worst that the club sheet could do was to catch an un-
wary sailor across the throat and give his Adam's apple a workout.

The owner of a vessel equipped with a forestaysail on a club obviously leads a
much fuller life than his contemporary who sheets his staysail home with winches
and who owns a foredeck free of large, violent pieces of wood. It's all a matter of
personal preference, cost, and efficiency. If you really want your vessel to perform,
forget about a club; have your forestaysail cut so that the clew comes aft of the
mast. The driving power of your mainsail will then be increased by the resulting
"slot" effect. There is no way a staysail on a club can achieve this.

And the cost of the club and all its gear versus a couple of winches? By the time a
staysail club is shaped, the gooseneck and end fittings are installed (some clubs even
have an outhaul and track), a pedestal with a swiveling eye or fork (the rest of the
gooseneck fitting) is bolted firmly forward, blocks and leads for sheet and topping
lift are purchased — a fair piece of change has been laid out. The price of a pair of
winches can have a man scraping the bottom of the money locker, as we know, but
there's probably not too much difference in cost between sheeting a staysail home
with a club or with winches.

Winches, though, can be utilized for other jobs — which is a distinction a club can
never claim. To use the genoa staysail, for instance, someone may suggest stowing
the working staysail below, unshipping the club, and reeving sheets for the genoa
staysail, which all adds up to a lot of toil aboard, say, a two-handed cruising boat.

And just how do you sheet the genoa staysail? With winches, of course! I say that once you've unshipped the staysail club, for whatever reason, never put it back. Keep it aboard, though, and swap the thing for a couple of bunches of bananas from a Pacific Islander sometime when you're cruising down that way. He'll chop it up and use it to dry his copra. That, in my book, is a suitable end for any staysail club.

Mizzens

A mizzen is a little mainsail in shape and construction. Being smaller than the mainsail, it is usually a lighter weight. Again, this varies from boat to boat; the mizzen on a ketch is often almost as large as the mainsail, while the mizzen on a yawl is quite small. Aboard some ketches, the mizzen might be two-thirds or more of the area of the mainsail and have as many rows of reef points, in which case it might be built of the same cloth. Whatever the size of the sail or the weight of its fabric, a mizzen for a cruising boat should be built with the same attention to strength as that paid to a mainsail.

I like to see a mizzen cut flat so there is less chance of its luffing or being backwinded by the mainsail when on the wind. When the vessel is running before the wind, the mizzen is usually hauled down because it blankets the mainsail, so the sail doesn't need to be cut full. When the wind pipes up, the mizzen is usually reefed or dropped, depending on its size and on how the skipper uses his rig to deal with the weather conditions. When I first put a mizzen in the *White Squall* to convert her from a cutter to a yawl, I had great visions of dropping the mainsail in a really hard breeze and proceeding safely and joyously under mizzen and jib, and/or staysail. I mean, it *sounded* good. It didn't work, though. I tried it a number of times and was never happy with the combination. With a great gap between mizzen and headsail once the mainsail was furled, I just wasn't getting the best out of my ship. So I would douse the mizzen, reef the main, and continue under this rig with one headsail (usually the staysail). Then I would occupy my time by gazing at the mizzen with great disillusionment, since I was towing it along and its only contribution was negative.

Some mizzens are cut flat so that, day and night, they can be kept up at anchor. There is a worldwide fraternity I've always thought of as the Mizzen Club. Anyone can join; the only qualification for membership is that you keep your mizzen up all the time while lying on a mooring or hook. It's a practice that sends sailmakers wild with joy; a member of the club is assured of an enthusiastic reception in any sail loft. Working on the theory that the more a sail flaps, the more it wears, members of the Mizzen Club voluntarily shorten the lives of their sails and contribute in a modest way to a sailmaker's income. Membership fees in the Mizzen Club are waived, since it is generally accepted that Club wallahs shell out enough in unnecessary sail repair to make the organization exclusive and expensive enough as it is.

I remember a night when a member of the Club dropped anchor alongside me at Peter Island in the British Virgins. It was a nice, calm, innocent-looking night, and during it he sailed into me twice. After all hands, gummy-eyed, had been up fending him off the second time, I asked him why he didn't pull down his mizzen (I used a few more words than this, actually), and he replied that it was because the mizzen

Member of the mizzen club. (Ralph Naranjo photo)

held his head into the wind. Now, I always thought that our schooner lay head to wind in the practically tideless Virgins. I must have been mistaken.

You meet these mizzen maniacs all over the world. One day when Minine and I were anchored in the *White Squall II* behind the island of Isabella in a fairly remote part of the Galapagos, she called excitedly down the hatch for me to come on deck, saying that one of my favorite sights was going past. At the time, we hadn't seen another human, let alone a boat, for more than a month, and I came from below thinking . . . no, it couldn't be. Sure enough, though, there he was, a full-fledged member of the Club, powering upwind with only his mizzen hoisted, and flapping to beat the band. A sight to make any sailmaker delirious with happiness.

I have a friend who actually found a use for a mizzen in a boat under 50 feet. (I won't give you his real name, because he hasn't got time to sit down and answer all the letters. I'll call him John.) He had a 38-foot yawl, which could sleep four and which he chartered in the Virgin Islands. His feeling for mizzens closely approximated my own, but he found that when four charter guests were aboard and he had to sleep in the cockpit, his mizzen enabled him to do it, come rain or blow.

John's hatch was offset to port, and when he was all fired up to retire for the night, he would slack the sheet to the mizzen, which had been left hoisted and flapping, and, with the foreguy, heave the boom about halfway out on the port side. The wind hitting the sail would cant the stern of his vessel to starboard, giving him a lee on the port side of the cockpit, over which wind could howl and rain could pelt while our ingenious sailor slept like a baby.

This commentary on mizzens would not be complete without once again making reference to a mizzen staysail, since there is hardly an occasion when I've sounded off about mizzens that an interjection concerning this sail hasn't been brightly, even triumphantly, delivered. Although I can carry on at great length about this sail when aroused, I will content myself with (in addition to what was said earlier in the book) just a few comments. First of all, even if you get one of these temperamental pieces of fabric up and drawing, you're living in the middle of a sail. Also, visibility forward quite often becomes a memory. And last, but by no means least, this sail doesn't help in cementing relations between skipper and cook; nothing, but nothing, can blow out the flame of a galley stove quite as successfully as the downdraft from a mizzen staysail.

Storm Sails

Never leave port on anything more than an afternoon's jaunt without your storm sails. A sensible, seamanlike approach to any kind of sailing is to plan that once you have poked your nose outside the breakwater, you should be able to deal with whatever conditions might arise *by yourself,* without hollering for help. It's a funny thing, but it seems that the more conscientious we are about readying our vessel and ourselves for the worst, the less the preparations are needed. But if we don't apply ourselves to all this before leaving port, we get it in the neck. If Murphy's law can be applied to any facet of human endeavor, it seems best suited to the life of the cruising sailor.

Just as important as a strong suit of cruising sails — and far more important than genoas and other light extras — are a storm trysail and a storm jib. I'm an advocate of storm trysails that are not more than 30 percent of the area of the mainsail. For a vessel with an unusual rig, an already tiny main, or an obviously oversized mainsail, the cooperation of a reliable sailmaker who is also an oceangoing seaman (not all of them are) should be enlisted to determine this area. The point to be remembered is that the trysail is for *storm conditions only.* A trysail that blows out in bad weather and starts flogging and whipping torn pieces of sail about the deck can injure someone. A storm trysail's strength must be beyond reproach. Don't let anyone talk you into putting battens in your trysail; have the sail cut with a hollow leech and either

*Switchover installed above
stacked mainsail slides to
enable trysail to use mainmast
track. (Courtesy Yachtspars)*

roped or taped heavily all around. The tack, head, and clew cringles must be built so that under no conceivable conditions will they part from the sail.

The storm jib, or storm staysail (what it's called depends on where it's used) must be just as strong as the storm trysail. The IOR (International Offshore Rule) recommends that the area of a storm jib be no more than five percent of I squared, where I is the above-deck height of the mast. This is the absolute maximum; in fact, four or even three-and-a-half percent is more realistic. If the ship has a strong working staysail that can be reefed, this can be carried with the trysail until it's time to heave-to. Then it's a job for the storm jib.

Always have your storm sails where you can get at them quickly. Buried under a bunk up forward or at the bottom of a pile of gear in a lazarette is no place to stow them. Aboard cruising boats whose skippers travel only in recommended seasons, storm sails are seldom used. They should be looked after carefully in port, however, and be ready for use without the need for foraging around to find them at the start of even a short passage.

A favorite (and good) location for the storm trysail is in a bag on deck at the foot of the mainmast. On small boats it is sometimes possible to reach above the stacked mainsail slides and feed the trysail slides through a gate and onto the main track. An alternative is to have a section of track leading from such a gate to the foot of the mast at one side, and to keep the trysail in a bag, yet with its slides already on the track. Best of all is the trysail in this last position, but on its own separate track, secured to the mast alongside the main track. This is an independent rig with less chance than any other of foul-ups when hoisting.

The sailcloth of a storm trysail is sometimes the same weight as the mainsail, but rugged strength is built into it through oversized strainer patches, tabling, and roping. The idea is that the lighter the weight, the easier it will be to set the trysail in a blow. I consider that a storm trysail should be one weight heavier than the mainsail, unless the mainsail itself is constructed of heavier-than-usual fabric. If the trysail lives in a bag at the foot of the mast, the fact that it's a weight heavier than the main won't make any difference at all to the hoisting and setting of the sail. It can make a big difference to a sailor's peace of mind, though, once it's up there. When you're lying hove-to in a gale of wind, it is no time to start having doubts about the strength of your storm sails.

A separate track for a storm trysail should be fastened very strongly to the mast over its full length. The top of the track should continue a couple of feet up past the head of the trysail. This point should have double fastenings to take the strain at the head of the sail, as well as a stop to prevent the trysail from being over-hoisted in a gale in the dark. You might also mark the pendant attached to the tack so that it can be made fast securely at a correct, predetermined height.

Don't mark the pendant with a splotch of paint or with a piece of colored wool poked between the strands; in extreme conditions at night, you'll never see it. Forget about aesthetics and tie a figure-eight knot — something you can feel. Provision for securing the pendant varies from boat to boat. If there is a strong hook or eye at the gooseneck, an eyesplice at the bottom of the pendant might be slipped under or shackled to this. It's handy to have a good cleat each side of the mast. The figure-eight in the pendant can be tucked under a cleat, ensuring the correct trysail height when hoisted. The pendant continues on around the forward side of the mast, back under the other cleat, once around the mast again, and makes fast to its standing part with two half hitches. However it is done, the pendant should be well secured before the trysail is hoisted.

So should the trysail sheets. Some seamen prefer to use a block and tackle such as a handy billy for each trysail sheet. I like two single sheets, each made fast to the trysail clew with a bowline. One sheet goes to port and the other to starboard. My reasoning is that a trysail in a bag at the foot of a mast with its luff slides on a track can only be considered ready to go if its pendant and sheets are also attached and in the bag. Block-and-tackle sheets can be in the bag, of course, but it is very easy to haul a tackle out of a bag and inadvertently turn over one of the blocks and twist the parts of the purchase. Rendering the line of a tackle in a gale can be a hell of a job, too, to say nothing of those blocks flailing around when hoisting the sail.

Tools are needed if tackles are used at the trysail clew. It's too risky to use snap-shackles on the sheet blocks, since they can flog open. This means that the bottom port and starboard sheet blocks have to be secured to pad eyes or eyebolts in the deck with screw shackles, which must then be tightened with a wrench beyond all question of loosening. If the vessel has no winches, then so be it — handy billies it is. But in a boat where a couple of good winches are available, lead a strong Dacron sheet to port and starboard from the trysail clew through single blocks, shackled solidly at deck level. Don't use snatch blocks, because these, too, can flog open. Each sheet should be given a minimum of four turns around a winch and belayed. The trysail is then ready to hoist.

The clew, when hoisted, should be clear of the main boom. If the boom can be positioned amidships in a strong crotch, or better yet, in a gallows frame, this greatly lessens the chance that trysail sheets will chafe the furled mainsail. If the lead of the lee sheet block puts the clew of the trysail an undesirable distance down to leeward, the windward sheet winch can be utilized to heave the clew toward the ship's centerline, achieving the same result as a tackle on a mainsheet traveler. When hoisting the trysail, keep clear of those sheets — a clout from one of them will make you think all your birthdays have come at once. As soon as the trysail is at full hoist, take the weight on the leeward sheet so as to take all flap out of the sail.

Aboard the 33-foot *White Squall,* we lashed the clew of the tiny storm trysail to the main boom before hoisting away. The furled mainsail was rolled to one side and the trysail sheet passed beneath the bolt rope on the foot of the mainsail and the boom, continued around under the boom, up over its standing part, back under the boom again to form a stopper hitch, passed around and around the boom for some six feet or so, and finished off with a clove hitch. This never moved. The boom was topped slightly to prevent unfair strain from coming on the leech of the trysail, and the sail was then hoisted. The advantage of this system is that the regular main boom equipment, such as mainsheet and foreguy, can now be used to control the position of the trysail.

With the more usual method of a trysail clew held by sheets to port and starboard, this last-mentioned system is sometimes used when a decision is made to run the vessel off. The windward sheet is eased, the boom is topped to within a few inches of the height of the trysail clew, and the sheet made fast to the boom. The lee sheet is slacked away and you're in business. Pad eyes or cleats affixed to the boom for the express purpose of securing the trysail clew might have something to recommend them. Once more, it comes down to personal preference. There seem to be a dozen ways of doing every job at sea; the best thing, perhaps, is to give a lot of thought to a system that works, and use it — but never stop keeping your eye peeled for a way that is better. The reason we used the method described to lash the trysail clew to the *White Squall*'s boom is that, when securing a line with strain on it in bad weather, I'm a nut for going round-and-round-and-round something.

Some vessels own a trysail big enough to be reefed. What this means, first of all, is that when it comes time to shorten the thing down to something resembling a pocket handkerchief, the weather is really turning it on. My tip is to lower the sail right down to the bottom of its track, tie in the reef, and hoist away again. When the wind feels like a smack in the face from a wet towel, it is no time to be standing up and trying to do like the slab-reefers do. Get down as close to that deck as you can.

The trysail of a gaff-rigger can be exactly the same as that of a marconi-rigged boat. I've never seen a trysail on its own track on a gaff-rigged mast, but you can bet that somewhere on this planet is a bloke who has his gaff and luff slides on a track, and right alongside it has a track for his trysail, too. If so, bully for him, because that's what I would do. A gaff in a saddle and a luff equipped with mast hoops cancels out a track for the trysail. The solution to the problem is a jackline spliced to the trysail head and going around and forward of the mast, back and through a luff eyelet, then forward *the same side,* around the mast, and back to pick up the next eyelet down, and so on. It works, too, although a few more acrobatics are called for than if the trysail were on its own track going to the foot of the mast.

There is, of course, a gaff trysail. This sail is bent to its own small gaff, complete with well-leathered jaws and parrel balls. The luff is held to the mast with a jackline.

This sail is not without a following; there are some dedicated gaff-or-nothing souls who wouldn't dream of hoisting anything without a gaff — and that goes for the trysail as well. They probably have a good reason for it, too; a gaff cutter with a center of effort that is well forward might not be happy with a marconi trysail.

The part I don't like about setting a gaff trysail — quite aside from wrestling that gaff up over the furled mainsail — is unshackling the peak halyards and securing them to the spar of the storm sail. Aboard the last gaff-rigger I owned (an ancient 38-footer), I riveted the pins of the screw shackles that held the two single-sheave peak halyard blocks to the wire gaff strops, and then I moused the eyes of these same pins with seizing wire. The thought of letting all this security go by the board, by nonchalantly unshackling in a gale of wind, is enough to make a man hunt for his beads. However, if a gaff trysail has to be set, there seems to be no other way out.

The storm jib, or storm staysail, should be constructed of the same material as the trysail, with similar attention paid to the strength of tack, head, and clew cringles. The design of the ship and her rig determines the distance forward of the mast that this sail occupies, but as a general rule in extreme conditions, the sail is set on a stay well aft of the bow — hence the term "storm staysail." Being well inboard, the sail can contribute a slot effect to benefit the drawing power of the trysail, while at the same time being far enough aft not to scoop up water.

Heaving-to is accomplished by hauling the storm headsail clew slightly to weather, heaving the trysail clew to within a few degrees of the ship's centerline, and putting the tiller to leeward or the wheel to windward. Deciding how much to windward the headsail should be, how far in the trysail should come, and where the helm should be positioned is the result of trial and error. The idea is to keep slow, controllable way on the vessel. The trysail provides drive ahead; the helm, adjusted to bring the ship into the wind, prevents the way from becoming excessive; and the slightly backed storm headsail stops the boat from coming about.

With the popularity of luff spar furling aboard oceangoing boats, we come, inevitably, to the question of how to set a small "iron-plated" storm headsail on a vessel that has both jib and staysail luff spar furling. Ideally, both of the roller-furling headsails should be off and stowed below decks by the time storm sails are needed. The chances of this, however, aboard a two-handed cruising boat caught in a gale at sea are rather remote. (How many among us can recognize an increase in wind as the forerunner of a storm?) When we're paddling along out there at sea and things have been going pretty well, it's easy to become complacent. We might sail from one side to the other of the largest ocean in the world without getting caught in a gale. On the other hand, we can be one day out of port and run into the mother and father of them all.

Aboard a shorthanded cruising boat that has roller-furling headsails set on a luff spar, the possibility must be faced that one day those sails might have to stay up in a gale. They might have to stay rolled around their spars because it's too dangerous for the crew to try to get them down. This doesn't apply to a vessel that has a complement of young, hirsute characters capable of doing all sorts of things at all sorts of times. It concerns long-range cruising boats, which, in general, don't have that kind of crew.

The windage presented by the rolled sails might, in extreme conditions, force a vessel's head downwind; here it depends on their bulk when rolled. A rolled sail set flying can be battled down in a gale because of its long, thin sausage shape; I know, for the simple reason that I've done it. A sail wound around a luff spar can't be lowered unless it is unfurled. As it comes down and slips out the bottom of its groove in the luff spar, someway, somehow, it must be muzzled down and stuffed in a bag. It boggles the mind to imagine one man achieving this in a gale, with that unfurled sail flogging like a demon.

Since a luff spar roller-furling headsail may have to stay up in a gale, the rolled bulk of each sail should present as little windage as possible. The smaller and tighter the roll, the better. If you intend to unfurl the sails in a breeze of wind, and then lower and stow them, make sure they are of a size that the crew (you, probably) can handle.

Using a tiny, unrolled piece of staysail as a storm headsail may be practical on some vessels. The skipper who intends to employ this tactic aboard his cruising boat had better acquaint his sailmaker with this revelation when the staysail is being built. Extra-strong strainers and an adequate clew should be built into the sail right at the outset. Other options include being clairvoyant enough to have the working staysail off and stowed, and the storm jib fed up into the groove of the roller-furling spar before the weather makes such an act impossible. An alternative is a strong, spare stay, which can be kept alongside either port or starboard shrouds, available to set up just aft of the roller-furling staysail. A storm headsail is hanked onto this and hoisted and sheeted in the usual manner.

This last is easier to write about than to do. In bad weather, it may require a great exercise of will to move oneself even three or four feet. Having to go through the drill of unlashing the temporary stay, and with the thing waving and threshing around, securing it to an eyebolt on the foredeck wouldn't appeal to many people. No, whatever is done in bad weather must be uncomplicated. I'll never forget wedging myself between a couple of bunks in my yawl and bolting together a heavy wooden sea anchor during a gale in the Southern Ocean. It was a hell of a job, and the memory has never left me. I had planned things badly; I had too many bits and pieces to fuss around with at a time when everything should have been at hand and ready to go.

The cruising man or woman who decides to use luff spar roller furling on the headsails of his or her boat had better be certain — absolutely — that the gear is rugged and simple. Have a storm jib that will fit the groove of your roller-furling spar, by all means, but make sure that the headsail itself is beefed up enough for a sliver of it to do the job of a storm sail if need be.

Manufacturers of roller-furling luff spars who tout their equipment as suitable for the shorthanded, long-range cruising boat have a big responsibility. Cruising couples, who often leave for five or 10 years with the intention of poking into odd corners of the world, rely on their equipment to perform as advertised. They expect this, for year after year. If they carry the roller-spar rig, the extrusion has got to be tough enough never to twist; if a spinnaker pole slams into it, nobody should have to worry. Its section must be small enough not to add unrealistically to the bulk of the rolled sail. Quite a tall order.

There is no doubt that a roller-furling headsail makes the cruising life easy. Our roller jibs aboard the schooner, which were set flying and therefore could be lowered in a gale when furled, made all the difference to Minine's and my handling of the 60-tonner. In the 1980 OSTAR, Phil Weld didn't have to effect a single headsail change, since both jib and staysail were luff spar roller furling. Phil Steggall, who finished third, approximately seven hours behind Weld, made 56 headsail changes during the race.

But in the seamen's lore handed down through generations of small-boat handling in extreme conditions, nothing stands out more clearly than the need for keeping down windage aloft to maintain stability. The headsails of luff spar roller-furling gear might be impossible for some people to get down and stowed in gale conditions. And if they're left up there, it's in direct contravention of long-established small-boat practice. A manufacturer of luff spar roller furling should ponder this before recommending his equipment as the answer for the shorthanded cruiser. The cruising man or woman should think about it, too.

The hoisting and setting of a storm trysail, and the hanking on or unfurling of a storm-sized headsail, should be practiced regularly. The first time, do the exercise in daylight and in good weather, when either moored or anchored. Run through the drill a few times, and then do it at night. A practice shot when sailing comes next — preferably at night when it is raining. If it's only you and your wife or husband who are going to be off and away cruising, make sure that no friend aboard lends a hand at any of these practice sessions. When and if it becomes necessary to use the storm sails at sea, you'll bless the fact a dozen times over that you've had a few solo dummy runs.

MEASURING AND ORDERING SAILS

In anticipation of the day when he will be called on to do some sail measuring, the cruising man is well advised to invest in a 100-foot tape.

Not many cruising yachtsmen concern themselves over the complexities of the I.O.R. (International Offshore Rule), which is an attitude I endorse heartily (I've been a rule-dodger all my life). However, for the cruiser who finds himself or herself some place where the ordering of sails necessitates familiarity with the mysterious code of the gang who dreamt up these rules, the following might be of interest:

I — height of foretriangle
J — base of foretriangle
P — mainsail hoist
BAD — boom above deck (sometimes BAS, where S is sheer)
E — foot of mainsail
SPL — spinnaker pole length
SPH — spinnaker pole height

For the person who already has an exact sail plan for a particular boat, with spars to match, the measuring of new sails presents no difficulty; the sailmaker can build sails to the size and shape indicated on the plan. This desirable state of affairs does not exist for all owners. A shorter mast or a longer boom than is shown on the original plan, an added bowsprit, a newly positioned inner forestay, a mizzenmast — any number of things can render a sail plan obsolete.

The surest way to get what you want when ordering a new sail is to take measurements of the space the sail will be expected to fill aboard your vessel. If it's a new mainsail, top up the boom to where you'll want it when the sail is bent and hoisted. Then stand off in your dinghy or walk along the dock to where you can see your vessel in profile, and give it the eye. If it looks good, go back aboard and take the measurements. I've done this with every boat I've owned. To arrive at a size and shape for the schooner's Yankee, I hoisted a length of Dacron line on the jib halyard and used this to simulate the leech. Another piece of line was the foot, and the forestay was the luff. I fussed around, lowering and hoisting and altering the length of foot and leech, until I had the outline of a jib up there with its clew held aft by a length of line, which was the "pretend" sheet.

After all this, I chugged across St. Thomas Harbor in my dinghy to Hassel Island to get Manfred the Sailmaker. Manfred eyeballed my effort from the dinghy, came aboard and made a few adjustments, went out in the dinghy again, and so on — until both he and I were satisfied. That jib, when it eventually was made and hoisted aboard, *really* fitted.

It is ideal if a sailmaker can come aboard and listen to your ideas — to which, perhaps, he can add some professional advice before going off and making the sail. Often you can coax him out for a sail in your boat, and that's even better. Once back in the bay, you can help him take measurements of the new mainsail or jib, or whatever it is you have planned. Always make certain he realizes that your intentions are to use the sail for world cruising, not just for an occasional weekend jaunt.

The chafe spots in an old sail should be noted carefully and referred to when ordering a replacement. If a local sailmaker will be building the new sail, take the old sail along and ask him to sew sacrificial chafing patches in the worn areas. These patches can take the brunt of the chafe on the sail fabric and stitching from spreader tips, shrouds, and the ends of wooden ratlines. If the sail being replaced has these chafing patches, lay the old sail on top of the new one and mark where the patches should be sewn on.

Ordering sails from afar is a different matter. It is possible, of course, to measure carefully the position of existing chafe patches on a sail being replaced, and to mark the exact position of the patches on the sketch accompanying the order. A description of their locations would also be included, but an element of doubt still enters in. If you are not sure you can communicate where to put the patches, or if you have no idea where such patches should be because the sail being ordered is a different shape or size than the others aboard, plan to sew on the patches yourself. Or get some sailmaker in the next country or group of islands to do it for you.

A way to mark the spots on a mainsail where it rests (and possibly chafes) against shrouds and spreaders when eased is to take a thick, soft-lead carpenter's pencil up in a chair. Mark the aft lower shroud each side, the topmast shrouds, the spreaders, and anything else the sail is likely to rest against. If the sail is a genoa, mark the spreader tips. Then go for a sail; that black pencil lead will tell you where the chafe spots are.

Something I would too often forget when placing an order for a new sail was a few extra square feet of the fabric. No matter how you try to take care of your sails, accidents do happen. I remember tripping over the windlass on the foredeck of the

White Squall when I was carrying a fisherman anchor; the point went clear through a couple of rolls of furled genoa. And the only cloth we had on board for sail repair was some mainsail material that was three ounces heavier.

Another time, years ago, during a cruise in a friend's sloop on the New Zealand coast, a spinnaker boom got whisked out of our hands on the foredeck and poked a hole in the mainsail. After the blame and breast beating was all over, we started hunting through the ship for a piece of fabric to effect a repair. The only thing we had was a canvas bucket. One of the crew, who had the (to me) unheard-of occupation of custom tailor, took the bucket to pieces and hand-sewed it over the rent in the sail. Norm's patch looked like hell, but it did the job; the hand-stitching was something else. So when placing an order for a sail, always ask for a few square feet of the same material. You just never know.

Of course, there are sailmakers and there are sailmakers. Some lofts specialize in racing sails, and the measure of their ability as sailmakers is associated closely with the success of the boats carrying their products. While their racing sails might be winners, it doesn't necessarily mean that their cruising sails are the greatest. Sometimes the man to patronize is the one with a small loft, because the boss does the measuring, the machine sewing, and the hand-stitching. On the other hand, this bloke's business might be small because his sails set like a fruit vendor's awning.

Always inquire about a loft's standard of work on cruising sails before choosing your sailmaker, and don't jump to patronize a guy just because he happens to be the cheapest. With the kind of strength you want worked into your wardrobe and the expertise required to accomplish this, you'll be spending more than peanuts. But just because a loft charges an arm and a leg for sails doesn't mean that they are the ones for you to order from, either. Ask the various cruising people you meet where they had their sails made, how satisfied they are with the products, and what the job cost. If the loft you decide on ultimately is close enough for a sailmaker to come aboard and spend some time with you, all well and good. If it's up to you to take your own measurements and mail complete specifications of the size and type of sails needed (and this often happens when a cruising boat is in a far-off port), make a sketch of each sail and include the following information on it:

(A) The exact measurement of foot, luff, leech, the type of cloth (e.g., soft, resin-free Dacron), the area, and the weight.

(B) The scale of the sketch.

(C) The length, width, and position of strainer patches, as discussed earlier in this chapter, drawn in with their measurements.

(D) The measurements of each row of reef points, taken upward from the foot of the sail. Draw in the strainer patches at luff cringle and reef cringle.

Other relevant information should be stapled to each sketch. A sample attachment might read: "Storm jib: (A) Luff to be ¼-inch, 7/19 stainless steel insulated wire rope. (B) Hanks to fit X inch (e.g., X might be $\frac{5}{16}$) stay, spaced X distance apart (typically, two-thirds of the distance between hanks in the working jib) up luff from tack and including head. (C) Sail to be X cut; seams triple-stitched with heavy Dacron thread. (D) Foot, luff, and leech to be taped heavily. (E) All cut edges to be heat sealed. (F) Dacron tape to be hand-sewn as well as machine-sewn over reinforcing strainer patches at head, tack, and clew."

The strongest storm sails probably are Scotch cut. The usual cut, with panels running from luff to leech, is still very popular, because with this cut the sail sets better.

If the sail halyard is wire, with a rope-to-wire splice, a 7/19 wire pendant should be ordered with the sail. The pendant is shackled to the head of the sail, so that the wire of the halyard is on the winch drum once the sail is hoisted. The pendant should have a hank at the top to control it while hoisting, and if necessary, another hank in the middle. The sail should be marked clearly at tack, head, and clew.

Attached to the sketch of a storm trysail should be another set of specifications, similar to those for a storm jib, except for the luff — which will be rope or heavily taped Dacron and be fitted with suitable track slides instead of hanks. Some trysails are roped all around, which makes a very strong sail, but it must be admitted that roping gives the leech a tendency to curl. For all that, the trysail I carried aboard my yawl was up-and-down cut and roped all around, and I never regretted it. The storm main staysail aboard the schooner was 12-ounce Dacron, Scotch cut, and heavily taped all around. I have no complaints to make about that sail, either.

There seems no question that heavy Dacron tape, sewn securely along foot, luff, and leech, makes a sail set better than if it were roped. Regular cut makes a sail set better yet. If the trysail is to be kept in a bag at the foot of the mast, order an extra-strong bag with webbing stitched down each side and across the bottom. A strong brass eyelet should be worked into a gathered double thickness of webbing each side at the bottom, so that the bag can be lashed down securely.

If the sail being ordered is a headsail, you can determine its size and shape much as we arrived at the dimensions of the Yankee for the *White Squall II.* Or the foretriangle can be measured, drawn to scale (not forgetting the sheer of the deck), and the headsail dimensions taken from this. A sketch of the headsail, with attached points A, B, and C, as previously outlined, should accompany the order. Point D would seldom be included in the sketch of a headsail — unless, of course, the sail were a heavy-weather jib or staysail and one wanted the option of reefing. Relevant information accompanying the sketch of a working jib or Yankee jib would be as follows:

(A) Luff to be X-inch 7/19 stainless steel insulated wire rope inside tabling.

(B) Hanks to fit X-inch stay, spaced X distance apart up the luff from the bottom hank and including the head.

(C) Bottom hank to be X distance above tack. (If the sail is tacked down at the bottom of a turnbuckle, the distance of the first hank up the luff must be above the turnbuckle jaws, toggle, or terminal fitting on the stay.)

(D) Tack pendant of X-inch 7/19 wire rope of X length, and head pendant of the same wire of X length. (A tack pendant to raise a headsail above a pulpit and prevent chafe is sometimes a desirable feature aboard an ocean cruiser. The head pendant is only necessary where the halyard is wire, with a rope-to-wire splice, and is intended to keep the wire on the winch drum when sail is hoisted. The sailor with an all-wire or all-rope halyard will not have this added expense.)

(E) Seams to be triple-stitched with heavy Dacron thread.

(F) Dacron tape to be hand-sewn as well as machine-sewn over reinforcing at head, tack, and clew, as shown on sketch.

(G) All cut edges to be heat sealed.

(H) A leech line leading out of the tabling to a plastic cam cleat above the clew, as shown in the sketch. (To control the chattering of the leech, the leech line can be tensioned and held securely by this cleat. But this is just one way of doing it. A jib, whose clew must pull around a staysail stay whenever the ship puts about, and that chafes the leech-line adjustment because of this, sometimes has a leech line that can be tensioned at the head. Such a line can be adjusted only when the sail is down, but the system still has a lot going for it, since it completely cancels out any chafe the line might suffer if it were to emerge near the clew.)

(I) Clew cringle to be a minimum diameter of X inches. (Always give yourself a big clew cringle to which, if necessary, you can hitch another line in addition to the sheets. You may want to pull the sail out to the end of a whisker pole sometime, or run a temporary sheet to the clew to save a winch for some other use.)

Information accompanying a staysail sketch would be the same as that for a working jib, with the probable exception of a tack pendant. If the staysail is on a club, a jackline (as previously discussed) would usually be ordered. There are cases when a staysail is on a club, but where a jackline is not necessary: if the staysail gooseneck is on a fore-and-aft sliding track or "horse," which is eased forward before sail is lowered, or if a clew outhaul is utilized to release right-angle luff-clew tension. In cases where a row of reef points or eyelets is considered desirable in a cruising boat's headsail, the relevant information would be:

(A) Reef points in position as per sketch.

(B) Each reef point to pass through a hand-sewn brass ring, which has a compressed brass grommet.

(C) Brass ring and grommet to be in the center of a diamond-shaped strengthening patch with X-inch sides.

If you're dreaming up a genoa jib for your cruising boat, don't plan to have the foot hug the deck. It's very easy to wash out a sail and have it fly to pieces after scooping up the lee bow wave or copping a wavetop from the windward side in the lower part of the sail (as we did). It doesn't take much water to make a ton. The clew of a cruising boat's genoa of, say, 120 percent of the foretriangle should be a good three feet from the deck when close-hauled. If you have no sail plan, and no old sail to measure from, mock up one, as we did, with pieces of line. Measure from these. Keep an eye out for possible chafe from spreaders and remember that this applies particularly to a vessel with wide spreaders.

The construction of the genoa, the leech line, and (possibly) tack and/or head pendants are done as for the working jib. If you're in a dilemma about the weight of the genoa, send the sailmaker the dimensions and displacement of your ship, and, in the absence of a sail plan, a photo of the boat in profile. So much the better if the picture is of the boat under sail. Give the approximate area of the working rig, and remember to make sure that the sailmaker knows that you're a *cruising* boat.

For a roller-furling headsail, the relevant information accompanying this sketch, in addition to the original points A, B, and C, are:

(A) Luff wire X-inch diameter, stainless steel 1/19 wire rope, insulated and well stitched inside the tabling.

(B) Head and tack luff wire terminals to be secured to the sail by external lashings to strong cringles in the sail at its head and tack.

(C) Head and tack terminals must be able to fit inside swivel jaws. Distance between swivel jaws is X inches. Sacrificial strip of X-ounce Dacron, X inches wide, to be sewn down the leech and along the foot of the starboard side of the headsail.

The 1/19 luff wire should be the same diameter as the vessel's headstay. The width of the sacrificial strip, which provides sun protection for the sail when rolled, varies with the cut of the sail, not with the area. A narrow sail with a long luff would, in general, need a wider sacrificial strip than a sail with a relatively short hoist and generous clew-luff distance. For some headsails, the width of the strip (typically, four-ounce cloth) is 12 inches; on other sails, a strip of 18 inches or wider is necessary. The rest of the construction of the roller-furling headsail is the same as for the working jib.

When ordering a jib for a roller spar, the company that makes the extrusion is the one to contact, as the sail luff must be of the exact size to fit the groove in the spar. Companies either supply their own sails or have a recommended set of specifications for constructing a sail luff. While the emphasis must be placed on strength when ordering sails for a cruising boat, the yachtsman should be aware that he can't go overboard on this with a headsail that rolls around a spar, for the two reasons already mentioned — that the spar adds its own bulk to the finished roll, and that the whole kit and caboodle might have to stay up in a gale.

For marconi mainsails and mizzens, in addition to a sketch, and items A through D, additional information would typically be:

(A) Seams to be triple-stitched with heavy Dacron thread.

(B) Dacron tape to be hand-sewn as well as machine-sewn over reinforcing strainer patches at head, tack, clew, and luff and leech reefing cringles.

(C) All cut edges to be heat sealed.

(D) Leech line to be included.

(E) Battens (four) to be included.

(F) Batten pockets to be sewn in the center of the panel, to be at right angles to the leech or to follow the seam angle from leech to luff — except that the batten between the first and second row of reef points, and the batten above the second row of points, will be parallel to the foot.

(G) A jackline to be used from the second row of reef points to the tack.

(H) Hand-sewn roping on foot and luff and over headboard, to be tapered off on leech. Foot roping to go around the clew cringle and up the leech past the second row of reef points, where it is tapered off.

(I) Tack cringle must be able to fit inside gooseneck jaw of X width.

(J) Clew cringle must fit inside outhaul jaw of X width.

(K) Slides attached to the foot, and to the luff from the second row of reef points to the head of the sail (as in the sample).

The jackline is only necessary if the sail is roller reefing and if sail slides would add their bulk to the rolled luff of the sail around the boom. A jackline is not used aboard a lot of vessels with slab-reefing mainsails, or on vessels with mizzens where there is a large crew to feed slides off and on the sail track. When you are cruising shorthanded, however, a jackline lets you hoist a sail again after reefing without having to feed sail slides back onto a track. Where the sail is roller reefing, an additional measure known as cut-back, or rub-back, should be indicated on the sketch and referred to in the relevant attachment. Cut-back is the distance aft of the sail track that the tack of a roller-furling main or mizzen is secured to the boom. This distance varies with the type of roller reefing installed. With worm-drive roller reefing, the cut-back distance is usually greater than for the type of roller reefing that has a spindle through the mast. It is advisable to have as many rows of reefing eyelets in a roller-reefing sail as you would if the sail were intended to be slab reefed. It is handy to have an additional reefing option.

Whether a sail is hand-roped or strengthened with heavy Dacron tape is a matter of personal preference — as is roping on the leech above the second row of reef points. This reinforcement can be Dacron tape or the usual tabling, with the leech strengthened only at the cringle at the end of a row of reef points. This last is common.

When ordering sails long distance, it may be necessary to include a sketch, as well as measurements, of the particular tack and clew fittings aboard the vessel. It is highly desirable that the sailmaker know these measurements and install cringles to fit the hardware aboard, so you won't start bending on your new mainsail and find that the jaws on your tack and outhaul fittings are too narrow. Send a sail slide as a sample, if you can, unless you're replacing a sail that is tired but still in use, and you want to re-use the same slides. In this case you put the slides on yourself when you have the new sail — no big deal.

I planned to do this with the slides of a mainsail I was using when cruising the west coast of Mexico in my yawl. The slides were worn in perfectly and it didn't make sense to replace them with new, awkward slides, which would take months to break in. I ordered the new mainsail and posted measurements and particulars from the most unpretentious post office (a room in a shack) that I'd ever seen. This was at Turtle Bay on the coast of Baja California, and I remember rowing back to my ship feeling as if there were more chance of my being struck by lightning than of that letter's reaching the sailmaker. In fact, a month or so later, I posted off a second identical letter from Acapulco. A few months later, when I picked up my new main in Panama, the accompanying note from the sailmaker said he'd lay his head on a block that he was the first guy ever to get an order from that post office on Baja. He never did receive the letter I sent from Acapulco.

If the sail being ordered is gaff-headed, a sketch with items A through D would be given, with the measurements from tack to throat and throat to peak taking the place of the usual luff dimension. Supply an additional measurement, from clew to throat, diagonally across the sail, or the spars will lie at the wrong angle. Other information is the same as for marconi mainsails and mizzens. It is usually up to the sailor to seize his own slides or hoops onto a gaff sail. If the gaff is run up on a hefty track that also carries luff slides, the chances are that the whole thing is custom built, in which case it's doubtful the sailmaker would have slides to fit. If the sail is on hoops, these stay on the mast. Some custom-built hoops incorporate a quick-release shackle to enable the easy removal of a gaff sail; often, though, the luff from throat to tack is seized to the hoops.

When seizing the luff of a gaff sail to riveted cane hoops, first cut off a fathom of strong lashing or spun yarn. Double this and make a lark's head in the center of the riveted join. Pass the two ends of the seizing through an eyelet in the luff from opposite sides, then back over the top of the hoop, then underneath and through the eyelet again. Go back underneath, over the top, and so on. Follow this procedure at least four times and finish off with a West Country whipping around the seizing between bolt rope and hoop. (A West Country whipping consists of a thumb (overhand) knot on top of the rope or lashing to be seized, another knot beneath, another knot up alongside the first knot, another beneath, and so on. The advantage of this whipping is that if any part of it is chafed through, it cannot ravel.) If you don't want to go through this rigmarole, forget all about the hoops and use a jackline. When our schooner had a gaff foresail, I cut off all the cane hoops, threw them over the side, and made a jackline from a ½-inch-diameter length of the slipperiest Dacron I could find. To take the initial slack out of the jackline, I would stand on the gooseneck and heave down on the line. Slack from that point down was taken from deck level. After the first dozen or so times the sail was hoisted and I settled on a length for this line, I made the bottom fast to the gooseneck and left it at that. This was for a tack-to-throat distance of about 24 feet.

Cunningham holes are specified by some yachtsmen when ordering mainsails, mizzens, and genoas. Some sailmakers whip in a Cunningham here and there whether the holes are ordered or not. First used by Briggs Cunningham when racing six-meter sailboats in the 1930s, a Cunningham is a cringle worked into the luff of a sail some 18 inches or less up from the tack and, on mainsails and mizzens, the same distance along the foot as well. Tension on either luff or foot can be adjusted by hitching a tackle onto a Cunningham and taking up on it. (Tightening the luff of a sail affects its shape by moving the draft forward.) A luff Cunningham hove down by a winch or purchase is another way of tightening the luff of a sail rather than using an extra heave on a halyard winch or a boom downhaul. A handy billy hitched or hooked to a foot Cunningham on a mainsail or mizzen does the same job as a boom outhaul.

The use of a Cunningham depends on how gung-ho you happen to be. The ocean-cruising sailor who wants to make like a racer, and is all geared to scamper up on deck and hitch onto his Cunningham, can have it. If that's your bag, have at it, but I'd rather give her a bit of a luff and take up on the halyard to tighten the hoist. The tension on the foot shouldn't change, anyway.

All the paraphernalia of a boom outhaul to tension the foot of a cruising boat's mainsail seems to me an unnecessary poultice to foist on the end of a boom. It's an expensive one, too. I've always hove out my clew with several turns of small, strong line rove between the clew cringle and a shackle on the boom-end fitting. To get the tension I wanted, I would lead each end of the lashing aft from the shackle to a purchase (filched temporarily from the mainsheet, staysail halyard, davit falls, or running backstays) and set up the foot. The lashing would then be stopped off with a seizing between clew and shackle (a distance of about three inches) and many more turns of lashing passed. And there it would sit — for years.

The tack of this mainsail is hitched under the starboard reefing hook. Note Cunningham in luff, sleeve in joined spar just above turning blocks, roller on shroud, lines between lifeline and rail to help confine sail during a foredeck sail-changing operation. (Courtesy Yachtspars)

Sail slides are often attached to the luff of a sail with small, strong, stainless steel D screw shackles, which pass through the eye of a slide. The luff goes between the jaws of the shackle and the pin passes through the eyelet. This method of attachment is fine as long as the shackles don't unscrew and there is adequate chafing material, such as tough plastic or leather, protecting the bolt rope or tape of the luff from the sides of the shackle.

Another way of attaching sail slides is with a strip of leather ½-inch to ⅝-inch wide. Take a strong, pliable piece of leather of the above width, about a foot long. Make a ¾-inch-long cut through the center of the leather, about ⅜ inch from one end. Pass the free end of the leather strip first through the eye in a slide, and then through an eyelet in the luff of the sail. Pull the strip through until the slotted end is about one inch from the eyelet. Now push the free end from the slide up through the ¾-inch cut and tie a sheet bend, working and tightening the knot until the eye in the sail slide is hard up against the luff. Cut the leather ½ inch clear of the knot. Don't worry if the slide chafes the sail luff; as soon as the sail is used, the knot will settle in and give an acceptable amount of slack.

Narrow Dacron tape can also be used to attach sail slides to luff eyelets. The tape can be sewn to the slide or made fast with a figure-eight knot and then wound round-and-round through eyelet and slide, with the slide positioned about one-eighth inch from the luff, until considerable strength has been achieved. The seizing is finished by a series of half hitches between bolt rope and slide. The end of the seizing is sometimes secured with a few stitches of waxed sail twine. I used the leather method of attaching sail slides for many years with complete success, but I found the system of using Dacron tape superior, because the finished seizing did not stretch.

On one of your visits aloft in a bosun's chair to inspect mast, tangs, terminal fittings, stays, shrouds, sheaves, or spreaders, smear the sail track for its full length with silicone paste. This paste need not be applied thickly; a thin coating is enough to bring a sail down with a rush. One application of this lubricant will last for months.

SAIL MAINTENANCE AND REPAIR

The care of a cruising boat's sails is of prime importance, and protecting the synthetic fabric from the sun's rays usually tops the list. With room below decks earmarked for furnishings, tankage, supplies, and a sensible amount of livable space, some of the sails that make up the wardrobe must live their lives topside even during a long stay in port. There just isn't room for them below. This applies to big boats as well as small ones; the bigger the boat, the bigger the sails, and the heavier they are to move. A 900-square-foot, 12-ounce mainsail, for instance, takes up an enormous amount of room below, and the task of taking the thing off and later bending it on again can make a man wonder what he's done to deserve the abuse.

A sail frequently left "as is" is a roller-furling jib, which has a sacrificial sun-strip sewn to the luff and leech. While every synthetic sail is all the better for being stowed in a dry, cool place, the strip does give fair protection. I remember leaving up our schooner's roller-furling jib — except for short intervals when I was servicing the swivels — for 2½ years at a stretch without any noticeable depreciation caused by the elements.

Sails left on booms must be well protected, too. A system of protection favored by the busy Virgin Islands bareboat fleet is to have a sacrificial sun-strip two to three feet deep (depending on the sail area) sewn to one side of the mainsail along the foot, from luff to leech. The drill when furling is to be sure to tuck the folds of the sail under the sun-strip to protect the sail completely when it is held to the boom by sail ties. The top few feet of the sail, which cannot be furled under the sun-strip, is shielded on each side by its own sacrificial piece of cloth.

This system is very successful in ensuring that the fabric of the sail is protected whenever it is furled, which is often twice a day. But one wonders about its suitability aboard a world-cruising sailboat, which needs more protection for her sails than a sacrificial strip can offer. She may be at anchor for months on end while the owners work ashore to build up the cruising kitty, and her sails must live on the booms because there is no other place for them. A horizontal surface takes a far worse beating from the sun than a nearly vertical surface — for example, a sail furled along a boom as compared with a roller-furled jib. It is claimed that some sailcloth has an ultraviolet shield incorporated into it during manufacture and that this greatly reduces its vulnerability to damage from sunlight. Even so, such a sail, when furled, should be protected by a sail cover during a stay of any duration in port.

One of the strongest reasons for using the protection provided by well-designed sail covers is the dirt in the air in some places — and not necessarily in big cities, either. Take Lautoka, Fiji — a place blessed with a good anchorage, equable climate, and beautiful scenery. When the wind is off the land at Lautoka (which is most of the time), thousands of tiny pieces of soot from the stacks of the sugar refinery blow aboard and have a marvelous time getting into the folds of furled sails and dirtying the ship. Sail covers seem to be the only answer in such a place. Another reason for sail covers is bird droppings. In some ports, birds play hit-the-deck with wonderful accuracy — and some of that stuff will even take off paint. Sun-strip or no sun-strip, and ultraviolet shield notwithstanding, there's not a sail in the world that would benefit from a direct hit with some of that goop.

There is a liquid marketed under the brand name of Duroseam, which is a great help in protecting the stitching of a sail. Duroseam, colorless when dry, is painted over the stitching on one side of a sail. The sail is hung up or left flat so the Duroseam can dry (overnight is sufficient), and then the stitching on the other side is given the same treatment. Duroseam penetrates and binds stitching together to such an extent that the stitching can be worn away completely along a seam, and yet the seam still holds. My old friend Max Carter, president of Yachtspars, tells me of an experiment he conducted with Duroseam.

Says Max: "We gave the Duroseam treatment to the stitching on both sides of a seam in a new piece of Dacron sailcloth. When dry, I had a good man with a disc sander sand the stitching (there were three rows) completely off both sides of the seam. He then did the same thing to the stitching of an untreated seam. The untreated seam fell apart immediately, but the Duroseamed part resisted all of our efforts to separate it. It was as if each little piece of Dacron thread still filling the hole in a seam was doing the job of a rivet.''

Regarding treatment of an old sail, Peter Dobson of Hood New Zealand has this to say: ''Duroseaming an old sail is possible only if all salt has been washed from the stitching. Special care should be taken to ensure that no salt remains in that part of a stitch that passes through the cloth in a seam.''

I know that Hood sail lofts stock Duroseam; probably other lofts and stores do, too. A can of this liquid has a place in every cruising boat's sailkit; it's a great way to ensure that even well-chafed seams stay together.

A well-made suit of sails can last for years, but only if two things happen: Careful attention must be paid to both chafe and exposure to sunlight, and worn sail parts must be repaired promptly. Here the coastwise cruiser or cruiser-racer, who is usually never too far from a sail loft, need not worry too much. The out-and-out racer is in pretty good shape, too, with spares on top of spares aboard, and a favorite sailmaker ashore who will attend to any repair in time for the flying machine to hurdle around the course the next weekend.

The bluewater cruiser seldom has these luxuries. If your mainsail needs a batten pocket resewn a couple of days before you raise Pitcairn Island, do you know what you do? You fix it your-bloody-self, that's what you do. If you can't and the sail starts to tear, you just might be in sad shape. (My wife has just interrupted to remind me that the natives on some islands weave sails from palm fronds — some option!)

About the only thing the old cotton sails had going for them was the ease of repair aboard. Putting a stitch in here and there was part of the game, and easy, too. A repair by hand is nowhere near as simple with some synthetic sails, however. At least not for the amateur. The reinforcing strainer patches on heavy Dacron sails, such as the 12-ounce mainsail I had built for the *White Squall II*, are almost impossible to push a sail needle through. Sometimes, when beefing up or renewing stitching in a clew or strainer patch of such a sail, it is necessary to drill each hole before passing the needle through.

Be wary of using a three-cornered sail needle on a synthetic sail that's had its fibers stiffened a bit by sunlight. Using a three-cornered needle, I have cut fibers in a Dacron sail I wanted another thousand miles out of. A round needle of the smallest size possible is much kinder to synthetic cloth.

A sewing machine is a handy piece of equipment to carry aboard a cruising boat. If you haven't got AC power aboard, search around for a hand-operated machine. J.J. and J. Read of England (327 Shirley Road, Southampton) sells a wonderful sewing machine designed to be used either by hand or with power. This machine is expensive but good, and it will zigzag-stitch, too. I was able to see one in use when Jeanne Moesly brought hers ashore to plug into AC power to make an awning for the *Rigadoon*. For any repairs aboard the vessel, she uses the hand attachment.

In the early days aboard the schooner, I had an electric sewing machine. To use it, we plugged into the 120-volt AC power supplied by the ship's Onan generator. We were in Oranjestad, Aruba, at the time, and I remember wandering along to the Singer dealer with a heavy, bilious-green piece of ship's tarpaulin in my hand. I folded the canvas twice, making four thicknesses of material, and asked if they sold a portable machine capable of sewing that much cloth. Sure enough, there was a small portable in stock that walked away with the job, so I bought the machine there and then, and it proved to be one of the best purchases I've ever made. It didn't stitch zigzag — a moot point. The important thing was that it could handle any sail aboard. Over the years, that machine has sewn sails, awnings, hatch and winch covers, curtains, bunk covers — everything except the 12-ounce mainsail I had built after the old one expired.

A sail repair kit should also include two or more sizes of sailor's palms and a variety of needles. The needles can be kept in a small jar filled with lube oil. If you're left-handed, take the time to hunt around for a left-handed palm; you may have to search, but such a tool is procurable. Carry several sizes of Dacron thread, including a spool of the largest size that your sewing machine (assuming you have one) can handle. Waxed Dacron thread also has a place in a cruising boat's ditty bag. Use this for hand-stitching strainer patches and roping, or for putting sailmaker's whippings on rope ends.

A lump of beeswax is important, too. Whenever a rope's end is rat-tailed to taper off the roping on a sail or to facilitate passing a line through a cringle, beeswax will help keep the fined-out strands together both during lay-up and after the tail is laid up and a whipping is stitched at its end. Treating unwaxed sail twine before a spate of hand-sewing or the seizing of jib hanks is another job for beeswax. A selection of sailcloth should also be carried.

A method of emergency sail repair was shown to me during the 1950s by Buzz Champion aboard the 36-foot Carol ketch *Little Bear*. I forget now where we were, but it was in some South Pacific anchorage. Buzz brought out a can of ordinary contact cement, saying, "I've stitched my last sail — this stuff is magic!" According to Buzz, all salt had to be washed from the part needing repair, and then it had to be dried thoroughly. After that, the cement was applied to both sail and patch, and when the glue was completely dry to the touch, the patch pressed firmly to the sail. It seemed to work OK.

A good repair kit, spare sailcloth, a sewing machine (either hand or electric), a grommet kit with a supply of brass grommets, and a book on sail maintenance and repair should be part of the equipment of a serious cruising boat. Keep your eye on your sails and always have your mind tuned to the possibility of chafe. With a cruising boat's wardrobe, the emphasis must be on service, with as little repair as possible along the line. If the need arises to put in a stitch here and there, you must have the wherewithal aboard to do the job. The beautiful lagoon at that remote island you're planning to sail to isn't likely to have a sailmaking loft hidden away among the coconut trees.

seven

Reefing Gear

An old handliner I knew used to take the slack out of his sloop's rigging by lashing port and starboard shrouds together with lines athwartships. Another character reefed his jib by tying an overhand knot in it about a third of the distance down from the head before hoisting away. That either or both of these techniques didn't catch on and haven't been copied by legions of sailors would probably mystify the two proponents if they were still around. They would conclude (and I knew them well) that no doubt it was because they were years ahead of their time.

An efficient system of shortening sail is necessary aboard every cruising boat. When the wind increases beyond the point where a boat can carry her normal working sails comfortably, the accepted tactic is to reduce sail area sensibly so that the ship can best handle the conditions. A reduction in sail area that suits his particular boat, that keeps her manageable and in balance as both wind and sea increase, should be the aim of the cruising sailor. A too-drastic reduction in sail area can cause a boat to hobbyhorse and get nowhere. Taking off a tiny amount of sail can mean that a half-hour later you're rolling out of your bunk and up there fiddling around again. Leaving full sail up when it comes on to blow can put an unfair strain on sails, mast, rigging, and hull. Such a practice can cause a vessel to be overburdened, and, in some instances, may be extremely dangerous. Experimenting to discover a realistic compromise of sail combinations to be used as the weather deteriorates should be one of the first things on the agenda of the new cruising boat owner.

There is no one system of sail reduction that applies to all vessels. An increase in wind can mean a genoa is taken off a sloop and replaced with a smaller headsail; a further freshening of the breeze might call for a reef in the mainsail as well. A cutter, under the same conditions, might drop and furl a headsail and reef her mainsail. A yawl might drop a headsail and then her mizzen; depending on the size of the main-

With two reefs in her mainsail and a small forestaysail, this cruising cutter moves right along. Note boom vang, lee running backstay taken forward, sturdy gallows frame. (Ralph Naranjo photo)

sail, that might need a tuck, too. A ketch might drop a headsail and, as the wind increases, reef her mizzen; here, it depends on the size of the mizzen in relation to the mainsail. If she's on a reach and she's hard-mouthed, she might only drop her mizzen. A schooner, gaff-rigged on the fore, might be happy with a tuck in the mainsail and the jib lowered and furled. A staysail schooner under identical conditions might end up sailing under forestaysail, main staysail, and reefed mainsail.

The above tactics are often used aboard variously rigged cruising boats as both wind and sea rise steadily. A sudden, dramatic increase in wind strength can call for other measures. Sometimes a vessel can be eased through a squall if a helmsman brings the ship just close enough to the breeze to keep her sailing, the intention being to spill wind from the sails without letting them flap. Or he might run her off before the wind. (A fine touch is needed to carry through either of these strategies successfully.) Other times — and navigable searoom has great bearing on this tactic — the safest and best method is to get the biggest sail down as quickly as possible.

There are parts of this world (the Tasman Sea is one) where a man can be sailing along blithely in good weather and quite suddenly lose the wind. During the day, he'll see what's looming up on him by watching the albatross and sundry feathered nomads wheeling along before it. At night (as is the usual case) he'll be entertained by what looks like the blackest piece of night he's ever seen, moving quietly toward him. And if he doesn't reduce the largest piece of sail he's got flying, faster than he's ever done it before, he might be in for an experience that will have him yearning for warm, tranquil nights by the fireside, or barns and chickens and things.

So far in this book we have discussed the different ways that a cruising boat's working and storm sails may be set and furled. With the aim of being able at all times to present the elements with an area of sail that will serve your needs safely and competently, the methods by which sails can be reefed and the equipment required for this exercise are the next means of sail-area control to warrant inspection.

SLAB REEFING

The mainsail is the sail most usually reefed aboard a cruising boat. The most popular way of accomplishing this seems to have gone full circle, back to where it was a hundred or more years ago. After a decade or so of roller reefing with variously shaped booms to pander to sail shape as sail is rolled down, the old system, now glorying in the title of "slab," is strongly at the fore.

With slab reefing, a pendant is led from a fixed point on the boom, up through a reef cringle in the leech of the sail, down through a cheek block on the boom, and forward toward the mast. Even 30 years ago the pendant was led to a handy billy on the boom. It now goes to a winch, which is a whole lot better than any block-and-tackle arrangement. Some hollow aluminum booms have provision for the pendant to lead inside the boom to an internal sheave, or, alternatively, to enter the boom after passing over the sheave of the cheek block. Once in the boom, the pendant leads forward, over a sheave in the boom (which also incorporates a line stopper) below the gooseneck, down to a turning block at the foot of the mast, and to a winch.

To put in a reef (those in the know now call it a "slab"), the topping lift is hardened to take the weight of the boom, the halyard is slacked, and the mainsheet is eased to allow the sail to luff slightly and drop to the desired height. Sometimes, aboard a racing boat, the luff is hove down with a tackle. If the sail luff is on slides up to the luff reefing cringle, the bottom track-stop must be opened to allow the slides to come off the track. If a jackline is used on the luff, this is not necessary. The luff reefing cringle is now secured to the end of the boom below the track. It is common for booms, nowadays, to have a stainless steel hook welded or bolted each side of the gooseneck fitting; the luff reef cringle hooks up to this. Or the cringle is lashed down — which is not as quick, but just as good.

The luff cringle must be secured before the leech is hove down by the reefing pen-

Pulling down a "slab." Standing part of the reef pendant is fast to loop of stainless steel on aft bottom part of cheek block. It passes under the boom, through the leech reef cringle, back over the sheave of the cheek block, and thence to a winch. (Carl Moesly photo)

dant. To create a desirable amount of tension along the row of reef points between luff cringle and leech, the cheek block (or internal sheave) and the standing part of the reef pendant are situated several inches aft of the cringle when it is hauled down to the boom. The luff cringle cannot be hooked or lashed in its required position if the leech is hove down first. Once the luff cringle is secured, the pendant can be turned up on a winch and the cringle cranked down to the boom. The halyard can then be tightened, the topping lift eased to allow the sail to set properly, and the mainsheet brought in.

Whether the reef points are tied before this is done and the ship gets going again depends on what sort of hurry you're in. I have always tied off the points and been satisfied that the reef was "looking good" before tightening the halyard, easing the topper, and bringing in the sheet. This wouldn't do aboard a racer, of course; in fact, it is common practice in the racing game for the bunt to be left untied and hanging or just tucked between the line of reef points and the boom after putting in a slab — especially if the leg from one buoy to another is a short one. The reef might be shaken out 10 minutes after it's put in.

Now while the cruising nut can learn a lot from his racing buddies (let's face it, the racer often finds out the hard way whether a fitting or system will work before we cruising blokes ever get a look at it), leaving the bunt hanging is a hand-me-down the cruiser can do without. The bunt of a reefed sail, left hanging between leech cringle and luff, forms a bag, which sheets of spray, the top of a wave, or even heavy rain can fill to the brim. If this happens aboard a racing boat, a clutch of muscle-bound characters will leap up and tumble the water out in the flick of an eye.

Not always so aboard a cruiser! I know a world-girdling couple who, both past the

A dummy run at pulling down a "slab" while still tied to a dock. Note all lines running to the cockpit. Windward running backstay is held in cleat after being tensioned by sheet winch. (Courtesy Yachtspars)

A neatly tied-in reef. But that reefing pendant should have been led under *the topping lift, leaving the lift free to use. Note slack preventer leading forward from single block. (Ralph Naranjo photo)*

half-century mark, left the bunt of their sail hanging after reefing down on a passage from Mauritius to Durban, South Africa. And a playful wavetop decided to fill it up. They had a hell of a job dealing with the situation, and at one point they seriously considered cutting a slit in the water-filled belly of their beautiful Dacron mainsail. They got rid of the water by hoisting the sail again; apparently it required a pretty hefty heave-ho on the halyard winch. They pulled down the reef once more, tied all the points (which they've done ever since), and proceeded — very much the wiser — on their way.

The manner in which the bunt of a reefed sail is held, after both luff and leech have been secured, is a matter of personal preference. There are two alternatives. Reef points can pass under the gathered bunt between sail and boom and be tied on the other side of the sail. Or a spiral lashing, which is rove by passing a line beneath the foot of the sail and through a row of eyelets, can be used.

Both methods have their champions. It is claimed that the spiral lashing makes a neater job and more evenly distributes the strain imposed by a weight of wind in the sail than a number of individual reef points. I have found the spiral lashing system to be a pain in the neck, especially when reefing a big sail shorthanded. (With a small sail — up to 300 square feet — holding a roll of the bunt and passing a lashing under the foot, up through an eyelet, under the foot, and so on, is no big deal even for one person.) A larger, and consequently heavier sail is a different matter.

Gathering up the bunt of a large mainsail and getting that spiral lashing tight is a long job for two people. We gave it a fair, honest try aboard our schooner, and before we were even halfway through the first exercise, we'd given it away. This was with the big, new mainsail we had built in St. Thomas. We had a couple of rows of eyelets installed instead of reef points, and when the main was hoisted, we were highly satisfied with the way it looked. The eyelets were a whole lot neater than hanging reef points. When we came to tuck in a reef on a trip to Curacao, however, we changed our minds. Gathering and holding the folds of more than 200 square feet of sail while we passed and tightened the spiral lashing was exhausting. The first job Minine and I tackled after arriving at Willemstad was to cut up that spiral lashing and install it in the mainsail as permanent reef points.

If you're a spiral-lashing-or-nothing buff, fine, but remember to have plenty of help if you're reefing a big sail. If your sail is equipped with reef points, pull down the luff and leech and gather the bunt as tightly as circumstances permit. As you work your way along it, tie each point with a reef bow, *not* a reef (square) knot. A reef bow can be loosened easily when it comes time to shake out the reef. The square knot might be so tight you'll have to work at it with a spike or a fid to get it undone — or you might even have to use a knife.

Passing the reef points between the foot of the sail and the boom assists in distributing, as evenly as possible, the strain each point takes.

Shaking out a reef is accomplished by hardening the topping lift and reversing the procedure for shortening sail. Each reef bow is released. The reefing pendant is eased away, slacking the leech. If the luff cringle is held by a metal hook, the halyard is slacked so that the cringle can be released. If the cringle is held by a lashing, the luff cringle can simply be let go, without slacking the halyard.

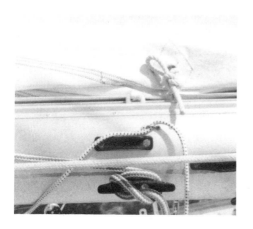

Left: *Triple-stitched heat-sealed seam, a reef bow, plastic slide fast to eyelet in the foot of the sail with Dacron lashing. Shock cord is passed over furled sail to hooks in other side of boom to effect a quick stow.* **Right:** *This luff reef cringle has a bronze ring each side of the sail joined by strong Dacron tape. Either ring can be used — it depends which one happens to be the most convenient. In the picture the starboard ring has been placed over the reefing hook and the ring on the port side is hard up against the reef cringle. (Carl Moesly photos)*

Once the luff cringle is released, sail can be hoisted. It may be necessary to ease the mainsheet to spill wind from the sail to accomplish this. If the luff is on slides to the reef cringle, they must be fed onto the track as the sail goes up; if a jackline is used, this is unnecessary. As soon as the sail is fully hoisted, the topping lift can be eased to allow the sail to assume its correct shape, and the sheet can be brought in. A most important step to be observed when shaking out a reef is that *all* the reef points are let go before the reef pendant is eased. Otherwise immediate and unfair strain can be taken by a reef point, with a chance that the sail will be torn.

It is common practice for booms (especially aluminum spars) to have an integral track into which the bolt rope on the foot of the sail fits. Having to pass the reef points around the boom is not the greatest practice. The foot of a cruising mainsail (or mizzen) should have slides or slugs that fit a track on a boom. This enables the reef points to pass between boom and sail.

A practice not usually included in the reefing drill of a racer, but one that I feel applies when cruising, is putting a lashing around the boom in addition to the reef pendant. A cruiser might have a reef or two in for a week. If the weather keeps kicking up, the ship might be reefed for an even longer period. To have the entire weight at the leech taken by one piece of line smacks too much of "all the eggs in one basket." I have always insisted on extra luff and leech reef lashings. The length of these lashings aboard my yawl was about one fathom; for the schooner, nearly two. I would rat-tail the ends carefully to permit many turns of line to be passed through either luff or leech cringles, and then stow the lashings under my pillow. This might sound like old-woman stuff, but when that leech cringle was hove down by its pendant, and, in addition, lashed securely to the boom with one of my tapered pieces of line, I'd think I was a hell of a fellow.

Now, I'm not much of a bloke at self-recrimination (given half a chance, I blame someone else). Aboard a two-handed boat, however, where the only crew is your wife (who'll give as good as she gets), this doesn't work. You're the skipper, and no matter what happens, *it's your fault.* To either would-be or practicing cruising skippers, I'll say this: Wind a good, strong lashing around your boom and through the reef cringle after the pendant has hove it down. Then the problem of finding someone to blame if the pendant does let go (and the sail tears) will never arise.

While the convenience of having reefing pendants constantly rove is reassuring, the specter of chafe cannot be ignored. On a long haul, where a man's eyes and mind are geared to prevent *anything* from chafing aboard the vessel — from clothes in a hanging locker to a flag halyard touching a shroud — permanently rove pendants should be viewed with a mighty suspicious eye. There are small things that can help avoid sail chafe from a pendant, all worthy of mention. Quite often the athwartships width of the metal reef cringle in the sail can help keep the pendant from touching the sail on its way to the boom. Sometimes the width of the boom, placing the standing part of the pendant and the cheek block a generous distance from the centerline — and the sail — cancels out chafe.

Investigate all this thoroughly before leaving on a cruise with reefing pendants rove permanently. Chafe can be avoided in some mainsails, especially those with a high aspect ratio, if a reefing pendant is placed under a light strain when sail is hoisted. The pendant will not chafe because the cheek block, or internal sheave and standing part, is close to the end of the boom, at the heavily strengthened and controllable part of the sail.

Because I was able to cash in on this last-mentioned circumstance, I could cruise in my yawl with two reefing pendants rove permanently. Aboard the schooner, it

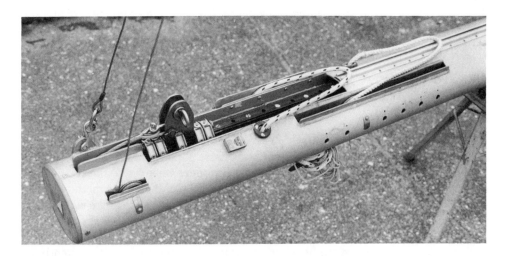

This boom still has to be fitted with bails. Note strong sliding car on outhaul track, wire topping lift with twisted shackle at standing end, internal anchorage and sheaves of color-coded reef pendants. The holes in the side of the boom are for changing the sheave position of the reefing pendants. (Courtesy Yachtspars)

was another story. The lower aspect ratio of the mainsail meant that the pendants would have to have been positioned proportionately farther along the boom than those of the yawl. With a feeling of "what do I have to lose?" I rigged two temporary pendants through the reef cringles in the schooner's main and went for a sail. During this dummy run, I came to the conclusion that permanently rove reefing pendants were something I just couldn't live with aboard that vessel. The distance of the pendants from the boom end meant that the pendant rested against the lee side of the sail, and, of course, against the stitching. That decided the issue for me.

It is possible to rig light "messengers" up from the boom, through reef cringles, and down again. When it comes time to reef, a messenger is married to the end of a pendant that is pulled through the cringle and down to an appropriate sheave. Personally, however, I'm too much of a nut about chafe even to trust a messenger. Also, I was never wild about putting to sea in a shorthanded cruising boat with any of the gear rigged temporarily. Aboard a racer, which is crawling with crew, OK — you can have them leaping and bounding about, reeving and rendering all sorts of things. A cruiser seldom has that much extra elbow grease available. I consider that the average little cruising boat should have all her running rigging permanently rove before leaving on a voyage, and have a reefing system that doesn't allow the possibility of chafe by pendants, messengers, or anything else. If permanently rove reefing pendants are going to chafe a sail, the cruiser could well do himself a favor by not reeving any of them. You can still shorten down when necessary; it just takes a little longer.

The way the two of us tucked in a reef aboard the *White Squall II* was to lower the mainsail and heave the 28-foot boom down into the gallows frame so that it was immovable. While the ship jogged along slowly under staysails, we would lash down the luff cringle, heave the leech reef cringle toward the end of the boom, and lash it securely around the spar. Then we'd tie the reef points. When the reef was "looking good," we'd hoist away and paddle along on the voyage again — no big deal at all. I can't recall ever having hurried the job, or thinking as we went through the motions leisurely that we should, perhaps, be doing it another way.

Shaking out the reef followed the same steps as for a sail hove down by a pendant. Then I'd be on my way below to stow the precious lashings, with their tapered ends, under my pillow. Sissy stuff . . . right?

ROLLER REEFING

As mentioned earlier, roller reefing seems to have fallen into disfavor alongside "slab" reefing (just can't get over that word). (I wonder what would have happened if someone had mentioned "slab" to Josh Slocum, who had used the method all his life and called it "reefing." The old boy would probably think the bloke was talking about a cut of bacon, or maybe it would send him scurrying below to hack off a slice of cheese . . . .)

The cruising game seems to be greatly influenced by the equipment currently in favor with the racing fleet. In the late 1950s and early 1960s, roller reefing was the rage with racing sailors. A number of companies were manufacturing really good, strong, roller-reefing gear (a lot of it worm-drive) complete with screw-type outhaul

Worm-drive roller reefing. Handle locates from port or starboard in slot in grease-filled gear casing. A sail used with this gear needs generous cut back, but the boom can be rotated no matter how the sheet is trimmed. (Courtesy Yachtspars)

fittings that were works of art. The wooden booms were, in general, larger at the after end to help retain sail shape and save the boom from drooping as sail was rolled down; a lot of booms were custom-built. It was the hollow aluminum boom, with reefing pendants, outhauls, and other lines inside, that brought a renewed interest in slab reefing: the boom was lighter, it didn't have to be shaped, the reefed sail set better, and it was possible for a well-trained crew to put in a reef more quickly than by roller.

Another reason, and as strong a one as any, for roller reefing's wane in popularity aboard racing boats was the arrival of the boom vang among the bigger classes. The boom vang, also known as the kicking strap, was for many years used only when racing small, open boats. The discovery that the big fellows could also control sail twist with the use of a vang — and so win races — meant that roller reefing got the heave-ho from the go-fast fleet.

It is possible to rig a vang to a roller boom by hooking a tackle to a sturdy lug pinned in a slot beneath the boom. But to reef the sail, the vang tackle must be taken off the lug to allow the boom to turn. This can be done, of course; the metal lug, an easy fit on a through-pin, obediently lies flush with the boom as sail is rolled down. However, unless a roller claw is used — and one of these can be tough on a sail if it is pulled from an oblique angle — a typical boom vang cannot be rigged once a reef is rolled down. (It has been suggested that a length of webbing with an eye at one end to serve as a boom anchor for a vang can be rolled into the sail as the boom rotates to reef the sail. For those who have a roller boom but who can't live without their vang, this system might be worth considering.)

However, be that as it may, roller reefing fell by the wayside overnight. Specially shaped booms ceased to be made and the roller-reefing gear itself played hard-to-get. Too bad, because it's good reefing gear for a shorthanded cruising boat. Aboard such a vessel, roller reefing is often quicker than slab reefing, and requires a lot less energy from the user, too. An advantage that roller reefing has over slab is that the sail area can be controlled strictly. With slab reefing, the sailor has to accept the amount of sail between the rows of reef points as the amount of sail he is able to

Boom sheet block or vang fitting for roller-reefed sail. (Courtesy Yachtspars)

take in. This is often too much for existing conditions — or too little. A roller-reefed sail can be shortened down exactly to whatever area suits.

I've never owned roller-reefing gear, for the simple reason that by the time I had my yawl ready to go cruising, I just couldn't afford it. The slab reefing I rigged for the yawl's mainsail cost the price of two galvanized sheaves (for the cheek blocks) and a couple of lengths of line. Although I would have liked roller reefing for the mainsail of *White Squall II,* the gear would have been so big that it's doubtful it could have been purchased anywhere. However, I have experienced the convenience of roller reefing in other vessels, and one occasion is worth mentioning.

It was nearly 30 years ago aboard the 29-foot, light-displacement sloop *Taurangi,* and we were beating around from Suva Harbor to Lauthala Bay between the barrier

Through-mast roller-reefing gear. Sail used with this gear does not need cut back (rub back), but boom must usually be hove well in before it can be rotated. (Courtesy Yachtspars)

reef and several inshore reefs. At the helm, I was thoroughly enjoying the windward ability of the light, well-balanced boat. Compared with my heavy-displacement 33-footer, it was like handling a sailing dinghy. As we progressed around the bulge of Viti Levu, the wind freshened, throwing warm spray across the vessel.

The difference at this point between a heavy- and a light-displacement boat is very noticeable. With the *White Squall,* I could have lumped full sail with ease; the *Taurangi* was definitely overcanvased. Peter, one of the owners, said nonchalantly, "We'll shorten down." The course was dead to windward, and we were doing short tacks — about 200 feet — between murderous reefs. And Pete was going to shorten down! I was on the point of asking how the devil he was going to accomplish this, but I decided in one of my rare moments of clairvoyance to keep my mouth shut.

The mainsheet was slacked a trifle and the topping lift hardened. Pete simply slacked the halyard with one hand and cranked up and down with a lever in a ratchet in the end of the boom close to the gooseneck. This rotated the boom, which rolled down the sail like a window blind. Pete belayed the halyard and slacked the lift, the mainsheet was trimmed — and now we were a little over a boat's length from a breaking reef. I was still in the driver's seat, so I put down the helm and the sloop shot about, away on a new tack with a comfortable amount of sail up. The reefing drill had taken only seconds, and it left me — the guy who sailed with permanently rove reefing pendants in his mainsail — more than a little envious.

There are those who will argue that a roller-reefed sail does not set as well as a sail shortened by the slab system, but to me, the convenience of being able to execute the drill just described far outweighs any small difference in the finished job. A person concerned about the set of a rolled sail, but seriously considering the use of this gear, might well consult a sailmaker regarding the shape of the boom. As previously mentioned, a boom should be of a larger diameter at the aft end to prevent the boom from drooping when sail is rolled down. This may not be the only consideration, however. The belly of a mainsail, especially a cruising sail, might call for the boom to be swelled toward the center.

A do-it-yourselfer with a yen to experiment might consider shaping a square-sectioned, solid, wooden boom, and set about planing up wooden shims to insert as sail is rolled down. Once the rolled sail has assumed a satisfactory shape, the shims are glued to the boom and the spar is finished carefully with plane and sander and then varnished or painted. This idea isn't new; it's one that has been used with success by many a cruiser willing to experiment to accomplish an acceptable set on a roller-reefed sail.

It's possible that proponents of hollow aluminum booms will level a remark or two at the cruising man who puts a solid boom on his boat; criticisms about weight and the necessity to run mainsheet, guys, preventers, vangs, and what-have-you from the end of the boom might be leveled with great accuracy. To which I say, phooey. There was a time when all we ever had were wooden booms — and solid ones at that. The 3½-ton *Taurangi,* with thousands of ocean miles under her keel, had a shaped wooden boom, and she wasn't any the worse for it.

I've heard it mentioned that a strike against roller reefing comes when a vessel is lying in a bay and the decision is made to reef down before sailing — that it is necessary for full sail to be hoisted, no matter how hard it is blowing, before sail can be shortened. This need not be so if the sail is fitted with luff and leech cringles and rows of eyelets where reef points normally would be. Before sail is hoisted, the luff cringle is lashed down, and the leech cringle is pulled toward the boom end by a lashing, which also secures the cringle to the boom. A spiral lashing is then passed through the eyelets and tightened, and the sail is ready to hoist. It's a case of slab reefing being used as a back-up to roller reefing. An alternative method for any job aboard a cruising boat is more to be desired than scorned. In fact, every roller main-sail would be just that much more versatile if a row of eyelets were installed in the deep-reef position while it was being built. This enables a worthwhile reef to be tied in, in a bay, and also provides protection in the event the roller gear packs up.

Roller-reefing gear, like a lot of other products, has a reputation for great variances in both the quality of available equipment and its design. Worm-type roller reefing, which has the gears inside a grease-filled casing, is operated by a handle engaged (usually from the windward side) on a shaft running from one side of the boom to the other near the gooseneck. This gear is usually very powerful. Because of the space used by the gear casing and its distance aft of the mast, it should be used only with a sail cut with a rub-back dimension, to ensure that the sail will not foul the shaft as the boom is rotated.

A more simple roller-reefing gear is the ratchet on the end of the boom, hard against the gooseneck, and the handle that swivels on the boom behind this. When cranked, the handle works a hooked pawl in the ratchet, a tooth at a time, to turn the boom. John Guzzwell sailed around the world with this rig in his 20-foot-6-inch *Trekka*. It's also used aboard the *Taurangi*. Then there is the roller-reefing gear that features a shaft running through the mast from the gooseneck, which incorporates a

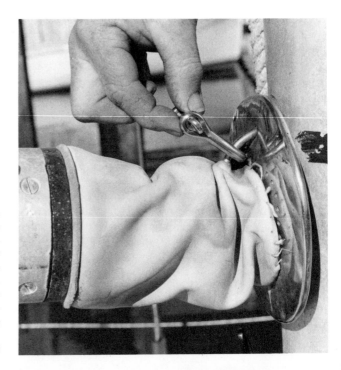

The toggles forming the universal joint of this through-mast roller-reefing system have been covered with chamois leather (which needs resewing to the flange). The chamois protects the luff of the reefed sail from chafe. The shackle is for the sail tack. (Courtesy Yachtspars)

handle at its end. This handle rotates the boom and the sail is rolled down. Like the pawl-and-ratchet system, this rig obviates the necessity for a rub-back dimension in the sail. Its disadvantage, compared with both worm-drive and pawl-and-ratchet systems, is that usually the boom must be hove hard in for sail to be shortened. Worm-drive and pawl-and-ratchet types of roller gear permit sail to be shortened with the boom in any position.

Types of roller-reefing gear used aboard ocean-cruising boats are not confined to what is manufactured and marketed commercially. Home-type and backyard models have sailed the world — some of them showing strong evidence of Rube Goldberg's guiding hand having been present during their construction. One of these masterpieces — a model that must have stretched Rube's inventive genius to its limit — was carried by George Dibbern aboard the 34-foot ketch *Te Rapunga*. George sailed the *Te Rapunga* from Germany to New Zealand in the early 1930s. The pride of George's life was his roller-reefing gear.

The *Te Rapunga* had an outsize hole drilled through her wooden mainmast from fore to aft at gooseneck level. Inside this hole wobbled a rusty shank, which protruded an inch or so out the forward side of the mast. When this shank was turned, the main boom was rotated through a system of universal joints; compared with the modern-day, through-the-mast type of roller reefing, it was an incredible affair. The *Te Rapunga* sailed a large slice of the world and crisscrossed among Pacific Island groups before and after World War II with this roller gear as the only way of reefing the mainsail. To shorten down, old George would wander up forward with an automobile crank handle that fitted the shank precisely. And no matter what the boom angle was, he'd wind away. Maybe Rube Goldberg was one of George's crew members . . . .

The Stoway system, where the sail winds around a vertical extrusion inside the mast, is another type of roller reefing. (We discussed it briefly earlier in this book.) The beauty of this rig is that no special boom shape is called for; there is no fiddling around with topping lift, halyard, and mainsheet while the operation is taking place. Sail shortening is very quick and the rolled sail is protected completely. A drastic sail reduction or a complete stowing of a mainsail takes place within seconds. That the sail disappears inside the mast (except for a tiny piece of clew) cancels out the need for a sail cover when anchored, or extra sail ties or lashings when hove-to in a gale at sea. The company advises that a track for a trysail be installed on the mast in the usual manner so that this sail also can be set.

The Stoway system should be of great interest to anyone contemplating either the reefing and sail-stowing gear of a new cruising boat or the complete re-rigging of a vessel for cruising. A person who already has an efficient rig aboard his boat would have to put out a fair piece of change just to revamp his reefing and furling gear for this system, since it requires the specially designed Stoway mast.

Another system of sailhandling that reefs and furls vertically is the Spool Reefurl, sold by Famet Marine (745 Second Avenue, Redwood City, California 94063). With this method, the sail does not disappear into the security of the mast, as with the Stoway system. However, existing spars and rigging may be utilized, since the sail is wound on an extrusion aft of the mast. This company also markets headsail furling/reefing gear.

Right: *Looking into a Stoway mast. Note that wire halyard leading to mast winch is such a length that both wire and splice are on the drum. (Courtesy Yachtspars)* **Below:** *External, roller-furled mainsail fitted to existing spar. Is the fitting below the drum strong enough to take the aft pull of the outhaul? (Ralph Naranjo photo)*

REEFING HEADSAILS

The reefing of headsails by points or spiral lashing does not, in general, enjoy the popularity it was once accorded. This, I feel, can be traced to the quick sail-changing methods developed in recent years: it is as quick or quicker to drop a sail, dump it down a hatch, bend on another, and hoist away as it is to reef. Although it's not as fast to increase sail area — it's quicker to shake out a reef in a headsail than to replace one sail with another — a "complete" sail of the same area as the reefed one will do a better job. Then there's roller furling/reefing, which we'll come to in a minute.

Reef points or a row of reefing eyelets are not included in modern headsails as a matter of course, but this does not mean that shortening a headsail this way should be disregarded. Aboard a cruising boat where stowage space is at a premium, the fact that a headsail can be reefed means precious room below decks need not be taken by an extra sail bag.

My yawl, a heavy little boat, was dead without a sail forward of the mast. Rather than take up stowage room below with another sail, I had a row of reef points installed in the staysail. When the wind freshened, I would drop the mizzen and then reef the staysail. A bit more wind would see a tuck in the mainsail. The next move would be to take the jib off her and perhaps put the second and last reef in the main. With a reefed staysail and double-reefed main, she could stand a lot of wind. Any further deterioration in the weather would see us dressing her in her storm clothes (trysail and storm staysail) and going below to draw off a mug of rum from the keg under the cabin table.

I do feel that a sail set on an inner forestay lends itself more readily to being reefed than a jib, because there is a lot more motion at the tack of the jib than at the tack of the staysail. Also, the jib is in a very narrow workspace when securing the luff cringle, regardless of whether there is a pulpit for support. The farther forward a person has to be to reef a sail, the more difficult and dangerous it is.

(Remember that a staysail equipped with a row of reef points should be constructed of the same weight of cloth as the mainsail, since it will be expected to do hard work when reefed in a weight of wind. And the same attention should be given to strengthening the luff and leech reefing cringles as is lavished on the sail's other load points.)

To reef the staysail aboard my yawl, I would always lower the sail completely and jog along under jib and mainsail while putting in the tuck. If things were a little damp on the foredeck, with sheets of spray occasionally whipping across, I would back the jib and heave-to until the reef was tied in (the hell with getting wet).

After the staysail was lowered, the lee sheet would be placed under firm (but not too hard) tension to stretch the sail from tack to clew. The staysail luff cringle would then be lashed to the tack and the leech cringle pulled toward the clew by several turns of lashing between cringle and clew, until the line of reef points was fairly stretched. Since the clew was held aft and at deck level by the sheet, this job was very easy. Once the cringle-to-clew lashing was fast, a separate lashing was used from the cringle around the foot of the staysail. The reef points were tied, the sheet slacked, and the sail was hoisted.

It was my own personal preference to lower the staysail completely to reef. It's possible that some experienced yachtsmen prefer to do the job with the sail still flying. I tried tying in a reef a couple of times with the sail still up, but each time the staysail luffed while I was busy with the cringle-to-clew lashing and whipped it out of my hand. Keep in mind that whenever it comes time to reef the staysail, the weather is starting to kick up, and if that sail flaps while you're working on it, it's like the crack of a whip — and mighty hard to hang on to. Once the sail's down on deck, the job's a piece of cake.

A sail on a club can be reefed in the same manner as a boomless sail. I suppose there are some fearless souls who have a forestaysail on a club and who reef the sail while it's still up. Of course, staysail clubs make a practice of wiping the foredeck clean every now and then in good weather, and I've never been game to let one of them show what it could do in a breeze of wind. To reef the forestaysail on the schooner, I would slack the halyard, and, standing by the foremast well aft of the boom, heave away on the downhaul until the sail was at the bottom of its stay. Then I'd bowse the staysail sheet down good and tight. After this, I would venture onto the foredeck and go about the business of tying in a reef.

When reefing a boomless staysail, some sailors prefer to move the staysail sheets to the reef cringle. There is something to be said for this approach to the exercise because of the direct connection between sheets and reef cringle. I always left the sheets where they were and used lashings to hold the cringle to the clew, since I didn't like the idea of having the staysail clew hanging below the reef cringle when the reefed sail was hoisted and drawing. Also, when it came time to shake out the reef, I thought it was easier, after letting go the reef points, to ease the lashings rather than to move the sheets from cringle to clew. The reason for using separate lashings from cringle to clew, and from the cringle under the foot of the sail, was simply to have one lashing be a back-up for the other.

LUFF SPAR HEADSAIL REEFING

Several reputable companies (Hood Sailmakers is one) recommend their luff spar roller-furling/reefing gear as ideal for the ocean cruiser. It is touted as reefing equipment that can be taken to sea and used as *the* means of shortening sail forward of the mast. On the face of it, it would seem that this is marvelous news for the cruising buff; gone are the days of swapping or reefing headsails. To take off sail forward, all that's needed is to pull a piece of string aft, and the sail winds up until whatever amount decided on is left drawing.

But is this really the be-all and end-all for the serious ocean cruiser? It is ideal for the Caribbean chartering and cruising scene, where the hops from island to island are short and the weather, in general, is good, but these conditions cannot be compared to those in the Pacific. And *anywhere* in the Pacific is a long way from home. If your gear goes on the blink, you're stuck with it.

When we talk about cruising, we're not talking about a one-shot deal; we're referring to a way of life. It is undeniable that experienced yachtsmen have taken this roller gear to sea and been happy with the reefing aspect of it. But have they been serious cruising nuts, out there year after year?

Small sloop with partly furled/reefed jib on luff spar. Note slightly bellied, uneven furl near masthead. You'd have to watch your head in this cockpit. (Courtesy Yachtspars)

Where you intend to cruise determines whether you use roller gear for reefing a headsail. Furling, yes — as mentioned in the last chapter, we've had a bit of experience with roller-furling gear at sea. But when I get to thinking about a trip during which we beat a large percentage of the way from New Zealand to the U.S. West Coast, I can't help but wonder how one of those luff spar reefing rigs would have stood up to it. Or how efficient that partly furled sail would be aboard a boat that was trying hard to get up to windward. If I'm wrong — and I hope I am — luff spar reefing is one of the best things ever to arrive aboard a cruising boat.

REEFING VERSUS AUXILIARY POWER

One of my first boats was a frail, narrow, old 38-foot gaff-rigger that leaked like a basket when sailed. As soon as we got underway, five-gallon cans of bilgewater would be passed up through the hatch and emptied over the side. A signal event, and cause for much jubilation among the bailers, was the installation of a large semi-rotary bilge pump that one of the crew rescued from a marine junk pile. An antique marvel, the pump was brought back to life by some rough-and-ready surgery, which included a couple of makeshift valves and a handle. This pump was operated nonstop by a succession of "volunteers" as soon as we hove the anchor aboard and got moving.

Since we were strictly "all sail" (we couldn't have afforded the fuel to run an engine even if we'd owned one), we were as alert as a covey of quail to any change in the weather once we anchored our ship in a bay. Contributing in great measure to this standard of vigilance was the belief that the old girl had a mind of her own. If she decided that the tack we'd chosen to get going on didn't suit, we could back jibs, run back and forth, shout, do all the things we thought were correct — and she'd quietly sag off onto whichever tack pleased her at the moment.

It never occurred to any teenage "manjack" aboard that this happened only because we didn't know what we were doing. So it wasn't seamanship that caused us to tuck a reef or two in the mainsail of the old *Mizpah* if we had any doubts about the weather when at anchor in an exposed bay. It was fear — fear of what she'd do if it started to blow and we had to get going in a hurry. The already-reefed mainsail was used time and time again. If there's any one thing that has remained with me from those days, it's the awareness of being ready to clear out if, through a wind change, there is the slightest likelihood that the ship might be caught at anchor on a lee shore.

The easiest way of dealing with this situation, of course, is to fire up the auxiliary and chug around to a sheltered anchorage, if such exists. Or, rather than beat out of the bay, to steam up to windward, hoisting sail as you go. The possibility should never be discounted, however, that an auxiliary engine — for any one of a variety of reasons — may decide to go on strike. And you can bet your favorite grandmother that if and when this happens, it'll be the time when you really need an engine.

No matter how dependable your auxiliary engine might be, if you anchor in a place that could become a lee shore in a wind change, have in mind the moves you would make if you had to clear out under sail. Never forget that the sails of the average cruising boat are a dependable power plant. I'm not suggesting that you put in a couple of reefs as a matter of course, as we did in those far-off days. (Ours was a case of the blind leading the blind, and with the old clunker we had, we were only accidentally doing the right thing.) What I'm referring to is the realization on the part of a cruising skipper that his sails can usually get him out of trouble if used properly. In case you think I'm making too big a thing of this, the following account of the completely preventable stranding and loss of a fine vessel might help drive the point home.

The ship, a 42-foot wooden ketch, was built in Tasmania and sailed across the Pacific to California. I'd seen the vessel in Auckland as she passed through, and I'd admired her greatly. It was with delight, then, that we anchored close to her in my yawl a few years later on a trip to Ensenada, Mexico. The next time we saw her was farther down the coast, lying on her starboard bilge and being picked clean as a bone by villagers. She'd dragged ashore slowly and steadily while her owner was trying to get his auxiliary engine going. Instead of putting a reef in the mainsail and clawing off in the 30-knot breeze under reefed main and staysail (or whatever sail combination suited), he'd pulled the starter motor off his engine and was busy examining it when she struck.

There isn't one of us incapable of making a wrong decision. I've made some marvelous booboos in my time, so I'm not about to point a finger at the other guy. But what a crying shame it was that the vessel's main means of propulsion was disregarded at a time when she needed it most. About the only good that can come out of such an event is the lessons that can be learned from it.

In this chapter we've discussed reefing, its various approaches, and the desirability of finding sail combinations to keep a cruising boat manageable and in balance as the wind rises. As can be seen, the ability to reef a boat's sails at sea calls for no great skill; neither does doing the same job at anchor. Knowing what combination of sails most suits a vessel in various wind strengths — whether she's a thousand miles at sea or sailing off a lee shore — does take some skill. It is this sort of knowledge that ranks the skippers of cruising boats.

Practice various reefing drills until you find a system that suits you and your boat. Don't wait for half a gale to learn how to put in a slab or roll down six feet of mainsail. Do it in good weather until you know the exercise backward and forward. Then, if you're caught in a bay with no engine and you have to clear out, or you're at sea and it comes on to blow, you won't feel unsteady. Be able to lay your hand on every piece of reefing equipment, from the crank handle of your roller gear to the spare lashings for the reef cringles, by day or night. Get in the habit of stowing them in the same place. A good place for tapered reef lashings is under your pillow . . . . But you already know that.

eight

Light Sails

While adequate working and storm sails are necessities aboard an ocean-cruising boat, it is highly desirable to have a selection of light sails included in her wardrobe. On some passages, with conditions ranging from near calm to perhaps only eight knots of wind for days on end, the progress of a heavily laden cruising boat, relying solely on working sails for motive power, can be painfully slow. The use of a light "extra" or two on such a voyage can sometimes shorten the trip by half and at the same time give the crew the satisfaction of sailing instead of just drifting along.

The number and size of the light sails carried *and used* aboard a cruising boat usually comes down to three factors: cost of the sails, number of crew to handle the sails, and room below deck to stow the sails when they're not set.

Cost of the sails often occupies top position on the list. After a vessel is equipped with everything needed for cruising, it is often beyond the financial ability of the owner to splurge on a great selection of light sails. A number of months may pass until our sailor finds a job along the way. Or time may be spent hanging fire until either Uncle Alf finally kicks the bucket and leaves that modest packet or those dividends come through. (Or, if he's a writer, until his royalties catch up with him — ho, ho!) With some cruising folk, all this can make a difference as to whether or not any light sails are carried.

Even where cost is no consideration, the number of crew and their ages and expertise should influence the choice of light sails carried. The type and size of any light extras should match the ability of the crew to handle them. A singlehander, for instance, must be wary of hoisting light sails, because not only must he do all the work of setting, trimming, or furling — he also has to sleep. A sudden freshening of wind while a singlehander is catching 40 winks can make for some strenuous and possibly dangerous work until sail is doused. A cruising couple can have their moments, too, for the same reasons. How comprehensive their vessel's light sail wardrobe is depends in great measure on the strength, agility, and experience of a couple — and how long and in what strength wind they can carry a large extra.

The cruising person today must be more aware of the danger of flying a big, light sail that he is marginally capable of handling in an emergency than was his counterpart who cruised in the days when sails were constructed of cotton. A light cotton sail used aboard a cruising boat usually would sacrifice itself by blowing out before the ship was endangered. (There were exceptions to this, of course; a very tender vessel with open hatches and clouds of canvas was always vulnerable.) Synthetic sails, weight for weight, are much stronger than the same sails constructed from cotton, especially if the cotton sail has had a year or so of wear. Synthetics hang on. It is possible for an extra-large, synthetic light sail, hoisted on, say, a 40-foot cruising boat, to overpower the vessel completely in a sudden strong squall. This is not intended to scare the pants off people who are all fired up to equip their cruising boat with an ensemble of light-weather sails, but in all fairness, it should be mentioned.

A cruising boat with three or more capable people aboard usually can carry every light sail in the book. The more experienced hands there are in a ship, the more this applies. It should be noted, however, that a vessel with a large crew generally is not one that keeps on cruising — unless, of course, the crew is changed every now and again. In choosing light sails for a cruising boat, the number of constant crew and the standard of each member's individual competence should be considered carefully.

Room below decks to stow sails, naturally enough, varies from boat to boat. A large cruising boat doesn't necessarily have plenty of room below decks for bags and bags of sails. Big boats mean big sails, which demand a lot of space for stowage. The crew that must be carried to handle those sails takes up a lot of room, too. A cruising couple or family, whose boat is their home, should think carefully about just what space is available below decks to stow light sails when they are not in use — both at sea and in port.

HEADSAILS

Because of the wide gulf separating different types of cruising boats, their sizes, and their rigs, it is impossible to be specific about a selection of light sails that would suit every kind of craft. There are very few sailing vessels that would not benefit from the use of a large headsail in light airs, however. The size and weight of the sail vary, of course, from one craft to another.

A genoa jib can put life into a shorthanded cruising boat like almost nothing else can. I remember when I first started ocean cruising in the 1940s, I read avidly all there was to read (and there wasn't much) about the game. Hulls, rigs, and aspect ratios were scrutinized with an inexperienced but determined eye. Sails, too — pictures of sailboats carrying what looked like acres of billowing canvas were examined with profound interest. When I launched my little *White Squall* in 1948, I vowed that when I could afford it, my vessel would also sport a light sail or two.

Mine was a case, however, of first things first. We were playing around down in the Roaring Forties at the time, and it made more sense for me to save for a really rugged trysail and storm jib. It was a great day when, with the century just 51 years old, a 4½-ounce cotton genoa of some 380 square feet was carried aboard tenderly. Then, amid wild excitement, it was hoisted for the first time, and my 10-ton cutter (it was another year or so before I changed her to yawl rig) became a different vessel. Even in light airs, with the eight-ounce working sails hanging slackly, the genoa would pull like a horse and tow the ship along.

I don't know how many times, over the years, I sat below stitching away, repairing that jib as my vessel sailed on her course. It got to the stage where my senses were tuned to just how much wind the genoa could stand before it blew out. I went through two of these sails before a Terylene (Dacron) genoa of the same size and weight came aboard in 1960. The efficiency of that synthetic sail, over the cotton genoa it replaced, was remarkable; the weight of wind it could take without tearing was a never-ending novelty.

In an effort to choose a selection of light sails suitable for a modern ocean-cruising boat, let's assume that you have a 40-foot marconi-rigged cutter with an aspect ratio (luff-to-foot) of 2½ to 1. As owners, and total crew, you are a couple who intend to use the vessel as a world-cruising home.

My choice of light sails for such a vessel would be two sizes of headsail. The first sail would be a six-ounce Dacron genoa of 120 percent of the foretriangle area; it would be cut with the clew a minimum of three feet above the deck. This sail could be carried in a fresh breeze with the vessel reaching, or close-hauled until the wind

The clew of this cruising cutter's genoa is a healthy height above deck. (Ralph Naranjo photo)

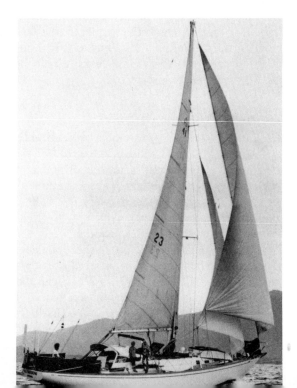

Nicely proportioned three-reef, four-batten mainsail. But that genny just might be low enough on the foot to scoop up a wave top. (Ralph Naranjo photo)

blew, say, 15 knots. The genoa would then be handed and stowed and the ship sailed under mainsail, boomless staysail, and working jib.

The second sail, for use in very light airs, would hoist on the jibstay and be cut as a drifter-reacher. This sail would be constructed of 1½-ounce nylon, and in area, it would be 150 percent of the foretriangle. Its clew would also be three feet above the deck. This light, nylon sail, possibly sheeted to the end of the main boom or boomed out to windward when running (see Chapter Nine), would be expected to tow the vessel along in the lightest of airs.

The reason for the clew height of both sails is, once again, an attempt to avoid scooping up the lee bow wave at sea. There is usually a far bigger slop on the open ocean than in sheltered waters with the same weight of wind. At sea there's a far greater chance that the foot of a low-cut headsail will collect the top of the lee bow wave.

STAYSAILS

The rig of the cruising boat is an influencing factor in deciding among other light sails. A staysail schooner, for instance, becomes a different vessel when a fisherman's staysail (literally, main topmast staysail) is hoisted in light airs. The easiest and safest way to handle this sail is to run it up on a track on the foremast. It is, in fact, good practice *always* to hoist a sail on a stay or a track; then, even if the wind rises suddenly, the sail can be controlled as it is brought down. A large sail set flying can contribute an unnecessary sting of excitement to the person dousing it in a breeze of wind.

(Here's another argument for holding the luffs of gaff sails to their masts with track instead of mast hoops. With track, you can have a second track for a fisherman's staysail; with mast hoops, you have to set the fisherman's staysail flying. A fisherman's staysail, its luff held by slides on a foremast track, is spread by a line from its peak to the main masthead and sheets lead from the clew to the end of the main boom or the after deck. On a staysail schooner, I prefer the sheets from a fisherman's staysail to lead to a deck block each side of the after deck and then to a winch, rather than to the end of the boom. With the sheets led to deck blocks, the sail can be handled in the same manner as a jib when tacking; the clew of the sail blows through the gap between the mainstay and the foremast and is sheeted to

Dolphin striker, staysail clubs, high-clewed Yankee — and maybe the main-staysail club is low enough to chafe on the jib sheet when eased. A handsome vessel, however. (Ralph Naranjo photo)

A staysail schooner with a fisherman "earning its keep." Note running backstay set up to windward. (Ralph Naranjo photo)

Looking up a schooner's mainmast at the peak of a fisherman's staysail. Aboard this schooner, two halyards are necessary, because the peak must be dipped under the lower triatic stay when tacking (or jibing). Here, the windward peak halyard is slack and is led under the lower triatic. When tacking, the lee side is slacked, the peak is dropped below the lower triatic and hauled up the other side. (Peter Otway photo)

leeward in the usual manner. If the sail is sheeted to the end of the boom, a block is necessary on each side at the end, for each sheet. There should be a winch on each side of the boom to take the sheets, and these winches should be close enough to the gooseneck so that they can be reached easily for trimming the sail when the boom is well out.)

The higher a sail is set, the more wind there is; a fisherman's staysail, hoisted way up on a schooner, can mean the difference between sitting and wallowing in light airs or making way through the water.

A cruising schooner with a large crew can set a sail known as a gollywobbler. This sail is an outsize fisherman's staysail, taking up the area between the foremast and the mainmast and coming down to within a few feet of the deck. A gollywobbler sheets to the end of the main boom. While some schooners have turned in fantastic runs by using this sail, a cruising schooner without a large crew is best advised to forget about a gollywobbler and settle for a fisherman's staysail of a size that suits the manpower available to handle it.

I can hear voices in the background from the mizzen staysail gang. Certain ketch and yawl owners become incensed when a bloke such as me takes a verbal swipe at mizzen staysails. I'll concede that we all see pictures from time to time of ketches or yawls bowling along with exotic mizzen staysails pulling as if their lives depended on it, but I'll also repeat what I said before — I've never had any luck with the sail. We would use it for anything from 10 minutes to 10 hours (don't think it ever saw a full day's service), and sometimes six months would pass before it was tried again hesitantly.

There are, of course, ketches with a great gap between mainmast and mizzenmast and an especially high-aspect-ratio rig, which allows for a permanent stay, to be set up from the mizzen masthead, on which a sail can be hoisted. The distance between masts is enough to allow clearance between this mizzen stay and the main boom. The mizzen staysail, hoisted on the mizzen stay, can be used on any point of sailing from hard on the wind to the point, off the wind, when it would be blanketed by the mizzen. When underway, such a vessel sometimes looks in profile like two high-aspect-ratio sloops, one closely following the other. This is an arrangement totally different from that on normal ketches or yawls without such clearance; they have to set their mizzen staysails flying.

If you're all fired up to buy your vessel a mizzen staysail, have at it. Tacked up to windward and with the sheet led to the end of the mizzen boom, you might get it drawing just long enough for a patient friend in another boat to take a picture. On the other hand, you might get it to work every time. There's every possibility that you're a better sailor than I am — and 10 chances out of 10 you have more patience.

As mentioned earlier, another way of carrying much the same sail as a mizzen staysail on a sloop or cutter is to take a single block, complete with halyard, and seize it to the permanent backstay, about a third or halfway up the stay. The sail is tacked up to windward to an eyebolt, pad eye, or chainplate, and hoisted away. The sheet leads to a block as far aft as possible on the lee side. When drawing, this sail will impose considerable strain on the masthead, but with rugged cruising gear, this shouldn't be too much of a problem. The chances of using the sail continually would seem to be the same as for a mizzen staysail.

A sail that some ketch owners claim will push a ship along is known as a "mule." This sail fills the gap between main masthead, mizzen masthead, and mainsail leech — sort of like an upside-down jib. When I was still damp behind the ears, my old buddy George Dibbern would speak with pride of his mule, and with extravagant gestures, pronounce it, " . . . one of my best sails!" I used to absorb George's pearls of wisdom in the manner of a sponge with a spill of beer. I didn't realize at the time that Rube Goldberg was one of George's key men. And Rube could make anything work.

Do I hear mumblings from the spinnaker team? A spinnaker, pulling as if an airplane had a towline on your vessel, can really make you cover the miles. Aboard ocean cruisers, however, the practice of setting a spinnaker is often taboo, because of the number, age, strength, or agility of the people running the ship. There are many world-girdling couples who just wouldn't be able to handle the spinnaker gear if conditions — such as a wind change at night — deteriorated in a hurry.

Again, if you have the energy and expertise, buy yourself a spinnaker and set it flying from a pole. During a spate of about 10 years, I'd feel so guilty when I didn't have a spinnaker set that I'd have all hands up in the middle of the night a thousand miles from nowhere getting the thing hoisted and drawing. I managed, thank the stars, to outgrow the habit. I became perfectly happy to use my genoa jibs for reaching in light weather; there are better cruising rigs than the spinnaker for running, as we'll see in the next chapter.

TOPSAILS

For gaff-rigged vessels, there is no doubt that a light, well-cut gaff topsail will soon show every reason for its inclusion in the ship's sail inventory. Not only will a gaff topsail catch the wind in airs light enough to barely fill the vessel's working sails, but also the topsail will keep the gaff from swinging and contributing its share of chafe to mainsail and running gear. A gaff topsail is held in such esteem by some sailors that quite recently I heard a gaff-rig buff declare that in light airs he placed the importance of his topsail ahead of his genoa jib. For a topsail to perform this well, it should be not less than one-third the area of the mainsail.

There are many ways of rigging a gaff topsail, but before settling on any particular one, the owner of a cruising gaff-rigger should first consider two things: Is the mainsail high peaked? Is the peak of the gaff above or below the masthead when sail is hoisted?

If the gaff is high peaked — that is, if the angle between gaff and mast is oblique enough (25 degrees or less) to give a deep, narrow space between gaff and mast — the chances of a useful topsail that sets well are not very good. If the gaff peak is such a distance below the masthead that a horizontal line drawn from peak to mast divides the vertical between gaff jaws and masthead in half (or near enough) — and the mast-gaff angle exceeds 25 degrees (45 to 50 degrees is preferred) — it should be possible to carry a well-set gaff topsail. Another way to say this is, if the head and foot of the topsail are of about equal length, there is a fair chance the sail will set well.

If the gaff peak is above, on a level with, or barely below the masthead, the topsail probably will have to be fitted with a jackyard to give its head enough height. To achieve this, it is often necessary for the luff of the topsail to be bent to the jackyard from the head nearly to the tack to enable the head to project above the masthead. The sail is hoisted by a masthead halyard and the lower end of the jackyard is held close to the mast by a line, or "leader." This line runs from a fixed point on the mast just above the position of the lower end of the hoisted jackyard, through a bull's-eye or cringle seized to the lower end of the yard, and to the deck.

Jackyards traditionally have been small-diameter hollow or solid wooden spars to which the topsail was bent with a lacing. When continual use of the gaff topsail was anticipated, the sail would be rolled around the spar and the bundle kept handy on deck. The topsail would be taken off the spar and stowed during a spell in port, or for a voyage that wouldn't see much use of the sail. I have heard of a hollow wooden dinghy mast with a typical luff groove (into which the topsail luff was fed) that was used as a jackyard for a small gaff topsail; the practice sounds ideal. Even better and stronger, perhaps, would be a small aluminum spar with an integral track.

There are, of course (for the bloke who *really* likes his sticks and string), club topsails. These sails, used mainly in very light weather, have a jackyard on the luff that takes the head of the sail well above the masthead, and a club on the foot to take the clew of the sail past the peak of the gaff. The club extends inboard along the gaff at least as far as it extends outboard, and the sheet is made fast to the club at the point opposite the sheet block on the end of the gaff.

To ensure that a gaff topsail will set on the wind, the sail should be made a little smaller than the space it will be required to fill. The topsail can then be hove tight and flat by its sheet to the peak of the gaff. There is nothing more frustrating than a gaff topsail that has been cut a little large. The only way you can flatten it is to ease the peak halyard, thus ruining the set of your mainsail.

On a number of large charter boats and school ships, a gaff topsail is hoisted on a

The cruising sailor has to decide whether or not a gaff topsail this small is worth the bother, and whether or not it would be worth having to deal with a longer jackyard to give the sail more area and a better shape. (This is a pinky schooner built to Howard Chapelle's design for the Glad Tidings.*)*

topmast to which the luff of the sail is secured by hoops, a track, or a lacing. Such a topsail sometimes is fitted with brails, which, when a decision is made to furl, gather the sail to the foot of the topmast. A crew member then goes aloft to complete the stow. Aboard the average small, gaff-rigged cruising boat, it is more usual for all the setting and furling to be done from the deck. With a little planning and forethought, this can be accomplished quite easily.

The halyard, of course, may be handled from the deck in any case. The clew is hauled to the peak of the gaff by its sheet, which runs along the length of the gaff to a block near the jaws and down to the deck. A line from the tack leads to the deck and also serves as a downhaul.

A jackyard topsail has its luff held by the jackyard and tension on the tackline. A thimble-headed topsail (not bent to a jackyard but hoisted from the deck as is) has its luff held close to the mast, once aloft, by tension on the halyard and tackline. A leader may be used on a thimble-headed topsail to ensure control over the topsail when either hoisting or lowering. The leader goes from a point on the mast between gaff jaws and masthead, through a thimble seized onto the topsail halfway down the luff, and to the deck; the strain on it helps stiffen the luff.

It is possible that the use of gaff topsails to augment a ship's wardrobe in light airs is a practice as old as gaff rig itself, for in the days of commercial sail, any opportunity to move a cargo vessel along a little faster was never overlooked. Extra time spent on a voyage because of light weather was money down the drain, and more than a few shipmasters hung onto their light topsails as the wind increased — and so, in proportion, did the speed of their command. Every now and again, aboard a fore-and-after, the gaff topsails would be left up in conditions "not fit for a parson's son." In weather, in other words, that the sails were never meant to stand. My old mentor, Francis B. McKenzie, whom I regarded as the original ancient mariner and who used to fill my young ears with horrific tales of wooden ships and iron men, told me about such an incident.

It was in the 1880s when Francis, 14 years of age, was deckboy aboard a heavy cargo schooner running from Australia to New Zealand. The ship had loaded general cargo in Auckland on this particular voyage and had sailed up the east coast of New Zealand with a "soldier's wind" right off the land. They had experienced a calm off North Cape before the wind came in from the northeast, giving them a fair wind to Sydney, some 1,000 miles west. Once clear of the land, the skipper celebrated this manna from heaven by going below, closing the door, and slamming the hatch shut over his cabin. Here, he started consuming bottle after bottle of whiskey — the Old Man was on a bender. Orders left with the mate were to "leave all the bloody rags up there" and to "call me when you see the light!" (Sydney Heads).

According to Francis, the wind freshened steadily all the first day, and just before nightfall, the mate, who for a few hours had been shooting uneasy glances aloft at the fore and main gaff topsails, sent Francis along to the skipper's cabin with the intelligence that "it's blowin' like stink an' them topsails gotta come off 'er!"

Francis, who was only on his second trip to sea, and who stood trembling in awe of ship's captains, knocked on the hatchway leading down to the master's cabin and delivered the message. This touched off a roar from below, and a comment, "Gotta come off her, do they? Well, you just get back along there and ask *mister* mate what the hell he thinks them topsails are, anyhow — whore's drawers?" The captain paused for breath and got going again. "You tell him that the topsails stay where they are. The moon'll be up soon and it'll scoff the wind."

This bulletin was duly relayed to the mate, who gazed up to windward at the big, curling seas and aloft at the bulging topsails. With the wind still increasing, the mate proceeded to chew his bottom lip with large yellow teeth. An hour after dark, with wind and sea still rising, the mate could stand it no longer. Francis was dispatched with another plea to let them take down the topsails. This message galvanized the ship's master into bounding up the companionway leading from his cabin to the deck and bellowing into the deckboy's face, through the partly opened hatch, "Get the hell back there and tell the mate the moon'll be up soon and it'll scoff the wind!" Francis almost turned a back somersault at this broadside and scurried back along the deck.

The next time the mate sent Francis to alert the skipper that things were even worse, an empty whiskey bottle, thrown with great force, exploded beneath the deckboy's nose. "Tell that bloody mate the moon'll scoff the wind!" Francis, heart hammering against the roof of his mouth, scampered back up onto the poop.

By now things were pretty bad. The schooner, down to her marks with cargo, was taking heavy water over the weather rail all along her waist: the freeing ports could be heard thudding as the vessel lifted on the top of a sea. The moon, rising astern, was the signal for the wind to increase even more. Two men were now needed at the wheel; the mate was chewing both his lips. When it seemed that the press of sail would bury the vessel, there was a report like a field gun from aloft. It was followed by an even louder bang, and the ship eased as if she'd been holding her breath. The mate swung briskly to Francis. "Run along to the captain's cabin, McKenzie. Give 'im my compliments. And tell 'im the wind's just scoffed the tops'ls!"

nine

Running Sails
Square Rig and Twin Spinnakers

At first thought, the term *running sails* might seem to refer to sails carried aboard a vessel for the express purpose of running downwind, but that definition is not always complete. In an effort to extend the usable range of a cruising boat's wardrobe, sails such as jibs, staysails, and genoas — sails intended primarily for serious on-the-wind work — are often set in strange but successful combinations to send a ship running before the wind.

Behind this diversification (in addition to the economics of making a sail do more than one job) is the search for a chafe-free downhill rig, and a rig that will give a ship lift, rather than just push her. To achieve this state of affairs, most sails hoisted for the sole intent of running are carried well forward in a sailing vessel.

In an attempt to discuss the options available to cruising people who may wonder what combination of sails would best enable their particular craft to run before it, we will start with a rig that has been around for a long time.

SQUARESAILS

The traditional running sail carried by vessels over the centuries is the squaresail (whose name is something of a misnomer, since the sail is more of a rectangle than a square). Hung from a horizontal yard, which pivots on the mast, a squaresail enables a vessel to run before the wind without risk of a jibe. There have been attempts by cruising sailors to get more service out of their squaresails by setting them on a reach, but by and large, the squaresail's even limited popularity aboard small sailing vessels stems from its use with the wind well aft.

A strong advocate of the squaresail as almost indispensable aboard a small cruising boat was Conor O'Brien, who sailed his engineless, 42-foot, 23-ton ketch, *Saoirse,* eastabout around the world. O'Brien sailed from Dublin, Ireland, on June

20, 1923, to keep a mountain-climbing appointment on New Zealand's South Island. After trying unsuccessfully to sell his vessel in Auckland, he carried on, running his easting down in the Southern Ocean. He returned to Dublin, after circumnavigating by way of the three great capes — Cape of Good Hope, Cape Leeuwin (Australia), and Cape Horn — on June 20, 1925, a neat two years after departing. *Across Three Oceans* (published by John de Graff) is a delightful, seamanlike account of the voyage.

Although the *Saoirse*'s captain could find fault with his vessel, he was adamant about the suitability of her square rig for cruising. "One is not long at sea before one realizes that the comfort and speed of a passage depends less on fore-and-afters than on square canvas," he wrote. In another book, a sail plan advocated by O'Brien as an oceangoing rig for a yacht of 52-foot waterline shows a brigantine-rigged vessel, all square on the foremast and with a Scotch-cut gaff mainsail, the miter running diagonally across the sail from clew to throat.

Aboard his gaff-rigged ketch, Conor O'Brien bent the foresail (as he called *Saoirse*'s squaresail) to a track screwed to the underside of a yard that pivoted on his mainmast. A strong bolt rope was sewn down the center of the sail from head to foot. This roping ended in a cringle, which, when time came to furl the sail, was bowsed down with a handy billy. Brails, running through thimbles seized first to this bolt rope and then to either leech, enabled the squaresail to be furled one side at a time. The total area of the sail was 320 square feet. Above the yard, two raffees were carried. The raffees, each of 90 square feet, were run up on twin forestays and were cut so that their clews hauled neatly to each yard end. This meant that when a decision was made to furl, the sails could be taken in from the deck (with a downhaul) and were always under control. When the mainsail and gaff topsail were carried in addition to the squaresail and raffees, the lee raffee, which the topsail would blanket, had its luff bent to a boathook that was lashed to the windward yard end. The raffee, hanging upside down from the yard, was used as a studding sail.

To enable the yard to be braced well around, the cap shrouds were each led over the tip of a swinging spreader; these shrouds then were set up to aft chainplates. When the yard was thus braced, the slackness of the lee rigging caused the spreader to be pushed farther aft, out of harm's way. When we talk about squaresails, raffees, and such, we are referring, of course, to a lot of string (and all aboard a 42-footer). There are outhauls, inhauls, downhauls, halyards, brails, tackles — you name it, they're all part of the scene. Apparently it wasn't all beer and skittles, either. Although the *Saoirse*'s squaresail was intended for windward work in addition to off-the-wind work, her master writes, "Tacking ship with it set was a heavy job for two," and "on a close reach great care was needed at the helm, for the sail would get aback in an instant, and then there would be the devil to pay." I'll bet there would!

I do consider that the cruising man contemplating rigging a squaresail on his ship should carefully evaluate the pros and cons of windage, weight aloft, and the large amount of running gear involved — and even then only allocate to the squaresail the task of running before the wind. Maybe in a vessel exceeding, say, 150 feet on deck, there is some excuse for a yard on the foremast, but for the average cruising boat of between 25 and 65 feet in length, a squaresail doesn't make sense to me. Conor

The squaresails and fishermen of this brigantine brail in to the foremast. (Ralph Naranjo photo)

O'Brien's dogma notwithstanding, there are many sails (such as a good, high-clewed genoa) that are more effective and a whole lot easier to handle when on a reach than a squaresail.

I must admit, however, that I've always admired a cruising vessel that sports a yard or two on her foremast. No two ways about it; it looks as salty as seaweed and smacks of deep water and all that. Now and again we'd anchor in some way-out bay alongside a vessel rigged as a topsail schooner, brigantine, or whatever, and I'd sit on deck with a toddy in my hand, admiring her — and thanking my lucky stars she didn't belong to me. Those yards and braces and things may give a ship a romantic look and project the onlooker back into another century, but that's all they do. You can bet your bottom dollar that the same vessel would be a whole lot more efficient, both on the wind *and* off, with a fore-and-aft rig and perhaps some sort of twin spinnaker setup for running downhill. All this probably curdles the ire of the square-rig gang, but that can't be helped — it's a fact.

That yard, up there permanently, represents weight and windage aloft that detract from the sailing efficiency of the vessel as almost nothing else can. If you're bent on hanging a yard or two on your foremast, then go to it; it's your ship. But for getting to windward, you'll probably have your auxiliary engine ticking over every inch of the way. Even off the wind, the amount of sail set from a yard can be disappointing. O'Brien's *Saoirse,* with all her paraphernalia of lines and rigging, carried only 320 square feet in her squaresail — not much for a 23-ton craft.

Two 90-square-foot raffees only brought the total area of *Saoirse*'s running sails to 500 square feet. We are not told how a boathook was secured to a yardend so that an upside-down raffee could be set as a studding sail, clipper-ship fashion, on a long downhill leg. From O'Brien's description of the caliber of *Saoirse*'s paid crew, who were recruited from various merchant marine shipping offices along the way, it seems probable that the job of lying along a yard and lashing on a temporary stuns'l spar would be attempted with a minimum of enthusiasm. Maybe the yard was lowered or cockbilled to accomplish this task. Maybe the master of the vessel clambered aloft, hand over hand, with the boathook clenched between his teeth.

To analyze further, we'll take a 45-foot gaff-rigged cutter with a moderate-to-heavy-displacement hull. If we want to detract from her sailing efficiency, we'll put another mast in her, making her a ketch or a yawl. Then, in an effort to *really* foul up the lady, we'll give her a yard on her mainmast as well. What length of yard will we hang up there? Twenty-two feet? All right, with her beam of, say, 12½ feet, that's fair enough; if the yard were any longer, we'd probably have trouble sheeting the clews. What'll we do about the squaresail's bellying out and chafing against the inner forestay? (Don't forget: if we pivot that yard too far below the inner forestay, we'll lose out on sail area.) Set a raffee above the yard and inner forestay? That means more string — another halyard, outhauls, downhaul, possibly inhauls. Hang the yard above the inner forestay and divide the squaresail in two, so there'll be no chafe on the stay? OK, that usually works. How deep will the squaresail be? Twenty feet? That will give us a sail area of 440 square feet. Is this relatively small sail area worth having a yard aloft, along with all its weight and windage, not to mention the additional windage of the furled, brailed, or rolled-up sail?

Why don't we forget all about the yard, and instead, hang two 15-foot aluminum booms down against the foreside of the mast, with their bottom ends, say, two feet from the deck. Or, if we don't like this idea, let them hang down each side against a shroud. Our twin "spinnakers" will hank onto two stays set up by quick-release levers to eyebolts in the deck, some six feet forward of the mast and about two feet apart.

I can hear an agonized howl or two in the background whenever I mention the word *spinnaker* to describe this rig. To refer to these sails as spinnakers — which are sails set flying — is being rather reckless with the word. The term *twin staysails* is probably nearer the correct mark. However, since I have always considered staysails to be smaller sails, spread by booms that clamp onto stays that carry the hoisted sails, I'll stick with *spinnakers.*

Setting these running sails is just a matter of hanking the sails to the stays, shackling the clews to the ends of the booms, and hoisting away. The leech of these twins will be reinforced strongly with tape to obviate the necessity of topping lifts. We'll have an adjustable line inside the tabling from the clew to the tack of each sail. These will be installed to control any flap or chatter induced in the sails by the guys, which run from the boom ends down to the afterdeck and which could cause slackness in the foot of each twin.

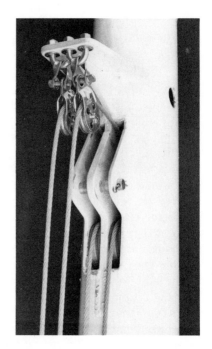

Suitable for larger fractional rigs, this four-sheave hounds fitting has two spinnaker and two headsail halyards. Note sturdy lugs and pin to take headstay(s). (Courtesy Yachtspars)

With the mast height of a 45-foot gaff cutter giving us, in our hypothetical case, an I measurement of 42 feet, a 35-foot luff for the twins can be accommodated easily. This will give us a total sail area of 525 square feet, compared with the 440 square feet provided by the squaresail. If our cruising boat is marconi-rigged (which rig, because of its widespread shrouds obstructing the bracing of the yard, lends itself less to the carrying of a squaresail than does a gaff rig), a hoist of 45 feet should be attained easily for the twins. This gives a sail area of 675 square feet — which is more like it!

The deck eyebolts to which the stays are secured are spaced apart so that the twins are hoisted each side of the staysail or inner forestay and therefore cannot chafe against it. To reef, the halyards are slacked or one twin is lowered and stowed.

What all this means is that a downwind, chafe-free rig is available immediately, without sacrificing the vessel's ability when close-hauled by the weight and windage of a permanent yard aloft. It is true that twin booms stowed up and down the mast or against the shrouds can cause a certain amount of windage. But the windage of stowed twin booms can in no way compare to that which is offered by a permanent yard — no matter how much the yard is braced around in an attempt to nullify this.

We now arrive at a highly debatable point. Is it really worth carrying sails designed specifically to enable a cruising vessel to run before the wind? Are they just another gimmick? Weigh carefully the points already discussed, and try not to be influenced by romantic-looking pictures. Then make your decision.

SELF-STEERING RIGS

One prime reason for the development of a rig designed solely for running before the wind has practically disappeared from the cruising scene. While freedom from chafe and the ability to impart lift, rather than push, are admirable features associated with such running sails, the rig resulted mainly from yachtsmen's experiments with ways to make a cruising boat steer herself. Captain Otway Waller, a pioneer in the evolution of self-steering, startled the ocean-cruising world in 1930 with a setup that enabled his little *Imogen* to sail successfully before the wind with nobody at the helm. This started a flurry of home-grown self-steering rigs, all designed for use when the vessel was running free. (Everybody wanted to be in the sack instead of at the tiller.)

Captain Waller fitted twin booms into goosenecks on the mast of *Imogen*. On the outboard end of each boom, he installed both a topping lift and a roller-furled sail. The sails were tacked down at the foot of the mast. The booms were eased 10 degrees or so forward of a right angle to the ship's centerline. A guy ran from the end of each boom to a quarter block, and back to the tiller. Foreguys were led from the ends of the booms to blocks on the end of the bowsprit and back inboard. Normally, these guys were left slack, their job being to control the boom while sail was set or to hold the spars if the sails were taken aback. Captain Waller's rig proved to be a success; any attempt by *Imogen* to yaw off her course downwind brought increased strain on the sail coming round to windward. The wind, pushing sail and boom forward, caused the guy to pull the tiller to windward and put the ship back on course.

The Frenchman Marin-Marie, who describes his running rig in his book *Wind Aloft, Wind Alow,* and who crossed the Atlantic singlehanded in his double-ended gaff cutter *Winnibelle,* in the 1930s, used a somewhat different system for self-steering. He set up twin staysail stays to the stemhead and clamped a double gooseneck fitting to these, a few feet up from the deck. Twin booms went from this fitting to the clews of staysails, which hoisted on the stays. Foreguys were used to the end of the bowsprit in the same manner as in the Waller rig, but it was found that the guys leading aft to the tiller had to be taken through a single block on each side, shackled to eyebolts up near the shrouds. This lead caused much additional friction, but it was found to be necessary to prevent the boom ends from lifting. (In his book, Marin-Marie gives a graphic account of how, besmeared with tallow, he accomplished all this.)

In Auckland, New Zealand, in the early 1950s, I copied *Winnibelle*'s self-steering running rig as faithfully as I could. I had a trip all planned in my yawl, and I hoped to blow along in the Roaring Forties under my twins for about 1,500 miles, and then head on up to Tahiti, carrying fore-and-aft sail. I started installing my running self-steering rig by going aloft in a chair and splicing another staysail stay around the mainmast of my yawl. Then I set the stay up to the stemhead, just like the Frenchman did in his book. Instead of a metal gooseneck clamp-fitting such as Marin-Marie used, I fashioned one out of a chunk of Australian hardwood. I installed a couple of spare eyebolts in it to take the goosenecks on the two 12-foot booms. Four ½-inch-diameter galvanized bolts clamped the staysail stays between my chunk of hardwood and a one-inch-thick, 6-inch-by-6-inch piece of plywood. Running home from the Great Barrier Island in a fresh northeaster one day, I tried out the rig.

The twin booms and their leads took a bit of fiddling around with, but the rig was successful. Instead of all-rope guys, liberally smeared with tallow in the nip of the blocks (as per *Winnibelle*), I used flexible galvanized wire with rope tails that went through quarter blocks to the tiller. It took half a gale to get my little 10-tonner moving with this rig, but, at least when we left on the trip a couple of months later, I had the satisfaction of knowing that there was self-steering equipment aboard.

Did we use it? No, not even on one occasion! Down where the much-vaunted westerlies were supposed to blow around and around the world, we encountered northerly, northeasterly, easterly, southeasterly, and southerly winds — the last, right off the ice. A few months later, when we started to trickle back down through the islands in the trades, the winds didn't blow hard or consistently enough to warrant rigging the twins. The only time they were ever used was the day of their dress rehearsal, on the way home from the Great Barrier Island.

TWIN RUNNING SAILS

With the development of various types of wind vanes that steer a ship on any point of sailing, the original reason for the creation of twin running sails (to enable the vessel to self-steer) disappeared. And so, to a great extent, have the sails themselves. With the availability of low-drain automatic pilots, and solar cells, wind chargers, and propeller-driven generators (the propeller is towed astern on a line) to keep the batteries topped up, the day might not be too far distant when even a wind vane is regarded as something of a novelty. So . . . is there any percentage in rigging twin running sails?

It depends on where you plan to go and the length of time you intend to be away. If tradewind passages are planned, which will (assuming the wind gods play ball)

Solar panels supply power to run automatic pilot — one of the original reasons for twin "spinnakers" gone by the board. (Ralph Naranjo photo)

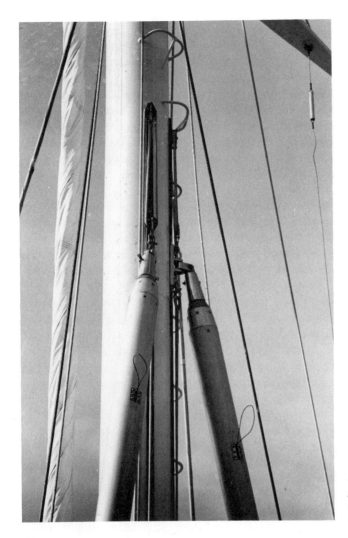

Running poles in stowed position. Note radio antenna on port spreader. (Courtesy Yachtspars)

keep the vessel running before the wind for weeks on end, then, yes, there's probably some justification in going to the expense and trouble of twins and all their gear. But for the cruiser who's on a one-shot deal, it just isn't worth it. It's far easier and simpler to sew chafe patches on each side of your mainsail (as discussed in Chapter Six) and balance this with a boomed-out genoa, or jib, on the other side.

Or do as I ended up doing in my yawl during various Pacific trips. When on a run in the trades with the wind well astern, we would rig a spinnaker boom complete with foreguy, after guy, and topping lift, on the weather side. The genoa would be hoisted, and the sheet led through the piston clip on the end of the boom and to the cockpit. If it looked as though we needed more sail and the weather was stable, we would furl the mainsail and guy the main boom out wide with mainsheet, foreguy, and topping lift. Our 600-square-foot spinnaker would be tacked to the end of the bowsprit, and the sheet would be led through a block on the end of the boom to a deck block and a cockpit winch. The next move would be to hoist away on the spinnaker halyard and trim the sheet. After this treatment, with 980 square feet of sail all forward of the mast (and all chafe-free), my little vessel would pick up her skirts and bustle along in fine style.

A safer and more controllable sail than a spinnaker — especially set in this manner — would have been more desirable. That was all I had, so that's what I used. Another genoa and a twin forestay for it to hank on would have been ideal (and we would have missed the odd moments of excitement that occurred when a change of wind told us that the 'chute had no right being up there). Although we did use this rig whenever conditions warranted it, I didn't feel it was used often enough to justify carrying permanent booms and the sails to go with them.

Again, it comes down to the crew and your energy level. It must be said that twin spinnakers, once they're up on deck and hanked on to their stays, are a piece of cake to set and to furl.

It is possible, of course, to carry a spinnaker in the usual manner aboard an ocean cruiser, and no sail pulls a vessel along more beautifully than this one. Expertise, agility, and strength come into it. I know that participants in long, singlehanded races fly spinnakers, and some of them make marvelous runs with these sails. A race is a race, though, and a singlehander in such a contest is conditioned specifically for it. Such conditioning doesn't necessarily apply aboard an ocean cruiser. There are people out on the briny, waddling along in their little floating homes, who've never hoisted a spinnaker in their lives.

The skipper of a cruising sailboat contemplating using a spinnaker in the usual way will find that it really helps to have some serious practice in light airs before leaving on a cruise. He or she might, perhaps, be interested in the following procedure. Stop the spinnaker every couple of feet with rubber bands that will break as the sail fills. (To help make this operation easy, the spinnaker can be pulled through a plastic bucket with the bottom cut out. Then a sufficient number of rubber bands can be stretched around the bucket. The bands are slipped off the bucket to snap around the 'chute as it's pulled through. Keep both luffs of the spinnaker together to avoid inducing a twist in the sail during this procedure.)

Assume we are sailing under mainsail, jib, and staysail, or mainsail and genoa. There are two of us aboard, and the ship is being steered by automatic pilot. The steps for setting the spinnaker would be as follows:

1. Put the ship on a broad reach and be certain she's holding the course.

2. Hook the spinnaker pole into its fitting on the mast, *piston up,* and secure foreguy and after guy to the forward end of the pole. Snap the topping lift to its bridle or to the end of the pole, positioned on deck near the headstay.

3. Carry the already-stopped spinnaker forward in its bag or turtle on the lee side of the headstay; if necessary, lash it in position.

4. Bring the spinnaker tack around the headstay from leeward and snap it to the pole. Clip the halyard to the spinnaker head and make the sheet fast to the clew with a bowline.

5. Make the sheet fast aft. (This is a just-in-case measure.)

6. Heave away on the topping lift until the pole is level with the mast fitting, ideally about head height. The spinnaker pole is still fore and aft, and the sail, still mostly in its bag, is to leeward of the jib.

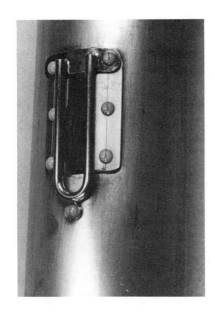

Spinnaker topping lift entry box with stainless steel halyard guard. This guard is insulated from the alloy box with polysulfide or neoprene, which is also used between the box flanges and the mast. Silicone on the threads of the roundhead machine screws ensures easy withdrawal of the fitting for inspection. (Courtesy Yachtspars)

7. Make the foreguy fast with enough slack to allow the boom to be squared off.

8. While one person takes the weight with the after guy with several turns around a winch drum, the other hoists the stopped sail.

9. The halyard man comes aft and puts the vessel on its downwind course.

10. While one person heaves away on the after guy, pulling the spinnaker boom square-off and the sail around the forestay, the other takes in the sheet, which causes the stops to break and the sail to fill. (Headsails, still hoisted, have assisted by blanketing the sail and preventing it from filling prematurely.)

Once trimmed, the spinnaker pole should be at right angles to the wind; if you want to be all gung-ho about it, tie a wool streamer to the pole to give an indication of the apparent wind direction. The pole should be horizontal to the mast and the spinnaker clew and tack should be level with one another and parallel to the water. With the ship dead on course, tension the sheet by easing away until about six inches of curl appears in the spinnaker luff. (This varies with the size of the sea running and the maximum angle the boat tends to yaw off course.) When running dead before it, the spinnaker need not be hoisted two-blocks. If the spinnaker head looks too close to the masthead, ease the halyard a couple of feet.

The attachment on a cruising boat's mast to which the spinnaker pole-end fitting snaps need not have up-and-down adjustment. A strong U of ⅜-inch-diameter stainless rod, welded to a plate of the same material and secured to the mast about six feet above the deck, is sufficient. It is important for a pole-end fitting to fit sloppily enough on the mast attachment for the pole itself to twist a little (such as when the sail fills and eases) without straining either fitting.

Arrival at a destination, a change of wind direction, a change of course, and an increase in wind strength are all likely to influence a decision to take down the spinnaker. When carrying a spinnaker, a cruising yachtsman aboard a shorthanded vessel must keep in mind an increase in wind. Since such an event is inevitable at some point, it is best to know how to get the sail off with a minimum of fuss.

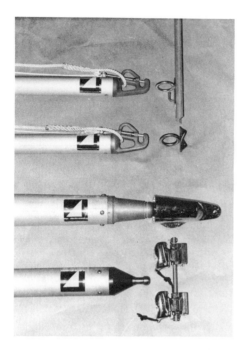

Left: *Mast fittings to suit various types of spinnaker pole ends.* **Above:** *Spinnaker pole fitting at left is designed for a male track. Lugs at each end of fitting are for uphaul and downhaul. Center fitting is for male track and is positioned by plunger. Right fitting uses female track and is positioned by threaded rod. (Courtesy Yachtspars)*

If your boat has a small mainsail that will not provide much of a lee to blanket the spinnaker as it is lowered, run up your jib and staysail, or genoa, and head up slightly to enable these sails to draw. While one person starts over-trimming the sheet as the spinnaker luffs, the other pulls the line to the piston clip on the end of the pole, releasing the spinnaker tack. (It may be necessary to ease the halyard a little to accomplish this.) He or she then lowers away on the halyard, and the spinnaker, blanketed behind the headsail, is gathered in by the person on the lee deck.

If the mainsail is large enough (or the spinnaker small enough) for this maneuver to be accomplished with the vessel still on her downwind course, there is no need to hoist the headsails until the spinnaker is down and stowed. In this case, the after guy is eased until the pole is against (or close to) the forestay, the tack is released from the end of the boom, and the sail is gathered in on the lee side of the mainsail as it comes down.

Some yachtsmen might not like the fact that we have used an after guy to the pole-end, and utilized the piston clip to both hold and release the spinnaker tack. Another way of doing the job is to run the after guy through the pole-end fitting and make the guy fast to the spinnaker tack. In this case, the spinnaker in its bag need not be taken any farther forward than the lee shrouds; all hoisting can be done from there.

I have described a system that calls for the tack and the after guy to be secured separately to the end of the pole in order to escape the constant chafe that an after guy is subject to when led through a piston-type end-fitting to the spinnaker tack. We happen to be ocean cruising, not racing from buoy to buoy; that spinnaker might be up there for days. If the after guy runs through a block on the end of the pole on its way to the spinnaker tack, then this is an altogether different kettle of

Spinnaker pole held in deck cradle by loop of shock cord. (Courtesy Yachtspars)

fish. As long as chafe is kept to an absolute minimum, this practice can be very efficient and enable a spinnaker to be set or downed with little fuss.

It is not unusual for two spinnaker halyards to be used on a long downhill run. The extra halyard is simply there as a back-up in case the halyard taking the weight carries away. While a spinnaker halyard seldom gives trouble, this scheme has a lot to recommend it aboard an ocean cruiser. Anything that can contribute to the safety of a sail-carrying exercise is worthwhile.

There are, of course, many variations to spinnaker drill, and here it is up to the cruising people to develop a system that works aboard their own particular vessel and doesn't overtax their physical capabilities. It will usually be found that the reason for the successful carrying of a spinnaker aboard, say, a two-handed ocean cruiser is the result of practice beforehand in calm water and light winds — practice that leaves each person knowing exactly what his or her job is when either setting or handing the sail.

Aboard the *White Squall II,* Minine and I used twin genoas as a method of running before it. For two people handling a 70-footer, it worked well enough. When we hauled the ship for a haircut-and-shave in Cartagena, Colombia, we had two 25-foot booms built, complete with fittings. To enable the poles to stow up and down the foreside of the foremast, I removed two belaying pins from the main staysail gooseneck and dropped the pins of the pole gooseneck fittings down these holes. Two nuts, threaded on the pins from underneath, completed this part of the job. A two-part mast band was bolted firmly around the mast a foot above where the pole-ends were hove up to their stowed position. Two single blocks with topping lifts were hung from this band, and the lifts were shackled permanently to the ends of the poles. Also rigged on the pole-ends were outhauls and fore-and-aft guys. These poles lived on the foremast for eight years.

To use this rig, we would lower the poles until the outboard ends were a desired height (about 10 feet) above the water. The fore-and-aft guys were then set up to hold the spars rigid. The clew of our largest roller-furling jib was hove out to the end of one pole, and the clew of the spare genoa, which was hanked onto the forestay, was set up to the end of the other spar. This wasn't as efficient as twins set on stays secured to the deck a few feet forward of the mast, because as the wind moved to one quarter or the other and the poles were braced to cater to this, the leech of the windward genoa would sometimes collapse. For two people running a fairly large vessel, though, the "twins" were easy to rig and to stow, and we'd run thousands of miles at a time in the trades with them pulling like a team of oxen.

At such a time, we would spread the big awning above the furled mainsail and let "Iron Michael" (our Wood Freeman automatic pilot) steer the course to within an nth of a degree — while we lay sleeping or reading atop the deckhouse. A really tough life! At times we would hoist the main staysail and haul it hard amidships to try to dampen down the roll. (Something that seems to go hand in hand with twin running sails is the encouragement they give a vessel to roll. You roll like you've never rolled before.) The compensation, of course, is lack of chafe, and although the combined area of the schooner's twin genoas was only 1,300 square feet, the rig was totally chafe-free, and that fact alone put any small measure of discomfort in its proper perspective.

ALTERNATE RUNNING RIGS

Rigs for running that have been adopted by cruising couples, or a couple with children, are many and varied. With wind vanes or automatic pilots now doing the steering, and twin running sails no longer needed for this job, it is quite usual for a cruising boat to run with the mainsail one side and a poled-out headsail the other. To be available for use on either side of the bow, and at the same time facilitate handling, a single pole is sometimes stowed up and down the mast. To use a single pole with a headsail when running before it, the pole is lowered and the headsail sheet rove through the end fitting on the pole. Held at a suitable height by its lift, the pole is swung out and positioned by a foreguy and an "after guy." The headsail sheet leads from the end of the pole, to a deck block, and to a winch.

A separate and permanent sheet for the headsail is sometimes rove through the boom-end fitting, or through a block shackled to the end. This is not a bad idea, because if a wind or course change makes it necessary to jibe, the lee headsail sheet is available immediately to trim the sail as soon as the permanent sheet to the end of the boom is eased.

An even simpler method than the permanent "mast-hung" pole for pushing out the clew of a headsail when running before the wind is the one used aboard Ralph and Lenore Naranjo's *Wind Shadow*. When running before it in light airs, Ralph hoists a drifter/reacher on the headstay and the working staysail on the inner forestay. A fairly short pole (in length about two-thirds the distance from mast to headstay) is clipped onto the mast fitting; its outboard end accommodates the sheets of both headsails. The staysail sheet runs through the fitting on the end of the pole, and the sheet from the drifter/reacher runs through a block also at the end of the

Opposite top: *Jockey pole being used to spread the angle between after guy and spinnaker pole end as the spinnaker pole is eased forward. It's about now that the cruising nut would be switching to genoa . . . . (Courtesy Yachtspars)* **Opposite bottom:** Wind Shadow*'s simple, no-chafe downhill rig. (Ralph Naranjo photo)*

The line leading through the small block on the underside of this boom end is the sheet for a "blooper" or "gennaker" — or whatever other exotic "extra" takes the skipper's fancy. (Courtesy Yachtspars)

pole. A foreguy is used to prevent the pole from swinging back and chafing the forward lower shroud, but no topping lift is needed. (If your pole is equipped with a bridle to take a lift, by all means use it if you feel inclined.)

This has proved to be an ideal rig when running before it, and it is carried until, as Ralph puts it, "the first whitecaps appear." To reduce sail, his seven-year-old son walks forward and stands within the ship's inner pulpit. Here, he gathers in the drifter/reacher as his nine-year-old sister eases the sheet from the cockpit, and Ralph lowers away. The boat then proceeds on her way, running under full main and poled-out staysail, steered all the while by her Aries wind vane. The staysail can still be left poled-out even after a couple of reefs have been tucked in the main. If a further deterioration of weather calls for the staysail to come down, this is catered to by easing the staysail sheet and halyard, whereupon both pole end and sail lower obediently to the foredeck.

Always be prepared to experiment to see which running sails best suit both you and your boat. The "flashers" and "gennakers" being touted as poleless running sails for cruising boats might be just the thing on a long trip. Remember: Give a sail a good try before you either approve or condemn it. A sail that's perfect for one boat might not suit another at all.

We sometimes see some wonderful sail innovations along the cruising beat. I remember a bloke who arrived in Honolulu with what was a brand-new rig to my eyes. Dick's gaff ketch was about 40 feet on deck and had a none-too-long yard on her mainmast. To add to the sail area when running, a staysail was hanked to a cap shroud on either side of the vessel and hoisted away. The next gimmick would have turned Rube Goldberg, and even Heath Robinson, pea green with envy. The handles of two dinghy oars were poked through the staysail clews and the blade of each oar, which had a U cut in the center of the tip, was fitted over an after shroud on either side of the ship. Each oar was held to a shroud by a lashing whose claim to distinction was a fuzzy whipping at both ends. An after guy led from the end of each oar to the cockpit.

We're not finished yet! When the blade of one of the oars started to split from the pressure of the base of the U against a shroud, Dick ferreted around in his tool locker and came up with a couple of six-inch C-clamps, which he utilized across the base of each oar blade to keep the grain together. When I met him, he'd just run a large part of the way from the mainland to Hawaii with these "shroudsails" and the small squaresail, and we hashed the whole thing over during a get-acquainted session in the Ala Wai yacht harbor. Dick, who had his wife and three kids along, told me he couldn't see any reason to change a thing. He was, after all, only on a sail around the world.

ten

Awnings

It is of small moment whether the hemisphere a sailor inhabits compels him to sail north or south to enjoy the world's warmer regions. Once he's arrived, the tropic sun will serve him up medium rare, done to a turn, or fried to a crisp — unless he has an awning.

A voyage to an area where there is warm water and *hot sun* is usually worth all the planning, the scheming, and the hard work. There are those of us who get so bitten by the warm-weather-cruising bug, and the thought of escaping from leaden skies and the patter of hail, that we sail again and again to the tropics and live and cruise aboard our boats in the sun for weeks, months, or even years. Some of us, minds reeling at the prospect of living continuously in an area of sun, blue sea, and tradewinds, finally say the hell with it — and organize our lives so that we become permanent inhabitants of the tropics. But none of us can do it without shade.

A sailor is not long in the tropics before he discovers that a good, well-designed awning makes all the difference to the pleasure of living aboard. Even a vessel with a profusion of ventilators can be hot below decks if no awning is spread topside. Awnings for ocean-cruising sailboats can be divided into two categories: those designed to shelter the crew from wind, sun, and spray while sailing, and those more suitable for use when the vessel is at anchor. The latter awnings are generally larger and cover more of the ship than is practical for a sailing awning. A large, well-thought-out awning makes a pleasant living area out of space that is not otherwise habitable when the ship is anchored.

An awning spread over a sailboat's deck induces a cool flow of air to be felt throughout the entire ship. Another bonus is that during a tropical shower, hatches and skylights, which might otherwise have to be closed, can be left open. There are other benefits, too. Until you've had a siesta on deck under your awning — maybe after a couple of cold ones before lunch — you haven't lived. Without that awning, you'd probably be sweltering below, waiting for the sun to go down.

Every little bit of shade helps . . . . (Ralph Naranjo photo)

Sometimes the extension of a cockpit dodger — such as a piece of material clipped to the dodger-top and positioned over the cockpit by lashings to mizzen shrouds or a spreader on a backstay — can be used as a sailing awning in good weather. In many cases, and especially if the dodger-front can be unzipped to allow a flow of air through, such a rig will suffice as an at-anchor awning as well. If the boat's cabintop and decks are insulated, she will probably be cool enough below with such an awning.

We kid ourselves if we believe that a small shelter over the cockpit area is all that's needed, and we sit huddled beneath it, because it represents the only place topside where there's any shade. The rest of the on-deck area is unusable for lounging, swinging a hammock, or even working comfortably at some project. Believe me, it's a whole lot more pleasant to dissect an outboard motor under the shade of an awning, or splice a few lines or put a stitch in a jib, than to do those same jobs in the sun.

The person who's planning to sail to the tropics and become as brown as a nut from all that sunshine should not feel that he or she is about to be shortchanged. The best tans are the ones that just happen along — the tan you get without trying will last a lot longer than the one acquired from lying in the sun smothered in goop. And while fairly launched on the subject of tans, I might comment that in all my years of warm-weather sailing and living aboard, I've never seen any of the dyed-in-the-wool tropic buffs (like me) sunbathing. What with dinghy trips, swimming, diving, fishing, sailing — you end up as tanned as an iguana anyhow. After having been on such an expedition, it's nice to know that you've got a good sun shelter to scamper back to. It's great, after a shelling venture, to clamber back aboard your 33-footer, grab a cold one out of your kerosene refrigerator, and sit like a swell under your awning. Try it sometime.

In addition to almost doubling the living area aboard, a good-sized awning provides a means of catching rainwater. Always have this in mind when planning your awning, for it is frequently impossible to fill water tanks in some of the paradises we anchor at when away on a cruise. Sometimes we can take containers ashore and fill them with water from a stream. They used to do all that romantic stuff in days of yore. You lug the water back aboard and empty it into the ship's tanks. Yo-ho-ho and all that. Ever had a go at this? No? Then keep it that way.

Sometimes, when consulting the Pilot for a worthwhile anchorage, we discover such information as, "at the N.E. head of the bay, good water may be found." Now, even though the novelty of watering ship from a stream that may have supplied Dampier or Captain Cook might appeal, take my tip and don't give way to temptation. Water *weighs.* A couple of such excursions with water casks (or plastic jugs) to a pretty, trickling stream, where mosquitoes the size of aircraft are waiting to gorge themselves on something new and tasty, can put a dent in the fervor of the most incurable romantic. Be a sport and carry a good, rain-catching awning, instead; it's surprising how much water can be garnered from a heavy tropic shower.

A cruising boat's awning should be strong, with strengthening patches at the load points to take both the strain of a squall while at anchor and the wear and tear occasioned by its use as a means of catching water. It is a mistake to construct an awning from lightweight material. A too-light awning will flap and chatter and bulge like a sail as soon as there is any wind. I made the mistake of designing such an awning for my yawl. I was going to be really clever about it and have an awning some 18 feet long and 11 feet wide — but built of lightweight material that would enable me to stow the cover in a tiny sailbag. It was stowable, all right, and the strainer patches sewn in at the corners and other load points permitted the awning to stay up when a stiff squall came riffling across the anchorage.

The racket it made was something again, though. Being lightweight Dacron, the awning crackled, popped, banged, and carried on in even 10 knots of wind. Another mistake I made was to use white Terylene (Dacron). The sun glared right on through, and it was even possible to be sunburned while sitting under it. Also, it leaked. The sun rotted it out in 15 months, however, and I wasn't sorry to see it go.

A dark-colored awning is very pleasant to sit under on a bright, tropic day. It's restful on the eyes, too. Grey-green Vivatex and blue Acrilan are ideal materials for awnings (and sail covers). They are also waterproof, another point in their favor.

Aboard the *White Squall II,* we made our own awnings, and this is something the neophyte cruising buff might well consider. There are not many cruising people who are capable of making their own sails, but one and all, if they so desire, can have a fling at constructing an awning for their vessel. If the awning you make is a bit baggy here and there, so what? It's good practice, and you can recut it and fuss around and eventually come up with an original, custom-built job. Don't be embarrassed about the trial-and-error part; very few sailmakers can construct an awning that fits perfectly the first time around.

The first awning I made for the schooner would have inspired a sailmaker to throw up his hands in despair. It was built of heavy, white, untreated canvas, which I picked up in Oranjestad, Aruba. It lasted exactly a year before, as rotten as a pear, it blew to pieces one night in a rainsquall. By then, I had a bit of an idea of what I'd done wrong. I hadn't bothered to install strainer patches; I'd run the seams fore-and-aft instead of athwartships; I hadn't beefed up the hoisting points; I'd made it a little too wide and too long; I hadn't bothered about side flaps.

The next awning we built aboard was of grey-green Vivatex. It was 28 feet long and 14 feet wide, which — in the manner of a nicely setting gaff topsail — was a little smaller than the space it was expected to fill. I made a drawing of it with a scale of an inch to a foot on the back of an old chart, and I cut patterns for strainer patches out of brown paper. As with the first awning, this one was sewn together aboard the ship with our little portable Singer sewing machine. We gave it 12-inch flaps as side curtains, and sewed a four-inch-wide reinforcing strip fore-and-aft along the center.

I then settled down with palm and needle and waxed thread, to hand-sew ½-inch Dacron rope along each side, across the front, and along the ridge. Four lighter lines for use as hoisting points were spliced into the ridge-rope before it was sewn on. These light (¼-inch) lines were at "guessed at" points and led to a common shackle that snapped onto the main halyard terminal fitting. When the fore-and-aft lines were snapped to rings on a forward mainmast shroud each side, then set up taut to the ends of a spreader on the topping lift, and hitched to the running backstays, the main halyard was tensioned to raise the center. This set up the awning tight and gave us plenty of headroom. The *White Squall II*'s awning — machine-sewing, hand-sewing, the lot — took 40 hours of work. That ½-inch roping took the strain away from the material when the wind piped up; it helped the awning lie quietly, too. I remember a time when we were anchored behind Nananu-i-Thake Island in the Fijis, with our anemometer reading 52 m.p.h. — and the awning still up there. I doubt this would have been possible were the awning not roped.

If you're getting a sailmaker to build an awning for you, have a definite idea of what you want before he comes aboard to measure. And don't make your awning too complicated; if it means you have to run half a hundred lines here, there, and everywhere, it'll take too long to put up and you'll be loath to use it for just that reason. There seem to be as many ways of making awnings as there are ways of making sails. The aim of the cruising sailor should be to find an awning of as simple a design as possible, but one that also caters to both him and his ship.

Some awnings are constructed with one or more battens to keep the cover stretched and well spread toward the sides of the ship. Another type of awning has no battens and is stretched between masts, shrouds, backstays, a spreader hung from a backstay, and anything else that's handy to hitch onto. And, as has been mentioned, an awning constructed from a piece of material clipped to a dodger-top and spread over the cockpit is not uncommon.

I've tried all three types. Aboard my yawl, I sewed a green, waterproof, canvas dodger together with palm, needle, and sail twine. It took a bit of trial and error, but in the end the dodger "fit like it was borned there." The canvas of the dodger was spread over laminated wooden hoops, which were pinned each side of the cockpit and enabled the cover to fold forward like the hood of a baby's carriage. The piece of canvas for a temporary awning, which I would clip to the after hoop of the dodger and position over the cockpit by lashing to the mizzen shrouds, gave fair shelter from the sun when at anchor, but for a stopover for any period longer than two days, I would rig the big awning.

This awning covered the boat from main to mizzenmast and had four athwartships battens. Each batten was 11 feet long and was constructed of two pieces of one-inch dowel (broomstick) each 5½ feet long and joined by a one-foot piece of stainless steel pipe. One batten fitted into a pocket across the front of the awning and another across the aft end. The other two battens were positioned at equal distances between these two. Fore-and-aft tension was achieved with a lashing from the forward end around the mainmast, and another at the aft end around the mizzen. The main halyard clipped onto a bridle coming from two lifting points along the center. Light lines were tied to the lifelines from the ends of the battens.

I found this awning to be too much trouble to rig. If we were only sailing from bay to bay, I would leave the battens in their pockets and carry the whole thing in a roll on the side deck. This wasn't too bad, as the awning thus packaged took only about 20 minutes to rig, once we were anchored. A passage of any length, however, would call for the battens to be removed from the awning, pulled apart (from the pieces of stainless steel pipe), and lashed up under the deck in the forepeak. Then the awning would be folded and stowed. When the awning was next rigged, it would take an hour, which is too long.

When I first designed this awning, I came up with the bright idea of extending the battens (and the awning) six inches or so on each side of the ship, to enable rain to run off without hitting the vessel (what an optimist!) and to give us more shade. This worked against me on several counts. The apparatus was wider than the boat, so I couldn't raft up with another vessel without the battens getting hooked in her rigging. Tying up to a dock with high fender pilings was a big deal, too. On one occasion when I was alongside in Aruba to take on fuel, a batten got around the side of a piling and tore the awning (beating of gums and complaints to the Almighty). But the worst of all occurred in Cristobal, in the Canal Zone.

We were tied up at the yacht club and I was doing a job on the port shoulder of a friend's boat. (His vessel had attacked the wall of one of the locks on its way through the Canal and had come off second best in the fight. His bow had taken on a strange shape.) It started to rain like it had never rained before, and the water running off my awning fell, as planned, in a direct drop to the sea. All this would have been fine and given me great reason to strut, except that the rainwater cascaded off the awning and onto the oil that floats about a half-inch thick on the water of this port. The oil splashed up over my topsides and made a hell of a mess. It was a full day's work to clean up, and the oil ate into the paint, too.

If you're still all fired up to have a battened awning, no matter what, Forespar (2672 Dow Avenue, Tustin, California 92680) will supply you with telescoping aluminum awning poles.

The *White Squall II*'s battenless awning was twice the size of the one I had aboard my yawl, and it took two of us only 10 minutes' easy work to get it up and fully rigged. We perfected this system during our chartering years when the awning was sometimes up and down twice a day. We made a half-dozen of these over the years and ended up settling for 12-inch side flaps. These flaps, which ran the full length of the awning each side below the roping, made all the difference in keeping down glare. Since we slept on deck, year in and year out, we had to have some way of preventing rain from driving under the awning from forward when we were anchored. We achieved this by unclipping the forward sides of the awning from the shrouds, bringing them amidships under the main boom, and hooking the clips into two brass eyes a few inches above deck level on the front of a skylight. Two 10-gallon plastic containers were usually stationed halfway under the front of the awning to catch the runoff from any rainsquall.

When we were in a bay for any length of time, we would also rig an awning between foremast and mainmast. We sewed a canvas funnel in the center of each side of this awning; a male hose fitting was seized in the bottom of both funnels. Regular female hose fittings screwed to these, and the hoses were led to a deck filler. It is possible to use Delrin through-hull fittings instead of canvas funnels; they're a whole lot easier and quicker to install. However, before settling on either funnels or through-hulls, look for the lowest, or most likely places to install the drains once the awning is rigged. Mark the spots, take down the awning, install whatever fittings you've decided on — and you're in business.

Use hoses of a generous inside diameter between your awning drains and deck filler; ⅝ inch or even larger is recommended for two reasons. First, a hose with a small (less than half-inch) inside diameter tends to become airlocked, especially if the run from drain to filler is of any length. Second, when you are trying to catch as much water as possible in a really heavy downpour and you ease the halyard and allow the center of the awning to droop, a great pool may collect. Large-diameter hoses will whisk away this water almost as fast as it falls. Hoses of small diameter take their time about it, and meanwhile, the canvas must hold the weight of the water.

Rain, more often than not, is accompanied by wind, which loves to shake the daylights out of an awning. In some cases this can make it difficult to collect water, because the wind gets under the awning and lifts it. Any water that's been collecting is thrown in the air and gets taken along with the breeze. In an effort to prevent this, we would make a line fast around each hose fitting at the bottom of the funnels and set them up under strain to a couple of handy eyebolts in the deck. This worked well and always held down the awning when it was both raining and blowing. We sewed a strong reinforcing patch around the opening to each funnel to distribute the strain resulting from this practice. Whenever it looked like rain, we would lower the sides

This nonbattened awning can be rigged in less than 10 minutes. Awning is spread by hitching or lashing to shrouds or running backstays and a spreader temporarily hung off the permanent backstay. The five light lines along the center of the awning go to a common snapshackle, which engages the terminal of the main halyard. Slight tension on the halyard tightens the awning. Lanyards from side flaps are made fast to lifelines. Note radial davits forward of main rigging. (Peter Otway photo)

at the forward end of the schooner's main awning in the manner described, so there was no chance that the water would blow away. The rain would hit the awning and run merrily down into our 10-gallon containers. Whenever it rained, we would channel as much as possible into our tanks, and sometimes months (on one occasion, 13 months) passed before we watered up at a dock.

The rig of a vessel and her beam (or lack of it) dictate the size and shape of her awnings. A ketch with a cockpit aft, for instance, often has a Bimini-type awning over the cockpit for tropical sailing, and a larger one between the masts when anchored for any period longer than a few days. A yawl is better than a ketch for this purpose, because, boat for boat, the distance between masts is greater and the awning covers the cockpit. A dodger-type sailing awning, if one is carried, can then be folded forward out of the way, and the crew of a yawl can experience the pleasure that goes with a long, large cover that reaches from mast to mast.

The same can be said of a sloop or a cutter. Although neither of these vessels has convenient mizzen shrouds to which to tie the after, outer corners of an awning, a spreader can be hung easily from the permanent backstay and used for the same purpose. The spreader (a common way of rigging it is to clip it to a ring seized to the backstay) is usually the same length as the beam of the vessel over which it is used. It is held horizontally by tie-downs at each end. The sides and center of the awning are set up by lines that go to the middle and both ends of the spreader.

A schooner rig lends itself to the spreading of a large awning aft of the mainmast. The after end of this awning can be stretched to the center and ends of a spreader as in the case of a sloop or cutter. Our main awning aboard the *White Squall II* was rigged in this manner, and during our 14 years of tropical chartering and cruising in this vessel, more time was spent on deck under the awning when at anchor than was spent below.

Gaff-rigged vessels add their own special problems. For an awning to be rigged above a furled gaff sail, something has to be done about the peak halyard, lazyjacks, and topping lifts. Sometimes, before spreading an awning aboard a gaff-rigger, the peak halyard blocks are unshackled from the gaff strops, and, with the halyard still rove, are carried forward to be lashed together at the mast. Here, it's a matter of preference. I'm a great believer in having the pins of peak halyard shackles both riveted and moused, so that in no way can they let go while that gaff is up. To take such shackles apart just to rig an awning is too big a deal. Some brave souls might be quite happy to unscrew the pins of their peak halyard shackles and take the whole lot forward before putting up their awning, but it wouldn't do for me.

I prefer to see a peak halyard of such length that it will allow enough slack to pull the bight of the halyard along the boom so that an awning may be spread. If the boom sits in a gallows frame, topping lifts and lazyjacks can be given the same treatment, being slacked and pulled along the boom. Aboard large gaff-riggers, an awning is sometimes spread beneath the boom. This way, halyard, lifts, and lazyjacks stay put. If the boom doesn't have a fixed gooseneck, it may be raised to give headroom under the awning.

Commercially built Bimini-type awnings are seen frequently aboard both center-cockpit and aft-cockpit sailboats. Some of these are first-class jobs with flaps each side that can be unzipped or spread over the decks between awning and rail. A removable front to allow a channel of air is common, too. A lot of these awnings are stretched over frames that allow them to fold forward, baby-carriage fashion, and this is a desirable feature. About the only thing the cruising sailor must watch here (apart from the ruggedness of the thing) is that the frames be truly nonmagnetic. The area that the awning shelters usually houses the ship's steering compass, so make sure the metal in the dodger frames doesn't have enough ferrous content to shake up your compass.

Whether an awning should be fitted with side flaps is a matter of some contention. Personally, I like flaps (or curtains, as they're sometimes called) along the sides of an awning. I've had awnings both with flaps and without, and I have discovered that their addition helps cut down glare and increases the shade. And even though a

Deck awning with side flaps on masthead cutter. Forward wind scoop looks capable of doing a fine job. (Ralph Naranjo photo)

vessel usually lies head-to-wind at anchor, it also plays a part in preventing rain from blowing under the sides.

Side flaps should not be too deep, however. If they are deep enough to interfere with visibility, the awning would have to be struck before motoring. A way around this, of course, is to have detachable side flaps. The 12-inch side flaps on the schooner's awning were the result of trial and error and didn't cut down visibility enough to make it difficult to handle with the awning still rigged.

While on the subject of awnings with detachable pieces, I might mention that if you really want to use the area beneath the awning as living space while at anchor in the tropics, you should consider having a front to the awning that either rolls up or clips on. As mentioned, we would lower the forward sides if a rainsquall came along, but this is not possible with some awnings, especially those with battens. If the awning has a front that can be rolled down quickly or clipped on, it can stop the rain from howling along underneath and driving everyone below.

With the tradewind blowing from an easterly direction, it is not uncommon for the stern of a boat in the tropics to be pointing at the source of all the warmth for an hour or so before the sun goes down. A trick to prevent the sun from inviting itself to your cocktail party is to carry a piece of densely meshed plastic screen and clip it across the back of the awning in the late afternoon. The ideal material is regular garden shade cloth with a triple-folded and sewn edge to take Push-Dot (or Velcro) canvas fasteners to clip to corresponding fasteners installed on the awning. This screen does a great job of filtering out sunlight and cutting down glare, and it makes it impossible for a blowtorch ray to interrupt the magic hour on deck. It's still possible to see what's going on through this type of screen, too. If a merry group on deck decides that a good sunset is in the offing, the screen can be taken down and all hands can get an eyeful of the event. They might, if they're lucky, even see something spectacular. If conditions are right, and they look carefully but not too often as the sun disappears, they might even see the green flash. Especially if they've had enough to drink.

eleven

Dinghies

I recently saw a "world cruiser" touted in an expensive advertisement in one of the world's foremost yachting magazines. The ad was in color, and it covered the first two pages of the magazine. Presented in this lavish splurge was a 60-foot ketch.

The guy responsible for the advertisement just can't have been out there. This boat's cabintop ran almost from one end of the ship to the other and was so studded with vangs, vents, winches, and bric-a-brac that there was no place to set down the subject of this chapter — a dinghy. (She also had a few other minor problems: few slipway operators in various parts of the world would care to deal with the nightmare of her little fin keel and spade rudder if asked to haul her for antifouling; she had no winch or windlass to handle ground tackle; and if the one stay forward of her mainmast carried away, she could well lose the mast — but we won't dwell here on these details.)

I couldn't even find a suitable spot for a liferaft on this ketch. There was a time when designers of cruising yachts showed, with a little dashed outline, the position on deck where a dinghy could be carried. And it's about time they did it again. There happen to be more boats engaged in cruising now than at any other time in history. To sell a man or woman a cruising boat that has no place on deck to carry a dinghy is shortchanging them, in my opinion. I hope that the serious cruising person won't be influenced by this type of advertising. Look before you leap; realize, if you're really going *cruising,* that you need a good dinghy and somewhere to stow it securely aboard.

CHOOSING A DINGHY

Rubber dinghies have a definite place in the long-range cruising scene, but not, I consider, as your number one shore boat. This observation might bring a little fire to the eye of a manufacturer of inflatables, and cause muttering in the ranks of those who own rubber dinghies, but that can't be helped. A rubber dink has several counts against it. For instance, it is expensive; it can be ripped and deflated; exposure to tropical sun can shorten its life greatly; and it can't be rowed in anything more than a slight harbor chop. This last is very important. I know that the present-day outboard motor is a reliable piece of equipment, but it can still break down. And when it does, mate, you pick up the oars and you row.

Minine and I were diving for shells one day outside the barrier reef at the entrance to Papetoai Bay, Moorea. When we clambered back into our 12-foot-8-inch fiberglass dink (which was anchored just inside the pass), I fired up the outboard motor, and as soon as I put the engine in gear, the propeller hit a coral head and sheared the pin — and I didn't have a spare. Careless? Sure. I've made some marvelous goofs in my time. I paid for this one, too; paid for it with a 2½-hour row against a stiff breeze to the head of the bay where our schooner was anchored. And I thanked my stars that our dinghy could be rowed. I have no confidence that I, or anyone else, could have rowed an inflatable against such a wind and slop as was in the bay that day.

Another thing. There are not too many of us who have been in the cruising game for a while who haven't now and again had to run out an anchor in a dinghy, or heave up an anchor with its rode and chain from a dinghy, or perhaps run a line ashore in a breeze of wind. These jobs can be accomplished in a rubber dinghy with a good outboard motor, but if there's a fresh breeze and any sort of chop, the work could be impossible under oars. If you really need to run out an anchor to kedge yourself off a sandbank and there's a bit of a chop — and you've got a rubber dinghy with an outboard that's temporarily *non compos mentis* — chances are you'll stay right there on the bank. A good rigid dinghy, however, can be handled easily under oars and can do such jobs in half a gale.

In a final attempt to drive the point home, I'll recount the time a big ketch from San Diego dragged anchor in Suva, Fiji. It was raining and blowing pretty hard at the time, but we could hear the couple aboard yelling above the noise of the wind. Minine and I got into our fiberglass dinghy and went over to find the vessel with her stern about 10 feet away from a coral reef known locally as the "dynamite patch." The ship's auxiliary engine was out of action, and their tender was an inflatable with no outboard. There is no way an anchor can be rowed to windward in a rubber dinghy in those conditions.

The guy managed to dump a 50-pound pick with a few fathoms of chain into our dinghy from the bow of the ketch. As our six-horsepower Johnson putted us off into the night (it was actually about two o'clock in the morning), he stood on his foredeck paying out nylon rode. We dropped the hook and went back to where the bloke was now winding away like a dervish on a hand windlass, while his girlfriend hauled at the line as it came off the surging drum. When he was about 30 feet clear and satisfied that this anchor was holding, he jumped down into our boat. We went hand-over-hand along his main rode and horsed up his anchor and chain. The anchor that had dragged was a Danforth that looked and felt to be of about 70 pounds. We took this lot way out to hell and gone and dropped it, after which we took him back to his vessel.

In the morning, apart from a few scratches here and there and a bucket or so of harbor mud from the Danforth's flukes, our dinghy had nothing to show for the experience. If we had had a rubber dinghy, though, I wouldn't have been too happy about having someone heave scratchy chain and a sharp-fluked anchor into it.

Carry a rubber dinghy that can be deflated and stowed in the lazarette, but have a rigid dinghy as well. This dinghy should be sturdy enough to carry ground tackle, fuel, stores, cases of booze, fish, shells, anything. And if you bump a rock or coral head, or run over a snag during one of your mini-cruises along a shoreline, out to a reef, or up a stream, the dink should be able to shrug it off as part of the game.

Carry as big a tender as your vessel's deck space permits. A 60-footer should have room on deck for a 12-foot dinghy. A 45-footer is poorly laid out on deck if there's not room for a 10-foot dinghy. My 33-footer carried a sturdy 8½-foot pram, which had oars, a sail, a centerboard, and a 2½-horsepower Seagull to send it along. Even though I wished the dinghy were bigger at times, this was an adequate setup for a small cruising boat. Aboard the *White Squall II,* we carried a 12-foot-8-inch fiberglass dinghy and a nine-footer built of the same material. Both saw hard use and both underwent surgery for the cuts and abrasions they picked up at various times.

In this day and age, there are not too many dinghies designed specifically as rowing boats. The evolution of good, dependable outboard motors has resulted in a crop of wide, flat-floored, bluff-bowed yacht tenders, which object strongly to being rowed. I consider the outboard motor to be one of the best things ever to arrive on the cruising scene, but I think it is unwise to become so enchanted by it that one purchases a dinghy that can't be propelled easily by oars. Make sure you have a dummy run (preferably in a bit of a chop) rowing any dinghy you're interested in purchasing as a tender for your cruising boat.

HOISTING A DINGHY ABOARD

It is quite usual for a cruising boat to tow her dinghy within the confines of a sheltered island group, or within a sound or harbor. For any open-sea passage, however — and this includes a cruise along a coast — bring your dinghy aboard. I realize that there are various tricks that enable a dinghy to be towed at sea, and I touched on a few of these in *The Charter Game.* But I still stand by bringing the tender aboard for any open-water passage. No matter whether you've bent an extra line to the painter and slacked away until the dink is riding on the windward side of the following sea, or put a little drogue over her stern to ensure that she trails dead straight along behind — she's still out there, sport. Besides giving you an excuse to chew a fingernail or two if it comes on to blow, she'll probably also take a knot off your speed.

Perhaps the simplest method of getting a dinghy out of the water and onto the ship is one I saw used for the tender of a 36-foot ketch. A lifeline was slacked and a couple of stanchions removed. A U-shaped wooden frame was fitted over the rail. Bolted to the top of the frame and running fore and aft was an axle with a grooved rubber wheel. The yacht's tender (a Sabot sailing dinghy) was brought aboard by a powerful heave on its bow, the keel of the little boat running in the rubber wheel, much as a runabout would be hauled onto a trailer. When the stern reached the rail, the dinghy was lifted bodily and stowed upside-down on the cabintop.

We would lift both of the schooner's dinghies out of the water with radial davits situated fore and aft of amidships on the port side. Each davit had a handy-billy tackle rove to disadvantage (the hauling part came from the double block at the davit head). Bronze snapshackles secured the bottom blocks to eyes, one inside the transom of each dinghy and the other inside the bow. When hove up two blocks, a dinghy would just clear the top of the lifelines as the radial davits swung it inboard. The big dinghy was lashed down on deck on the port side. The nine-footer stowed upside-down atop a couple of deckboxes under the main staysail boom. Even better than block-and-tackle falls to hoist the boats would have been an all-wire winch mounted on each davit, with the wire leading through a sheave incorporated in the davit head. With this arrangement, the davits could have been lower, because a foot or more of height was wasted by the length of the blocks.

Though radial davits are used with great success aboard Freedom 40s, this type of hoisting equipment is not usually practical for the average small cruising boat. Aboard my 33-footer, radial davits would have been ludicrous. For hoisting the dinghy out of the water and onto this vessel, we used the main halyard. We would first of all bring the dinghy alongside and lash the oars to the center thwart, paying particular attention to the position of the rowlocks (oarlocks). I always used ring rowlocks and made a practice of ensuring that each of these stayed on its oar by tacking a strip of leather around the shaft to build up a shoulder between the rowlock and the handgrip. (Some marine stores sell thick neoprene rings that slide down the oar and do this job admirably.) When lashing the oars to the dinghy seat, I would make a point of passing the line over both oarlocks to hold them still when the boat was stowed upside-down. This tactic stemmed from a trip when those rowlocks clinked against each other, day after day, and nearly drove us around the bend searching through the vessel to find the noise that wouldn't let us sleep.

To lift the dinghy aboard, we would make the painter fast to the main halyard and heave away. The boat would be prevented from bruising the topsides by pushing it off and keeping it clear until the transom cleared the lifelines. At this point, the stern of the dinghy would be carried aft as the halyard was eased and the boat would settle into its place on the cabintop. To have a dinghy hanging vertically from a main halyard might not seem too elegant, but it was a simple and very quick method of accomplishing the job. A genoa halyard could be used in the same manner to hoist and launch from the foredeck.

Another way of hoisting a dinghy (and one that gives the job a little more class) is to make up a sling that snaps to rings inside the dinghy at bow and stern. A marlinspike hitch is made in the center of the sling and a shackle inserted. The shackle is secured to the main halyard and the dinghy is hoisted level, and kept clear of the topsides in the same way described for a boat lifted by its painter. A dinghy lifted with a sling can be lowered into a cradle on deck, if the intention is to carry the boat right side up, or turned over if the dinghy is to be stowed upside-down.

There are several ways of turning the dinghy over. If the dinghy is small, or light,

*Radial davits on Freedom
40. (Ralph Naranjo photo)*

two people can easily lift the boat and turn it over once it's on deck. If this is not possible, the sling can be secured to an eye *outside* both the bow and the stern of the dinghy. A wooden spreader of the same length as the distance between these eyes is then used to keep the sling apart and prevent it from binding on bow and stern as the dinghy is flipped upside-down while in the air. This job can be done without a spreader, but here it depends on the weight of the dinghy and the length of the sling. Any sling that a dinghy is to be turned in should be of a generous length, not less than 1¼ times the length of the dinghy. A sling not kept apart by a spreader, but used to turn a dinghy inside it, should be as long as possible.

A dinghy can also be lifted aboard by using the main boom as a derrick. The main halyard is secured to the end of the boom to double up on the topping lift, and the boom is raised to the required height. This height is calculated by plumbing the lower mainsheet block above the centerline of the dinghy when the boat is alongside. The sling is shackled to this block and the mainsheet used as a tackle. (A sailboat with a short boom and a mainsheet taken from a point, say, a quarter or a third of the way along toward the gooseneck might find difficulty in using her boom in this way. Once the boom is topped to a height that enables the dinghy to clear the rail, the mainsheet, being so far from the end of the boom, might not plumb over the dinghy's centerline.)

The possibility of using the main boom as a cargo derrick is one that every ocean-cruising nut should keep in mind. I used the main boom and mainsheet tackle of my 33-footer to lift my auxiliary engine aboard; and I used to go alongside a dock and rig the same gear to lift my motorcycle on and off as well.

An old schooner trick for hoisting small boats aboard was to have a single block hung from the tips of both fore and main spreaders. Each block was the top block of a single Spanish burton, which has a mechanical advantage of 3-to-1. With the hook of a burton in the forward lifting ring of a dory, and another at the aft end, and a couple of seamen on each hauling part, the boat would be whisked aboard. This system needed pretty rugged spreaders to be successful, with each spreader tip often supported by its own shroud. Hardly suitable hoisting gear for a cruising yacht, but effective equipment aboard a large vessel with many hands.

A similar system for lifting a dinghy aboard can be employed by using the main halyard and mizzen staysail halyard of a ketch. The main halyard goes to a ring either inside or outside of the stem of the dinghy, and the mizzen staysail halyard is snapped or shackled to a ring at the transom — again, either inside or outside of the boat. Both halyards lift the dinghy clear of the water and up onto the deck of the ship. If the halyards are fast to external rings, the dinghy can be turned upside-down easily before being lowered into place.

The methods described so far for hoisting a dinghy aboard have applied to a vessel at anchor or on a mooring. Comes the time, however, when the job might have to be done underway. This should be avoided like the plague aboard a shorthanded boat, but if the event is a necessity, the following method might be considered. The vessel is first hove-to by hauling the headsails to windward. The next move depends on the rig of the vessel. The object in heaving-to is to take way off the ship and give her an angle of heel that will assist the exercise. A cutter or sloop will probably lie quietly with headsails backed, the mainsail in a nearly close-hauled position, and the helm adjusted so the wind is about six points (67.5 degrees) on the bow. A ketch or yawl might need a mizzen adjustment. If possible, the lee lifelines should be slacked to enable the removal of any stanchion that might be in the way.

With the stage now set, the dinghy painter is taken well forward along the lee side until the tender is in a position to be lifted aboard over the rail. From here on, it depends on the weight of the dinghy, the available manpower, and the height of the lee rail above the water. If it's impossible to horse the dinghy aboard with a huff and a puff, then the regular lifting method by halyard or davit must be employed. I've never been able to do this job without putting a few dings in my topsides, but there's bound to be someone who can (or says he can) do the drill in a right smart manner without a bump or a scratch.

It does no sailor any harm to be confronted with the job of bringing the dinghy aboard at sea — especially if his topsides have just had a new paint job or his rail a fresh coat of varnish. It's a sure-fire way of ensuring that from then on, the dinghy gets stowed on deck before he leaves the bay, no matter what.

Before hoisting or launching a dinghy, the skipper of an anchored vessel is well advised to have a good look around the bay to see if a passing motorboat is going to cause a roll that will interfere with the operation. If somebody's chugging in or out of the bay, wait until his wash subsides before starting any boat drill; it can make all the difference between a smooth job and a bouncy, difficult one. Sometimes, though, no matter how we plan it, the unexpected happens and nothing goes right.

A few years ago, with a charter party aboard, we sailed from St. Thomas across to Buck Island, St. Croix, in the *White Squall II*. We had an aluminum 13-footer as a tender at the time, and before leaving Charlotte Amalie, we had hoisted it aboard and lashed it down on deck. We had a good sail across, and the 36-mile run was sloppy enough to make me happy that the boat was aboard and not being towed astern. We rounded up off Buck Island, dropped the hook, and furled the sails. Our intention was to make a run in through the reef in the dinghy and snorkel over the coral. One of our gang was a gung-ho photographer and was all fired up to use his new underwater movie camera.

We hitched the falls from the radial davits to an eye inside the transom of our dinghy, and, since there was no similar eye inside the bow, we made the painter fast to the bottom block of the forward falls. We then hove the dinghy up two blocks and pivoted the davits so the dinghy swung clear of the lifelines and out over the water. All this was our usual drill — so far, that is. On this occasion, however, the towing eye of the dinghy carried away before we even had a chance to start lowering. The dinghy was suddenly hanging by its stern from the aft davit. All sorts of stuff cascaded into the water — oars, outboard tank and hose, glass-bottomed bucket, bailer, sponge, dinghy anchor and rode, a couple of cushions, a fish scaler, three or four sets of snorkeling gear . . . .

Someone jumped over the side to start retrieving this equipment while, to the tune of a few colorful comments, the hauling part of the aft fall was taken off its cleat to prepare for lowering the stern into the water. It was at this moment that a runabout roared out toward us from the beach at Buck Island. My first thought was that they had come to offer assistance, which we didn't need, but which I was prepared to appreciate as a gesture. It didn't turn out that way, though. The runabout tore around and around our vessel several times, setting up a ferocious roll and making the dangling aluminum dinghy whang mightily against the ship. The three occupants of the runabout had come to take photos of the mishap. With a cheerful wave, they disappeared off into the distance in a cloud of spray, leaving all hands in the throes of a marvelous outrage at all "fizzboat" operators. The discussion was so satisfying that it upstaged the accident.

Mention of a roll brings us to the damage, in the form of dings and gouges, that a dinghy can score in a vessel's topsides. A good fender around a rigid dinghy is a must, as are fenders for the tender to lie against when hauled alongside. Sometimes, however, fenders are not enough, nor is tailing the dinghy astern when at anchor. It'll creep up during the night and give the mother ship "a good one."

Aboard the *White Squall II* we would sometimes rig a dinghy boom in a surging anchorage. We would use one of our twin running poles, but a regular spinnaker pole will do equally as well.

The pole is rigged with topping lift, foreguy, after guy, and outhaul, square out on whichever side of the ship suits. The end of the pole should be high enough above the water so that the deepest roll in that direction will place the pole-end no closer to the surface than a couple of feet. The dinghy painter is made fast to the outhaul and hove to the end of the pole. A line from the dinghy's stern is taken well aft on the ship and made fast. The painter and stern line must be adjusted so that the dinghy lies comfortably between pole-end and ship. It's possible, with a little adjusting and playing around, to position the dinghy so that no matter what antics it gets up to, it is still clear of the ship but available for almost instant use. The alternative to this, of course, is to hoist the dinghy aboard.

STOWING A DINGHY

I remember when we were building my 33-footer in the late 1940s, spending a great deal of time figuring out where to stow the dinghy. In the end, the cabintop was

Sturdy, double-ended cruising cutter with her dinghy stowed on the foredeck. (Ralph Naranjo photo)

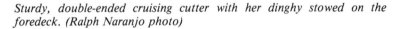

Thirty-foot Wanderer III *with her dinghy stowed snugly on deck aft of the mast. (Ralph Naranjo photo)*

designed so that an 8½-foot pram could fit snugly between mainmast and doghouse. Ringbolts were installed in the cabin sides to take the lashings. When the dinghy was stowed upside-down in its allotted place, its painter was made fast to the mainmast and a half-inch line was passed back and forth over the bottom of the little shore boat from the eyebolts in each coaming. No matter what the weather, this dinghy never moved.

A rigid dinghy can be carried on the foredeck, but this is a poor location for a

Mainsail and mizzen of this Chesapeake Bay three-sail bateau are on mast hoops instead of tracks and slides. Deck layout enables rigid dinghy to be stowed on cabintop. How about that length of free spar on the jib foot? (Ralph Naranjo photo)

tender. A dinghy on the foredeck presents an object for headsails and sheets to chafe against and can make an obstacle course for sailhandling. However, the way a lot of cruising boats' decks are laid out nowadays, there is no place but the foredeck to carry a dinghy, which is one of the reasons we see a lot of rubber dinghies among the cruising fleet. A rubber dink can be deflated and stowed below.

Space on deck to stow a rigid dinghy can sometimes be utilized to accommodate more than one tender by nesting a larger boat with a smaller one. Nesting necessitates the removal of the seats in the larger dinghy. Typically, the smaller dinghy is stowed upside-down on either deck or cabintop. The larger dinghy is hoisted aboard and the seats are removed. It is then placed upside-down over its smaller companion and secured by lashings. This system has a lot to recommend it; one set of lifting gear does the job of hoisting and launching both tenders. Most important, probably, is that the space on deck does double duty.

CARRYING A DINGHY IN DAVITS

In some circles it is popular to carry a dinghy in davits hung over the stern, and there is no question about the convenience it offers. Using the dinghy is just a matter of screwing in the drain plug, letting go the gripes, and lowering away. To hoist the dinghy, you bring it under the falls, hook on and wind (or heave), and up she comes. Some boats, though not many, cruise the world with this rig, and I take off my hat to their skippers. You can't beat success. No way can you tell a guy who's just sailed around the world with his dinghy hanging over the stern in a couple of davits that what he's doing is wrong. It's the way to get a thick ear or a black eye.

For all that, carrying a dinghy in such a manner means there's more chance of losing it than if the boat were lashed down securely on deck. A dinghy turned upside-down on either cabintop or deck and well lashed to eyebolts can go through as much bad weather as the ship. Freeboard is a big consideration in carrying a dinghy in stern davits. If your vessel is big and buoyant and has a lot of freeboard aft — enough height so that the dinghy when hoisted has a minimum of six feet of clearance between its bottom and the sea — you might get away with it. It also depends a lot on where you cruise.

Heavy, all-gaff "character" schooner with her dinghy in stern davits. Note good-sized main topsail. The ketch at right is towing a speedboat too big to hoist on board. (Ralph Naranjo photo)

I always wished I could carry a dinghy in davits over the stern of the *White Squall II*. Our bumpkin, however, prevented this, so I made do with the radial davits. I have no doubt, though, that were it not for the bumpkin, our dink would have lived in a couple of davits over the stern. It wouldn't have had a long life, though. I always considered the *White Squall II* to be a good vessel when running, and the six-foot clearance between dinghy and water would have been easy enough to arrange.

There were two occasions when we were well and truly pooped, and I've wondered ever since how a dinghy in davits over the stern would have fared.

One incident happened at night when we were running along the coast of Venezuela, but the second, a far more spectacular occurrence, was off the Kermadec Islands in the South Pacific in the early 1970s. We were running under bare poles, and just after dawn one day, we were swept by two tremendous seas that climbed over the stern and galloped down the deck, filling her bulwark to bulwark. There were three of us aboard that trip, and we were all on deck, well clipped on with harnesses, when it happened. We were washed in a heap back and forth across the afterdeck by both of these seas, and if we had had a dinghy hanging over the stern in davits, it would have been right there tumbling around with us. Any yachtsman bent on carrying his dinghy in this manner would do well to ensure that his gear is mighty rugged (and still keep his head down when it comes on to blow).

twelve

Summing Up

It is impossible, in any one book or series of books, to cover completely every aspect of rigging, for more equipment is thrown among us as each year passes. The approaches to the problems of rigging a cruising boat and the strategies for solving them discussed here have all been used on ocean passages. Most rigging methods are still with us; some are good, some are excellent, and some leave a lot to be desired. Some rigging, such as deadeyes and lanyards and the use of hemp-cored 6/7 wire, has long been discarded and may be seen only on character boats. Other rigging, such as swaged terminals, is relatively new.

It is up to the sailor to make his or her own choices, to decide which rig will best suit a particular need, to mull over the types of spars, standing rigging, running rigging, terminals, sails, and cordage. My advice to anyone doing this is never to be too quick to embrace a new product. Keep a weather eye trained on new equipment and watch how it performs — but don't go falling all over yourself to be a guinea pig. If you're really going cruising and a new "failproof" product you've bought decides to quit halfway between, say, the Galapagos and the Marquesas (it seldom happens *before* you leave), it's a long way back for a refund. And if the so-called failproof gear causes your mainmast to go over the side, you could be in for more than your share of strife before things are sorted out.

The cruising nut should watch closely his racing counterpart. There are some mighty good sailors in the racing game, and a lot of our cruising equipment first cut its teeth aboard racing boats. Watch methods of sailhandling, too; sometimes the cruiser can pick up a few worthwhile moves. (Leaving the bunt hanging after putting in a slab is one we can do without, but those "Kayzee" headfoil cartridges, discussed in Chapter Six, are winners for the cruiser who is bent on using a luff spar.)

Although modern, well-proven rigging may be wonderful to have, the cruiser need not despair if his pocket cannot stretch to the prices such gear commands. There is

This cruiser has been running before the wind with the clew of her jib hauled out to starboard by the starboard jib sheet led through the end fitting of the spinnaker pole (still rigged). A change of wind, or course, has led to the starboard sheet being slacked and the port sheet being utilized. The spinnaker pole can be taken down at leisure — or, for that matter, left where it is for the time being. (Ralph Naranjo photo)

Boat boom rigged, starboard killick "at the hawse," all her sails harbor-furled — and the end of that jibboom is a long way from home. (Ralph Naranjo photo)

nothing wrong with galvanized wire and galvanized tangs, terminals, and turn-buckles. Treated once a year, such equipment will last as long, or longer, than any other. As far as dependability is concerned, remember that galvanized turnbuckles sailed around Cape Horn hundreds of times before the first bronze or stainless job ever saw Cape Stiff.

Putting this book together has been a lot of work and a lot of fun, and inevitably has evoked its share of memories of the sometimes-bizarre methods people have employed to keep a mast in a ship. I remember a 36-foot double-ender sailing across the Pacific and then all the way back to California with the galvanized wire used on telephone poles for rigging. Mast-anchorage splices were accomplished by halving the strands, passing them each side of the mast, and winding the ends around each halved side until they met at the standing part. Ends and standing part were clamped together with a wire rope clip. The bottom "terminals" were galvanized thimbles around which the wire was bent and held with wire rope clips. This vessel kicked around the Pacific for years, and while her rigging might not have aroused envy in the breast of a beholder, the proof of any pudding is in the eating. Her mast, no matter what the weather, stayed in the ship.

We haven't recommended telephone wire and galvanized clips as the ideal rigging for an ocean cruiser, even though this may mystify the skipper of the 36-footer, if he's still around. There happen to be better, neater ways of keeping the stick standing. I mention it to point out the importance of keeping an open mind when faced with the job of rigging a sailboat for the long-range cruising scene. It's not necessary to follow slavishly the system of rigging aboard the boat you saw in the next slip, or across the way, or at the boat show last week.

When starting from scratch, revamping, or beefing up the rig of a cruising boat, examine the masts and wire setup — both standing and running — of as many vessels as possible. Consult this book, and any other book you can lay your hands on; pore over magazines. Don't hesitate to criticize. If you see any weakness in the rig of a boat comparable to your own, if you consider there is the slightest possibility that the vessel you're inspecting might lose her mast if any one fitting carried away, be sure not to make the same mistake when rigging *your* ship.

A safe, efficient cruising rig is worth a lot of planning and forethought. Once it's accomplished, such a rig imparts a sense of confidence to a cruising sailor that is equaled only by the seaworthiness of the vessel in which it is installed.

Index